PSYCHOLOGY IN THE LEGAL PROCESS

Edited by

Bruce Dennis Sales, J.D., Ph.D.
Director, Law-Psychology Graduate Training Program
University of Nebraska

S P Books Division of
SPECTRUM PUBLICATIONS, INC.
New York

Distributed by Halsted Press
A Division of John Wiley & Sons

New York   Toronto   London   Sydney

To My Wife

SPECTRUM PUBLICATIONS, INC.
175-20 Wexford Terrace, Jamaica, N.Y. 11432

Library of Congress Cataloging in Publication Data

Main entry under title:

Psychology in the legal process.

    Bibliography: p.
    Includes index.
    1. Law–Psychology–Addresses, essays, lectures.
2. Psychology, Forensic–Addresses, essays, lectures.
3. Criminal psychology–Addresses, essays, lectures.
4. Judicial process--United States–Addresses, essays,
lectures. I. Sales, Bruce Dennis.
K487.P75P78   340.1'9   77-3580
ISBN 0-89335-012-5

Distributed solely by the Halsted Press Division of John Wiley & Sons, Inc.
New York, New York
ISBN 0-470-99180-1

Contents

III ISSUES IN THE CRIMINAL AND CORRECTIONAL PROCESSES

IV POLICY AND PROFESSIONAL ISSUES

Contributors

WILLIAM AUSTIN, Ph.D.
Department of Psychology
University of Virginia
Charlottesville, Virginia

JOHN BERMAN, Ph.D.
Department of Psychology
University of Nebraska
Lincoln, Nebraska

F. JOSEPH BOSTER, Ph.D.
Department of Communication
Michigan State University
East Lansing, Michigan

RICHARD A. BLUNK, B.A.
College of Law
University of Texas
Austin, Texas

STANLEY L. BRODSKY, Ph.D.
Department of Psychology
University of Alabama
University, Alabama

BERT P. CUNDICK, Ph.D.
Department of Psychology
Brigham Young University
Provo, Utah

LARRY C. FARMER, Ph.D.
School of Law
Brigham Young University
Provo, Utah

ABRAHAM FENSTER, Ph.D.
Department of Psychology
John Jay College of Criminal Justice
New York, New York

ALVIN GOLDSTEIN, Ph.D.
Department of Psychology
University of Missouri
Columbia, Missouri

ROBERT J. HOWELL, Ph.D.
Department of Psychology
Brigham Young University
Provo, Utah

C. BLAKE KEASEY, Ph.D.
Department of Psychology
University of Nebraska
Lincoln, Nebraska

REX E. LEE, J.D.
School of Law
Brigham Young University
Provo, Utah

DAVID LEVINE, Ph.D.
Department of Psychology
University of Nebrasks
Lincoln, Nebraska

BERNARD LOCKE, Ph.D.
Department of Psychology
John Jay College of Criminal Justice
New YorkNew York

GERALD R. MILLER, Ph.D.
Department of Communication
Michigan State University
East Lansing, Michigan

JOHN MONAHAN, Ph.D.
Program in Social Ecology
University of California
Irvine, California

C. KEITH ROOKER
School of Law
Brigham Young University
Provo, Utah

BRUCE DENNIS SALES, J.D., Ph.D.
Department of Psychology and College of Law
University of Nebraska
Lincoln, Nebraska

R. KIRKLAND SCHWITZGEBEL, J.D., Ed.D.
Department of Psychology
California Lutheran College
Thousand Oaks, California
    on leave from
Department of Psychiatry
Harvard Medical School
Cambridge, Massachusetts

ALICE M. PADAWER-SINGER, Ph.D.
Jury Project
Columbia University
New York, New York
    and
Department of Educational Psychology
Long Island University
Broklyn, New York

ANDREW N. SINGER, J.D.
Monash, Chazen, and Stream
Attorneys at Law
New York, New York

RICKIE L.J. SINGER, J.D.
Davis, Polk and Wardwell
Attorneys at Law
New York, New York

JUNE LOUIN TAPP, Ph.D.
Revelle College
University of California
San Diego, California
    on leave from
Department of Criminal Justice and Studies and
Department of Psychology
University of Minnesota
Minneapolis, Minnesota

MARY KRISTINE UTNE, M.A.
Department of Sociology
University of Wisconsin
Madison, Wisconsin

CARL F. WIEDEMANN, Ph.D.
Department of Psychology
John Jay College of Criminal Justice
New York, New York

David Levine, Professor of Psychology at the University of Nebraska—Lincoln, was a past treasurer of the American Psychology-Law Society and a member of its Board of Directors. During 1974-75, Professor Levine was on sabbatical at the Institute of Criminology in Cambridge, England. A partial product of his efforts during that year is contained in his chapter in this book. His excitement and enthusiasm for psycho-legal studies and the use of psychology to promote justice was an inspiration for all. During the 1975-76 year, he was writing a book on dangerousness when he died unexpectedly on March 5, 1976. The shock and loss that I and my colleagues feel are a testament to his quality both as a person and as a scholar, but his memory will live on and the goals that he fought for will remain vital to those of us who knew him well.

Preface

In the summer of 1974, the American Psychology-Law Society held its first national convention. Much of the material presented in this volume is expended from talks originally given in the second national convention of the Society held in Chicago in September, 1975. These include the chapters by Tapp; Farmer, Williams, Cundick, Howell, Lee and Rooker; Padawer-Singer, Singer and Singer; Fenster, Weidemann and Locke; Berman; Keasey and Sales; Austin and Utne; Monahan; Goldstein; and Woody. The remaining chapters, contributed by members of the organization, were solicited by the editor.

The society will be publishing the best papers of succeeding national conventions, the next of which is to take place in the Summer of 1977, in Snowmass, Colorado. With the rapid development of the law-psychology interface, compilations of original writings such as are contained in this volume will hopefully keep both scholars and practitioners abreast of the most current thinking within the two fields.

Bruce Dennis Sales
November, 1976

I

Introduction

Psychology and Law: A Look at the Interface[1]

JUNE LOUIN TAPP

The field of psychology-law, although currently enjoying great popularity, is neither a U.S. nor a new invention. Indeed, psychology-law overtures date back to Sigmund Freud's suggestion to judges, in 1906, that they ought to look to psychology for useful information on ascertaining truth in events of law (1959). Before that, Wilhelm Stern, in his 1903 book, suggested that psychology had a great deal to contribute to law and lawyers, especially in the field of testimony. Roughly during the same period, Hugo Munsterberg (1908) produced the first substantive work, *On the Witness Stand,* interestingly subtitled *Issues in Psychology and Crime.* After that, in 1909, William Healy established the first psychological clinic attached to the juvenile court in Chicago and, in 1915, he authored a book called *Honesty* which described the causes and treatments of dishonesty among children. By 1913, J.B. Watson, expressing his dissatisfaction with psychology, suggested to jurists that they could utilize empirical data in a practical way as soon as psychologists could obtain relevant data!

The fact is that some 70 years later, when dealing with sociolegal problems of greater complexity and sophistication, the "proven" knowledge of psychology still awaits its turn for *full* acceptance and recognition within the law—whether in terms of procedural or of substantive implications. Despite its having been an early 20th-century concern of such prominent psychologists as the Austrian Freud, the German Stern, and the American Watson, the past 70 years have not exhibited astounding growth between psychology and law. In the past 5 to 10 years, there is increasing evidence, however, of something happening that qualitatively and quantitatively departs from past patterns. To depict the nature of this "happening," I attend to some key indicators that demonstrate the shift from an interstitial to interfacial[2] relation between psychology and the law.

INDICES AT THE INTERFACE

Historical Overview.

A perusal of history suggests that, in the early 1900s, interest in the relation of psychology and law primarily focused on the courtroom. In the 1920s, there were the efforts of lawyer Robert Hutchins and Yale psychologist Donald Slesinger on the topic of evidence. Among others, they wrote an article (1929) entitled "Legal Psychology."[3] By 1931, psychologist M.E. Burtt published a book called *Legal Psychology*. E.S. Robinson's 1935 psychology book, entitled *Law and the Lawyers,* was followed, in 1943, by U. Moore and C.C. Callahan's "Law and Learning Theory," a 15-year study done at Yale University. The latter, a psycholegal study of traffic, was deemed mundane and trivial. It made only a minimal impression on lawyers and psychologists.

In fact, from the 1930s to the 1960s, the main empirical and theoretical contributions between the behavioral sciences and law came from anthropology, sociology, and psychiatry. They included such monumental examples as lawyer Karl Llewellyn and anthropologist Adamson Hoebel's work on *The Cheyenne Way* in the 1940s, psychiatrist Thomas Szasz's attack on *Law, Liberty and Psychiatry* in the 1950s, and the jury studies by lawyer Harry Kalven and sociologist Hans Zeisel in the 1960s.

In the late 1960s, psychologists renewed their active pursuit of research in legal settings (Tapp, 1969). During this current wave of activity, the work has expanded its limits beyond forensic questions and situation-specific problem solving. John Thibaut and Lauren Walker's research on *Procedural Justice* (1975) is illustrative of the marked advancement over the courtroom and jury studies of the earlier decades. This work, done respectively by a lawyer and a psychologist, is typical of psycholegal research in the 1970s; that is, there is the noteworthy impact of jurisprudential constructs on psychological paradigms and the reverse.

Over two decades ago, psychologists Lee Cronbach and Paul Meehl (1955) underscored the need for congruence in theoretical and methodological constructs. Later, Meehl (1967) emphasized the need to go beyond point-to-point predictions, and Cronbach (1975) stressed that we seek explanations beyond the first interaction and proceed with historical and ahistorical cautions. These all suggest that to ask—or answer—a question from the legal side requires some comparability from the psychological side as well. Investigators from psychology in the 1970s are more likely to require such construct congruency, judging by recent research and reform efforts (e.g., Hogan, 1975; Lerner, 1975; Monahan, 1975; Parke, 1977; Tapp & Levine, 1974, 1977; Thibaut & Walker, 1975).

Unlike legal science from previous periods, psychologists and lawyers in the 1970s are not merely talking the interdisciplinary game. They are in active dialogue about the theoretical and empirical meanings of legal experiences such as the administration of justice (e.g., Thibaut & Walker, 1975), the acquisition of rules (e.g., Friedman, 1975; Hogan, 1976), the operation of a just community (e.g., Kohlberg et al., 1974), the socialization of an ethical legality (e.g., Tapp & Levine, 1974), and the effect of the rehabilitative ideal (e.g., Schwitzgebel, 1975; Shuman, 1977). The work of the 1970s suggests that both disciplines are seeking the same thing: a better question to yield a better answer.

Although a scan of the psycholegal literature of the last 5 to 10 years, compared with the earlier decades, reveals differences in emphases, the overriding themes throughout this century are: (1) the union of psychology and law can promote justice and science; (2) psychology can and has offered ways of systematically documenting a sociolegal and psycholegal event; and (3) the phenomena of both psychology and law require new views of science and society. The difference in contemporary patterns is that now psychology and law have begun to address these goals in more intellectually sophisticated and less parochial ways. With such basic and shared goals, it is no wonder that Friedman (1974, p. 1070) suggested that "a couple of areas, so far neglected, will enjoy . . . something of a minor boom. One is psychology and the law. This is long overdue."

Conferences

The change in relationship between the two fields is well chronicled by conferences including both psychologists and lawyers. For example, 1975 was the first year that the American Psychology-Law Society (hereinafter APLS) had a Distinguished Lecturer on the topic of "Psychology and Law"; in 1974, APLS inaugurated its First National Convention for psychologists and lawyers. Additionally, in 1975, the University of Nebraska-Lincoln sponsored a national conference on "Psycholegal Issues in the Criminal Justice System," and the Battelle Institute held a meeting on "Psychological Processes in the Legal System." These are but four precursors. Generally, the range and magnitude of psychologists involved in legal matters, as well as the range and magnitude of lawyers using psychological matter, is substantial now, if conferences are a measure.

Indexing Systems

Another indicator of the growth of psychology-law research can be found in the indexing systems of the two fields. For example, in the 1965 *Psychological Abstracts (PA),* there were 111 articles listed under such categories as crime, criminal law, government, prisoners, and prisons. While there were over 100 articles in 1965, there were 493 in 1968, and 718 in 1972. Even with a limited psychological abstracting system, there was an obvious increase. In 1973; *PA* changed its method of indexing its annual volume. Entering the new system with some 70 descriptors drawn from the old *PA* Thesaurus, I added a few "new" ones, like legal decisionmaking and fairness. With the new system, I found 2221 articles in the five-year period from 1967 to 1972; however, for the two-and-a-half-year period from January 1973 to May 1975, I found 1771! Evidently, there is an explosion, regardless of categories. Something has obviously happened!

Examination of the traditional and equally limited *Index of Legal Periodicals (ILP)* afforded equally interesting findings. Of the *ILP* categories, only three were useful for this analysis: mental health, psychology, and psychiatry. In these areas, there were as many entries for the one-year period of 1973-74 as there had been for the preceding three-year period. The greatest number of listings was in the psychiatry category.

What do these data mean? At the very least, they mean that lawyers more typically have used psychiatrists as their expert witnesses in the courtroom and have accepted psychiatrists as sources of their information about the psychological growth of normal/abnormal notions about law and justice. However, there is some shift in the *ILP* publication pattern as well. The number of articles categorized both in mental health and in psychology has increased over the past few years. Moreover, there are several articles that I, as reader or reviewer, would have put in the psychology category rather than elsewhere. On balance then, the psychology-related offerings in law-related publications have increased too.

Organizational Trends

Similarly, traditional organizations have changed. For example, the American Bar Association (ABA), for the first time in its history, has more than token psychologists around. Several ABA Advisory Commissions and Committees include psychologists in their membership and, thus, in the decisionmaking. Additionally, the American Bar Foundation, the research affiliate of the ABA, has retained at least one psychologist on its staff since 1967.

The emergence of newer organizations, such as APLS, affords another good indicator. In 1968, Jay Ziskin chaired a psychology-law symposium at APA in San Francisco; 15 people stayed to convene the American Psychology-Law Society. Today APLS' membership is over 500, and it is one of several new associations aimed at law-psychology interaction.

Similarly, the *American Psychological Association* is now more active in the area. In 1965, there was a single APA presentation in the annual convention program that could be described as at the law-psychology interface. By 1973 and 1974, the number had increased to 28 and 33 respectively; this included symposia, individual papers, and workshops. The 1975 APA Program revealed a numerical and conceptual explosion. For the first time, there were two major addresses on law and psychology issues: Isidore Chein's Kurt Lewin Address entitled "There Ought to be a Law—But Why?" and Al Pepitone's Presidential Address on "Social Psychological Perspectives in Crime and Punishment." Both presentations were sponsored by Division 9. Historically, Division 9 (the Society for the Psychological Study of Social Issues) has been the primary place where many kinds of social issues initially appeared. However, as the 1975 Annual Program revealed, psychology and law had made a dramatic debut generally. While 9 was still the most active, Divisions 8, 12, 13, 14, 18, 22, 25, and 27 had papers or symposia dealing with issues in law and psychology. Different from any previous APA "happening," the pattern continued, as evidenced by Division 9's theme, "Law, Legislation and Human Behavior," and a general explosion of the psychology-law area in the program offerings of the 1976 Annual Convention.

In addition, if one compares the *American Psychologist's* offerings of 1972-1975 to those of 1969-1972, one finds the expanded law-psychology titles noteworthy. Topics include a diverse array of issues such as the rights and kinds of treatments for offenders, utilization and training of psychologists for the criminal justice system, scientific method in assessing attitudes toward law, and conditions for compliance. Inspection of the past year's offerings show continuation of this pattern.

The Academy

Historically, many law and society programs at the graduate level were nourished by the Russell Sage Foundation (see Ladinsky, 1975). Memorable examples include the Law and Society Center at the University of California, Berkeley, the Law and Social Sciences program at Northwestern University, and the Russell Sage Fellows at Yale University. In most ventures, the emphasis was law and sociology. Throughout all of the programs, there is only an occasional psychologist. Until recently he or she typically came from Northwestern (the residence of distinguished psychologist Donald Campbell).

With the support of the National Institue of Mental Health, the University of

Nebraska-Lincoln formally inaugurated, in 1974, a J.D.-Ph.D. Program in Law and Psychology. Informally, the possibility today of simultaneously pursuing the double degrees without the aide of a formal joint program is a phenomenon occurring much more widely from Minnesota to Florida and from Stanford to Chicago.

Federal Support

A survey of one federal agency's "law and society programs" revealed that most of its support was not channeled to psychological research but to sociological or psychiatric plus law. In contrast, another agency reported that, in the 1960s, about 28% of its grants went to psychologists; in the early 1970s, the figure was still higher—about 40%. By the mid-1970s, increasing numbers of agencies—national and international (e.g., Canada)—had "law" or "justice" in their budgetary format for use in psychological work. Whatever the source of support—local or state, public or private—psychologists will have to be as scrupulous about their roles and goals in accepting "justice money" as they were, or should have been, about accepting "poverty money" in the 1960s.

There is some indication that the law and society emphasis of the 1960s and the emergent law and psychology of the 1970s is shifting toward a "criminal justice and ... " emphasis. A serious decision for those at the law-psychology interface is whether to deal with the total legal structure of which the criminal justice system. To choose the latter option may be to reduce research and reform to discrete "crime" projects instead of building a body of knowledge on law and justice.

The balance that must be struck is a delicate one. Researchers and policymakers must attend to the source of funding, aware that, while psycholegal research is not particularly value-free, its findings should not be controlled by the demands or whims of the supply source (i.e., the money). To do this fully, the investigator must weigh his or her responsibilities to the recipient (i.e., the "subject" or society) and to the sponsor of research. The ethics area is no longer of minimal concern to either psychology or law. Lon Fuller, speaking to lawyers, discussed the ethics of their role (1969c); Donald Campbell has done likewise to psychologists (1969, 1974); lawyer David Wexler cautioned both (1973), as did psychologist Robert Boruch (1974). Increments in support for psycholegal research evidently extend one's ethical, legal, scientific, and social responsibilities.

Publications, Materials, and Courses

What about publications as an indicator? *The Law and Society Review* has been published for some 10 years. In that period, only 3.5% of their publications were psychological. Yet, among others in the past several years, two journals—one devoted to psychology and law and one to criminal justice behavior—will have appeared: *Law and Human Behavior and Criminal Justice and Behavior.*

Several other publication efforts are noteworthy. For example, in 1974, the *Stanford Law Review* devoted two issues to law and psychology (June, 1974, and November, 1974) and in 1975, Brigham Young University proffered a *Symposium on The Use of Video Tape in the Courtroom.* Overall in the 1970s, both law reviews and law-related journals increasingly accepted psychologists' articles—a rare thing in the 1950s or 1960s—and fewer of those articles were calls for action—a frequent thing in the 1950s or 1960s.

In fact, many efforts from the 1920s to the 1960s were, at most, calls for action and, at the least, arrays of information or insight. Exemplary is the work by Hans Toch. Toch's *Legal and Criminal Psychology* (1961) was probably the best compendium in the 1960s. Although this 14-chapter book contained offerings from as many sociologists and lawyers as psychologists, it was not a vehicle that stimulated interaction. Generally, little was produced in the way of substantive and substantial teaching or research materials until the 1970s. The year 1977 will witness the appearance of several new psychology-law efforts: the first volume of a book series entitled *Perspectives in Law and Psychology* (Sales, 1977) and the first SPSSI-sponsored volume on *Law, Justice, and the Individual in Society: Psychological and Legal Issues* (Tapp & Levine, 1977) are examples.

While universities increasingly listed courses at graduate and undergraduate levels, until lately there were few course-related materials in the tradition of psychology or law texts. Most people who taught courses—whether called law and psychology, legal socialization, crime and justice, or law and society—picked through the "literature" and developed their own syllabi, their own books, their own reference lists. What is needed, beyond the efforts described above, is a clearinghouse for materials that would reflect the research that is upcoming and out and the programs that are in process. My 1976 *Annual Review of Psychology* chapter on law and psychology (Tapp, 1976) can only initiate this effort; some organization, dedicated to educational exchange between law and psychology, ought to consider a clearinghouse function.

GROUNDS FOR INTEGRATION

In part, the explosion of interest in psychology and its paradigms has occurred because the function of law has changed in the culture. Many question whether the law is merely a mechanism for social control. Some say it should be an instrument of social change; others, a mechanism for facilitating access to the benefits of society and to the individual's selfhood; still others depict it as a vehicle toward a socialization of rights and the pressing of individual and institutional claims (see Friedman, 1971, 1975; Tapp, 1971, 1973, 1976; Tapp & Levine, 1974, 1977). But to all, there is increasingly a greater understanding of the law's function as a mobility belt—socially, psychologically, economically, and politically.

Also, slowly, there has come recognition of a myth about the relation of law and psychology. These two disciplines are in no way dissociated or discordant (Tapp, 1974, 1976). Their coterminality in understanding rule acquisition or justice norm-setting is both substantive and substantial.[4] While they may not be isomorphic in approach, they are both certainly interactive and public in their pursuits. Among others, both Freud and Fuller—some 60 to 70 years apart— attest to those qualities in describing their respective as well as mutual enterprises (cf. Freud, 1959, to Fuller, 1969b). To lawyer Fuller, law as a public enterprise and a shared activity is best explained by underlying "moral and psychological forces" (1969a, 1969b, 1977). Such a position is amenable to post-Freudian psychologists as well, who are also steeped in the traditions of group dynamics, field theory, and socialization processes.[5]

Since both law and psychology are value-conscious and evidence-minded and few psycholegal research activities are undertaken "value-free," investigators must be cautious to dismiss psychological or legal evidence, theoretical or empirical, that are found wanting. Such evaluation is critical to facilitate movement beyond conceptual debate or legal fiction. The role of psychology, as already partially described elsewhere (Tapp, 1976), involves recognition of its own brands of empiricism and research *plus* the systematic generating of questions, mapping of data, and translating of legal notions. Psychologists need to translate significant experiments (e.g., attribution and exchange theory *or* perception and cognition theory) into language available to the legal profession. For example, many legal problems related to the eyewitness identification process suffer precisely because the psychological "stuff" in perception or memory is simply not translated or made available in ways useful to lawyers.

Similarly, actors in the legal system must revise their approach. Lawyers must ask questions with fewer conditional whereas's to obviate the feeling of signing a contract instead of answering a question. Lawyers, too, must recognize their educative role, especially as the law becomes a prime and primary socializing agent. To do this effectively, legal scholars have to recognize the multiple roles of law and extend their empirical and research notions accordingly (Meehl, 1971; Tapp, 1969). After all, the law, like the home and like the school, is one of the "controlled" environments which influences people's attitudes (beliefs) and actions (behaviors) and shapes their lives.

What is "true" for research and reform in law then is certainly as "true" (i.e., conditional, antecedent) for psychology. More than one case is needed to demonstrate a point; more than one laboratory setting is needed to determine the antecedent. On balance, the criteria for research and reform should be, if it is not now, more similar than different. Such an approach to methodology and policy in assessing legal events is likely to produce a mandate not "to stamp out crime (or poverty, or discrimination, or inflation)," but one "to embark, wholeheartedly but skeptically, upon the social experiment to see whether or not it works [Meehl, 1970, pp. 20-30]." Mindful of these issues, psychologists and lawyers in concert can better clarify the problems and the procedures. In part, this appears to be in the process of happening.

ISSUES FOR FUTURE CONCERN

What are some outstanding issues in need of psycholegal attention? The work to be done in rights is preeminent because understanding the social and legal aspects of rights is basic to developing claims-consciousness and to entering the sociolegal order as a critical consumer (e.g., Friedman, 1971; Gallatin, 1975; Koocher, 1976; Tapp & Levine, 1974). Yet to date, whether in law or psychology, the notion of rights has involved more rhetoric than research. To move beyond this stage, comprehensive investigations have to be done on the theoretical, empirical, and practical meanings of rights that would encompass the legal, psychosocial, and developmental viewpoints *plus* incorporate the perspectives of adult and child, individual and institution (e.g., parent and child rights in the court, meaning of a right and "right").

A topic related to rights is the role and function of law. How can we describe competence and control or compliance and choice when we are ignorant of the public's attitudes toward the law? What do people really think and feel in response to constructs such as "law," "justice," "crime," "police"? Individually and institutionally, do these words produce different "clutches" (i.e., pits in the stomach) depending on the society or the situation? How were these attitudes produced? Only by understanding the process of legal socialization—that is, how the individual came to reason on matters "legal" or "just"—can we come to understand and extend the ethical limits of the law and the capacity of the organism to deal with law effectively. Both sets of understanding are necessary in order to assure the establishment of a just community.

Another major area for study is the judicial process—how decisions are made in courtrooms by jurors and juries. Decisionmaking involves a way of processing information. Many psychological findings on these variables can be made explicit; psychologists should "educate" lawyers about mediating processes in the decisionmaking process. In a survey of jury research over the last 10 years, James Davis and colleagues (1977) persuasively argued that most research had been on the "juror" rather than the "jury." Further, much of it has been done with university students in simulated situations using stimulus materials that are not "real" and typically have stressed demographic rather than interactive variables.

Considering that only 3-5% of most U.S. crime is adjudicated by juries, why has the jury process caught both the ire and imagination of psychologists? Why has the psychologist's role in several trials of national prominence evoked debate on the ethical and legal, conceptual and practical aspects of such psycholegal cooperation (also see Shapley, 1974)? One reason may involve the fact that some psychologists became advocates as well as experts and redefined the boundaries of *in situ* or action research. Another is that those who actively participated in courtroom practices raised the "role" question for the psychologist: Should the psychologist function as advocate or as expert in the legal system? While the decision—to be or not to be an advocate—is, of course, a personal question, perhaps the emphasis in jury research (given the small percentage of such trials in the whole legal system) is the more demanding professional *and* psychological question. Such considerations raise serious questions about the role of any "expert" and of any "witness" in an adversary legal system.

The implications of the issues, however, extend beyond the jury selection process. For example, when asked by a lawyer to help select a jury, should the psychologist function as an advocate *or* should the psychologist help select the fairest jury possible? If the latter is the task, then in a just system, psychologists on both sides presumably would pick the same "fair" people.

The criminal justice system is another setting in which the psychologist can engage in research and advance reform (see Brodsky, 1972). Concomitant with the growing doubts about the rehabilitative model and concerns about guaranteeing "due process" rights of patients and prisoners, the question of what the psychologist should be doing in criminal justice settings is under review. For example, Paul Meehl has argued (personal communication, 1975) that the psychologist in a prison setting is simply a psychologist treating a person with a particular emotional disturbance, whether it is alcoholism or schizophrenia. But does this model really apply? Is the psychologist's responsibility altered in the context of an involuntary total institution where the parameters of choice and competence are greatly reduced?

The ethical problems over conflict of interest loom large too; that is, the psychologist's responsibilities vis-à-vis the individual, the institution, and society. Since there is mixed evidence that any kind of treatment consistently moves anyone closer to "rehabilitation" or "resocialization," psychologists, however unintentionally, may help to perpetuate a myth of rehabilitation for the incarcerated and to the outside world.

Another problem is that the ability to predict dangerousness is so limited that psychologists face serious questions about whether or not they should be involved in involuntary commitment proceedings or other legal decisionmaking that requires such predictions. As E.I. Megargee emphasized, no test "has been developed which will adequately *post*dict, let alone *pre*dict, violent behavior [1970, p. 145] ." With concerns over the inability to predict or treat effectively and the dilemma of the psychologist's role in the criminal justice system, psychologists working in prison and mental health settings have steadily moved toward a justice model involving contractual rights and responsibilities for all parties.

Israel Goldiamond, in an incisive piece (1974) entitled "A Constructional

Approach to Social Problems," formulated a contract paradigm for persons in total institutional contexts, whether prisons or hospitals. His major reference was the U.S. Constitution; his major concern, the conflict present in therapy regardless of the type of therapy. Goldiamond cogently argued that any kind of therapy—behavior modification, psychoanalysis, primal therapy, or whatever— involves behavior change and modification. To him, such definitional quibbling is miniscule in magnitude compared to the establishment of a contractual arrangement so that the patient or prisoner is not the only person paying the price for ineffectual treatment. Focusing on the responsibility and accountability of the institution and the professional, as Goldiamond does, may force the psychologist to review his/her role in all total institutions, whatever their custodial purpose.

Similarly, psychologist-lawyer R.K. Schwitzgebel in the August, 1975, *American Psychologist* described a contractual approach denoting the ethical and legal liabilities that go with "giving" treatment. Basic to his model is the concept that informed consent and explicit mutual exchange can protect persons from intrusion and coercion. His approach to rehabilitation is particularly interesting given an earlier book with R.E. Schwitzgebel (1963) on psychotechnology that advanced the use of electronic devices to control patients or prisoners. However, it is reflective of a rising ethical-legal consciousness.

CONCLUSION

Whether one examines the legal socialization process, the judicial process, or the criminal justice process, concerns about justice pervade all these areas. In each area, there is substantial recognition that the social-situational context (e.g., the legal setting) plays a vital role in structuring human behavior. For example, Haney and Zimbardo's highly illuminating, although simulated, Stanford prison experiments (1977) described how 21 normal, healthy, American young men became pathological in 6 days of role-playing prisoners and guards. Unknowingly, they were socialized to criminality and exhibited inhumane, unjust behaviors. Kohlberg, Scharf, and colleagues' work in prisons and in establishing a "just community" is also indicative of the power of cognitive *and* situational structures (1971, 1974). These investigators found that movement in moral stages among inmates could not occur beyond a certain level due to the low-stage moral attributes of the prison clime. Both pieces of research, built on a "justice" model (one simulated, one *in situ*), have significant implications for the enterprises of science and society.

On balance, given the complex problems of law and society, the psychologist and the lawyer, the community and the citizen, seem to be better off today than just a short time ago. While there are still enormous gaps—substantive and theoretical, methodological and empirical—the difference today is that we *can be* more systematic, *are* more committed to documenting events descriptively, and *may be* more willing to ask questions from more than one frame of reference. Both law and psychology have become less parochial and do seek interdisciplinary experiences. "Interdisciplinary" does not simply mean between law and psychology, but among different kinds of psychologies and different kinds of law as well. This expansion means that both psychologists and lawyers can frame a question in a number of ways and seek an answer in more than just one ecologically valid setting. Answering and asking the question in this manner should yield a pattern of congruence, if not "truth."

FOOTNOTES

[1] This chapter is a revised version of Dr. Tapp's presentation, as the first Distinguished Lecturer/Discussant, at the 1975 National Convention of the American Psychology-Law Society [Ed.'s Note].

[2] In an interstitial position, the boundaries of the principles are close but the two bodies of matter have a chink or space beside them. In an interfacial position, there is a shared or a common boundary.

[3] Hutchins, interviewed in 1975 about his most vivid memories in education, recalled these articles with Slesinger. He had hoped that those psycholegal articles would evoke paradigms for action and research affecting the Law of Evidence as well as the teaching of law. His observation, some 35 years later, was that not very much had happened in either arena. That is an arresting comment to which lawyers and particularly psychologists of the 1970s must address themselves.

[4] As a case in point, philosopher John Rawls explicitly utilized psychology to validate his construct of a "sense of justice" as "natural" and indicative of an inherent capacity in humankind to be facilitated by the social structure (1971).

[5] Another case in point are Thibaut and Walker (1975), who, among others (e.g., Tapp & Levine, 1974), expressly continue the search for construct congruency, drawing upon the philosophical and jurisprudential models of Fuller and Rawls.

REFERENCES

Boruch, R.F. *Costs, benefits and legal implications in social research.* Evanston, Ill.: Northwestern University Press, 1974.

Brodsky, S.L. (ed.) *Psychologists in the criminal justice system.* Urbana, Ill.: University of Illinois Press, 1972.

Burtt, M.E. *Legal psychology.* Englewood Cliffs, N.J.: Prentice-Hall, 1931.

Campbell, D.T. Reforms as experiments. *American Psychologist,* 1969, *24,* 409-429.

Campbell, D.T. *Qualitative knowing in action research.* Paper presented as the Kurt Lewin Award Address to Division 9 (The Society for the Psychological Study of Social Issues) at the annual meeting of the American Psychological Association, New Orleans, September 1974.

Chein, I. *There ought to be a law—but why?* Paper presented at the annual meeting of the American Psychological Association, Chicago, September 1975.

Cronbach, L.J. Beyond the two disciplines of scientific psychology. *American Psycholo-*

gist, 1975, *30*, 116-127.

Cronbach, L.J. & Meehl, P. Construct validity in psychological tests. *Psychological Bulletin*, 1955, *52*, 281-302.

Davis, J.H., Bray, R.M., & Holt, R.W. The empirical study of decision processes in juries: A critical review. In J.L. Tapp & F.J. Levine (Eds.), *Law, justice, and the individual in society: Psychological and legal issues*. New York: Holt, Rinehart & Winston, 1977.

Fadiman, C., & Hutchins, R.M. Get ready for anything. *Center Report*, 1975, *8*, 20-24.

Freud, S. Psycho-analysis and the ascertaining of truth in courts of law. In *Clinical papers and papers on technique: Collected papers* (Vol. 2). New York: Basic Books, 1959.

Friedman, L.M. The idea of right as a social and legal concept. *Journal of Social Issues*, 1971, *27*, 189-198.

Friedman, L.M. Remarks on the future of law and social science research. *North Carolina Law Review*, 1974, *52*, 1068-1078.

Friedman, L.M. *The legal system*. New York: Russell Sage, 1975.

Fuller, L.L. Human interaction and the law. *American Journal of Jurisprudence*, 1969a, *14*, 1-36.

Fuller, L.L. *The morality of law*. (Rev. ed.) New Haven: Yale University Press, 1969b.

Fuller, L.L. Two principles of human association. In J.R. Pennock & J.W. Chapman (Eds.), *Voluntary associations: Nomos XI*. New York: Atherton, 1969c.

Fuller, L.L. Some presuppositions shaping the concept of "socialization." In J.L. Tapp & F.J. Levine (Eds.), *Law, justice, and the individual in society: Psychological and legal* issues; New York: Holt, Rinehart & Winston, 1977.

Gallatin, J. The conceptualization of rights: Psychological development and cross-national perspectives. In R. Claude (Ed.), *Comparative human rights*. Baltimore: The Johns Hopkins University Press, 1975.

Goldiamond, I. Toward a constructional approach to social problems: Ethical and constitutional issues raised by applied behavior analysis. *Behaviorism*, 1974, *2*, 1-84.

Haney, C. & Zimbardo, P.G., The socialization into criminality: On becoming a prisoner and a guard. In J.L. Tapp & F.J. Levine (Eds.), *Law, justice, and the individual in society: Psychological and legal issues*. New York: Holt, Rinehart & Winston, 1977.

Healy, W. *Honesty: A study of the causes and treatment of dishonesty among children*. Indianapolis, Ind.: Bobbs-Merrill, 1915.

Hogan, R. Theoretical egocentrism and the problem of compliance. *American Psychologist*, 1975, *30*, 533-540.

Hogan, R. Legal socialization. In G. Bermant, C. Nemeth, & N. Vidmar (Eds.), *Psychology and the law*. Lexington, Mass.: D.C. Heath, 1976.

Hutchins, R.M. & Slesinger, D. Legal psychology. *Psychological Review*, 1929, *36*, 13-26,

Kalven, H., Jr. & Zeisel, H. *The American jury*. Boston: Little, Brown, 1966.

Kohlberg, L., Kauffman, K., Scharf, P. & Hickey, J. *The just community approach to corrections: A manual part I*. Cambridge, Mass.: Moral Education Research Foundation, Harvard University, 1974.

Kohlberg, L., Scharf, P. & Hickey, J. Justice structure of the prison. *Prison Journal*, 1971, *51*, 3-14.

Koocher, G.P. (Ed.) *Children's rights and the mental health professions*. New York: Wiley-Interscience, 1976.

Ladinsky, J. *The teaching of law and social science courses in the United States*. Working Paper No. 11, Center for Law and the Behavioral Sciences, University of Wisconsin-Madison, 1975.

Lerner, M.J. (Ed.) The justice motive in social behavior. *Journal of Social Issues*, 1975, *31*(3).

Llewellyn, K.N. & Hoebel, E.A. *The Cheyenne way: Conflict and case law in primitive jurisprudence.* Norman, Okla.: University of Oklahoma Press, 1941.

Meehl, P.E. Theory-testing in psychology and physics: A methodological paradox. *Philosophy of Science,* 1967, *34,* 103-115.

Meehl, P.E. Psychology and the criminal law. *University of Richmond Law Review,* 1970, *5,* 1-30.

Meehl, P.E. Law and the fireside induction. *Journal of Social Issues,* 1971, *27,* 65-100.

Megargee, E.I. The prediction of violence with psychological tests. In C. Speilberger (Ed.), *Current topics in clinical and community psychology.* New York: Academic Press, 1970.

Monahan, J. (Ed.) *Community mental health and the criminal justice system.* New York: Pergamon, 1975.

Moore, U. & Callahan, C., Law and learning theory: A study in legal control. *Yale Law Journal,* 1943, *53,* 1-136.

Munsterberg, H., *On the witness stand: Essays on psychology and crime.* New York: Clark, Boardman, 1908.

Parke, R. Socialization into child abuse: A social interactional perspective. In J.L. Tapp & F.J. Levine (Eds.), *Law, justice, and the individual in society: Psychological and legal issues.* New York: Holt, Rinehart & Winston, 1977.

Pepitone, A. *Social psychological perspectives in crime and punishment.* Paper presented at the annual meeting of the American Psychological Association, Chicago, September 1975.

Rawls, J. *A theory of justice.* Cambridge, Mass.: Belknap, 1971.

Robinson, E.S. *Law and the lawyers.* New York: Macmillan, 1935.

Sales, B.D. *Perspectives in law and psychology: The criminal justice system.* Volume I. New York: Plenum, 1977.

Schwitzgebel, R.K. A contractual model for the protection of the rights of institutionalized patients. *American Psychologist,* 1975, *30,* 815-820.

Schwitzgebel, R.L. & Schwitzgebel, R.K. *Psychotechnology: Electronic control of mind and behavior.* New York: Holt, Rinehart & Winston, 1963.

Shapley, D. Jury selection: Social scientists gamble in an already loaded game. *Science,* 1974, *185,* 1033-1034, 1071.

Shuman, S.I. Why criminal law?: Parameters for evaluating objectives and response alternatives. In J.L. Tapp & F.J. Levine (Eds.), *Law, justice, and the individual in society: Psychological and legal issues.* New York: Holt, Rinehart & Winston, 1977.

Stern, W. *Beitrage zur psychologie der aussage.* Leipzig: Verlag Barth, 1903.

Symposium, *The use of videotape in the courtroom.* Provo, Utah: *Brigham Young University Law Review,* 1975.

Szasz, T.S. *Law liberty, and psychiatry: An inquiry into the social uses of mental health practices.* New York: Macmillan, 1963.

Tapp, J.L. Psychology and the law: The dilemma. *Psychology Today,* 1969, *2,* 16-22.

Tapp, J.L. (Ed.) Socialization, the law, and society. *Journal of Social Issues,* 1971, *27*(2).

Tapp, J.L. *Cross-cultural and developmental dimensions of a jurisprudence of youth.* Working Paper No. 5, Law & Society Center, University of California, Berkeley, 1973.

Tapp, J.L. The psychological limits of legality. In J.R. Pennock & J.W. Chapman (Eds.) *The limits of law: Nomos XV.* New York: Atherton, 1974.

Tapp, J.L., Psychology and the law: An overture. In M.R. Rosenzweig & L.W. Porter (Eds.), *Annual review of psychology* (Vol. 27). Palo Alto, Calif.: Annual Reviews, 1976.

Tapp, J.L. & Levine, F.J. Legal socialization: Strategies for an ethical legality. *Stanford Law Review,* 1974, *27,* 1-72.

Tapp, J.L. & Levine, F.J. (Eds.) *Law justice, and the individual in society: Psychological and legal issues.* New York: Holt, Rinehart & Winston, 1977.

Thibaut, J. & Walker, L. *Procedural justice: A psychological analysis.* Hillsdale, N.J.: Lawrence Erlbaum Associates, 1975.

Toch, H. (Ed.) *Legal and criminal psychology.* New York: Holt, Rinehart & Winston, 1961.

Watson, J.B. Psychology as the behaviorist views it. *Psychological Review,* 1913, *20,* 158-177.

Wexler, D. Token and taboo: Behavior modification, token economies, and the law. *California Law Review,* 1973, *61,* 81-109.

II

Issues in
the Jury and
Trial Processes

Three Images of the Trial: Their Implications for Psychological Research

GERALD R. MILLER
F. JOSEPH BOSTER

Legal professionals and social scientists have only recently begun a persistent, if somewhat hesitant, intellectual courtship. To be sure, history has witnessed occasional attempts by one suitor to woo the affections of the other, but these infrequent advances have resembled shotgun weddings more closely than mutually compatible professional marriages. Events of the last few decades, however, have strengthened the vows of both parties, and future annulment or divorce grows increasingly unlikely.

To some extent, the prior reluctance of both principals to contemplate scholarly matrimony has stemmed from perceived incompatibility. The testable hypotheses, statistical paraphernelia, and ostensibly value-free milieu of the social scientist have been viewed as a world apart from the rule-governed, rhetorical (in the best sense of that term), and value-laden environment of the legal professional. And while phrases such as "two different worlds" make for romantic popular song lyrics, they do not herald potentially harmonious professional and intellectual wedlock.

Not surprisingly, this chapter rests on the assumption that at least some of the activities and objectives of the social scientist—in particular, the psychologist—are congruent with those of the legal professional—in particular, the legal professional within the confines of a specific judicial institution, the courtroom trial. More specifically, one common objective of the psychologist and the judicial participants in a courtroom trial carries considerable import for the stance taken in this chapter: *both groups render judgments on the probable truth or falsity of certain factual statements.*[1] At first glance, this asserted equivalence may disturb some classically trained psychologists who continue to see their mission as the search for absolute truth in a rigidly deterministic behavioral universe. Nevertheless, we will defend it as a useful working premise; the statements "There is a *[probable]* positive relationship between one's status and the number of communications directed at him or her" and "Jones is *[probably]* guilty of murder"[2] share many of the same logical attributes.

Moreover, for both psychologist and legal professional, differences in the evidential grounds for arriving at a judgment will affect the relative perceived probability that the factual statement is true.[3] For instance, it is a truism of social science that one is more certain of the truth of a statement describing an empirical finding if that finding has been replicated—"certain," of course, in the psychological rather than logical sense of the term. Although no direct analog to replication exists in the legal system, an appeal can usefully be thought of as a rough approximation, for it involves a request for a second objective expert, or experts, to examine the "data" and to reach an independent judgment on their validity. Thus, if an appellate court upholds the verdict that Jones is guilty of murder, our certainty in the truth of the factual statement "Jones is guilty of murder" is usually increased.

In a similar vein, a simple study that we conducted recently yielded the less than startling finding that different kinds of evidence influence the certainty with which individuals attribute guilt to a criminal defendant (Miller & Boster, 1975) All participants received the following brief scenario and instructions:

> Jones has harbored ill feelings toward Smith for some time because of gambling losses. Both Jones and Smith work on the fourth floor of an office building. One evening Smith is shot and killed in his office. Assume that Jones is accused of the crime and that you are a juror at his trial. Further assume that the prosecution bases its case against Jones primarily on the following evidence. After reading the evidence, answer the two questions concerning it from the perspective of your role as juror.

A randomly selected one-fourth of the participants then received a single item of circumstantial evidence (specifically, that the murder weapon belonged to Jones and that Jones was working at his office the night Smith was killed); one-fourth received the information that an eyewitness who was not acquainted with either Smith or Jones testified that he had seen Jones fire at Smith from the door of Smith's office; one-fourth received the same testimonial account attributed to a witness who was acquainted with both Smith and Jones; and one-fourth received the information that Jones had confessed to the police and that the confession was introduced at the trial. All participants were then asked, given the evidence, (1) how likely they would be to find Jones guilty of Smith's murder, and (2) how certain they would feel about Jones's guilt.

We expected participants in the confession condition to report the highest likelihood of a guilty finding and the highest certainty of Jones's guilt, followed by participants in the familiar witness condition, the unfamiliar witness condition, and the circumstantial evidence condition. Table I reports the mean scores for participants in the four conditions. It can be seen that the means order according to prediction, save for the reversal on likelihood for the unfamiliar witness and circumstantial evidence conditions. Participants in the confession condition were significantly more likely to find Jones guilty than participants in the unfamiliar witness condition, with no other comparisons significant. In terms of certainty, participants in the confession condition were significantly more certain of Jones's guilt than their counterparts in the other three conditions.

Most germane to the present discussion, however, is the fact that even the likelihood and certainty means for the confession condition fall considerably short of the upper limit of the scale. This is hardly surprising since most people have been privy to public discussion of the issues surrounding police interrogation and the obtaining of confessions from suspects. Thus it appears that while differences in the kinds of evidence presented may affect the likelihood of a guilty finding and one's certainty concerning the truth of the factual statement "This defendant is guilty," even the strongest evidence—*i.e.,* a confession of guilt—does not remove the judgment from the realm of probability.

Again, some rough analogies to this situation exist in psychological research, some of which are based on fallacious thinking. For example, it has been demonstrated that most psychologists are more certain of the truth of an empirical finding when it is based on large rather than small samples, even though there is no logical basis for such a belief.[4] Also, greater certainty is often attached to the truth of a finding that is significant at the .01 level than to the truth of one that is significant at .05. Finally, in a somewhat different methodological realm, it seems reasonable to attach greater certainty to the truth of an experimental finding (or, at a minimum, the theoretical interpretation of that finding) if there are no obvious sources of bias and if all of the appropriate control groups have been employed in the study.

Though we have argued that research psychologists and legal professionals involved in trials share the common task of rendering judgments on the probable truth or falsity of certain factual statements, and though we have contended that different types of evidence give rise to different levels of psychological certainty about the truth of factual assertions, we must now underscore a crucial point for the major thrust of this chapter: *To say that this task is shared does not imply*

TABLE I

Mean Scores on the Likelihood and Certainty Measures for
Participants in the Four Conditions*

	Confession	Familiar Witness	Unfamiliar Witness	Circumstantial Evidence
Likelihood of guilty verdict	4.55a**	4.30ab	3.89b	4.15ab
Certainty of Jones's guilt	4.28a	3.42b	3.22b	3.21b

*For both responses, 6 = maximum and 1 = minimum.
**Means with a common letter do not differ significantly (p < .05).

that either psychologists or legal professionals agree universally on the best strategy for arriving at the evidence needed to make their judgments, nor does it even mandate that they believe this to be their most important task. For example, social psychologists who argue for a rule-following approach to the study of social behavior (e.g., Harré & Secord, 1972; Mischel, 1974) have a radically different conception of the kinds of empirical statements that should be generated and the types of evidence that should be used in generating them than their colleagues who hew to classical causal models of theory construction. In short, the two groups have sharply different images of the scientific process and of the nature of the outcomes accruing from the process.

Similarly, legal professionals—and others, for that matter—have differing images of the trial process and of the major functions served by trials, two which seem to imply a common function and one which rests on an entirely different functional assumption. The distinctions we will draw are not mere exercises in logic-chopping; rather, they suggest varying priorities concerning the kinds of questions the psychological researcher should ask about the trial process. Stated differently, the theoretical importance and the applied implications of psychological findings relating to the trial can only be assessed within the context of a particular image of the trial process; consequently, commitment to one image dictates attention to research questions different from those dictated by commitment to another.

IMAGE 1: THE TRIAL AS A RATIONAL, RULE-GOVERNED EVENT

Although we have no empirical evidence for this claim, we suspect that the conviction that trial outcomes should be decided on the grounds of the facts, evidence, and reasoned arguments presented by the contesting parties is one of the most consensually shared values of members of our legal system. Such a value reflects a vision of the trial as a rational, rule-governed event involving the parties to a courtroom controversy in a collective search for truth. Since this image so pervades many people's thinking about the primary function of the trial, we shall deal with it first.

Certainly, the pervasiveness of this image is hardly surprising. The concept of *dialectic* represents a common thread in a 2,400-year-old tapestry of Western philosophy; Aristotle said, "Dialectic lies along the path to the principles of all methods of inquiry" (1960, p. 279). Underlying this faith in dialectic is the commonsense assumption that objective events actually occur and that what is necessary is a method for ascertaining what "really exists" or what "really happened." Dialectic supposedly provides this method through the vehicle of rational, rule-governed argument among reasonable persons who are capable of both knowing and reporting what *is* the case. In a sense, dialectic guides those engaged in it along the path of *episteme* in much the same way that several persons assemble the pieces of a puzzle.

Clearly, this faith in the supremacy and efficacy of dialectic has been embraced by many legal scholars. As a consequence of commitment to dialectic's judicial hegemony, the trial proceedings are viewed as an attempt to discover what "really happened" in an encounter, or in a series of encounters, between two or more involved parties. The process of discovery takes the form of presentation of evidence from witnesses who are supposedly able to tell "the truth, the whole truth, and nothing but the truth," and who will, in fact, perform to the utmost of their capabilities.[5] The assumption that witnesses are capable of knowing and reporting events completely and accurately is further underscored by the attitude of that famous television police officer Joe Friday, whose bland "I only want the facts, ma'am" is familiar to all of us.

The task of marshaling evidence is performed by two trained dialecticians, or teams of dialecticians, who represent the contesting parties.[6] Here, legal philosophy and practice depart from the classical view of dialectic. In the latter, the participating parties are presumed to be objective, disinterested, and aloof from individual bias, concerned only with pursuing the veracity of knowledge claims. Their concern requires them to argue several positions so as to ascertain whether a given position culminates in a logical contradiction. By contrast, our legal system operates somewhat differently. Attorneys are bound to present only one side of a case: their client's. This form of *interested dialectic* represents the method by which evidence is to be presented. Attorneys present arguments supporting their client's position and buttress these arguments with evidence given by witnesses whose testimony provides substantiation.

Finally, either a judge or a jury hears the information contained in the arguments and evidence, and, after weighing it, decides whether or not the defendant is guilty "beyond a reasonable doubt." Throughout the entire proceedings, the sanctity of the dialectical search is supposedly preserved by adherence to a set of rules which ostensibly prevents the introduction of rule-violating, biasing factors into the decisional equation.

This rational, rule-governed image of the trial is reflected, to a large extent, by such popular television courtroom programs as *Perry Mason.* A typical script centers on a trial governed by rational argument, with both attorneys conforming closely to the rules. In most cases, the protagonist (be it Perry Mason, Petrocelli, Kate McShane, or whoever) emerges victorious simply because of his or her ability to bring novel information to bear on the case, information that clearly demonstrates that the defendant is not guilty.

What are the implications of this particular trial image for the research psychologist? First, it should be emphasized that the image itself is factually suspect. Stated differently, while it may represent a desirable vision of what a trial *should be,* it may not accurately mirror the psychological and sociological realities of what a trial *actually is.* Consequently, one investigational priority suggested by this image consists of a concerted attempt to assess the extent to which participants in the trial process are capable of processing information and arriving at decisions in ways conforming to this rational, rule-governed image. A brief consideration of several representative research problems will exemplify this priority more specifically.

As indicated above, a vision of the trial as reasoned dialectic presumes the ability of witnesses to observe and to report events accurately. Nevertheless, it is a psychological commonplace that perception is notoriously capricious; while "seeing is believing," it is also frequently the case that "believing results in seeing." Given the numerous studies demonstrating that perception is influenced by needs, attitudes, situational context, and a host of other variables, there is surely room for a healthy skepticism concerning the ability of trial witnesses to recount accurately events they have observed or to identify correctly persons responsible for criminal acts. Such skepticism is further buttressed by the results of several studies dealing with the accuracy of eyewitness identifications (Buckhout, 1974; Wall, 1965). In general, the findings indicate that eyewitnesses are very suggestible and quite prone to error in subsequent identifications, a less than startling finding when one considers that the initial observations of the witness are often made under extremely stressful conditions, in a brief time span, and under less than optimal observational circumstances— *e.g.,* relative darkness or poor lighting. Thus, in our simple study described earlier, the participants who received evidence based on eyewitness identification were probably justified in their uncertainty about the defendant's guilt, particularly when the identification was made by a witness who was unacquainted with the defendant. To assess the extent to which the rational, rule-governed ideal can be realized in the courtroom, then, psychological researchers should assign high priority to questions relating to the ability of individuals to observe and report events accurately, as well as seek to identify the variables that inhibit and facilitate this process. While some helpful inferences can probably be gleaned from the substantial literature dealing with perception and information-processing, numerous predictions remain to be tested in the "real world" environs of the courtroom.

Even if it could be demonstrated that witnesses are able to report information accurately—or, alternatively, that conditions could be structured to maximize the fidelity of their reports—achievement of a rational, rule-governed trial process would still hinge on the ability of decision-makers to weigh this information rationally. In other words, jurors would have to lay aside their prejudices and preconceived views regarding the case and replace such biases with a dispassionate analysis of the arguments and evidence. Again, there is reason to question the extent to which such an ideal can be realized, and several important aspects of the general issue are fair investigational game for the research psychologist.

Consider, for instance, the potential impact of pre-trial information on the juror's objectivity. It is, of course, obvious that the event our society labels "a trial" does not occur in a psychological and sociological vacuum. Thus events extrinsic to the trial often provide additional, potentially biasing information for jurors. Considerable research supports the notion that potential jurors are influenced by such pre-trial publicity (*e.g.,* Hoiberg & Stires, 1973; Jaffee, 1965; Kline & Jess, 1966; Tans & Chaffee, 1966), although the effect is hardly simple, with numerous individual difference variables intervening. To counteract the influence of exposure to certain kinds of pre-trial information, the legal system has developed rules aimed at minimizing its impact. Thus the voir dire permits attorneys and judges to determine, among other things, the extent to which pre-trial publicity has affected potential jurors, while the change of venue permits geographic relocation of the trial when bias and prejudice are so extreme as to preclude the possibility of a fair trial at the original site.

Nevertheless, application of these rules may pose as many problems as it resolves. For example, in this era of heavy mass media exposure, it is unlikely that certain cases can be relocated in *any* geographical area where potential jurors have remained psychologically unscathed by pre-trial publicity. At a more basic level, we are unaware of any data revealing whether the very information that a change of venue has occurred may be sufficient to affect the information-processing of jurors. In other words, knowledge that a trial has been shifted from its original site may itself create biases and expectations that interfere with rational information-processing and decision-making, a possibility worthy of research.

Furthermore, although one purpose of the voir dire is to eliminate jurors who may be biased toward either of the two parties, the process is often ineffective (Siebert et al., 1970). As we shall indicate in greater detail when discussing the second trial image, pre-trial publicity is not the only factor that may influence jurors' ability to process information and to reach decisions objectively. Such variables as the personal attractiveness of the defendant (Landy & Aronson, 1969) and the presentational skills of the witness (Miller et al., 1975a) also affect juror behavior. In short, it may be difficult, if not impossible, to control all factors that may cause jurors to deviate from a rational path in assessing the evidence and in reaching their verdicts. To the extent that this is so, the rational, rule-governed image will remain an ideal rather than a reality, but, as we have sought to emphasize, more research is needed before any firm conclusions can be reached.

Since we have already mentioned the questionable psychological effectiveness of certain legal rules, we will close our discussion of the rational, rule-governed trial image by considering one of the more suspect conventions: the charge to the jury to disregard inadmissible material. Obviously, this charge springs from certain assumptions about what constitutes relevant and acceptable information for arriving at a verdict, assumptions closely allied with the ideal of the trial as dialectic. To approximate this ideal, however, members of the jury must be psychologically capable of complying with the judge's instructions. A key question for research, then, concerns the extent to which such behavioral compliance is possible, or, alternatively, the conditions under which it is possible to disregard inadmissible material as opposed to the conditions under which it is not.

Several studies (*e.g.,* Sue et al., 1973) have revealed that a single instance of extremely damaging inadmissible evidence is sufficient to influence the verdicts of jurors even though they are instructed to disregard it. For the most part, however, these investigations do not closely approximate the actual courtroom environment; typically, role-playing jurors (or, as they are often labeled, *simulated jurors)* are provided with brief, written synopses of the trial which vary as to whether or not they contain the inadmissible evidence. After reading these synopses, the role-playing jurors then render their verdicts, and the judgments of the two groups are compared. Because they are far removed from the physical milieu and the legal trappings of the courtroom, these studies are often criticized by members of the legal community on grounds of dubious generalizability or ecological validity.

In an extensive program of research dealing with the possible effects of video-taped trial materials on juror response (*e.g.,* Miller, 1976; Miller et al., 1975a), we have conducted several studies aimed at assessing the influence of inadmissible material on juror information-processing and decision-making.[7] One ostensible advantage of videotape, of course, is that it permits the deletion of inadmissible material before the jurors hear the trial, thus assuring that such rule-violating information will not intrude on their psyches. In other words, deletion of inadmissible material presumes the possible ineffectiveness of the judge's injunction and substitutes actual expunging of the material from the ongoing trial.

As yet, we have detected no evidence that the presence of inadmissible testimony exerts a systematic effect on juror verdicts; *i.e.,* there have been no significant differences in the verdicts of jurors exposed to varying amounts of inadmissible testimony. In this research, we have achieved a much more realistic simulation of the typical courtroom environment than have previous investigators (Miller et al., 1974). Actual groups of impaneled jurors, led by the presiding judge to believe they were participating in a real trial, have viewed the reenactment of an entire three-and-one-half-hour civil case involving an automobile injury claim. The various versions of the trial differ only in the amount of inadmissible testimony they contain, with a range from zero to six items of inadmissible testimony. These items, however, are not highly damaging or psychologically colorful instances; rather, they are intended to approximate typical kinds of objections that occur in the everyday conduct of trials.

Naturally, as underscored earlier in footnote 3, interpretation of findings of no differences—*i.e.,* results based on failures to reject the null hypothesis—must be made cautiously. Still, we have tried to minimize sources of Type II error in most of the research: substantial samples of jurors have been used, measuring instruments have been carefully pretested, control of potentially relevant extraneous variables has been pursued rigorously, and, as indicated above, studies have been conducted in highly realistic courtroom environments. Consequently, we have considerable psychological confidence in our findings of no differences in juror response even though we are unable to specify the precise level of statistical credence that can be placed in them.

To the extent that our confidence is justified, it leads to the commonsense conclusion that the relationships between use of inadmissible material and subsequent juror behavior are complex. Rather than seeking simple, sovereign generalizations, the best plan of attack lies in systematic variation of both the *qualitative* and *quantitative* aspects of inadmissible material so as to determine how such variations influence juror response. Moreover, we are presently seeking to determine what features of the rule-governed communicative interchanges accompanying introduction of inadmissible material play a role in shaping jurors' perceptions. For example, the content of the inadmissible material may sometimes be relatively unimportant; rather, what may matter is the heightened salience of the material resulting from the lodging of an objection and the subsequent communicative interplay occurring between the judge and the contesting attorneys. If this is so, an attorney's best strategy may sometimes rest in ignoring his opponent's introduction of inadmissible material, even though such a move may not seem to square intuitively with an image of the trial as a rational, rule-governed process.

Since we have expressed skepticism about the likelihood of achieving trial circumstances that are fully congruent with the rational, rule-governed ideal, it may appear that we have lingered excessively on this image. Our preoccupation rests on the following assumption: even if such an ideal cannot be fully realized, greater understanding of the variables affecting trial processes and outcomes should allow the legal system to conduct trials more closely approximating ideal dialectical circumstances. The debate about the limits of humanity's rationality is one of Western civilization's most venerable philosophical disputes. Despite considerable pessimism about the extent to which rationality is possible, most persons seem to agree that systems of rational decision-making are a desirable goal. When applied to the trial situation, this fact implies that any contributions psychologists can make toward understanding the information-processing and decision-making of trial participants may bear fruit in the form of an improved courtroom climate for rational decision-making.

IMAGE 2: THE TRIAL AS A TEST OF CREDIBILITY

We commenced this chapter by emphasizing that the task of judicial participants in a courtroom trial closely resembles the mission of the social scientist; specifically, both groups must render judgments about the probable truth or falsity of certain factual statements. In the trial setting, contingency is a necessary consequence of incomplete and conflicting sets of factual information. Stated differently, a trial is by nature historical and retrodictive; the contesting parties scrutinize and investigate the past and eventually select samples of available evidence and information which best support their respective positions. Again, this task is closely akin to that of the social scientist, with the exception that trial adversaries are not expected to sample randomly or representatively. Instead, they are required to sample selectively; *i.e.,* as indicated above, they incorporate into their cases only those items of information and evidence that bolster their client's position.

Obviously, this inherent bias in sampling creates serious judgmental problems for those charged with rendering a verdict. Furthermore, these problems again underscore the practical limitations of an image of the trial as a rational, rule-governed process, for if factual information is incomplete and deliberately biased this dialectical ideal is difficult, if not impossible, to achieve.

Consequently, an image of the trial as a test of credibility emerges. Such a vision conceives of information-processing in a broader context than the previous image. Since factual information and evidence are necessarily incomplete and biased, those charged with decision-making, whether they be judges or jurors, must not only weigh the information and evidence, but must also evaluate the veracity of the opposing evidential and informational sources. Making these judgments of credibility demands attention not only to the factual information presented, but also to the *way* in which it is presented, the apparent qualifications of witnesses, and numerous other relevant factors. In short, the judge or jurors must survey the rich field of stimuli that constitutes the trial setting and select cues which permit judgments about the probable trustworthiness and/or competence of particular witnesses.

We hasten to add that this image of the trial is not necessarily incongruent with, or mutually exclusive from, a vision of the trial as a rational, rule-governed process. Both images rely heavily on the assumption that the primary function of a trial is to arrive at the soundest possible judgment concerning the criminal guilt or civil responsibility of a defendant—in other words, to determine the probability of the truth or falsity of the relevant factual statement on the best grounds possible. Where the two images diverge is in the relative emphasis they place on weighing information and evidence per se as opposed to evaluating the believability of the *sources* of such information. Thus we grant that the difference between the two images is one of degree, not kind.

Even this difference in degree, however, has important implications concerning legal and research priorities. To illustrate: Suppose a researcher demonstrated empirically that jurors can better retain relevant trial-related information and more successfully identify logical fallacies in arguments if they read the information and arguments from a written transcript rather than hear them presented orally.[8] Since both retention of relevant information and identification of logical fallacies are important ingredients of the dialectical process, proponents of Image 1 might argue that trial procedures should be changed to permit jurors to read arguments and testimony instead of hearing them. Such a change, however, would drastically reduce the information available to jurors. More specifically, the nonverbal and paralinguistic cues of witnesses and attorneys would be purged from the proceedings, and, as a result of this sharply curtailed stimulus field, jurors would be deprived of information needed for making inferences about witness and attorney credibility. In short, jurors would be forced to take the truth of the information and evidence as a given, and in cases where factual information conflicted they would be hard-pressed to arrive at grounds for discriminating between contradictory accounts. Thus an advocate of Image 2 would probably contend that gains in information retention and logical analysis would be more than offset by losses in information required to form intelligent judgments about credibility.

Of course, the extent of congruity between the two images depends partially on the cues that jurors actually use in arriving at judgments of credibility. Unfortunately, although there is certainly no shortage of conventional wisdom about the matter, social psychologists and communication researchers have yet to develop a taxonomy of behaviors that clearly qualify as valid indicants of questionable credibility. In the absence of such defensible indicants, jurors probably make use of a variety of cues, some of which may be rationally justified and some of which may not.

By far the most dubious cues are those representing *fixed attributes* of the individual—*e.g.,* physical appearance, race, or sex. In their most unsavory form, judgments of credibility based on fixed attributes become nothing more than exercises in stereotyping; a defendant or witness is perceived as untrustworthy and/or incompetent solely on grounds of skin color, gender, or an "unpleasant" or "sinister" countenance. Particularly (though not exclusively) when the outcome of a case hinges on chosing the more credible of two directly conflicting accounts—*e.g.,* when an alleged rape victim testifies that a sexual act was forcibly consummated but the defendant testifies that the "victim" voluntarily entered into it—such stereotypes may exert a powerful influence on juror responses. Just how these judgments interact with such variables as the type of case—*e.g.,* whether certain stereotypes regarding blacks are more likely to influence decisions in rape cases than in embezzlement cases, or, for that matter, whether these stereotypes may operate to a defendant's advantage in one type of case and to his or her disadvantage in another—is still largely unknown. To be sure, some recent work stemming from an attribution theory perspective indicates that physically attractive persons are likely to be less severely punished for transgressions than are relatively unattractive individuals (Dion, 1972; Efran, 1974), and that physical attraction interacts with the type of crime to influence severity of punishment (Sigall & Osgrove, 1975): specifically, when a crime is largely unrelated to physical attractiveness (*e.g.,* burglary), attractive defendants receive more lenient sentences; when a crime is perceived as attractiveness-related (*e.g.,* a swindle), however, attractive defendants are accorded harsher treatment. Although suggestive, these studies have limited implications for an image of the trial as a test of credibility: first, it is not clear that the observed differences stem from discrepancies in perceived credibility; second, the studies deal exclusively with defendants and provide no data concerning the extent to which similar processes are at work when jurors assess the credibility of witnesses. Thus, until considerably more research has been accumulated, the effects of fixed-attribute cues on judgments of credibility will remain a mystery.

A second category of cues for evaluating credibility lies in the behaviors a witness *exhibits* when presenting testimony. On the face of it, these cues appear to have a stronger rational justification and to converge more closely with the previously discussed image of the trial as a rational, rule-governed process. Even here, however, the matter is not this simple, for participation in a trial is likely to engender considerable anxiety, and persons vary widely in their responses to anxiety arousal. As a consequence, a flushed face, a nervous twitch, or a halting delivery—all of which may be used as cues for inferring questionable trustworthiness and/or competence—may reflect nothing more than an attack of extreme anxiety. On the other hand, persons who have developed good control of their communicative behaviors may be perceived as highly credible, even if they deviate from the straight-and-narrow in their answers to questions.

As mentioned earlier, some recent research of our own bears upon this possibility (Miller et al., 1975a,b). Role-playing jurors, randomly assigned to one or the other of two conditions, heard the same testimony presented by a strong or a weak witness. To control for other possible contaminating factors (physical appearance, sex, etc.), a professional actor portrayed both witnesses. In the strong witness condition, the actor responded to the attorney's questions in a confident, assertive way, displaying few distracting nonverbal and paralinguistic behaviors. By contrast, his responses in the weak witness condition were halting, unsure, and accompanied by a number of nervous bodily and vocal behaviors. After hearing the testimony, all role-playing jurors completed an instrument designed to measure their retention of the information presented by the witness, their perceptions of the witness's credibility, and their verdicts in the case.

Although verdict was not significantly affected by witness strength, both retention of information and ratings of credibility were. In two separate studies, jurors who heard the strong witness retained significantly more of the testimonial information and rated the witness as significantly more credible. Thus, holding both message content and the fixed attributes of the witness constant, presentational skill exerted a strong impact on juror response. These results would indicate that the grounds for arriving at judgments of credibility may sometimes bear little relationship to the personal integrity of the witness or the substantive merits of his or her testimony. In short, the test of credibility used by jurors may not square closely with rational, reasoned criteria for assessing the believability of witnesses.

As indicated above, a major problem lies in the researcher's present inability to specify the cues that signal deception or prevarication on the part of the witness. Given such a knowledge gap, one alternative research strategy involves the study of conditions that inhibit or facilitate a person's ability to detect deception. This approach permits researchers to beg the question of *precisely what* cues are associated with deception and to concentrate instead on displays of various *sets* of facial and bodily cues. For example, a study by Ekman & Friesen (1974) revealed that persons could better detect deception from bodily cues than from facial cues. In this research, a group of persons were videotaped responding truthfully and untruthfully about emotions they experienced while viewing a film. A second group of subjects then viewed the taped responses: half of the subjects saw only the head and half saw only the body. Since the audio track was eliminated, judgments of truthfulness were based entirely on the available nonverbal behaviors. Subjects who saw the body-only shot were more successful in detecting deception than were subjects who saw the head-only shot.

Obviously, the procedures employed in Ekman & Friesen's study are far removed from the practical realities of the courtroom. The day has not yet come when jurors are denied visual access to the heads of witnesses, nor is it feasible to eliminate the verbal messages that convey information and evidence to jurors. In ongoing research of our own, however, we have extended the Ekman & Friesen paradigm to take account of these realities (Hocking et al., 1975; Miller et al., 1975a). Observers make judgments of the veracity of witnesses under a variety of observational conditons, summarized in Table II. Furthermore, while the witness present truthful and untruthful answers to questions dealing with their emotional states (a situation akin to that studied by Ekman & Friesen), they also respond truthfully and untruthfully to questions about an event they have witnessed, a task more closely related to the content of typical courtroom testimony. Thus two accuracy scores are calculated for each observer: one representing degree of success at detecting emotional deception and the other indexing degree of success at detecting factual deception.

Although the research is not yet completed, several preliminary find ngs deserve mention. First, like Ekman & Friesen, we found that observers' accuracy in detecting emotional deception was greatest in the body-only conditon. This superiority did not, however, hold for factual deception; when attempting to identify instances of factual lying, observers in both the head-and-body and the head-only conditions were more accurate than their body-only counterparts. This discrepancy between optimal observational conditions for rendering the two types of judgments illustrates one of the many problems encountered in generalizing the results of laboratory studies to the courtroom environment, for it indicates that application of Ekman & Friesen's findings to courtroom testimony could be quite misleading.

When compared with visual information only, visual *plus* audio information resulted in higher observer accuracy for both factual and emotional judgments, though this difference was significant for factual judgments only. Thus, while nonverbal cues may provide an important source of information for drawing inferences about possible deception, the addition of paralinguistic cues and other vocal behaviors appears to produce an increase in judgmental accuracy. Since jurors in a courtroom are unlikely to have a chance to sample the nonverbal behaviors of witnesses apart from their verbal responses, this finding is encouraging for proponents of Image 2.

A final preliminary finding does raise several serious questions about the image of a trial as a test of credibility, at least as trials are now conducted. Overall accuracy was greatest for observers in the transcript condition; in other words, persons who read the transcribed answers of witnesses, without the benefit of any nonverbal or paralinguistic cues, were most successful in identifying untruthful responses. Although this result is perplexing and counterintuitive, several specialists in nonverbal communication have indicated that it is consistent with previous research, and we are presently scanning the literature to locate this prior work. Moreover, we are beginning a study aimed at evaluating several possible alternative explanations for the higher accuracy of observers in the transcript condition. Perhaps written communication permits greater detachment, thus making observers less susceptible to distracting or skillfully deceptive nonverbal behaviors. Certainly, a written transcript provides more redundancy; whereas the verbal and nonverbal behaviors of oral testimony are fleeting, a

TABLE II

**Various Observational Conditions Under Which Judgments of
Emotional and Factual Deception Were Made.[a]**

	Head Only		Body Only		Head and Body		
	Audio and Visual	Visual only	Audio and Visual	Visual only	Audio and Visual	Visual only	
Color							Audio only
Black-and-white							Transcript only

[a]For all observational conditions, observers made judgments of both emotional and factual reports.

transcript can be examined and reexamined for clues concerning possible discrepancies. In a similar vein, effective processing of transcript information does not demand continuous attention, while oral testimony that is lost because of inattention or distraction cannot be retrieved. Whatever the explanation, the finding casts doubt on much of the conventional wisdom regarding the efficacy of nonverbal and paralinguistic cues as data for making accurate inferences about the motives and dispositions of communicators.

This latter finding also underscores our chief concern about the image of a trial as a test of credibility. Unquestionably, courtroom decision-makers do make inferences about the credibility of witnesses, attorneys, and contesting parties, and these inferences undoubtedly figure heavily in the eventual judgment. Whether these inferences have a solid basis *in fact* is another issue; as we have tried to indicate, they may often be grounded in stereotyping, folklore, or "commonsense intuition." An important priority for the psychological researcher, then, is not only identification of the specific cues used to make credibility judgments, but also a concerted effort to determine the circumstances that enhance or detract from the accuracy of such judgments. Until more is known about these questions, the extent to which decisions based on weighing the relative credibility of trial contestants are consistent with accepted legal values regarding just decision-making in the courtroom remains questionable.

IMAGE 3: THE TRIAL AS A CONFLICT-RESOLVING RITUAL

A widely held sociological generalization states that if societies do not develop acceptable institutions for peacefully resolving conflicts, they will be resolved by violent means. In American society, the legal system, in general, and the courtroom trial, in particular, are important institutions for facilitating the orderly and peaceful resolution of conflict. "Legal and political procedures, such as trials and elections," says Kenneth Boulding, "are essentially social rituals designed to minimize the costs of conflict" (1975, p. 423). His remark captures the image of a trial as a conflict-resolving ritual.

How does this viewpoint differ from the two images previously discussed? At the risk of oversimplification, we suggest that it removes primary attention from the concept of *doing justice* and transfers it to the psychological realm of *creating a sense that justice is being done.* Lest we be misunderstood, we do not believe that the two concerns are unrelated or diametrically opposed (though history has recorded instances when they seemed to be) nor do we think that those who advocate an image of the trial as a conflict-resolving ritual are unconcerned about the quality of individual decisions. What is involved is a shift in priority: while a proponent of the rational, rule-governed image would assert that the primary function of a trial is to approach "the truth" as closely as possible in any given case, a supporter of the conflict-resolving ritual image would contend that the outcome of any particular trial is less important than maintaining the shared perception that our legal system provides an efficient means for resolving conflict peacefully.

A specific example should clarify this rather abstract distinction. In our research on the use of videotape in courtroom trials, we have sometimes encountered the criticism that the use of such materials as prerecorded videotaped trials and videotaped depositions "dehumanizes" the trial. Obviously, issues concerning the most humanistic way of dispensing justice are complex and multifaceted. Suppose, for instance, that use of videotaped trial materials permits more rapid scheduling of cases. Certainly, it seems eminently humane to grant economically disadvantaged persons, faced with the hardship of medical and hospital bills, their "day in court" as promptly as possible. Or consider the plight of the alleged rape victim, forced to recount the details of the harrowing, psychologically debilitating experience in a crowded courtroom. Might it not be more humane to videotape the victim's testimony, as well as the subsequent cross-examination, away from the threatening confines of the courtroom? The list of such possibilities is almost endless.

As we have conversed with these critics, however, we have discovered that they usually equate "dehumanizing" with "an absence of, or a reduction in, face-to-face courtroom confrontation." In other words, interpersonal contact is viewed as a good thing, and any reduction of it is perceived as a threat to our trial system. When asked to provide a rationale for their position, these critics often assert that the substitution of mediated communication technology for direct interpersonal confrontation will detract from the "dignity" or "majesty" of the court—that it will culminate in a lack of public confidence in the legal system. In other words, once the humanistic rhetoric is stripped from the argument, these critics stand revealed as advocates of Image 3: *Their chief concern is with a possible loss of collective faith in the trial as an equitable means of resolving conflict peacefully.*

We do not mean to treat this concern lightly; in fact, we have no serious quarrel with the ideological thrust of Image 3. Nevertheless, questions about the impact of procedural changes on our society's attitudes and perceptions about the trial system are empirical ones, and we have discovered little research dealing with them. Without such investigations, Image 3 can become a barrier to needed legal changes; *any* change can be labeled a threat to the image of the trial as a conflict-resolving ritual. To embrace such a position is to ignore the fact that changes in the rituals and procedures associated with various social institutions occur constantly without any apparent loss in the public's confidence in the institution. For example, few, if any, university professors now meet their students in academic robes; many large classes are taught on closed-circuit television; and in some areas programmed instruction has largely replaced "Mark Hopkins on the other end of a log." Despite the laments of some traditionalists, we are unaware of any convincing evidence that such procedural changes (changes in educational ritual, one might say) have produced a serious decline in public confidence in our educational system. This is not to state that our schools are entirely immune to a "credibility gap," but only to suggest that the causes for lack of confidence do not appear to spring from changes in institutional rituals and procedures.

The preceding analysis suggests two research priorities relating to our final image. First, the extent to which people presently share positive attitudes and perceptions about the trial as a conflict-resolving ritual should be systematically assessed. Some proponents of Image 3 seem to feel that the status quo reflects an ultimate triumph in institutional effectiveness—as one jurist has been cited, "they are 100 percent in favor of progress and 1,000 percent opposed to change." Perhaps such caution is warranted; changes in the procedures and trappings of the courtroom trial may engender a wholesale crisis in confidence. On the other hand, certain segments of our society manifest considerable skepticism about contemporary versions of due process; they view the courts as an instrument for legitimizing and perpetuating the present power structure, rather than as a just, equitable system for peacefully resolving conflicts. In some cases, disenchantment with the legal system has culminated in attempts to resolve conflicts by employing force and violence, by going "outside the system" for redress of real or imagined grievances. What features of our present trial system foster these negative attitudes? What are the psychological characteristics of individuals who deny the effectiveness of present trial procedures, and how do these persons differ from those who place their confidence in the courts? Although there is a smattering of research and a multitude of folklore dealing with these kinds of questions, considerable fertile investigational soil remains unturned.

If one accepts the crucial need for viable institutions that facilitate peaceful resolution of social conflict but at the same time grants that the effectiveness of such institutions may often be enhanced by change, a final research issue is suggested: what strategies and methods can be used to foster needed changes in trial conduct while at the same time maintaining a shared consensus of positive attitudes toward the legal system? Concern with this general question combines a realization of the value of change with an awareness that a sense of relative stability is often an important ingredient of public confidence. Perhaps even more important, it underscores the fact that our final image is not necessarily discordant with the two discussed earlier: careful planning and research should make it possible for citizens to have their justice and their sense of it, too.

SUMMING UP

In this chapter, we have sketched three contemporary images of the trial and have examined some of the implications of each for psychological research dealing with legal problems. As we have sought to indicate throughout, the three images are neither exhaustive nor mutually exclusive; to a large extent, they reflect differences in degree, rather than in kind. Even so, each image suggests certain investigational priorities for the researcher. Obviously, we have provided only a sampling, not a complete inventory, of the questions implied by each trial image. Still, we believe the distinctions that have been drawn possess utility for psychological researchers, primarily because the conduct of research and the interpretation of research findings can be accomplished more effectively if the investigator begins with a clear conception of both the nature and primary functions of the trial process.

FOOTNOTES

Actually, as this paper progresses, it will become apparent we are also concerned with trial participants who are not legal professionals—specifically, that decision-making body called the jury.

[2] Here the factual statement refers to whether or not Jones actually slew another person

under circumstances consistent with the legal definition of murder, not to whether he was or was not judged guilty. For the latter situation, the appropriate factual statement would be "Jones was found guilty of murder," an assertion the truth or falsity of which does not often involve probability considerations.

[3] We will avoid the phrase "or false" for two reasons: first, because it is stylistically cumbersome; second, to avoid a lengthy digression into the problems involved in attempting to falsify certain relational statements in social science, *i.e.,* the failure to reject the null hypothesis chestnut. Obviously, however, this problem has considerable import for some psychological research dealing with the trial process. For instance, if researchers were studying the impact of the use of a communication medium such as videotape on jurors' responses, they might expect it would result in responses comparable to those presented in a live trial *i.e.,* that there would be no significant differences in the responses of jurors viewing live and videotaped trials. Such a finding requires them to confront squarely the logical hazards associated with failure to reject the null.

[4] In fact, the implications of a small sample finding may be more profound, since the effect must be large to offset the sampling error.

[5] The extreme importance of such optimal performance is underscored by the severe legal penalties (*e.g.,* perjury) that follow for not doing so.

[6] People who lack such dialectical competence are discouraged from active participation; thus jurists usually advise against litigants foregoing an attorney and representing themselves.

[7] This research was supported by NSF Grant #GI 38398, Gerald R. Miller and Fredrick S. Siebert, Principal Investigators.

[8] Later we will discuss preliminary findings from our own research which do, in fact, suggest that observers are more successful in detecting deceptive communication from written transcripts than from oral testimony.

REFERENCES

Aristotle. *Topica,* E.S. Forster (trans.). Cambridge, Mass.: Harvard University Press, 1960.

Boulding, K.E. Truth or power. *Science,* 1975, *190,* 423.

Buckhout, R. Eyewitness testimony. *Scientific American,* 1974, *231,* 23-31.

Dion, K. Physical attractiveness and evaluation of children's transgressions. *Journal of Personality and Social Psychology,* 1972, *24,* 207-213.

Efran, M.E. The effect of physical appearance on the judgment of guilt, interpersonal attraction, and severity of recommended punishment in a simulated jury task. *Journal of Research in Personality,* 1974, *8,* 45-54.

Ekman, P. & Friesen, W.V. Detecting deception from the body or face. *Journal of Personality and Social Psychology,* 1974, *29,* 288-298.

Harré, R. & Secord, P.F. *The explanation of social behaviour.* Totowa, N.J.: Littlefield, Adams, 1972.

Hocking, J.E., Bauchner, J.E., Kaminski, E.P. & Miller, G.R. *Detecting deceptive communication from verbal, visual, and paralinguistic cues.* Unpublished manuscript, Department of Communication, Michigan State University, 1975.

Hoiberg, B.C. & Stires, L.K. The effect of several types of pretrial publicity on the guilt attributions of simulated jurors. *Journal of Applied Social Psychology*, 1973, *3*, 267-275.

Jaffee, C. The press and the oppressed—A study of prejudicial news reporting in criminal cases. *The Journal of Criminal Law, Criminology and Police Service*, 1965, *56*, 1-17.

Kline, F.G. & Jess, P.H. Prejudicial publicity: Its effect on law school mock juries. *Journalism Quarterly*, 1966, *43*, 113-116.

Landy, D. & Aronson, E. The influence of the character of the criminal and his victim on the decisions of simulated jurors. *Journal of Experimental Social Psychology*, 1969, *5*, 141-152.

Miller, G.R. Jurors' responses to videotaped trial materials: Some recent findings. *Personality and Social Psychology Bulletin*, 1975, *1*, 561-569.

Miller, G.R. The effects of videotaped trial materials on juror response. In G. Bermant (ed.), *Psychology and the law: Research frontiers*. Lexington, Mass.: D.C. Heath, 1976, pp. 185-208.

Miller, G.R., Bender, D.C., Boster, F.J., Florence, B.T., Fontes, N.E., Hocking, J.E. & Nicholson, H.E. The effects of videotape testimony in jury trials. *Brigham Young University Law Review*, 1975a, *1*, 331-373.

Miller, G.R., Bender, D.C., Florence, B.T. & Nicholson, H.E. Real versus reel: What's the verdict? *Journal of Communication*, 1974, *24*, 99-111.

Miller, G.R. & Boster, F.J. *Effects of type of evidence on judgments of likelihood of conviction and certainty of guilt*. Unpublished manuscript, Department of Communication, Michigan State University, 1975.

Miller, G.R., Boster, F.J., Fontes, N.E., LeFebvre, D.J. & Poole, M.S. Jurors' responses to videotaped trial materials—Some further evidence. *Michigan State Bar Journal*, 1975b, *54*, 278-282.

Mischel, T. (ed.). *Understanding other persons*. Oxford, England: Basil Blackwell, 1974.

Siebert, F.S., Wilcox, W. & Hough, G. *Free press and fair trial: Some dimensions of the problem*. Athens, Ga.: University of Georgia Press, 1970.

Sigall, H. & Osgrove, N. Beautiful but dangerous: Effects of offender attractiveness and nature of the crime on juridic judgment. *Journal of Personality and Social Psychology*, 1975, *31*, 410-414.

Sue, S., Smith, R.E. & Caldwell, C. Effects of inadmissible evidence on the decisions of simulated jurors: A moral dilemma. *Journal of Applied Social Psychology*, 1973, *3*, 345-353.

Tans, M.D. & Chaffee, S.H. Pretrial publicity and juror prejudice. *Journalism Quarterly*, 1966, *43*, 647-654.

Wall, P.M. *Eyewitness identification in criminal cases*. Springfield, Ill.: Charles C. Thomas, 1965.

Persuasion During the Voir Dire

RICHARD ALAN BLUNK
BRUCE DENNIS SALES

I. THE PURPOSE OF THE VOIR DIRE EXAMINATION[1]

It is the right of many individuals accused of a criminal offense, as well as both parties in a civil litigation, to have the issue at question determined by a disinterested and impartial jury.[2] For example, the court in *Scribner v. State,* 3 Okla. Crim. 601, 603, 108 P. 422, 423, 35 L.R.A. (n.s.) 985, 988 (1910) called this right one of the "cardinal principles" of our system of jurisprudence; Justice Weaver in *State v. Crofford,* 121 Iowa 395, 399, 96 N.W. 889, 891 (1903) described it as "absolutely essential to the proper administration of justice." However, determining what degree of fairness and impartiality is necessary to qualify jurors to serve constantly arises in actual practice.[3] This difficulty is acute since the partiality of even one juror vitiates the jury as a whole,[4] requiring that the verdict reached by such a partial jury be set aside.[5]

The opportunity to prove or disprove impartiality among the prospective triers of fact is inherent in the guarantee of the right to an impartial jury,[6] and the voir dire examination is- in theory, at least, the process through which the trial judge discharges his obligation to dismiss those veniremen who are not fit for jury duty.[7] Incompetency under statute is a question of law; however, since

39

the statutory delineation of certain grounds of incompetency does not preclude the exclusion of jurors on other grounds,[8] in cases where the statutes are not inclusive incompetency becomes a question of fact to be determined by the trial court in the exercise of sound discretion.[9] While it is recognized that the trial judge ordinarily has great discretion in conducting the voir dire,[10] which will not be disturbed unless blatantly abused,[11] some statutes dictate that the court must, on the motion of either party, examine the prospective jurors to determine their competency.[12] It has been suggested, however, that the more convenient and efficient practice is to allow counsel to conduct the examination under judicial supervision and direction.[13] This practice is consistent with counsel's being allowed X number of peremptory challenges which may be used to eliminate a prospective juror when the judge refuses to act for cause.[14]

Although the trial judge can limit the extent of the voir dire examination on any of the venireman's particular qualifications[15] and rule upon the propriety of the form of the questions,[16] his discretionary power is nonetheless subject to the essential demands of fairness.[17] Therefore, to ensure judgment by a fair and impartial jury the trial judge should allow counsel reasonable latitude in their examination of the veniremen.[18] For example, the court in *State v. Higgs,* 143 Conn. 138, 142, 120 A. 2d, 152, 154 (1956) stated that "in exercising its discretion, the court should grant such latitude as is reasonably necessary to fairly accomplish the purposes of the voir dire." In light of such reasoning, the latitude of questioning is not generally limited to those questions formulated by statute but, as the court in *Pinder v. State,* 27 Fla. 370, 370, 8 So. 837, 838 (1891) noted, should be "so varied and elaborated as the circumstances surrounding the juror under examination in relation to the case on trial would seem to require."

Generally, the voir dire examination by counsel is proper so long as it attempts to discover the veniremen's state of mind on issues directly and indirectly related to the litigation in question;[19] therefore, questions which go primarily to ascertain any ground of incompetency leading to a challenge for cause are universally permissible.[20] Although the scope of the inquiry is not always confined strictly to these areas,[21] the court in *Vega v. Evans,* 128 Ohio St. 535, 191 N.E. 757, 757 (1934) stated that if it extends beyond such subjects and goes toward establishing a peremptory challenge, it must be conducted in "good faith with the object of obtaining a fair and impartial jury and must not be likely to create bias or prejudice [for or against any side]." Although the voir dire examination is not supposed to afford counsel an opportunity to influence the veniremen, such may not be the case in actual practice.

II. STRATEGIES FOR THE VOIR DIRE EXAMINATION

There are two philosophies[22] on the importance of the voir dire examination among members of the bar. One acknowledges the potential benefits of thorough questioning; the other, as Brody notes, does not:

> There is one school of thought which holds that any twelve good men and true will do; that picking a jury is a wasteful, futile pastime. . . .Disciples of this school say that all jurors are fair and impartial, at least in theory, and anyhow there is no way of finding out who is fair and who is not by merely asking questions. . . .Take the first twelve men, put them in the box, swear them in, and—on with the trial.[23]

While some fatalistic attorneys simply accept the first twelve veniremen with neither questioning nor ceremony,[24] a strategy more commonly used by proponents of this school involves counsel's histrionically declining the opportunity of questioning the veniremen with a "grand gesture"[25] while explicitly stressing his faith in the ability of the jury system in general, and these veniremen in particular, to render a fair and just verdict. Counsel's "sincerity" implies that a fair and just verdict for the case at bar will be one favorable to his client. This "grand-stand play"[26] is, therefore, a covert ingratiatory ploy. In pursuit of this goal, advocates of this strategy believe that the veniremen's impressions of counsel, especially *first* impressions, are crucial in increasing the juror's receptivity toward counsel's position. Schweitzer, for example, notes:

> The old adage, "first impressions stick," may not contain a truth applicable to all situations, but at least it contains a thought counsel should bear in mind in selecting a jury. Where counsel acts in such a manner before the jury as to create a feeling of annoyance at his tactics, or some suspicion of his honesty and sincerity, he begins his case with a decided handicap, which all his ingenuity during the course of the trial may not serve to eradicate. . .
>
> Counsel should bear in mind that juries frequently decide issues on the basis of their like or dislike for counsel. . . .[27]

Goldstein believes similarly; he warns that:

> In most cases it is found that the jury "tries" the lawyer rather than the clients. . . .It, therefore, becomes important that the attorney should never lose sight of the fact that he is appealing to the jury to return a favorable verdict.[28]

The courts have been aware of such juror proclivities and counsel's attempts to make use of them. The court in *Skidmore v. B. & O. Railroad,* 167 F. 2d 54, 61, 62 (1948), for example, notes:

> In a series of pamphlets on trial practice, recently published under the auspices of the American Bar Association, one author writes that "the advocate*** must always recognize that the jury is judging the lawyer as well as the witnesses, quick to take sides because of the protagonists rather than their opinion of the testimony;" another says that the jurors' reaction to trial counsel "may be more important than the reaction to the client, for the client

appears on the stand only during a relatively brief period, while the lawyer is before the jury all the time."[29]

Although the proper use of this "grand-stand play" technique may be very beneficial, it is neither universally accepted nor practiced:

> Should the first twelve be selected? This is a "trick" which counsel assumes impresses the jury with the sincerity, the justifiableness of his cause and his complete satisfaction and delight with 12 such honest people. It may also be supposed to convey that counsel is willing to try his case, it is so good, before anyone, any first twelve.
>
> I believe that such tactics do not impress the jury, unless adversely to the lawyer so conducting his voir dire. Frequently a jury may feel this lawyer to be careless about this lawsuit, every juror deciding that he wouldn't want his case to be tried in this manner. . . .[30]

Belli's sentiments above are shared by many others who also believe in the importance of the voir dire examination.[31] Although the specific reasons given for utilizing the voir dire vary,[32] members of this second school of thought believe that: (1) counsel's in-depth questioning of the veniremen, not a bombastic prefatory statement, is more effective in achieving the purpose of the voir dire, such purpose being to reveal prejudices and/or biases possessed by the veniremen at the outset of the trial for or against either party to the litigation, and (2) the veniremen's first impressions of counsel are important.

According to proponents of this strategy, all human beings possess biases and prejudices which color their perception of the world and may influence their verdict in any given case. For example, Morrill states:

> Regardless of anything to the contrary, all human beings are prejudiced. Not only are all human beings prejudiced, but these feelings spill over into many areas.[33]

This strategy is, therefore, a direct attempt at eliciting those answers which would enable counsel to have the obviously prejudiced veniremen removed by a challenge for cause and the possibly prejudiced rejected peremptorily.

Advocates of this strategy note two potential benefits which rebound with its exclusive use: (1) Counsel is theoretically enabled to exclude from the jury those initially hostile to his cause; his case is presented to triers of fact divested of any predilections or prejudgments. Indeed, since prejudice is part of the human frailty, some work in the area of assessing biases and prejudices is warranted, (2) though of less importance to proponents of this strategy, counsel's questioning, if handled with professional decorum, may make a favorable impression on the veniremen. Wolfstone, for example, makes the following statement:

> The voir dire is the first event, and this is the time when the first impression is made. The voir dire, of course, cannot be a substitute for the opening

statement, but when the trial lawyer has completed the voir dire examination, the jurors have already developed their first-impression beliefs, and if the examination was successful they should firmly believe that counsel is an honest, sincere man who is frank and candid and talks "straight from the shoulder."[34]

There are, however, several difficulties inherent in the use of this strategy: (1) People may possess prejudices which they will neither recognize nor accept as such. "The difficulty with prejudices," according to Palmer, ". . . is that most men regard their opinions as convictions."[35] (2) It may be difficult to elicit answers which truly reflect the state of the venireman's mind, for, as Hafif notes, "the most difficult things to rout out of people are prejudices and biases."[36] Morrill states, "It is safe to say that [an attorney] will never find a juror who will stand up and say, 'I am prejudiced,' and then start listing the categories in which he is prejudiced, for and against."[37] (3) Although verbal reports (such as the veniremen's answers on voir dire) presumably have some predictive validity, they may not provide an adequate basis for the prediction of subsequent behavior. (4) Counsel's inquiries may fail to investigate the correct prejudice[38] or the veniremen may simply lie on the voir dire.[39] (5) The veniremen may resent this method of questioning, as Israelson warns:

> If the attorney sets up a barrage of objections and challenges, or asks questions that seem to be prying, he will run two risks: first, he may alienate the jurors before the case is even begun, and second, the jurors whose qualifications survive the probing of counsel are likely to gain the impression that counsel is attempting to withhold the entire truth. What appears to the legally trained mind as proper grounds for disqualification of a juror tends to merge in the layman's mind with the feeling that counsel will adopt any means to win his client's case. The attorney may thus find that he has succeeded in alienating a large segment of the panel in the process of weeding out the few undesirable jurors.[40]

(6) Perhaps the most noted deficiency of this strategy is that it may not make the most effective use of the opportunities available during the voir dire examination. For example, Belli notes:

> Even if counsel has advanced knowledge of each individual juror, still he overlooks the other (though perhaps originally unintended) opportunity of voir dire, i.e., the occasion to become friendly with the jury, to meet each individual juror and to impress them, briefly, of course, with certain rules of law and "slogans."[41]

While questioning to reveal prejudices and/or biases attempts only to extricate evidence of such proclivities, another technique has developed around it: the indoctrinational strategy. This may well be the most energetic and judicially deprecated use of the opportunities available during the voir dire.[42] Its objectives listed in order of importance to advocates of this stragegy are: (1) to ingratiate the attorney to the veniremen, (2) to make the veniremen aware of, and to test their reactions to, certain aspects of the case (*e.g.,* counsel's theory of the case, germane rules of law, judicially acceptable defenses, etc.), and (3) through the use of hypothetical questions, to analyze potential areas of veniremen prejudice which may arise during the trial. Indoctrination has been described as the process in which "the question itself is designed to have an influence on the juror and his answer thereto is only incidental or of little significance."[43] The philosophy behind the introduction of specific aspects of the case during the voir dire is quite ingenious: Counsel is theoretically able to recognize those veniremen who are capable of becoming acclimated to those items while he still wields the power of challenge over the panel. Holdaway describes the inculcating potential of such a process:

> Often the purpose of the question will be to advise, in an interrogatory form, the juror of certain rules of law, defenses, or facts expected to arise in the case in such a way as to ally the juror with the counsel's side or theory of the case. For example, the following question does not really anticipate a negative response: "Do you agree with the rule of law that requires acquittal in the event there is reasonable doubt?" The rule of reasonable doubt is one of the fundamental principles of our criminal law and is known as such by most of our citizens; therefore, even in the instance where a [venireman] did not particularly agree with the rule, he would hardly acknowledge so in open court. The real reason for such a question is, in a sense, to put the [venireman] on notice right from the start that there might be reasonable doubt in the case and to get him mentally familiar with the rule in the hope that he will look for reasonable doubt in the case and vote to acquit. It makes it more likely, furthermore, that in the decision-making process the [venireman] will be more aware than he otherwise would have been of the principle of reasonable doubt. . . .and perhaps by emphasizing it at the voir dire and, of course, during summation, the rule will be enlarged in his mind.[44]

While the committing tendency of this type of question will be considered later, a belief in the efficacy of such a strategy in securing the jury most sympathetic to one's cause is widely held by members of the bar.[45]

The indoctrinational strategy is by far the most complex voir dire strategy in that the three potential functions it serves may be inextricably interwoven; indeed, the subtleties of its application are legion. For example, Bryan advocates an indoctrinational method known as the "piggyback"[46] technique, wherein one suggestion which is, or will readily be, accepted by the veniremen is connected to another suggestion which is not accepted in order to allow the veniremen to mentally connect the two.

Although opinions vary on the purported benefits of the three voir dire techniques (the "grand-stand play," questioning to discover prejudices and/or biases, and the indoctrinational strategy), there is little empirical evidence on the relative effectiveness of each. The data that do exist are in conflict. Broeder, in an observational study of jury trials in a Midwest federal district court, presented a pessimistic picture of the success of this function. He concluded:

> Voir dire was grossly ineffective not only in weeding out "unfavorable" jurors but even in eliciting the data which would have shown particular jurors as very likely to prove "unfavorable"....
>
> As an institution for sifting out "unfavorable" jurors, voir dire cannot be effective. A lawyer simply cannot anticipate many of the factors in the jurors' background which will affect their thinking....[47]

However, Diamond & Zeisel, after contrasting the verdicts of juries selected with voir dire to the verdicts of veniremen excused by either the prosecution or the defense, concluded that both "generally succeeded in eliminating jurors un-friendly to their sides."[48] Another study[49] supports this latter finding wherein it was found that jurors selected with voir dire tended to: (1) be more sympathetic toward the historical extent of crime in general and the precipitating factors involved in any particular crime, (2) be apparently less influenced by pretrial prejudical information, (3) display a greater tendency to follow the letter of the law, and (4) display lower shifts of opinion during deliberation than those jurors selected without a voir dire examination.

While not conclusive, these studies are important in that they attempt to measure the effectiveness of the voir dire. They do not, however, focus upon one of the principal psychological processes that counsel attempts to initiate and control during this stage of the trial—that is, persuasion, especially in the indoctrinal approach. The remainder of this chapter will present a psychological conceptualization of the voir dire that should suggest a sound rationale for theoretically oriented, empirically sound research on this topic.

III. A PSYCHOLOGICAL CONCEPTUALIZATION OF THE VOIR DIRE EXAMINATION

A. Increasing the Veniremen's Receptivity to Counsel's Persuasion.[50]

Although many other theories of attitude change have been advanced, the Yale Communication and Attitude Change Program[51] is certainly one of the most prolific and renowned conceptualizations of attitude change to date.[52] The "Yale approach" utilizes an information-processing paradigm which

> attempts to tease out exhaustively the logically necessary steps between being presented with a persuasive communication and ultimate compliance with its directives. It further analyzes as exhaustively as possible the components of the communication and considers how each of them will affect each of the behavioral steps into which the persuasion process has been analyzed.[53]

This paradigm consists of two variables: (1) the independent variable, "communication," which is analyzable into source variables dealing with "variations in the purported, rather than actual, source of the persuasive communication,"[54] message variables, channel variables, receiver variables, and destination variables, and (2) the dependent variable, "being persuaded." There are six behavioral steps leading to persuasion: presenting the message, directing the receiver's attention toward it, the receiver's comprehending the message, his yielding to what is comprehended, his retention of attitude change, and carrying out the overt behavior urged by the communication. Persuasion is theoretically the end result of this six-step chain.[55] Although similar work has been done with all components of the independent variable, the present inquiry will concentrate solely on those qualities of the source which may enhance his persuasive impact.

The source, which may be defined as the originator of the message in communication, has been analyzed into three perceived characteristics: *attraction, credibility,* and *power.* Although necessary for experimental rigor, the isolation of source components is an artificial misrepresentation.[56] Therefore, the term "source valence,"[57] which is generally regarded as the composite effect of these components, must also be used in a conceptual assessment of how counsel's "impression management"[58] during the voir dire examination (*i.e.,* how the attorney presents himself to, or "handles" himself in front of, the veniremen) may affect his persuasive impact.[59]

1. *Attraction*

Assessments of the efficacy of source attractiveness in increasing persuasive impact have been varied. While several have deferred final judgment until definitive research is done,[60] some have deemphasized the importance of attraction;[61] many researchers, however, consider it to be a major determinant of message acceptance.[62] King & Sereno,[63] for example, note two germane lines of research which support the efficacy of high rather than low source attraction in increasing the receiver's receptivity to his persuasion. The first depicts attraction as a function of attitudinal similarity,[64] value similarity,[65] similarity of previous experience,[66] similarity of personality,[67] similarity of need,[68] and similarity of economic background.[69] The second, which has investigated the relationship between interpersonal similarity and persuasion directly, suggests that not only are similar sources more attractive to the recipient of the message, but they are also more persuasive.[70] McGuire, who suggests that the attractive source need not present evidence for the veridicality of his position to enhance his persuasive impact, describes the process as follows:

> Presumably the receiver, to the extent that he perceives the source to be like himself in diverse characteristics, assumes that they also share common needs and goals. The receiver might therefore conclude that what the source is urging is good for "our kind of people," and thus changes his attitude accordingly.[71]

Although McGuire's suggestion that the perception of certain similarities may lead to the expectation of others has been repeated by many,[72] not all similarities lead to an enhanced persuasiveness. Specifically, support has been found for the suggestion that the only influential similarities are those which are relevant to an acceptance of the position advocated.[73] The logical extention of these findings would seem to be: *(Proposition 1)* Counsel may increase his persuasive impact on the veniremen by developing a perception of relevant similarities with them. This point may be particularly useful to the advocates of the "grandstand play" strategy since their prime objective is to establish the perception of such similarities (*e.g.,* a shared belief in the effectiveness of the American system of jurisprudence).

2. *Credibility*

There are many reviews of the literature dealing with source credibility.[74] King & Sereno, for example, claim there is a widely held belief that "the greater the perceived credibility of the source, the greater will be his persuasive impact."[75] While the multidimensionality of source credibility has been noted repeatedly,[76] only two dimensions are used by the Yale approach: expertise (*i.e.,* the source's "perceived ability to know the correct stand on the issue"[77]) and objectivity (*i.e.,* his "motivation to communicate this knowledge without bias."[78]) Hovland et al. describe the Yale group's position as follows:

> An individual's tendency to accept a conclusion advocated by a given communicator will depend in part upon how well informed and intelligent he believes the communicator to be. However, a recipient may believe that a communicator is capable of transmitting valid statements, but still be inclined to reject the communication if he suspects the communicator is motivated to make nonvalid assertions. It seems necessary, therefore, to make a distinction between 1) the extent to which a communicator is perceived to be a source of valid assertions (his "expertness") and 2) the degree of confidence in the communicator's intent to communicate the assertions he considers most valid (his "trustworthiness"). In any given case, the weight given a communicator's assertions by his audience will depend upon both of these factors, and this resultant value can be referred to as the "credibility" of the communicator.[79]

Indeed, considerable evidence has been collected which supports the commonsense notion that (all things being equal) the greater the source's perceived expertise, the greater the recipient's attitude change in the direction he advocates.[80] There may, however, be such a thing as too much expertise: for example, research has indicated that while children tend to be influenced more by others somewhat older than themselves, they are less influenced by those considerably older.[81] Similarly, other experiments[82] suggest that a highly prestigious person may actually become more attractive if he commits a social faux pas (*e.g.,* spilling a cup of coffee).

It would appear, then, that the initial hypothesis was too simplistic. McGuire states that this nonmonotonic relationship between the source's perceived expertise and his persuasive impact is due to

> a tendency for people to be influenced by those who know more than themselves [perceived expertise] and a tendency to be influenced by those who are similar to themselves [perceived similarity], with the usual proviso of everything else being equal. However, since most people do not perceive themselves as being expert on the usual communication topics, these two processes tend to go in opposite directions, with the more expert source gaining from his being perceived as having a greater fund of knowledge but losing from being perceived as very different from the recipient.[83]

Although counsel walks a thin line between losing the potential benefits of perceived similarity while gaining those of perceived expertise, the following conclusion appears to be the logical extrapolation from the studies just reviewed: *(Proposition 2)* To the extent that counsel is able to develop perceived expertise in the eyes of the veniremen (specifically through a demeanor of confidence, efficiency, and moderate display of knowledge) his persuasive impact will be enhanced; however, emphasis on recondite points of law or a pedantic display of legal expertise may alienate the veniremen by a loss of perceived similarity. Testimonials to the efficacy of perceived expertise and similarity on persuasion both are legion throughout the trial tactics literature,[84] particularly among those who advocate indoctrination or questioning to reveal prejudices and/or biases.

Similarly, the source's perceived objectivity tends to enhance his persuasive impact. For example, sources who would benefit from the listener's being persuaded are judged as being less fair and, on occasion, have been less persuasive than more objective sources.[85] Listeners who are highly involved in an issue have been found to be more influenced by persuasive sources who seem unaware that they were being overheard.[86] There is also evidence that the source's refutation, rather than ignorance, of the opposition's arguments produces more resistance to subsequent countercommunications.[87] Indeed, these studies validate Jones & Wortman's "ingratiator's dilemma," which states that "tactics *obviously* designed to enhance attraction are going to be less effective precisely in those settings where attraction is most important."[88] Such results lead to the following conclusion: *(Proposition 3)* To the extent that they view the attorney as being objective and unbiased, the veniremen should be more receptive to his persuasion. Therefore, counsel must be cautious in any persuasive attempt during the voir dire since juror awareness of such an intent could damage his valence; arguments should be couched in terms of "Clear evidence will show that . . ." or "The prosecution must prove beyond a reasonable doubt . . . Evidence that falls short of that dictates that the defendant must be acquitted . . . The Constitution of the United States and our American system of justice demands this result."

3. *Power*

Although perceived power does not directly enhance the source's persuasive impact, it may be very useful in explaining the "lack of candor"[89] among the veniremen. Kelman, for example, suggests that the perception of source power may lead the recipient to respond to the source's questions with what the recipient believes to be the "correct"[90] answer (*i.e.,* the "socially desirable"[91] response). This would occur, for example, when a venireman who wants to serve on a particular case realizes that those who conduct the voir dire examination have the power to remove unfit members from the panel. While the difficulty of obtaining answers which are truly indicative of a venireman's state of mind has been lamented by many in the trial tactics literature,[92] an application of the concept of social desirability to the voir dire examination does not seem to have previously appeared in the literature.[93]

B. The Immunization of Prospective Jurors

While the effectiveness of the indoctrinational technique is unknown, conceptually it appears to be an attempt to acclimate the veniremen to specific legal principles and/or to immunize them against the influence that certain facts about counsel's client, the action itself, or evidence in the case may have on them. Considerable evidence has been collected on the effectiveness of two immunization techniques which could be extremely beneficial in such a voir dire examination: the commitment approach and the anchoring approach.

The anchoring approach to immunization against persuasion involves

> making the belief resistant to persuasion by tying it in with already held cognitions, either by establishing new links or by making pre-existing links salient. The already held cognitions would include the believer's accepted values, his other beliefs, or his valued sources and reference groups. Such linkages are assumed to produce resistance to persuasion because a change in the given belief would then require the receiver's changing these other linked beliefs correspondingly. Alternatively, he would have to endure cognitive inconsistency, which (it is assumed) he is motivated to minimize.[94]

Theoretically, anchors- reference points which give individuals a sense of orientation on judgmental scales—are extremely influential when an individual has had little previous experience with a particular reference scale.[95] Several theorists[96] have suggested that linking beliefs to accepted values makes those beliefs more resistant to change to the extent that they are "perceived as instrumental to the attainment of positively valenced goals."[97]

Both rational[98] and empirical[99] support have been found for the contention that a belief may be made more resistant to persuasion by merely sensitizing an individual to the fact that it is logically related to many beliefs which he already holds. McGuire, for example, has found that simply asking an individual to rehearse related beliefs which he already possesses may increase the salience of linkages to a given belief, thereby making that belief more resistant to subsequent attack.[100] The new belief may also be anchored to a positively valenced source, either a reference group[101] or a specific individual,[102] for it is assumed that "if the believer is made to see that his opinion is shared by others whom he values highly, the opinion will be more resistant to subsequent attack."[103] This result suggests the following hypothesis: *(Proposition 4)*. Since such abstract values as justice and equality before the law are positively balanced by the majority of the American public,[104] linking these propositions to rules such as the *presumption* of innocence and proof *beyond* a reasonable doubt should minimize the impact of potentially damaging aspects of the case.

The commitment approach to immunization against persuasion utilizes the central notion of the psychological consistency theories by assuming that "the individual tries to keep his internal beliefs, his verbal statements, and his gross behavior in agreement with one another."[105] This approach

> involve(s) the believer's taking some more or less irrevocable step on the basis of his belief, thereby committing himself to it. Insofar as commitment makes changing the belief dangerous, costly, awkward, or at least harmful to self-esteem, it strengthens the believer's tendency to resist social influence attempts aimed at this belief.[106]

Although the irrevocability of such commitments is debatable, there are several ways in which they may be created. For example, some researchers have found that external commitment,[107] which occurs when "an external source attributes to an individual a particular opinion prior to exposure to an attempt to effect [attitudinal] change,"[108] as well as internal commitment, which may occur by simply asking an individual to come to the private decision that he holds a certain belief,[109] both confer resistance to subsequent persuasion. Others have found that the strongest commitment appears to be that instilled by the public avowal of belief.[110] Research into the effects of such public statements has shown that under certain conditions (*e.g.,* high volition[111]) counterattitudinal avowal may bring private opinion in line with public action. However, in light of the evidence that veniremen occasionally lie during the voir dire,[112] counterattitudinal avowals unfortunately seem to leave the veniremen's proclivities and prejudices intact. Perhaps the blatancy of the socially desirable answer and the situational pressures to appear objective and unbiased vitiate the dissonance-arousing effects of such statements.

A second line of research has revealed that consonant commitment produced by the public avowal of one's true beliefs seems to have no direct effect on attitude; it serves only to direct reactions against an attack on one's belief.[113] Although an intrusive pursuit of those beliefs to which veniremen are committed[114] or which are an integral part of their self-concept[115] may result in a "boomerang" effect (*i.e.,* an intensification of initial attitude in reaction against a persuasive communication) which could damage counsel's "valence," no evidence exists which defines such commitments as irrevocable.

The research demonstrating the effectiveness of both approaches to immunizing against persuasion leads to the following conclusion: *(Proposition 5)* To the extent that counsel may present specific aspects of the case to the veniremen including facts about the defendant and judicially acceptable defenses, the anchoring and the committing approaches to immunization against persuasion should serve as helpful voir dire techniques.

IV. CONCLUSION

This article, in its conceptualization of the voir dire examination, has made several suggestions which may aid counsel in enhancing his persuasive impact (*e.g.,* by establishing perceived similarity, objectivity, and expertise before the veniremen) and referred attention to the applicability of two methods of immunization against persuasion to a specific voir dire tactic. However, much theoretical and empirical work remains to be done on the psychological processes operating during the voir dire examination as well as the legal process as a whole. While the ethical implications of manipulative research within the courtroom must be considered,[116] the intention of this chapter is not only to provide a legitimate basis for further inquiry on the voir dire examination but also to serve as a paradigmatic contribution which psychology is capable of making to the study of the legal process.

FOOTNOTES

[1] Only a representative group of cases and psychological studies will be cited to support any contention made in the text since a complete listing of all the germane material is unnecessary to substantiate the points contained herein.

[2] Jackson v. United States, 408 F.2d 306 (9th Cir. 1969); Singer v. United States, 380 U.S. 24 (1965); United States v. Daily, 139 F.2d 7 (7th Cir. 1944); United States v. Napoleone, 349 F.2d 350 (3rd Cir. 1965).

[3] Billmeyer v. St. Louis Transit Company, 108 Mo. App. 6, 82 S.W. 536 (1904); Dennis v. United States, 339 U.S. 162 (1950); United States v. Woods, 299 U.S. 123 (1936).

[4] State v. Mott, 29 Mont. 292, 74 P. 728 (1903); United States v. Chapman, 158 F.2d 417 (10th Cir. 1940).

[5] Coughlin v. People, 144 Ill. 165, 33 N.E. 1 (1893); Hughes v. State, 43 Tex. Crim. 511, 60 S.W. 562 (1902); Naylor v. Metropolitan Street Railroad Company, 66 Kan. 407, 71 P. 835 (1903); People v. Riggins, 159 Cal. 113, 112 P. 862 (1910).

[6] Dennis v. United States, *supra* note 3; Morford v. United States, 339 U.S. 285 (1950).

[7] Dennis v. United States, *supra* note 3; Frazier v. United States, 335 U.S. 497 (1948); United States v. Chapman, *supra* note 4.

[8] Crawford v. United States, 212 U.S. 183 (1908); Gaff v. State, 155 Ind. 277, 58 N.E. 74 (1900); Lyles v. State, 41 Tex. 172 (1874); Lester v. State, 2 Tex. App. 432 (1877).

[9] Block v. State, 100 Ind. 357 (1884); Coppersmith v. Mound City Railroad Company, 51 Mo. App. 357 (1892); State v. West, 69 Mo. 401 (1879).

[10] Aldridge v. United States, 283 U.S. 308 (1931); Sherman v. William M. Ryan & Sons, Inc., 126 Conn. 574, 13 A.2d 134 (1940); State v. Higgs, 143 Conn. 130, 120 A.2d 152 (1956).

[11] Bratcher v. United States, 149 F.2d 742 (4th Cir. 1945); Ippolito v. United States, 108 F.2d 668 (6th Cir. 1940); Rhea v. State, 63 Neb. 461, 88 N.W. 789 (1902).

[12] State v. Gidron, 211 S.C. 360, 45 S.E.2d 587 (1947); State v. Royster, 181 S.C. 269, 186 S.E. 921 (1936).

[13] Pinder v. State, 27 Fla. 370, 8 So. 837 (1891); State v. Guidry, 160 La. 655, 107 So. 479 (1926).

[14] B.D. Sales, Who should conduct the voir dire? A paper presented at the Annual Convention of the American Psychology-Law Society, San Francisco, 1974. A challenge for cause may be defined as an "objection to a juror made on voir dire for cause stated, that is pointing out the ground upon which the juror is disqualified." W. Anderson, Ballentine's Law Dictionary 190 (1969). A peremptory challenge may be defined as "an arbitrary and capricious species of challenge to a certain number of jurors without showing any cause, and it is not essential to such a challenge that any bias or prejudice on the part of a juror be shown." 14 Am. Jur. Jury 882 (1969).

[15] See, e.g., Carpenter v. Hyman, 67 W. Va. 4, 66 S.E. 1078 (1910); Corens v. State, 185 Md. 561, 45 A.2d 340 (1946); Jones v. State, 20 Okla. Crim. 154, 201 P. 664 (1924); Sherman V. William M. Ryan & Sons, Inc., supra note 10.

[16] See, e.g., Coy v. State, 78 Tex. Crim. 184, 180 S.W. 264 (1915); State v. Foster, 150 La. 971, 91 So. 411 (1922); State v. Williams, 230 La. 1059, 89 So. 2d 898 (1956).

[17] Aldridge v. United States, supra note 10; Brown v. United States, 338 F.2d 543 (D.C. Cir. 1964); Sellers v. United States, 271 F.2d 475 (D.C. Cir. 1959); United States v. Napoleone, supra note 2.

[18] Aldridge v. United States, supra note 10; Connors v. United States, 158 U.S. 408 (1895); United States v. Daily, supra note 2.

[19] Bryant v. State, 207 Md. 565, 115 A.2d 502 (1955); Corens v. State, supra note 15; Loveland v. Nieters, 79 N.D. 1, 54 N.W. 2d 533 (1952).

[20] Alexander v. R.D. Grier & Sons Co., 181 Md. 415, 30 A.2d 757 (1943); Casey v. Roman Catholic Archbishop, 217 Md. 595, 143 A.2d 627 (1958); State v. Lloyd, 138 Wash. 8, 244 P. 130 (1926).

[21] Duffy v. Carroll, 137 Conn. 51, 75 A.2d 33 (1950); Pearcy v. Michigan Mutual Life Insurance Co., 111 Ind. 59, 12 N.E. 98 (1887); State v. Higgs, supra note 10.

[22] Although we speak of only two philosophies regarding the voir dire examination, there are three techniques for conducting it that will be elaborated in this section.

[23] Brody, Selecting a jury—art or blindman's bluff, 4 Crim. L. Rev. 67, 67-68 (1957).

[24] See Broeder, Voir dire examination: An empirical study, 38 S. Cal. L. Rev. 503 (1965).

[25] Nizer, The art of the jury trial, in S. Gazan, Trial tactics and experiences. 165, 168 (1958).

[26] Field, Voir dire examination—A neglected art, 33 U. Mo. K.C.L.R. 171, 173 (1965).

[27] S. Schweitzer, Cyclopedia of trial practice 2006 (1954).

[28] I. Goldstein, Trial technique 152 (2d ed. 1962).

[29] Citing H. Gair and R. Conason, The trial of a negligence action 36 (1946); H. Bodin, Selecting a jury 50 (1945).

[30] 1 M. Belli, Modern trials 803-804 (1954).

[31] See Gazan supra note 25; A. Morrill, Anatomy of a trial (1968); B. Palmer, Courtroom strategies (1959).

[32] For example, Nizer in Gazan supra note 25 at 168 emphasizes the desirability of choosing the triers of fact, calling it a "precious opportunity;" Schweitzer supra note 27 at 2008 praises the opportunity to make a brief prefatory statement to the panel.

[33] Morrill *supra* note 31 at 4. Indeed, ample evidence exists to support this claim. For example, for evidence of the distorting effect of prejudicial attitudes on the recall of factual information see the following: T.G. Apler & S.S. Korchin. Memory of socially relevant material. *Journal of Abnormal and Social Psychology,* 1961, *62,* 35-40; F.C. Bartlett, *Remembering: A study in experimental and social psychology.* London: Cambridge, 1932; K.B. Clark, Some factors in influencing and remembering of prose material. *Archives of Psychology,* 1940, *36* (No. 253); A.L. Edwards, Political frames of reference as a function influencing recognition. *Journal of Abnormal and Social Psychology,* 1941, *36,* 34-50; E.E. Jones & R. Kohler, The effect of plausibility on the learning of controversial statements. *Journal of Abnormal and Social Psychology,* 1958, *57,* 315-320; J. Levine & G. Murphy, The learning and forgetting of controversial material. *Journal of Abnormal and Social Psychology,* 1943, *38,* 507-517; R. Taft, Selective recall and memory distortion of favorable and unfavorable material. *Journal of Abnormal and Social Psychology,* 1954, *49,* 23-29; W.S. Watson & G.W. Hartman, The rigidity of a basic attitudinal frame. *Journal of Abnormal and Social Psychology,* 1939, *34,* 314-335. For similar evidence of the effect of prejudicial attitudes on subsequent reasoning see the following: N.M. Prentice, The influence of ethnic attitude on reasoning about ethnic groups. *Journal of Abnormal and Social Psychology,* 1957, *55,* 270-272; H. Schuman & J. Harding, Prejudice and the norm of rationality. *Sociometry,* 1964, *27,* 353-371; D. Thisthlewaite, Attitude and structure as factors in the distortion of reasoning. *Journal of Abnormal and Social Psychology,* 1961, *62,* 184-186.

[34] 14 Am. Jur. Trials Glass Door Accidents 101, 173 (1968).

[35] Palmer *supra* note 31 at 160.

[36] Hafif, Adequate voir dire—A right and a necessity, 44 J. State B.A. Calif. 858, 868 (1969).

[37] Morrill *supra* note 31 at 5.

[38] See Broeder *supra* note 24; E. Hartley, *Problems in prejudice* (2d ed.). New York: Octagon Books, 1969.

[39] See Broeder *supra* note 24.

[40] 5 Am. Jur. Trials Selecting the Jury 143, 201 (1968).

[41] Belli *supra* note 30 at 804.

[42] See, *e.g.,* Christian v. New York Central Railroad Co., 28 Ill. App. 2d 57, 170 N.E.2d 183 (1960); Vega v. Evans, 128 Ohio St. 535, 192 N.E. 757 (1934).

[43] Holdaway, Voir dire—A neglected tool of advocacy, 40 Military L.R. 1, 2 (1968).

[44] Id. at 3.

[45] See Belli *supra* note 30; W. Bryan, *The chosen ones* (1971); Morrill *supra* note 31.

[46] Bryan *supra* note 45 at 202.

[47] Broeder *supra* note 24 at 505-506. Broeder was, however, somewhat more optimistic about the efficacy of the indoctrinational strategy. Specifically, after noting that approximately 80% of the counsel's time was spent indoctrinating the veniremen, he stated: "Voir dire is utilized much more effectively as a forum for indoctrination than as a means of sifting out potentially unfavorable jurors." Id. at 528. Since the voir dire examination does not theoretically afford counsel the opportunity to influence the veniremen, this abundant use of indoctrination may be interpreted as an abuse of judicial leniency. There are, however, two factors which may facilitate the use of such a tactic. First, counsel's true intention in asking any specific question is a state of mind, and as such, is not easily discernible, *e.g.,* Morrill *supra* note 31 at 13. Secondly, there is precedent to the effect that the court cannot infer that a question was asked for an ulterior motive if it is, on the surface at least, a proper question. See Blair v. M. McCormack Construction Co., 123 App. Div. 30, 107 N.Y. Supp. 750 (1907); Grant v. National Railway Spring Co., 100 App. Div. 234, 91 N.Y. Supp. 805 (1905).

[48] S. Diamond & H. Zeisel, A courtroom experiment on juror selection and decision

making. A paper presented at the American Psychological Association Annual Convention, New Orleans, 1972, 2.

[49] Padawer-Singer, Singer & Singer, Voir dire by two lawyers: An essential safeguard, 57 Judicature 386 (1974).

[50] Conceptually, increasing the veniremen's receptivity to counsel is quite similar, if not identical, to enhancing counsel's persuasive impact upon the veniremen since both increase the possibility of the veniremen's changing their attitudes in line with counsel's arguments or statements and thereby being persuaded by him.

[51] C.I. Hovland, L. Janis & H.H. Kelley, *Communication and persuasion.* New Haven: Yale University Press, 1953; W.J. McGuire, The nature of attitudes and attitude change. In G. Lindzey and E. Aronson (eds.), *The handbook of social psychology* (Vol. 3). Reading: Addison-Wesley, 1969(a).

[52] See, *e.g.,* C.A. Kiesler, B.E. Collins & N. Miller, *Attitude change.* New York: Wiley, 1969, at 103, where they call it "one of the major forces shaping contemporary research and theory on attitude change."

[53] W.J. McGuire, Persuasion, resistance, and attitude change. In I. de Sola Pool, F.W. Frey, W. Schramm, N. Maccoby & E.R. Parker (eds.), *Handbook of communication.* Chicago: Rand McNally, 1973, 228.

[54] McGuire, 1969a, *op. cit.,* 177.

[55] See W.J. McGuire, Personality and attitude change: an information processing theory. In A.C. Greenwald, T.C. Brock & T.M. Ostron (eds.), *Psychological foundations of attitudes.* New York: Academic Press, 1968.

[56] J.A. Daly & V.A. Richmond, A review of selected literature on the source variable in communication. Unpublished manuscript, University of West Virginia, 1970.

[57] McGuire, 1969a, *op. cit.,* 178.

[58] E. Goffman, *The presentation of self in everyday life.* Garden City: Doubleday, 1959.

[59] Although the majority of the studies cited in this article used a prevalenced source, the legitimacy of the inferential leap necessary to apply their findings to the following conceptualization rests upon the precedent of those studies in which: (1) source valence was developed in uncontrolled interaction between source and receiver, *e.g.,* L. Festinger, S. Schachter & K. Back, *Social pressures in informal groups.* New York: Harper, 1950; R. Lippit, N. Polansky, F. Redl & S. Rosen, The dynamics of power. *Human Relations,* 1952, *5,* 37-64; T.M. Newcomb, *Personality and social change.* New York: Dryden, 1943 and (2) source valence was developed by the source's proficiency at performing a task, *e.g.,* M.D. Croner & R.H. Willis, Perceived differences in task competence and asymmetry of dyadic influence. *Journal of Abnormal and Social Psychology,* 1961, *62,* 705-708; H.C. Kelman, Effects of success or failure on "suggestibility" in the autokinetic situation. *Journal of Abnormal and Social Psychology,* 1950, *45,* 267-285.

[60] K. Giffin, The contribution of studies of source credibility to a theory of interpersonal trust in the communication process. *Psychological Bulletin,* 1967, *68,* 104-120.

[61] H.W. Simons, N.N. Berkowitz & R.J. Moyer, Similarity, credibility, and attitude change: a review and a theory. *Psychological Bulletin,* 1970, *73,* 1-16.

[62] E. Berscheid, Opinion change and communicator-communicatee similarity and dissimilarity. *Journal of Personality and Social Psychology,* 1966, *4,* 670-680; T.E. Brock, Communicator-recipient similarity and decision change. *Journal of Personality and Social Psychology,* 1965, *1,* 650-654; H.C. Kelman, Processes of opinion change. *Public Opinion Quarterly,* 1961, *25,* 57-78; McGuire, 1969a, *op. cit.*

[63] S.W. King & K.K. Sereno, Attitude change as a function of degree and type of interpersonal similarity and message type. *Western Speech,* 973, *37,* 218-232.

[64] D. Byrne, Interpersonal attraction and attitude similarity. *Journal of Abnormal and Social Psychology,* 1961, *62,* 713-715; D. Byrne, Response to attitude similarity-dissimilarity as a function of affiliation need. *Journal of Personality,* 1962, *30,* 164-177; D. Byrne,

G.L. Clore & W. Griffit, Response discrepancy versus attitude similarity-dissimilarity as determinants of attraction. *Psychonomic Science*, 1967, *25*, 397-398; D. Byrne & W. Griffit, Similarity versus liking: a clarification. *Psychonomic Science*, 1966, *25*, 295-296; D. Byrne, W. Griffit & C. Golightly, Prestige as a factor in determining the effect of attitude similarity-dissimilarity on attraction. *Journal of Personality*, 1966, *34*, 434-444; D. Byrne & O. London, Primacy-recency and the sequential presentation of attitudinal stimuli. *Psychonomic Science*, 1966, 193-194; D. Byrne & C. McGraw, Interpersonal attraction toward Negroes. *Human Relations*, 1964, *17*, 201-213.

⁶⁵E. Berscheid, The effects of communicator-communicatee value similarity and dissimilarity upon value change. *Dissertation Abstracts International*, 1966, *27*, 1108-1109A; J.A. Precker, Similarity of valuings as a factor in selection of peers and near-authority figures. *Journal of Abnormal and Social Psychology*, 1952, *47*, 406-414; A.J. Smith, Similarity of values and ifs relations to acceptance and the projection of similarity. *Journal of Psychology*, 1957, *43*, 251-260; D.D. Stein, The influence of belief systems on interpersonal preference: a validation study of Rokeach's theory of prejudice. *Psychological Monographs*, 1966, *80* (No. 8).

⁶⁶Brock, *op. cit.;* C.F. Vick & R.V. Wood, Similarity of past experience and the communication of meaning. *Speech Monographs*, 1969, *36*, 159-162.

⁶⁷M.E. Bonney, A sociometric study of the relationship of some factors of mutual friendships on the elementary, secondary, and college levels. *Sociometry*, 1946, *9*, 21-47; W.R. Griffit, Interpersonal attraction as a function of self-concept and personality similarity-dissimilarity. *Journal of Personality and Social Psychology*, 1966, *4*, 581-588; H.E. McGuckin, The persuasive force of similarity in cognitive style between advocate and audience. *Speech Monographs*, 1967, *34*, 145-151.

⁶⁸C.E. Izard, Personality similarity and friendship. *Journal of Abnormal and Social Psychology*, 1960, *61*, 47-51.

⁶⁹D. Byrne, G.L. Clore & P. Worchel, Effects of economic similarity-dissimilarity on interpersonal attraction. *Journal of Personality and Social Psychology*, 1966, *4*, 220-224.

⁷⁰K.W. Back, Influence through social communication. *Journal of Abnormal and Social Psychology*, 1951, *46*, 9-23; E. Berscheid, Opinion change and communicator-communicatee similarity and dissimilarity. *Journal of Personality and Social Psychology*, 1966, *4*, 670-680; Brock, *op. cit.;* E. Burnstein, E. Stotland & A. Zander, Similarity to a model and self-evaluation. *Journal of Abnormal and Social Psychology*, 1961, *62*, 257-264; J. Mills & J.M. Jellison, Effect on opinion change of similarity between the communicator and the audience he addressed. *Journal of Personality and Social Psychology*, 1968, *9*, (2, Pt. 1), 153-156; Precker, *op. cit.;* E. Stotland, A. Zander & T. Natsoulas, Generalization of interpersonal similarity. *Journal of Abnormal and Social Psychology*, 1961, *62*, 250-256; W. Weiss, Opinion congruence with a negative source on one issue as a factor influencing agreement on another issue. *Journal of Abnormal and Social Psychology*, 1957, *54*, 180-186.

⁷¹McGuire, 1969a, *op. cit.*, 187.

⁷²Burnstein, Stotland & Zander, *op. cit.;* T.M. Newcomb, The prediction of interpersonal attraction. *American Psychologist*, 1956, *11*, 575-586; Stotland, Zander & Natsoulas, *op. cit.*

⁷³Brock, *op. cit.;* King & Sereno, *op. cit.;* B. Moya, E. Connolley & H. Gerard, The interactive effect of source and message on attitudinal change. Paper presented at the Western Psychological Association meeting, San Francisco, April, 1971; Simons, Berkowitz & Moyer, *op. cit.*

⁷⁴K. Anderson & T. Clevenger, A summary of experimental research in ethos. *Speech Monographs*, 1963, *30*, 59-78; King & Sereno, *op. cit.;* McGuire, 1969a, *op. cit.*

⁷⁵King & Sereno, *op. cit.*, 220. A partial reference list of others who have also advocated the efficacy of high, rather than low source credibility in effecting more attitude change and/or creating a more favorable interpretation of the source's position would include:

E. Aronson, J. Turner & M. Carlsmith, Communicator credibility and communicator discrepancy as determinants of opinion change. *Journal of Abnormal and Social Psychology*, 1963, *67*, 31-36; A.R. Cohen, *Attitude change and social influence.* New York: Basic Books, 1964; H.H. Johnson, J.M. Torcivia & M.A. Poprick, Effects of source credibility on the relationship between authoritarianism and attitude change. *Journal of Personality and Social Psychology*, 1968, *9*, 179-183; C.I. Hovland, L. Janis & H.H. Kelley, *op. cit.*; C.I. Hovland & W. Weiss, The influence of source credibility on communication effectiveness. *Public Opinion Quarterly*, 1951, *15*, 635-650; M. Myers & A. Goldberg, Group credibility and opinion change. *Journal of Communication*, 1970, *20*, 1974-1979; H. Sigall & R. Helmreich, Opinion change as a function of stress and communicator credibility. *Journal of Experimental Social Psychology*, 1969, *5*, 70-78.

[76] R.L. Applbaum & W.E. Anatol, Dimensions of source credibility: a test for reproductibility. *Speech Monographs*, 1973, *40*, 231-237; E.S. Baudin & M.K. Davis, Scales for the measurement of ethos: another attempt. *Speech Monographs*, 1973, *39*, 296-301.

[77] McGuire, 1969a, *op. cit.*, 182.

[78] *Ibid.*

[79] Hovland, Janis & Kelley, *op. cit.*, 21.

[80] E. Aronson & B.W. Golden, The effect of relevant and irrelevant aspects of communicator credibility on attitude change. *Journal of Personality*, 1962, *30*, 135-146; Hovland, Janis & Kelley, *op. cit.*; McGuire, 1969a, *op. cit.*

[81] K.G. Stvkát, *Suggestibility: a factorial and experimental analysis.* Stockholm: Almquist & Wiksell, 1958.

[82] E. Aronson, B. Willerman & J. Floyd, The effect of a pratfall on increasing interpersonal attraction. *Psychonomic Science*, 1966, *4*, 227-228; R. Helmreich, E. Aronson & J. LeFan, To err is humanizing—sometimes. *Journal of Personality and Social Psychology*, 1970, *16*, 259-264.

[83] McGuire, 1973, *op. cit.*, 230.

[84] Goldstein, *op. cit.*; R.K. Soonavala, *Advocacy: Its principles and practice.* Bombay: Tripathi, 1953.

[85] C.I. Hovland & W. Mandell, An experimental comparison of conclusion-drawing by the communicator and by the audience. *Journal of Abnormal and Social Psychology*, 1952, *47*, 581-588; C.I. Hovland & W. Weiss, *op. cit.*; H.C. Kelman & C.I. Hovland, "Reinstatement" of the communicator in delayed measurement of opinion change. *Journal of Abnormal and Social Psychology*, 1953, *48*, 327-335.

[86] E. Walster & L. Festinger, The effectiveness of "overheard" persuasive communications. *Journal of Abnormal and Social Psychology*, 1962, *65*, 395-402.

[87] A.A. Lumsdaine & I.L. Janis, Resistance to "counter-propaganda" produced by one-sided and two-sided "propaganda" presentations. *Public Opinion Quarterly*, 1953, *17*, 311-318; W.J. McGuire, Inducing resistance to persuasion: some contemporary approaches. In L. Berkowitz (ed.), *Advances in experimental social psychology* (Vol. 1). New York: Academic Press, 1964.

[88] E.E. Jones & C. Wortman, *Ingratiation: an attributional approach.* Morristown: General Learning Press, 1973, 2.

[89] Broeder *supra* note 24 at 506.

[90] Kelman, *op. cit.*, 62.

[91] The socially desirable answer may be defined as one which the veniremen perceive as conforming to the "(c)onsensus judgment as to what behavior, feelings, and attitudes win social approval in American society." W.E. Fordyce, Social desirability in the MMPI. *Journal of Consulting Psychology*, 1956, *20*, 171-175, 171. For a further discussion see D.P. Crowne & D. Marlowe, *The approval motive.* New York: Wiley, 1964; A. Edwards, *The social desirability variable in personality assessment.* New York: Dryden Press, 1957. Social

desirability may also cause the juror to respond identically to the majority of the veniremen. This process, which works independently of the perceived power of the attorney, deals with the tendency to conform as discussed by Asch (*e.g.*, S.E. Asch, Group pressure. In S.E. Asch, *Social psychology*. Englewood Cliffs: Prentice-Hall, 1952, 451-465) and others. Also see Sales, *op. cit.* Since a more detailed elaboration and analysis of juror responses is in preparation for publication at a later date, these processes will not be discussed in detail here.

[92] Hafif, *op. cit.;* Morrill, *op. cit.*

[93] See Sales, *op. cit.*

[94] McGuire, 1969a, *op. cit.,* 262.

[95] Kiesler, Collins & Miller, *op. cit.*

[96] E.R. Carlson, Attitude change through modification of attitude structure. *Journal of Abnormal and Social Psychology,* 1956, *52,* 256-261; M.J. Rosenberg, Cognitive structure and attitudinal effect. *Journal of Abnormal and Social Psychology,* 1956, *53,* 367-372; R.B. Zajonc, The process of cognitive tuning in communication. *Journal of Abnormal and Social Psychology,* 1960, *61,* 159-167.

[97] McGuire, 1969a, *op. cit.,* 262.

[98] R.P. Abelson & M.J. Rosenberg, Symbolic psycho-logic: a model of attitudinal cognition. *Behavioral Science,* 1958, *3,* 1-13; F. Harary, On the measurement of structural balance. *Behavioral Science,* 1959, *4,* 316-323.

[99] M.J. Rosenberg & R.P. Abelson, An analysis of cognitive balancing. In M.J. Rosenberg, C.I. Hovland, W.J. McGuire, R.P. Abelson & J.W. Brehm (eds.), *Attitude and attitude change.* New Haven. Yale University Press, 1960.

[100] W.J. McGuire, Cognitive consistency and attitude change. *Journal of Abnormal and Social Psychology,* 1960a, *60,* 345-353; W.J. McGuire, Direct and indirect persuasive effects of dissonance-producing messages. *Journal of Abnormal and Social Psychology,* 1960b, *60,* 354-358.

[101] W.W. Charters & T.M. Newcomb, Some attitudinal effects of experimentally increased salience of a membership group. In E. Maccoby, T.M. Newcomb & E.L. Hartley (eds.), *Readings in social psychology.* New York: Holt, 1958; J.E. Dittes & H.H. Kelley, Effects of different conditions of acceptance upon conformity to group norms. *Journal of Abnormal and Social Psychology,* 1956, *53,* 100-107; H.H. Kelley & E. Volkhart, The resistance to change of group-anchor attitudes. *American Sociological Review,* 1952, *17,* 453-465; H.H. Kelley & C.L. Woodruff, Member's reactions to apparent group approval of a counternorm communication. *Journal of Abnormal and Social Psychology,* 1956, *52,* 67-74.

[102] Kelman & Hovland, *op. cit.;* P.H. Tannenbaum, Initial attitude toward source and concept as factors in attitude change through communication. *Public Opinion Quarterly,* 1956, *20,* 413-425.

[103] McGuire, 1964, *op. cit.,* 197.

[104] J. Harding, H. Prohansky, B. Kutner & I. Chein, Prejudice and ethnic relations. In G. Lindzey & and E. Aronson (eds.), *The handbook of social psychology* (Vol. 5). Reading: Addison-Wesley, 1969; G. Myrdal, *An American dilemma: the Negro problem and modern democracy* (2nd ed.), New York: Harper, 1962.

[105] McGuire, 1969a, *op. cit.,* 261.

[106] McGuire, 1964, *op. cit.,* 194.

[107] M.E. Rosenbaum & D.E. Franc, Opinion change as a function of external commitment and amount of discrepancy from the opinion of another. *Journal of Abnormal and Social Psychology,* 1960, *61,* 15-20; M.E. Rosenbaum & I.M. Zimmerman, The effects of external commitment on response to an attempt to change opinion. *Public Opinion Quarterly,* 1959, *23,* 247-254. But see C.A. Kiesler, *The psychology of commitment.* New York:

Academic Press, 1971, for a statistical explanation of these results.

[108] Rosenbaum & Zimmerman, *op. cit.,* 247-248.

[109] E. Bennett, Discussion, decision, commitment, and consensus in "group decisions." *Human Relations,* 1955, *8,* 251-274.

[110] A.R. Cohen, J.W. Brehm & B. Latane, Choice of strategy and voluntary exposure to information under public and private conditions. *Journal of Personality,* 1959, *27,* 63-73; M. Deutsch & H. Gerard, A study of normative and informational social influences upon individual judgments. *Journal of Abnormal and Social Psychology,* 1955, *51,* 629-636; S. Fisher, I. Rubinstein & R. Freeman, Intertrial effects of immediate self-commitment in a continuous social influence situation. *Journal of Abnormal and Social Psychology,* 1956, *52,* 200-207; C.I. Hovland, E. Campbell & T. Brock, The effect of "commitment" on opinion change following communication. In C.I. Hovland (ed.), *Order of presentation in persuasion.* New Haven: Yale University Press, 1957.

[111] J.W. Brehm & A.R. Cohen, *Explorations in cognitive dissonance.* New York: Wiley, 1962.

[112] See Broeder *supra* note 24 at 506.

[113] Kiesler, *op. cit.*

[114] D.O. Sears, J.L. Freedman & E.F. O'Connor, The effects of anticipated debate and commitment on the polarization of audience opinion. *Public Opinion Quarterly,* 1964, *28,* 615-627.

[115] Compare J.L. Freedman & D.O. Sears, Warning, distraction, and resistance to influence. *Journal of Personality and Social Psychology,* 1965, *1,* 262-266, with W.J. McGuire & S. Millman, Anticipatory belief lowering following forewarning of a persuasive attack. *Journal of Personality and Social Psychology,* 1965, *2,* 471-479.

[116] B.D. Sales, The psychological voir dire: an ethical and legal dilemma for psychologists, lawyers, and the legal profession. A paper presented to the Annual Convention of the American Psychology-Law Society, San Francisco, 1974.

4

The Effect of the Method of Presenting Trial Testimony on Juror Decisional Processes[1]

LARRY C. FARMER, GERALD R. WILLIAMS
BERT P. CUNDICK, ROBERT J. HOWELL,
REX E. LEE AND C. KEITH ROOKER

Over the past five years there has been a growing interest in applying video-tape technology to the judicial process. Proponents have suggested a variety of possible applications, including the use of prerecorded videotape to present witness testimony in jury trials. This suggestion has led to judicial experimentation with prerecorded videotape testimony in a number of jurisdictions and to the cautious liberalization of rules relating to the admissibility of electronically recorded evidence at a trial. Although the legal literature has been generally optimistic about these developments (McCrystal, 1974; Morrill, 1971; Kornblum, 1972), occasional questions have been raised about them (Doret, 1974; Stiver, 1974) and researchers from a number of disciplines have tested for possible undesirable effects of videotape presentations on jurors (Bermant, 1975; Bermant & Jacoubovitch, 1975; Bermant et al., 1975; Grow & Johnson, 1975; Williams et al., 1975; Miller et al., 1975). The research reported in this chapter builds on the findings of prior research by seeking to experimentally manipulate the jury verdict by interchanging two alternative methods of testimony presentation.

There are three primary contexts in which videotape may be employed to present testimony evidence at trial. First, it may be used to present the testimony of a witness who cannot be present. It might happen, for example, that a particular witness is seriously ill or is otherwise unable to personally attend and testify. In such cases, courts are generally willing to allow the absent witness's testimony or deposition to be taken outside of the courtroom and preserved for a later presentation at trial. The usual means has been to record it stenographically and have the resulting transcript read to the jury during the trial. In a number of instances, videotape recording and replay of deposition testimony have replaced the transcript method (NCSC, 1974).

Given the relative convenience and utility of videotape presentations, a second use has been suggested, that of prerecording the testimony of expert witnesses for later playback at trial, thus allowing them to give their testimony at a convenient time prior to trial and saving the parties the costs of paying them to sit through several days of trial waiting their turn to testify. It should be noted that in such instances videotape is being used as a substitute, not for a read transcript, but for the live appearance of the witness.

The third proposed usage goes the next step and suggests prerecording all of the testimony to be used at trial, editing the tapes of objectionable material, then replaying them to the jury without the necessity of the judge, attorneys, parties, and witnesses being present. This has been tried experimentally and is known as the videotape trial (McCrystal, 1974).

The videotape trial has received far more public and scientific attention than the other possible uses, perhaps because of its innovative aspects and potential efficiencies. In spite of the impressions generated by this publicity, the prerecorded videotape trial is still in the experimental stage and is the least frequently employed of the video applications. As with depositions of expert witnesses, it involves substituting videotape testimony for live appearances of the witnesses, and requires a number of procedural and behavioral changes from the way jury trials are traditionally conducted that may affect the interests of litigants and the public generally. These concerns have been the subject of considerable discussion and experimentation by the commentators previously noted.

On the other hand, without the fanfare accompanying the concept of the videotape trial, videotape depositions are being used on a much wider scale. For example, a recent national survey of trial attorneys and judges indicates that one-half of the respondents had been "exposed by use or observation to at least one trial-related application of videotape" (Grow & Johnson, 1975) and that, among those so exposed, experience with videotaped depositions exceeded experience with videotaped trials by a ratio of eight to one. Also indicative of this trend is the fact that Federal Rule of Civil Procedure 30 (b) (4) has recently been revised to allow depositions to be electronically recorded and Canon 3 (a) (7) of the ABA Code of Judicial Conduct now expressly provides for the use of electronic means to present evidence in the courtroom. Motivation for the use of videotape depositions has developed from a sense of frustration with the read transcript procedure, in particular the tedium associated with the reading of a lengthy deposition into evidence at trial (Wright & Miller, 1970). In contrast, trial attorneys and judges who have seen videotape presentation of depositions have been quite satisfied with their experience (Grow & Johnson, 1975).

Assuming the trend for the use of videotape depositions will continue, attorneys faced with the necessity of presenting a witness by deposition may be called upon to decide whether to present the witness by videotape or by read transcript. Though this question may at first seem trivial, it involves not only issues of cost and convenience, but also a fundamental tactical choice deriving from potential differences of impact on the jury.

A previous study suggests that videotape may have an impact on the jury significantly different from that of read transcript (Williams et al., 1975). That study involved the use of five alternative means for presenting identical testimony to jurors: live appearance, color videotape, black-and-white videotape, audio tape, and read transcript. The perceptions and reactions of jurors who viewed the live presentation of the trial testimony were compared to those of jurors who viewed the identical testimony presented by the alternative methods. It was found that substantially more and greater differences in juror perceptions occurred between the live and read transcript methods than between the live and color video, black-and-white video, or audio methods. It was concluded that the transcript method was markedly inferior to either of the videotape methods in its ability to reproduce the perceptions and reactions of live trial jurors.

The Williams et al. study was designed to compare juror decisions and perceptions which resulted from testimony presented by different media in separate trials. Only one medium was used in each experimental trial and comparisons were made across trials. In the transcript trial, for example, the testimonies of both witnesses were presented to the jury using the read transcript method. This technique for comparing different methods of presenting trial testimony ignores an important and frequently occurring element in the trial process: the mixing of testimony presentation media in the same trial. The most frequent use of videotape and transcript methods is the presentation of deposition testimony in an otherwise live trial. This is an inherently mixed media situation in which the bulk of the trial testimony is presented live and the deposition is entered into the proceedings by videotape or transcript.

The mixed media trial introduces new variables not present in the single medium trial. When mixed media are used, one medium may be more effective in communicating certain qualities of a witness, or of his testimony. than another. Other possible variations exist. For example, one medium may be inherently more persuasive than another, or more likely to inspire feelings such as empathy in jurors. These considerations indicate the need for a different design from the one used in the Williams et al. study, one which examines whether the use of more than one medium to present testimony in a single trial introduces important additional influences on the jury.

As mentioned, the most common mixed media trial situation occurs when

	Trial A	**Trial B**
Witness I (Landowner)	Color videotape	Transcript
Witness II (Expert witness)	Transcript	Color videotape

Fig. 1. Representation of the experimental design.

transcript testimony is read to the jury in an otherwise live trial. Given the problems inherent in replicating a live trial, this format for an experimental test was rejected in favor of one which would allow for more precise control; thus for this experiment videotape and transcript presentations of the Williams et al. land condemnation trial were counterbalanced in two experimental trials (see Fig. 1). This particular match of presentation methods, while quite unlikely to occur in ordinary trials, provides a basis for testing a number of questions. First, it supplies information on the general question of whether mixing the media used to present testimony may affect the decisions and perceptions of jurors. Second, it extends the experimental findings about the relative merits of videotape and transcript testimony presentation methods developed in the Williams et al. study. In addition, the experiment addresses the following questions:

(1) Does testimony presented by videotape have more influence on the preferred verdicts of individual jurors than the same testimony presented by read transcript?

(2) Does testimony presented by videotape affect the attitudes of jurors toward the trial participants differently from testimony presented by read transcript?

(3) Do jurors prefer the videotape or read transcript method of presenting testimony?

(4) Do jurors evaluate videotape and read transcript methods differently with regard to interest, ease of observation, clarity, and fatigue?

On the basis of the results of our previous study, it was hypothesized that a witness presented by color videotape would have greater positive influence on jurors than a witness presented by read transcript. Applied to the experimental design, this suggested that the most favorable outcomes for each witness should occur after the color videotape presentation of his testimony, with the landowner receiving his highest award and generally having the greatest positive influence on the jurors in Trial A and the city's expert witness receiving his most favorable outcomes in Trial B (see below). Also, it was expected that the jurors would prefer the color videotape method to the read transcript method.

METHOD

Subjects

Subjects for the study were 46 experienced jurors from previous jury panels of the local state trial court. Letters were sent to 130 jurors requesting their participation in the research, notifying them that they would be compensated at the usual per diem rate of $8, and asking them to return a preference form indicating the times they would be available to participate. Approximately 80% of the jurors responded. From this pool of potential subjects, jurors indicating availability for either of the two trials were randomly assigned, while jurors indicating availability for one of the trials were assigned in accordance with their preferences; this resulted in panels of 31 and 30 jurors, respectively. Although 30 jurors were actually present at the second trial, it was necessary to eliminate 8 of them from the data analysis because the video monitor they were viewing failed.[2]

Table I contains demographic information on the participating jurors. The age and educational characteristics of the jury panels in each trial were compared by means of t tests and no differences were found between the two groups.

The Stimulus Trial

A stimulus trial developed for previous research was used in this study, and is described in grater detail by Williams et al. (1975). In short, the case was an actual dispute that had been settled between the parties shortly before it was to have gone to trial. Experienced trial attorneys were selected and commissioned to complete preparations on the case and conduct a trial just as if the case were still a live dispute. The dispute was precipitated by the action of a local municipality in condemning approximately two-thirds of an acre of prime residential property in order to use it for street-widening purposes. The land was located near a prominent new building and was well-known to most of the participating jurors. As is usual in such cases, there was no question as to the right of the city to acquire the property nor as to how much of the property should be taken. Thus the dispute between the city and the landowner was over the amount that the city should pay the owner of the land as compensation for the property taken. Accordingly, the sole issue for the jury to decide was the value of the property taken.

TABLE I

Demographic Characteristics of Participating Jurors

| | No. of Jurors | | | |
	Male	Female	Mean Age	Mean Education
Trial A	13	18	50.1	13.3
Trial B[a]	10	12	53.9	13.6

[a]Eight additional jurors were present at this trial, but they were excluded from the data analysis due to the failure of the video monitor they were watching.

At trial, one witness was presented for each side. The property owner testified that the value of the property taken was $15,960, based on a per acre evaluation of $24,000. A real estate agent who qualified as an expert witness testified, on behalf of the city, that the rounded amount of just compensation for the property taken was $8,000, based on a per acre value of $12,000. Both witnesses agreed that the highest and best use of the property, both before and after the taking, was for residential development, and both based their judgments primarily upon the price paid in recent sales of comparable land. The major difference in approach was that the witness for the city relied upon unimproved acreage transactions while the landowner relied upon developed lot sales. Consequently, the major issue between the two witnesses was whether transactions involving unimproved acreage or developed lots were more comparable to the taking of the subject property. Although this issue was not precisely one of credibility, it did involve a difference of opinion as to the proper approach to the controlling issue of fact.

In addition to the landowner and the expert witness previously mentioned, the trial participants included counsel for the respective parties, a judge, a bailiff, and separate jury panels at each trial (see below). Counsel for both the landowner and the city were experienced trial attorneys. The bailiff normally assigned to the courtroom used in this study served as the court bailiff during each presentation of the stimulus trial. A law professor with previous judicial experience served as the trial judge. In short, the participants in this trial were people typically associated with jury trials, serving in their usual courtroom roles.

The Physical Setting

The setting for the experiment was a courtroom made available through the cooperation of the judges of the local division of the state trial court. The courtroom was large enough that the jurors could be conveniently seated in front of the railing dividing the court and the public sections.

Procedure

In its simplest terms the procedure was to test the relative impact of the read transcript and color videotape methods of delivering testimony by presenting two opposing witnesses by each of the two methods in an experimental design The trials[3] were held on consecutive evenings, and on each evening the entire proceeding occupied slightly more than three hours. On the first night (Trial A), the examination and cross-examination of the landowner (Witness I) were presented by color videotape, and the examination and cross-examination of the city's expert witness (Witness II) were read from a typed transcript by the attorneys who had conducted the original examinations. On the second night (Trial B), this procedure was reversed. The examination and cross-examination of the landowner were read from a typed transcript by the attorneys who had conducted the original examinations, and the examination and cross-examination of the city's expert witness were presented by color videotape.[4] Both the color videotape and the typed transcript were obtained from the original live trial recording.

In summary form, the procedure in each of the two trials was as follows: *Presented live in both trials:* (1) jurors met and seated in a preassigned random order by the bailiff; (2) bailiff announced the judge; (3) judge made introductory remarks and explanations; (4) jurors sworn by the bailiff for the voir dire examination; (5) voir dire examination conducted by the judge; (6) jurors granted five-minute recess; (7) jurors sworn to try the case. *Presented by color videotape in both trials:* (8) opening statement presented by counsel for the city; (9) opening statement presented by counsel for the landowner. *Presented by color videotape in the first trial and by transcript in the second trial:* (10) landowner examined; (11) landowner cross-examined. *Presented by transcript in the first trial and by color videotape in the second trial:* (12) expert witness examined; (13) expert witness cross-witness cross-examined. *Presented live in both trials:* (14) judge instructed the jury; (15) bailiff took jury to jury room; (16) jurors received instruction for completing the questionnaire; (17) jurors completed questionnaire; (18) jurors debriefed about the purposes of the trial, thanked, and dismissed.

The questionnaire was constructed to obtain the following information from the jurors: (a) predeliberation dollar award preferences, (b) forced-choice preferences for either of the two witnesses, (c) bipolar ratings of the competency, honesty, and friendliness of the witnesses, (d) estimation of the impact of the status of the expert witness, (e) forced-choice preference of either the color video or the transcript presentation method, and (f) bipolar ratings of the color video and transcript presentation methods.

Results

Predeliberation awards.

The jurors' predeliberation dollar award preferences in Trial A were significantly higher than the awards given in Trial B, t (50) = 2.53, $p < .01$ (one-tailed test) (mean dollar awards given in Table II). Thus, in accordance with the primary experimental hypothesis, the awards moved in a direction favorable to whichever party was presented by color videotape.

Impact of the expert witness.

Jurors were asked to indicate, on a nine-point, bipolar rating scale, how much they were influenced by "the fact that Mr.——was an expert at real estate evaluation" The scale ranged from "very much influenced" at one end to "not at all influenced" at the polar end. As predicted, in Trial B, the condition in which the testimony of the expert was presented by color videotape, jurors rated themselves as influenced by his status as an expert more than did the jurors in Trial A, the condition in which his testimony was read from a transcript. The mean rating given by the Trial B jurors was a "somewhat influenced" 4.05, while the mean rating given by the Trial A jurors was a slightly negative 5.55; this difference was significant: t (51) = 2.37, $p < .01$ (one-tailed test).

Competency, honesty, and friendliness ratings.

The jurors were asked to rate each of the witnesses in the trial on a set of seven-point bipolar rating scales used by Williams et al. (1975). Subsections of the overall scale were used to obtain information concerning the jurors' evaluations of the competency, honesty, and friendliness of each witness. These subsections were developed by Williams et al. from a larger set of items using factor analytic techniques. (See Table III for a list of the bipolar items used in each scale.)

On the basis of the results of the previous study, it was expected that the Trial A transcript presentation of the expert witness would result in ratings which were more negative than the ratings he would receive after his video presentation in Trial B. Also, it was expected that the Trial A ratings generally would produce less divergence between the expert witness (transcript) and the landowner (videotape), reducing the advantage in ratings enjoyed by the expert witness in previous single media presentations of the trial. In contrast, greater divergence was expected in the jurors' ratings of the two witnesses in Trial B (expert video, landowner transcript).

Table III contains the mean ratings and t test comparisons of the ratings of the expert witness and the landowner in Trials A and B. For purposes of reading the table, note that low scores reflect ratings closer to the left bipolar term and high ratings reflect mean evaluations closer to the terms on the right. Thus

TABLE II

Predeliberation Awards

	Mean Dollar Awards	S.D.
Trial A	11.240.	2609.
Trial B	9,786.	1558.

Note: The range of possible awards was between the $15,960 evaluation of the landowner and the $8,000 evaluation of the expert witness.

very positive ratings are indicated by scores near 1 and very negative ratings are indicated by scores near 7.

As expected, the differences in juror impressions of the competency and honesty of the expert witness and the landowner were reduced in Trial A. The expert was rated significantly more positively than the landowner on only 3 of the 15 terms on the competency and honesty scales. In Trial B, the expert witness, in striking contrast, was rated significantly more positively on all 15 terms in the two scales. Additional t tests comparing the ratings of the expert witness after his transcript and videotape presentations indicated that he was rated significantly more negatively on 13 of the 15 bipolar terms after his transcript presentation. When the video and transcript ratings of the landowner were compared, it was found that the landowner was rated more negatively after the transcript presentation on 14 of the 15 items, but only significantly so on 5 of the 15. Thus the comparative similarity between the ratings of the two witnesses on the Competency and Honesty scales in Trial A was primarily as a result of the more negative ratings given the expert after his transcript presentation.

Quite a different result occurred when the ratings of the two witnesses were compared on the items of the Friendliness scale. The expert witness was rated significantly more positively than the landowner on all 5 items in the scale in Trial A and on 4 of the 5 items in Trial B. Thus transcript presentations of testimony did not appear to meaningfully reduce the jurors' ability to discriminate between the two witnesses on "friendliness" items. When the video ratings of the expert were compared to his transcript ratings, it was found that he was rated more negatively in the transcript condition on only one item in the scale. The ratings of the landowner were quite differently affected. He was rated more positively after his transcript presentation than after his video presentation on 3 of the 6 items of the Friendliness scale. Apparently, the landowner, who had been consistently seen as somewhat unfriendly, was benefited on this dimension by the use of the transcript method to present his testimony. It appears, therefore, that the warmth and friendliness of the expert were not meaningfully lost

TABLE III

Jurors' Mean Bipolar Ratings of Witnesses

Competency

Bipolar Term	Trial A[a]			Trial B[b]		
	Landowner Video	Expert Trans.	p	Landowner Trans.	Expert Video	p
Precise-vague	5.0	4.8		6.2	2.4	**
Confident-hesitant	5.0	3.7	**	3.7	1.7	**
Certain-uncertain	4.2	4.2		3.9	2.5	**
Accurate-inaccurate	4.8	4.5		6.4	2.7	**
Knowledgeable-uninformed	3.5	4.2		4.2	2.4	**
Consistent-inconsistent	3.8	4.5		4.8	2.3	**
Clear memory-faulty memory	4.6	3.9		5.6	2.3	**
Convincing-unconvincing	4.7	4.6		5.6	2.2	**
Reasonable-unreasonable	4.4	3.5		4.6	2.5	**

Honesty

Bipolar Term	Landowner Video	Expert Trans.	p	Landowner Trans.	Expert Video	p
Trustworthy-untrustworthy	4.3	3.9		5.5	2.9	**
Telling truth-not telling truth	3.9	3.5		5.4	2.0	**
Sincere-insincere	3.8	3.5		4.4	2.2	**
Honest-dishonest	4.2	3.1	*	4.6	2.3	**
Fair-unfair	4.7	3.5	*	5.2	2.8	**
Logical-not logical	4.6	3.7		4.9	2.2	**

Friendliness

Bipolar Term	Landowner Video	Expert Trans.	p	Landowner Trans.	Expert Video	p
Friendly-unfriendly	4.6	2.3	**	3.5	2.2	**
Warm-cold	5.1	3.6	**	3.5	2.2	**
Well-mannered-ill-mannered	4.0	2.5	**	2.6	1.9	
Nice-not nice	3.9	3.1	*	3.6	2.0	**
Pleasant-annoying	4.6	2.8	*	3.2	1.8	**

[a]One tailed t test, $df = 30$, n = 31.
[b]One tailed t test, $df = 21$, n = 22.

*$p < .05$.
**$p < .01$.

during the transcript presentation of his testimony, but the negative cues of the landowner were attenuated during his transcript presentation.

Friendship preferences.

The jurors were asked to make a forced-choice selection between the witnesses by responding to the following question: If you had to choose between the two witnesses, whom would you prefer to have for a friend? This question was asked of the jurors in the Williams et al. (1975) study and the jurors' preferred awards were found to be significantly related to the forced-choice preferences. Given this relationship, this study was designed to test the effects of media upon the jurors' friendship shoices. It was hypothesized that the overwhelming preference for the expert witness which occurred in the previous study would be reduced when the expert's testimony was presented by transcript in contrast to a video presentation of the landowner's testimony (Trial A). The resulting selections are given in Table IV.

The expert was selected as a friend by 85% of the jurors after the color videotape presentation of his testimony and by 63% of the jurors after the transcript presentation of his testimony. Correspondingly, the landowner was preferred as a friend by 37% of the jurors after the color video presentation of his testimony and by 15% of the jurors after the transcript presentation of his testimony.[5] A directional test for a difference between two independent proportions revealed a tendency for both the landowner and the expert witness to be more frequently preferred after the color video presentation than after the transcript presentation: $z = 1.60, p = .055$.

Preferences for color video or transcript presentations.

In order to compare juror reactions to the two presentation methods, the following question was asked: "As a result of your experience this evening, which method do you prefer for presenting the testimony of witnesses who cannot appear in person?" When juror responses from the two trials were combined, the color video method was preferred three to one over the transcript method (see Table V). The percentage of jurors, 64%, preferring the color video presentation in Trial B was proportionately, but not significantly, lower than the 81% of the jurors preferring the color video method in Trial A. The less frequent preference for videotape in Trial B may have been attributable to malfunctions of the equipment during the trial.[6]

Ratings of the two presentation methods.

The jurors were asked to make an evaluation of the two testimony presentation methods by rating them on each of 5 bipolar scales. The polar terms and mean ratings are contained in Table VI. The Trial A jurors rated the video presentation as significantly more interesting, easier to pay attention to, more

TABLE IV

Jurors' Friendship Preferences
for Either Landowner or Expert Witness

Trial	Preferred Landowner	Preferred Expert Witness
Trial A[a]	11	19
Trial B	3	19

[a]One juror did not indicate a preference.

TABLE V

Jurors' Preferences for
Color Video or Transcript Presentations

Trial	n	Color Video	Transcript
Trial A	31	84%	16%
Trial B	22	64%	36%
Combined preferences	53	75%	25%

refreshing, clearer, and more stimulating than the transcript method; in every comparison, the difference between the ratings of the two methods was significant beyond the .01 level. In marked contrast to Trial A, the Trial B jurors did not rate the color video method significantly better than the transcript method on any of the bipolar pairs, a result that may have been influenced by difficulties with the color video monitors in Trial B.[7] The transcript method received essentially the same negative evaluation by the jurors in each trial, while the jurors in Trial B were significantly less favorable disposed to the video presentation on all items than were the Trial A jurors.

TABLE VI

Bipolar Ratings of
Color Video and Transcript Presentation Methods

	Interesting-Dull		Easy to Pay Attention-Difficult to Pay Attention		Refreshing-Fatiguing		Clear-Confusing		Stimulating-Tedious	
	Video	Trans.	Video	Trans.	Video	Trans.	Video	Trans.	Video	Trans.
Trial A	2.97	5.10	3.03	5.16	3.94	5.58	2.77	4.52	3.71	5.48
Trial B	4.57	4.76	4.81	5.14	5.38	5.33	3.86	4.52	5.00	5.71

Note: Lower mean ratings reflect a more positive evaluation. A 7-point scale was used.

DISCUSSION

The specific question under study in this experiment was whether, in the trial setting, color videotape presentations of deposition testimony are more persuasive than transcript readings of the same testimony. Four types of information bearing on this question were obtained from the subject jurors: (a) preferred awards, (b) perceptions of the expert witness's influence, (c) ratings of the witnesses, and (d) preferences for the witnesses. The overall results generally support the conclusions that the verdicts and preferences of the jurors were consistently more favorable for whichever side of the case was presented by color videotape. First, the landowner received a comparatively larger award when he was presented by videotape and his opponent witness by read transcript (Trial A), and he received significantly less for his property when he was presented by read transcript and his opponent witness by color videotape (Trial B). Second, the jurors perceived themselves as more influenced by the status of the expert witness after the videotape presentation of his testimony than after the transcript presentation. Third, the witnesses generally received more positive ratings as to their competency and honesty after their respective videotape presentations. Fourth, the jurors' friendship preferences for the landowner and the expert witness were respectively higher when each was presented by videotape. On the basis of this evidence, it appears that the witnesses were more influential when presented by the color videotape method than by read transcript.

In order to limit the complexity of the experimental trial used in this study, the number of witnesses was kept at two: the landowner and the opposing expert witness. As it turned out, these two witnesses made quite different impressions on the participating jurors and on four experienced trial attorneys who attended the trials. In the opinion of the trial attorneys, the landowner was a very poor witness with respect to both the content of his testimony and the manner of his presentation. The expert witness was perceived by these attorneys as a generally excellent witness. It seems intuitively correct that the persuasive, effective expert witness would benefit from a videotape presentation over a transcript reading of his testimony, but why would a very poor and perhaps detrimental witness benefit from a videotape presentation? Did this in fact happen? Was the landowner made more persuasive or effective by his color videotape presentation when it should have more clearly portrayed his negative qualities as well as his relatively sparse positive qualities as a witness? It is not necessary to presume that the poor witness's impact on the jury was enhanced by his videotaped presentation to explain the preferred verdicts. For example, the observed results could have occurred if the landowner's testimony affected the jurors similarly in both his video and transcript presentations while the expert witness's positive impact was comparatively reduced by the transcript presentation in Trial A.

Examination of the results of the competency, honesty, and friendliness ratings indicates that something very close to this may well have occurred. The landowner was not rated as dramatically more competent or honest after his video presentation than after his transcript presentation. Also, unlike the expert, he was rated as more friendly after the transcript presentation of his testimony. In receiving a larger award in Trial A, the landowner may have benefited more from the reduced impact of the testimony of the expert witness than from the increased impact of his testimony due to the use of videotape. Given this observation, the safest conclusion is the more cirsumscribed statement that, relative to the transcript presentation, the videotape presentation significantly benefited at least one of the witnesses in the trial.

Given the current practice of allowing deposition-type testimony to be presented in otherwise live trials it is important to determine what happens to jurors' perceptions and decisions when more than one method of presenting testimony is used in a trial. In our previous study, when the same medium was used to present all of the testimony in a trial, the jurors' perceptions of the witnesses remained (with a few important exceptions) relatively constant and similar to those of the original live trial. In this experiment, in which different media were used to present testimony in the same trial, the jurors' perceptions shifted quite dramatically in many cases, and, more importantly, the outcome of the trial was affected.

These results raise a number of theoretical questions concerning the practice of presenting testimony by different methods in the same trial. The task for the jurors in a trial is to weigh the evidence presented and make a decision on the basis of the evidence and the relevant law. It is probable that the weight given the testimony of one witness is very much dependent upon the impact of other witnesses in the same trial. Testimony, then, is not judged entirely in the abstract, but in its relationship to the other testimony presented at trial. Thus the use of a "weaker" medium to present a witness's testimony may not only reduce the impact of his testimony, but, due to the lack of effective counter-testimony, cause the testimony of an opponent to have greater comparative impact.

The finding that significant differences in the predeliberation verdicts occurred when videotape and read transcript methods were counterbalanced in separate trials emphasizes the need for concern about differences in relative persuasiveness in other possible combinations of presentation methods, most notably the combination of live and videotape or live and read transcript methods. These pairings occur whenever deposition testimony is presented by transcript or videotaped testimony in an otherwise live trial. If impact differences do exist between live and videotaped presentations, then the trend in some legal jurisdictions to routinely present the testimony of expert witnesses by videotape rather than by live trial appearance bears careful scrutiny. While the procedure holds a promise of considerable cost-saving for litigants and time-saving for experts, if videotaped testimony, individual attorneys and litigants may well be sacrificing more than they gain by using it.

FOOTNOTES

[1] The authors wish to thank the Research Division of Brigham Young University and the J. Reuben Clark Law School for providing the funding for this research and the judges and staff of the Fourth Judicial District Court of Utah for their generous assistance.

[2] The jurors sat in three groups in the courtroom, and each group viewed a different monitor. The eight jurors who were dropped from the sample were watching a monitor that lost both its sound and its picture within a few minutes of the beginning of the expert witness's testimony. Thus these jurors heard only the audio portion of his testimony from the other courtroom monitors. No attempt was made to accommodate the jurors viewing the faculty monitor, as that would have necessitated a significant change in viewing conditions for the unaffected jurors.

[3] Three 19-inch color video monitors were used at each trial. They all received their signals from the same playback unit.

[4] At the beginning of the expert witness's testimony, the amplifier attached to the central playback unit began to fail. The result was a slight but audible electronic distortion of the audio and some deterioration of the video picture on all three monitors. The primary form of the video deterioration was a "snowy" quality to the picture. In spite of the problems, the experimenters judged the video picture to be of sufficient quality to continue the trial at this point.

The possibility of such equipment failures raises a number of issues. If this had been a real trial, the failure of the amplifier could have presented some serious questions as to proper procedure. For example, if the testimony were stopped while the equipment was replaced or repaired, where in the testimony should the replay begin—at the beginning, at the point where the equipment began to fail, or at the point where it was turned off? Another problem arises as to who should determine whether the quality of the video replay is adequate—the judge, attorneys, bailiff, court reporter, etc.?

[5] By the time Trial B had been completed, the stimulus trial had been presented to jurors under varying conditions on eight different occasions. At each presentation, the jurors had been asked to indicate their choice of one or the other of the witnesses as a friend. Excluding the preferences reported in this study, the percentages of jurors selecting the landowner in each trial have been as follows: 8%, 11%, 21%, 12%, 22%, and 15%. Thus the proportion of preferences for the landowner in Trial B tends to be not only higher than in Trial A but also higher than the pattern of preferences that has occurred in all of the previous presentations of the trial.

[6] A directional test for a difference between two independent proportions was computed to determine whether the smaller proportion of jurors preferring the video method in Trial B was significant; the result was an insignificant but concerning z of 1.38, $p < .08$. Because of the problems with the video equipment in Trial B, one would expect the jurors to be less satisfied with the video presentation; therefore, this result was not surprising. The reason for concern was the possibility that some factor in the person or testimony of the expert witness tended to produce a lower level of satisfaction with the color video method in Trial B jurors. There were two reasons to conclude that the smaller number preferring the color video method in Trial B (if it were not, in fact, a random event) was due to the quality of the video picture and to equipment problems rather than to the characteristics of the testimony being presented. First, when the expert witness was presented by color videotape in Experiment 2, the jurors greatly preferred the color video method to the alternative audio method. Second, the one-tailed test used to determine if the number preferring video was significantly lower in Trial B than in Trial A could not be validly used to test for other types of differences. Since there was no a priori basis for thinking the color video method would be selected less frequently in Trial B for other than equipment problems, the proper tests

TABLE VII

Bipolar Ratings of
Color Video and Audiotape Presentation Methods

	Interesting-Dull		Easy to Pay Attention- Difficult to Pay Attention		Refreshing-Fatiguing		Clear-Confusing		Stimulating-Tedious	
	Video	Audio	Video	Audio	Video	Audio	Video	Audio	Video	Audio
Experiment No. 2	2.00	5.00	1.87	4.27	3.27	5.72	2.13	4.40	2.87	5.47

Note: Lower mean ratings reflect a more positive evaluation. A 7-point scale was used.

for other questions had to be nondirectional. The two-tailed probability of a difference was a much less concerning $p < .16$.

[7] This conclusion is also supported by the results of a subsequent experiment in which we compared jurors' ratings of videotape and audiotape methods of presenting trial testimony. In this experiment, we used the same procedures as in Trial B, except that an audiotape was used to present the landowner's testimony rather than the transcript method used in Trial B. The jurors' ratings of the two presentation methods used in this subsequent condition are reported in Table VIII (compare to Table VI). Not only was the color videotape method significantly rated as superior to the audiotape method in this presentation of the trial, but this use of the color video method was also significantly more positively rated than the identical use of the color video presentation of Trial B, in which the quality of the video picture was lessened by the partial failure of the video recorder and amplifier.

REFERENCES

Barber, J.P. & Bates, P.R. Videotape in criminal proceeding. *Hastings Law Journal*, 1972, *24*, 1-8.

Bermant, G. Critique–Data in search of theory in search of policy: Behavioral responses to videotape in the courtroom. *Brigham Young University Law Review*, 1975, 467-85.

Bermant, G. & Jacoubovitch, M.-D. Fish out of water: A brief overview of social and psychological concerns about videotaped trials. *Hastings Law Journal*, 1975, *26*, 999-1011.

Bermant, G., Chappell, D., Crockett, G.T., Jacoubovitch, M.-D. & McGuire, M. Juror responses to prerecorded videotape trial presentations in California and Ohio. *Hastings Law Journal*, 1975, *26*, 975-998.

Bermant, G., McGuire, M., McKinley, W. & Salo, C. The logic of simulation in jury research. *Criminal Justice and Behavior*, 1974, *1*, 224-232.

Doret, D.M. Trial by videotape–Can justice by done? *Temple Law Quarterly*, 1974, *47*, 228-268.

Farmer, L.C. *Juror evaluation as a function of live, color video, black and white video, audio, and read transcript presentations of trial testimony.* Unpublished doctoral dissertation, Brigham Young University, 1975.

Grow, R. & Johnson, R. Opening Pandora's box: Asking judges and attorneys to react to the videotape trial. *Brigham Young University Law Review*, 1975, *2*, 487-527.

McCrystal, J.L. The videotape trial comes of age. *Judicature*, 1974, *57*, 446-449.

Miller, G., Bender, D., Florence, T. & Nicholson, H. Real versus reel: What's, the verdict. *Journal of Communication*, 1974, *24*, 100-111.

Miller, G.R. & Siebert, F.S. *Effects of videotaped testimony on information processing and decision-making in jury trials.* Progress Report No. 2, 1975, Michigan State University, Grant GI-38398, RANN, National Science Foundation.

National Center for State Courts. *Video support in the criminal courts*, 1974, III, A-2-A-29.

Stiver, C.E. Video-tape trials: A practical evaluation and a legal analysis. *Stanford Law Review*, 1974, *26*, 619-645.

Taillefer, F.J., Short, E.H., Greenwood, J.M. & Brady, R.G. Video support in the criminal courts. *Journal of Communication*, 1974, *24*, 111-112.

Williams, G., Farmer, L., Lee, R., Cundick, B., Howell, R. & Rooker, C. Juror perceptions of trial testimony as a function of the method of presentation: A comparison of live, color video, black and white video, audio, and transcript presentations. *Brigham Young University Law Review*, 1975, *2*, 375-421.

5

An Experimental Study of Twelve vs. Six Member Juries Under Unanimous vs. Nonunanimous Decisions*

ALLICE M. PADAWER-SINGER
ANDREW N. SINGER
RICKIE L.J. SINGER

The United States Supreme Court, in landmark decisions, has ruled that states may decide (1) whether trials by jury in state courts necessitate a twelve- or less-than-twelve-member jury (*Williams v. Florida,* 1970) and (2) whether jury verdicts in state courts need be unanimous or nonunanimous (*Apodaca v. Oregon,* 1972; *Johnson v. Louisiana,* 1972). Since the states vary greatly in their adoption of smaller juries and/or nonunanimous verdicts in different types of trials, and since there is a paucity of empirical data as to the impact of such changes, major legal and social policy problems have emerged.

Arguments in favor of changes toward six-member juries and nonunanimous verdicts (*e.g.,* Wiehl, 1972; Bogue & Fritz, 1972; Devitt, 1971) have emphasized time and money savings and avoidance of hung juries and retrials, and have assumed that deliberations and the basis for decision-making would not differ relative to types of juries. Arguments in opposition to changes (*e.g.,* Baum, 1973; Kaufman, 1972; Stevens, 1971) stress that group deliberations may not be as

*This study was funded by the National Science Foundation, Division of Research Applied to National Needs, NSF-APR-73-07911-A02.

"robust" in smaller juries with nonunanimous verdicts, that different types of interaction take place, that holders of the majority opinion will not pay much attention to holders of the minority opinion, and that the majority is not necessarily "correct" thus attaching value to a hung jury. The strong polarization of members of the bar and the judiciary concerning the desirability of such changes calls for empirical data to determine the consequences of changes in jury size and in jury decision rule.

Over the years, the jury has attracted the attention of researchers from various disciplines and perspectives, including psychology, law, sociology, political science, communication, and journalism. Different aspects of the jury have been studied: comparisons of actual decisions and what would have been judges' decisions in these cases (Kalven & Zeisel, 1966); the influence of the socio-economic status of jurors (Strodtbeck et al., 1957), of news media publicity (Padawer-Singer & Barton, 1975), of voir dire and pre-trial publicity (Padawer-Singer et al., 1974), and of reduction in jury size (Kessler, 1973); and changes from unanimous to nonunanimous decisions (Saks, 1974) on juror decision-making. Thus jury research proliferated before and after the extensive review of jury research by Erlanger (1970).

Specific research and literature on changes from twelve- to six-member juries and/or changes from unanimous to nonunanimous verdicts have adopted a variety of approaches: comparisons of actual twelve- and six-member juries in civil cases in New Jersey (Stoever, 1972) and in Washington (Bermant & Coppock, 1973); predictions of outcomes derived on statistical grounds from specific assumptions (Zeisel, 1975; Zeisel & Diamond, 1974; Walbert, 1971; Feinberg, 1971; Friedman, 1972); and experimental research involving psychology students (Davis et al., 1975) and political science students (Valenti & Downing, 1975).

There are several problems in this research. First, as to experimental laboratory studies, although Kessler (1973) writes in favor of the use of student jurors because of their "greater availability and lower cost," whether the results of such studies can be generalized to "real juries functioning in real trials" (Bermant et al., 1974) is doubtful. For instance, jury studies which involve students as jurors cannot measure (1) the variation of demographic characteristics of jurors, (2) how jury size affects the community representation in each jury, or (3) the relationships of demographic characteristics to other variables such as voting. In other studies, adults were asked to serve as jurors: Miller and Hamilton (1975) used adults whose names were drawn from street listings, and Saks (1974) recruited "former jurors." These populations are more similar than college students to the actual jury population, but they are still mainly self-selected samples.

Another problem in the prior research is that no real voir dire took place. Voir dire refers to the jury selection process in which the judge and the lawyers question prospective jurors to uncover possible biases and prejudices. Prejudiced jurors may than be challenged and excused from serving. In a previous study on the Free Press-Fair Trial issue, Padawer-Singer et al. (1974) posited and found that voir dire is an essential element in jury selection.Yet Davis et al. (1975), for example, handed jurors a "written" voir dire questionnaire (as contrasted to real voir dire, which is oral) without the usual follow-up, namely, the elimination of some jurors on the aforementioned legal bases.

Finally, previous studies have used mainly short, fabricated trials on video-tapes (Kessler, 1973), audiotapes, or slide-and-tape presentations (Valenti & Downing, 1975) in artificial settings such as laboratories (Miller & Hamilton, 1975). Judges' charges to the jury were brief and given by the experimenters (Davis et al., 1975; Miller & Hamilton, 1975; Buckout, 1975). Only a half-hour to an hour was allotted for deliberations, after which juries were declared hung (Davis et al., 1975; Miller & Hamilton, 1975; Buckout, 1975). It is no wonder, then, that critics of laboratory-based jury studies speculate on the degree to which such data can be extrapolated. Rosenthal (1963), Orne (1962), and others have elaborated on the differences in expectations and behavior which occur as a function of laboratory vs. "real world" settings.

Field studies presenting fewer problems of external validity of data might be afflicted with other problems. In one study (Stoever, 1972), time comparisons between twelve- and six-member juries were not conclusive because the more complex cases were tried by twelve-member juries at lawyers' requests. Another study (Bermant & Coppock, 1973) found no difference between twelve- and six-member juries in finding for plaintiffs in compensation cases; however, these cases could be either jury or bench trials and lawyers could agree, if they wished, to have a jury of less than twelve. Thus random or "nonsystematic" assignment of certain types of cases to a particular size jury could not be assured. Erlanger (1970) urges that studies be conducted on jury populations with a systematic approach to the collection of data. Such data would meet with greater accep-tance from members of the judiciary, the bar, the news media, and the behavioral/social sciences.

The present study of decision-making in twelve- vs. six-member juries and unanimous vs. nonunanimous decisions has attempted to control independent variables and yet achieve the highest degree of realism to date in any experi-mental jury research. This is the only experimental study of jury size and types of decisions to be conducted with a population of jurors who came from the central jury room, in the authentic setting of the court,[1] and who were selected with voir dire examinations by real lawyers. A videotape over three hours long, reenacting a real trial and retaining the words of the lawyers, judges, and witnes-ses, was presented to the jurors. Further realism was introduced by having the judge, as opposed to the experimenter, give the jury instructions on the video-tape. Finally, as in real trials, jurors were allowed as much time to deliberate as they required, two or three days if necessary. If a jury felt it was deadlocked, the Allen Charge[2] was read to encourage the jurors to go back to the jury room and try again to reach a verdict. If, after additional deliberations, jurors announced that they were still deadlocked, the jury was declared hung.

This was an experimental study carried out in the "real world." Such a procedure achieved an atmosphere which induced our jurors to behave as real jurors, to take their responsibility seriously and not to dismiss the proceedings as a game or academic exercise. Their behavior, including the content and length of their deliberations, indicated the importance they attributed to this part of jury duty.

EXPERIMENTAL DESIGN

The present study was designed to test the effects of the main independent variables, group size twelve- vs. six-member juries and unanimous vs. non-unanimous decisions, on the main dependent variables, predeliberation opinion alignment, time taken to reach a verdict, jury verdicts, and the occurrence of hung juries. Data on other variables[4] were collected and studied in the course of the research. There were twenty-three juries in each of four different combinations.

About 1,500 jurors called for jury duty to the Queens County Supreme Court in New York participated in this study. The data reported are based on 828 jurors who were selected after voir dire examinations. They formed a heterogeneous group in terms of demographic characteristics, age, sex, education, ethnic background, and occupation.

The videotape, with all names and dates changed, was based on the transcript of a real murder trial. A woman was shot, apparently during a struggle along a canal path; a man was observed bending over the body; later, a man found in the vicinity was identified, arrested, and indicted. The trial presented mainly circumstantial evidence and the defendant did not take the stand. Government exhibits,[3] such as a map and pictures of the area, were reproduced and shown to jurors.

The experimental sequence was as follows: (1) Jurors were called into the assembly room by a jury clerk and escorted to the courtroom by a court officer. (2) Jurors were asked to participate in the study, that is, to watch a videotaped reenactment of a real trial, to deliberate, and to give their views on various aspects of the jury system and the administration of justice. They were assured of anonymity since each juror who participated received a number which substituted for his name for the duration of the study. (3) Two lawyers and a judge (a lawyer acting as a judge) entered the courtroom. (4) Either seven jurors (six plus one alternate) or thirteen (twelve plus one alternate) were called from the larger body of jurors and were questioned, retained, or excused during a voir dire. (5) When a jury was satisfactory to the defense and the prosecution, the judge asked the jurors to rise and swear that they would pay attention to the evidence presented and to the judge's charges. (6) Jurors returned the next day, watched the videotape, voted independently, then retired to deliberate as long

TABLE I

Research Design

| | Types of Decisions | |
Jury Size	Unanimous	Nonunanimous
6 jurors in each jury	23 juries	23 juries
12 jurors in each jury	23 juries	23 juries

as necessary and returned a verdict. (7) Finally, jurors answered an extensive anonymous questionnaire.

Jurors' deliberations were recorded with their knowledge and informed consent. Evidence from a previous study including the reports of jurors in the anonymous questionnaire and the free expression of thoughts and feelings in the taped deliberations showed that tape-recording did not interfere with deliberations.

RESULTS AND DISCUSSION

In this chapter, the data reported will emphasize the effects of jury size and decision rule (twelve- vs. six-member juries, unanimous vs. nonunanimous decisions) on predeliberation opinion alignment, time taken for deliberations, jury verdicts, and the occurrence of hung juries.

Jurors indicated anonymously their opinions about the defendant (guilty or not guilty) after viewing the trial and before entering the jury room for deliberations. A tally of predeliberation opinions in the different juries reveals that in eleven (23.9%) of the 6-member juries there were five or six jurors who held similar opinions about the defendant, thereby constituting a consensus. Thus the verdict is almost predetermined before deliberations start. In contrast, no twelve-member jury entered the jury room with twelve or eleven similar opinions. Only two (4.3%) of the twelve-member juries started deliberating with ten similar opinions. The difference in occurrence of an overwhelming predeliberation majority for guilty or not guilty between twelve- and six-member juries is significant ($x^2 = 7.25$, p $<$ .01).

It is logical to assume that the more agreement there is among jurors before deliberation, the less time it should take to deliberate. Indeed, the average deliberation time of juries in which the alignment of jurors is five or six for guilty or for not guilty (before deliberations) is 77.27 minutes. One jury took two

TABLE II

**Number and Percentage of Hung Juries by
Jury Size and Decisions**

Size	Unanimous	Nonunanimous	
12	5	5	10
	21.7%	21.7%	21.7%
6	4	0	4
	17.4%	0%	8.7%
	9	5	14
	19.5%	10.9%	15.2%

minutes and another took ten minutes to deliberate. This average is much lower than the average deliberation time of 154.63 minutes for the remaining six-member juries. The difference within the six-member juries is statistically significant at the $p < .05$ level ($t = 2.22$, 44 df). Thus the Supreme Court assumption that all six-member juries will deliberate thoroughly is not borne out. There appears to be an element of greater "instability" in six-member juries; chance factors and curtailed deliberations seem to determine the verdicts in almost one out of four six-member juries, while this is not the case in twelve-member juries.

Given the greater likelihood of diverse opinions in twelve-member juries than in six-member juries, it is logical to predict that the former are more prone to hung verdicts (see Elwork & Sales, 1977). A comparison of the number of hung juries between twelve- and six-member juries yields a statistically significant difference ($x^2 = 3.03$, $p < .05$) using a one-tail test (see Table II). This is due primarily to one type of jury—the six-member nonunanimous, in which there were no hung juries.[5] Since homogeneous opinions are more likely in six-member juries, the nonunanimous decision rule will further decrease the probability of a hung jury (Elwork & Sales, 1977).

This finding refutes the Supreme Court assumptions that a nonunanimous decision will preclude the occurrence of hung juries in twelve-member juries and that six-member juries deciding under the unanimous rule will have fewer hung decisions than their twelve-member counterparts. In our study, only the extreme type of jury—6-member nonunanimous, not recommended by the majority or by the minority views of the Supreme Court—leads to verdicts only.

TABLE III

**Verdicts as a Function of Jury Size and Types
of Decisions***

Jury Size	Unanimous Juries		Nonunanimous Juries		Total
	Not Guilty	Guilty	Not Guilty	Guilty	
6	11	8	14	9	(42)
12	10	8	9	9	(36)

*Differences in the total number of juries within each conditions are due to the omission of hung juries.

Regardless of the value and meaning of a hung jury in the administration of justice, changing to nonunanimous decisions in twelve-member juries or to six-member unanimous juries will not preclude the occurrence of hung juries.

Table III presents the number and kind of verdicts as a function of jury size and types of decisions. A comparison of these verdicts yields no significant differences.

This last result, though consistent with most prior studies, should be interpreted cautiously. It may be due to the type of case chosen, the small number of juries tested in each condition, or the fact that there may be differences but not in directionality. One study (Valenti & Downing, 1975) reported more guilty verdicts in six- than in twelve-member juries in a case with high apparent guilt of the defendant. A closer look reveals that what were called "non-convictions" in twelve-member juries were actually hung juries. These "non-convictions," with a majority of jurors for guilty, were added to "acquittals" and constituted the basis for a finding of more convictions in six-member juries. Had Valenti & Downing noted the direction of the majority, and not called every hung jury a "non-conviction" to be added to "acquittals," the results would also have been no apparent difference in verdict.

Lempert (1975) compared a few "ideal" and "next to ideal" experimental designs and demonstrated the difficulty of detecting true differences in verdicts. He believed that "the Court ought to be more concerned with Type II error, the possibility that available research has failed to reveal true differences between the verdicts rendered by different size juries." Our findings that (1) an overwhelming predeliberation opinion majority occurs more often in six-member juries, (2) in consequence, deliberations are curtailed and take less time, (3) hung juries occur with equal frequency in twelve-member unanimous, twelve-member nonunanimous and six-member unanimous juries, and (4) in only the extreme type of jury, the six-member nonunanimous, did juries not end in hung decisions, indicate that different deliberation processes and greater chance factors take place in six- as compared to twelve-member juries and that verdicts may not be the most appropriate measure of differences between juries since real but small differences would require a few thousand experiments to become statistically significant.

We must pay attention to other data such as predeliberation alignments and their relationship to time taken for deliberations, to hung juries, as reported above, and to taped deliberations, community representation within each jury, and jurors' preferences for certain juries. Such data will illustrate the impact of changes in jury size and types of decisions, and will provide the empirical data base for state legislative decisions and policy-making. Our findings echo and support the concerns of Justices Brennan and Douglas in the following statements:

> When less than unanimity is sufficient, consideration of minority views may become nothing more than a matter of majority grace. (Justice Brennan, Dissenting Opinion, *Apodaca v. Oregon,* 1972)

> Human experience teaches that polite and academic conversation is no substitute for the earnest and robust argument necessary to reach unanimity. (Justice Douglas, Dissenting Opinion, *Apodaca v. Oregon,* 1972)

FOOTNOTES

[1] This study was made possible by the permission and cooperation of Queens County Supreme Court Judge Charles Margett; Mr. Alexander Potruch, Secretary to Judge Margett; Mr. Edward Hughes, Jury Administrator; the whole staff of the court; and the Queens County Bar Association, with the cooperation of Mr. Jules Haskell and Professor Graziano, President of the Association.

[2] The Allen Charge asks jurors who have reported that they are deadlocked to resume deliberations and try to reach a verdict.

[3] Maps and photos of the scene of the crime were reproduced thanks to the cooperation of Mr. Al Hantman, District Attorney, Washington, D.C.

[4] Other data not yet analyzed will be reported at a later time. The data collected in this study included: (1) anonymous predeliberation opinions about the defendant (guilty or not guilty); (2) taped jury deliberations; (3) a questionnaire on (a) demographic characteristics, (b) previous jury and court experience, (c) perception of difficulty of decision, (d) perception of group pressure, (e) recall of favorable and unfavorable facts, (f) perception of defendant's motives, (g) attitudes toward criminal issues, sentencing and rehabilitation, the jury system, jurors' roles, news media, and (h) features of the experiment (videotape, tape recorder); (4) experimenters' ratings of jurors' characteristics and experimenters' comments about each jury; (5) postdeliberation opinions of each juror and verdicts; (6) occurrence of hung juries; and (7) time taken for deliberations.

[5] This type of jury was studied in order to examine (among other variables) at what point the occurrence of hung juries stops.

REFERENCES

Apodaca v. Oregon, 406 U.S. 404 (1972).

Baum, V.J. The six-man jury—the cross-section aborted. *The Judge's Journal 12,* 12 (1973).

Bermant, G. & Coppock, R. Outcomes of six- and twelve-member jury trials: an analysis of 128 civil cases in the State of Washington. *Washington Law Review 48,* 593 (1973).

Bermant, G., McGuire, M., McKinley W. & Salo, C. The logic and simulation in jury research. *Criminal Justice and Behavior 1,* 224-233 (1974).

Bogue, A.W. & Fritz, T.G. The six-man jury. *South Dakota Law Review 17,* 285 (1972).

Buckout, R. 6- and 12-Member juries, unanimous and non-unanimous decisions. Paper presented at the Eastern Psychological Association, April, 1975.

Davis, J.H., Kerr, N.L. & Atkin, R.S. The decision processes of 6- and 12- person mock juries assigned unanimous and 2/3 majority rules, *Journal of Personality and Social Psychology 32,* 1-14 (1975).

Devitt, E.J. 6-Member civil juries gain backing. *American Bar Association Journal 57,* 1112 (1971).

Elwork, A. & Sales, B.D. Psycholegal research on the jury and trial processes. In C. Petty, W. Curran & L. McGarry, *Modern Legal Medicine and Forensic Science.* Philadelphia, Pa.: F.A. Davis, 1977.

Erlanger, H.S. Jury research in America. Its past and future. *Law and Society Review 4,* 345 (1970).

Feinberg, W.E. Teaching the type I and type II errors: the judicial process, *The American Statistician* 30-32 (June, 1971).

Friedman, H. Trial by jury: criteria for convictions, jury size and type I and type II errors. *The American Statistician* 21-23 (April, 1972).

Johnson v. Louisiana, 40 U.S.L.W. 4524 (May 22, 1972).

Kalven, H. & Zeisel, H. *The American Jury.* Boston: Little, Brown, 1966.

Kaufman, I.R. Harbingers of jury reform. *American Bar Association Journal 58,* 696 (1972).

Kessler, J. An empirical study of six- and twelve-member jury decision-making processes. *Journal of Law Reform 6,* 712 (1973).

Lempert, R.A. Uncovering "non-discernible" differences: empirical research and the jury-size cases. *Michigan Law Review 73,* 4 (1975).

Miller, F.D. & Hamilton, V.L. Decision-making processes in simulated juries. Paper presented at the Public Choice Meeting, Chicago, April, 1975.

Orne, M. On the social psychology of the psychological experiment. *American Psychologist 17,* 776-783 (1962).

Padawer-Singer, A.M. & Barton, A.H. Free Press-Fair Trial study. In Rita Simon (ed.), *The Jury System in America: A Critical Overview.* Beverly Hills, Calif.: Sage Publications, 1975.

Padawer-Singer, A.M., Singer, A.N. & Singer, R.L.J., Voir dire by two lawyers: an essential safeguard. *Judicature 57* 386 (1974). (A few crucial errata appeared in this article. Corrections are available from the first author.)

Rosenthal, R. On the social psychology of the psychological experiment. *American Scientist 51,* 268-283 (1963).

Saks, M.J. Jury decision-making as a function of group size and social decision rule. Dissertation, University of Ohio, 1974.

Stevens, W.L. Constitutional law: defendant's right to a jury trial—is six enough? *Kentucky Law Journal 59,* 997 (1971).

Stoever, W.A. A comparison of six- and twelve-member civil juries in New Jersey superior and county courts. The Institute of Judicial Administration, Inc., 1972.

Strodtbeck, F.L., James, R.M. & Hawkins, C. Social status in jury deliberations. *American*

Sociological Review 22, 713-719 (1957).

Valenti, A.C. & Downing, L.L. Differential effects of jury size on verdicts following deliberation as a function of the apparent guilt of a defendant. *Journal of Personality and Social Psychology 32,* 655-663 (1975).

Walbert, D.F. The effect of jury size on the probability of conviction: an evaluation of *Williams v. Florida. Case Western Reserve Law Review 22,* 529 (1971).

Wiehl, L.L. (Judge) A state looks at the six-member jury. *The Judge's Journal 11,* 31 (1972).

Williams v. Florida, 90 S.Ct. 1893 (1970).

Zeisel, H. Personal communication, 1975.

Zeisel, H. & Diamond, S. Convincing empirical evidence on the six-member jury. *University of Chicago Law Review 41,* 281 (1974).

III

Issues in
the Criminal and
Correctional
Processes

6

Police Personality — Social Science Folklore and Psychological Measurement

C. ABRAHAM FENSTER
CARL F. WIEDEMANN
BERNARD LOCKE

At the present time the police officer is playing a crucial role in the history of the United States. Police as a factor in riot situations cannot be ignored. In 1968 the U.S. Riot Commission Report stated that "almost invariably the incident that ignites disorders arises from police action." (206) There have been recent instances where a single act on the part of an individual policeman has been said to have triggered a community-wide disturbance. Niederhoffer (1967), for example, reports that police action provoked a series of racial disturbances in Rochester, Philadelphia, Harlem, Watts, and Newark.

The significant role played by each policeman in community relations makes it important that all psychologically deviant policemen be identified and studied further so that their suitability or lack of suitability for police work can be determined (Rankin, 1959). The notion that emotional disturbance, instability, or neuroticism is related to poor police performance has found verification in a comprehensive study designed to establish general standards and effective procedures for the selection of patrolmen (Baehr et al., 1971).

Many research studies and other writings would seem to indicate that the police personality is psychologically unhealthy. As compared with average individuals, policemen were either found or suggested to be mentally unstable (New York *Times,* 1964; Rankin, 1959), schizoid (Rapaport, 1949), secretive (Clark, 1965; Glaser, 1958; Stoddard, 1968; Westley, 1951, 1956), suspicious (Glaser, 1958; Matarazzo et al., 1964; Mills, 1969; Niederhoffer, 1967; Rhead et al., 1968; Roberts, 1961; Verini & Walker, 1970; Westley, 1956), mentally unfit and cynical (Bain, 1939; Bohardt, 1959; Kates, 1950; Preiss & Ehrlich, 1966; Skolnick, 1966; Westley, 1951; Zion, 1966), corrupt (Smith, 1965; Steffens, 1931; Stern, 1962; Westley, 1951), prejudiced (Banton, 1964; Bayley & Mendelsohn, 1969; Black & Reiss, 1967; Calame, 1970; Ferdinand & Luchterhard, 1970; Heussenstamm, 1971; Kelly & West, 1973; Pilliavin, 1973; Preiss & Ehrlich, 1966; Sayre & Kaufman, 1960; Schleifer et al., 1968; Sikes, 1971; Skolnick, 1966; Wallach, 1970; Westley, 1970), of low intelligence (Bain, 1939; Terman et al., 1917; Thurstone, 1922), less masculine* (Terman & Miles, 1936), suicide-prone (Niederhoffer, 1967), authoritarian (Carlson et al., 1971; Leiren, 1973; Marshall & Mansson, 1966; Matarazzo et al., 1964; Trojanowicz, 1971; Walther et al., 1973), incompetent (Johnson & Gregory, 1971; Rotter & Stein, 1971), motivated to maintain the status quo (Astor, 1971; Bayley & Mendelsohn, 1969; Dodd, 1967; McGaghy, 1968; Niederhoffer, 1967; Walther et al., 1973), and prone to hypochondriasis, compulsive ritual, and the unwarranted abuse of power (Niederhoffer, 1967). Moreover, a recent study, showing that the personalities of correctional officer applicants are similar to those of prisoners (Berman, 1971), indicates that mental pathology may not be foreign to the personalities of those in the field of criminal justice.

Indeed, the psychological literature is replete with suggestions that occupational choice represents, at least in part, a psychological defense against the recognition of certain unacceptable impulses in oneself (*e.g.,* Roe, 1956; Shaffer & Shoben, 1956; Super, 1957). More specifically, psychologists and other social scientists have suggested that the occupational choice of becoming a policeman may be dictated by certain aggressive or authoritarian needs. Accordingly, Rapaport (1949) suggests:

> This adjustment of a patrolman may have been, in many cases, an effort of sublimation or the choice of a mode of life where their restlessness or aggression found a socially acceptable form of expression. (28)

While the research described above seems to paint a very negative picture of police personality, it should be noted that many investigators feel that such negative characteristics are mainly a function of the role demands of the police

---

*While much of the literature portrays policemen as highly heterosexual, there are many literary allusions to police homosexuality (*e.g.,* Buckley, 1967; Cory & LeRoy, 1963; Genet, 1964; Horwitz, 1967; Rechy 1963.)

job and not a function of personality defects of policemen. Thus Niederhoffer (1967) says that the "police officer swings his club in response to the thrust of organizational and occupational imperatives." Similar views are presented by others (*e.g.*, Astor, 1971; Bayley & Mendelsohn, 1969; Brown, 1971; Dodd, 1967; Murphy, 1965; Radano, 1968; Westley, 1953; Whelton, 1971).

While general emotional disturbance is probably related to poor police performance (Baehr et al., 1971), one must realize that certain traits which are ordinarily socially undesirable (perhaps isolation, suspiciousness, and aspects of authoritarianism) are useful—perhaps even necessary—for effective police work. Also, investigations should distinguish between general personality attributes and specific occupational role demands (Balch, 1972; Clark, 1965; Rhead et al., 1968).

There are a fair number of recent research studies and professional opinions that are more favorable in their evaluation of police. Thus, while most research finds police personality adjustment and intelligence to be about average (and some are more negative), Matarazzo et al. (1964) found a sample of accepted police applicants to be at the healthy end of each of three personality scales employed. Symonds (1970) and Lefkowitz (1971) also are favorable in their clinical evaluations of police.

While it may well be that maladjusted personalities do not perform well as policemen, the above studies provide limited evidence on the actual level of maladjustment among policemen for the following reasons: (a) many of the references implying neuroticism, stupidity, lack of masculinity, authoritarianism, etc., among policemen are (albeit professional) speculations that do not present psychometric or other research evidence (*e.g.*, Bain, 1939; Bohardt, 1959; Glaser, 1958; Myrdal, 1944; New York *Times*, 1964; Niederhoffer, 1967; Rankin, 1959; Sikes, 1971; Skolnick, 1966; Turner, 1965; Westley, 1951; Zion, 1966). (b) Other researchers (*e.g.*, Kates, 1950; Rapaport, 1949; Terman et al., 1917; Terman & Miles, 1936) used inadequate samples and instruments of questionable reliability (Anastasi, 1968). (c) While there is some evidence (Berman, 1971) that maladjusted and otherwise unsuitable candidates often apply for positions in the criminal justice field, very strict procedures for screening police applicants exist in almost all major cities; e.g., in New York City less than 15% of those applying for police positions have been accepted (Eilbert et al., 1961; Murphy, 1965; Niederhoffer, 1967). Even more stringent requirements are enforced in other jurisdictions (*e.g.*, Bohardt, 1959; Matarazzo et al., 1964; Wilson, 1964). It is hoped that such strict screening would eliminate maladjusted applicants. (d) Many of the reports or studies cited deal only with applicants or successful candidates who have *just* become members of the police force. We need to know about the intelligence and personality of the *typical* policeman, not the newly appointed one. The quality of police recruits is quite variable, being unduly sensitive to the current crime rate and to economic, social, and political conditions (McManus et al., 1970). (e) No direct comparisons are made between police maladjustment and that of civilians. In the 1968 riots, New York City policemen were alleged to have passively stood by while "hardhats" mercilessly clubbed college students. This raised questions as to the relative levels of emotional stability of both the hardhats and police (Fact Finding Commission on Columbia Disturbances, 1968). Also, social commentators have felt that college students often act in neurotic and authoritarian fashion (Feuer, 1969). (f) No distinction is made between the maladjustment indices of college-educated and non-college-educated policemen. College- and non-college-educated policemen have been found to differ significantly from each other on authoritarianism and intelligence (Guller, 1972; Leonard, 1964; Smith et al., 1967, 1968, 1970; Thurstone, 1922). It is important for us to know whether policemen who attend college on a part-time basis differ from other policemen with regard to maladjustment (and consequently police performance). (g) Since we are implicitly comparing police maladjustment with that of non-police, and maladjustment of college-educated police with that of non-college-educated police, it is probably desirable to test *all* police and non-police subjects with the same test batteries at the same time.

Accordingly, the present study tested a representative sample of college- and non-college-educated policemen (rather than applicants or newly appointed recruits) as well as representative samples of college-and non-college educated civilians (*i.e.,* non-police). Because of the ambiguity of previous research, we made no predictions but limited our hypotheses to the following questions:

(1) Is there a difference between the scores obtained by non-college-educated police and non-college-educated civilians with regard to intelligence, neuroticism, dogmatism, and masculinity?

(2) Is there a difference between the scores obtained by college-educated police and college-educated civilians on these measures?

(3) Is there a difference between the scores obtained by college-educated police as compared with those of non-college-educated police?

(4) Is there a difference between the scores obtained by college-educated civilians as compared with those of non-college-educated civilians?

In addition to seeking empirical information about the *adequacy* of police personality functioning (in terms of normality and intelligence), this research endeavors to seek empirical evidence as to police personality *types* and characteristic motivational *patterns.* Jung (1933) was the first psychoanalyst to emphasize the importance of understanding personality *types* in addition to understanding the quality and level of abnormality. This kind of focus can be very useful in understanding differences among essentially "normal" personalities and in understanding personality differences not based *in toto* on personality disturbance (see Gray, 1949). Perhaps the major differences between police and non-police are in type of motivation and type of personality rather than in degree of psychopathology. Indeed, this possibility is similar to the position somewhat tentatively advanced by Lefkowitz (1975). Thus we asked the following four questions about personality-motivational patterns which parallel our original questions about level of police (mal)adjustment:

(5) Is there a difference between the personality-motivational patterns of non-college police and non-college civilians?

(6) Is there a difference between the personality-motivational patterns of college-educated police and college-educated civilians?

(7) Is there a difference between the personality-motivational patterns of college-educated police as compared with those of non-college-educated police?

(8) Is there a difference between the personality-motivational patterns of college-educated civilians as compared with those of non-college-educated civilians?

METHOD

Subjects

A total of 722 male subjects were included in this study, as follows: (a) 250 Ss were identified New York City patrolmen who were enrolled in various introductory psychology classes in a college of the City University of New York where about 50% of the student body are police officers who attend the college on a part-time basis. (b) 238 Ss were individuals who were identified members of the New York City Police Department who worked with the first group and were procured by them, and who were *never* enrolled in any college course (according to both the forms they filled out and to the testimony of the police officers who procured them for the experiment). (c) 127 Ss were part-time students in introductory psychology classes at several other units of the City University of New York with admission standards equivalent to the unit from which college-oriented police were chosen. These students were never policemen according to their testimony. (d) 107 Ss were adult civilians who had never been to college and had never served as policemen. These were adults who volunteered for the experiment and who testified that they had never enrolled in any college course and had never served in any police department. They were procured for the study by the experimenters and other civilian students. The average ages of each group (non-college-educated police: $\overline{X} = 28.55$, $\sigma = 7.85$; college-educated police: $\overline{X} = 29.53$, $\sigma = 7.45$; non-college-educated civilians: $\overline{X} = 30.93$, $\sigma = 10.20$; college-educated civilians: $\overline{X} = 24.04$, $\sigma = 5.60$) were not significantly different except that college civilians were significantly lower in age than each of the other three groups ($p < .01$).

The sampling procedure was not "random" in the technical meaning, so that the samples are "representative" only in an approximate sense. Yet it was felt that the technique of having students, both police and civilian, bring a friend who had never gone to college was a good compromise between use of available subjects and obtaining a cross-sectional sample. It could be argued that friends of college students will be atypical to begin with, perhaps more like their college acquaintances than would be police and civilians at large. If this is true, however, the samples would be more like matched than random, and any significant contrast between college- and non-college-educated groups would be more meaningful.

Procedure

The Eysenck Personality Inventory, Form A, was given to all subjects in several group administration, according to the standardized instructions appearing in the test manual (Eysenck, 1968). The test yields scores in the key traits of personality (Eysenck, 1964), which are neuroticism and extraversion. The test also has a "lie scale," which taps defensiveness, or "faking good." The Otis Quick-Scoring Mental Abilities Test, Gamma Test, Form C (1939), was administered to all Ss in several group administrations, according to the standardized instructions appearing in the test manual. The M-F scale of the MMPI and Form I of the Wechsler Interest Inventory were administered to all Ss according to a standard group-testing procedure. Both tests yield scores of masculinity-femininity. Modified Rokeach (1960) and Piven (1961) scales were given, as well as a combined version, to test for authoritarianism. Each of these scales test different aspects of authority: Rokeach was interested in attitudes toward socialized authority, and Piven was concerned with the authoritative responses of social workers toward clients. The Rokeach scale was used rather than the one developed in *The Authoritarian Personality* (Adorno, Frenkel-Brunswick, Levenson, and Sanford, 1950) because the latter scale has been criticized for its major focus on fascist authoritarianism. The questionnaire, which was self-administered, contained instructions which indicated that the responses were confidential. Each of the items was rated on a Likert-type scale. The subjects were asked to respond to each item in terms of several degrees of agreement or disagreement, as follows:

1. I agree a little
2. I agree on the whole
3. I agree very much
-1. I disagree a little
-2. I disagree on the whole
-3. I disagree very much

Each item was set up in such a way that the most favorable response earned a value of +3 while the least favorable response was given a -3. For purposes of scoring, the responses were converted to values of 1 through 6, with 1 being the least favorable and 6 the most favorable. Finally, the Edwards Personal Preference Schedule was given. It was group-administered and consists of 210 forced-choice items designed to measure the 15 needs of Murray's Manifest Need System. It is unusual in that it uses ipsative scores to measure *patterns* of needs. The strength of each need is expressed not in absolute terms but in relation to the strength of the individual's other needs.

RESULTS

All variables were subjected to a 2 x 2 analysis of variance (Edwards, 1960), where the factors were Police vs. Non-Police, College vs. Non-College, and the interaction. In addition, a Duncan Multiple Range Test (Kramer, 1956) was performed on each variable to test for differences between subgroups such as Plain (Non-College-Educated) Police vs. College (-educated) Civilians. Finally, for each variable the coefficient eta-squared, η^2, was computed to reflect the degree of association between group membership and the dependent variable. Specifically, it reflects the percent reduction in squared errors of prediction by use of the subject's group mean rather than the grand mean, often more important than the significance of a difference in means. Table I summarizes the results of these procedures for the dependent variables Otis-I.Q.; Piven, Rokeach, and Combined dogmatism scores; Eysenck neuroticism, extroversion, and lie scales; and the Wechsler Interest Inventory and MMPI masculinity-femininity scale, both measures of masculinity. Table III presents the same results for the Edwards scales. Table II shows the group means for the measures of dogmatism, intelligence, neuroticism, and masculinity, and indicates which means differ significantly by the Duncan test, thus giving the direction of the effect in Table I. Table IV yields the same information for the Edwards scales.[1]

Table I offers some guidance as to where to begin. The three variables having the greatest number of significant discriminations (7) are also those variables with the largest coefficients of association, Otis-I.Q., Wechsler masculinity, and MMPI masculinity. Reference to Table II clarifies the direction of the results. With respect to I.Q., the results are easy to state. College students as a group, whether civilians or police, do not differ from each other in I.Q., but college students as a whole are superior to both plain police and plain civilians. In addition, and perhaps more germane, plain police have significantly higher I.Q.'s than do plain civilians . In terms of masculinity, as measured by the Wechsler, the pattern is similar to that of I.Q., but the groups are realigned. Civilians as a unit differ from police, who are higher in masculinity, and college vs. plain does not discriminate civilians. Further, college police, though significantly higher in masculinity than all civilians, are significantly lower than their plain co-workers. The MMPI measure of masculinity has a somewhat dissimilar flavor. The most different groups are plain police (most masculine) and collge civilians

TABLE I

Summary of Differences Between Police and Civilians, College Students and Non-Students, on the Psychological Dimensions of Neuroticism, Dogmatism, Intelligence, and Masculinity

	Neuroticism			Dogmatism			Intelligence	Masculinity		Number of Variables Where Significant
	Eysenck Neuroticism	Eysenck Extroversion	Eysenck Lie	Rokeach	Piven	Combined	Otis-I.Q.	MMPI	Wechsler	
Police vs. Civilians	(c)	(a)		(b)	(c)	(c)	(c)	(c)	(c)	8
College vs. Plain				(c)		(b)	(c)	(c)	(c)	5
Plain Police vs. College Police			(a)				(c)	(b)	(c)	4
Plain Police vs. College Civilians	(b)	(c)	(a)		(b)		(b)	(c)	(c)	7
Plain Police vs. Plain Civilians	(c)			(c)	(b)	(c)	(c)	(a)	(c)	7
College Police vs. College Civilians			(c)		(a)			(c)	(c)	4
College Police vs. Plain Civilians	(c)			(c)	(b)	(c)	(c)		(a)	6
College Civilians vs. Plain civilians	(a)		(a)	(c)		(b)	(c)	(c)		6
Degree of association (η^2)	.048	.012	.028	.041	.025	.040	.139	.073	.087	
Number of significant comparisons	5	2	4	5	5	5	7	7	7	

(a) Significant at p < .05 level.
(b) Significant at p < .01 level.
(c) Significant at p < .001 level.

TABLE II

Means of the Four Groups on the 9 Variables Measuring
Neuroticism, Dogmatism, Intelligence, and Masculinity

Eysenck Neuroticism	PP 7.49	CP 7.95	CC 8.98	PC 10.47
Eysenck Extroversion	CC 12.08	CP 12.54	PC 12.59	PP 13.16
Eysenck Lie	CP 2.07	PC 2.42	PP 2.49	CC 2.87
Rokeach	CP -16.72	CC -15.11	PP -11.91	PC - 1.97
Piven	PP 1.46	CP 1.90	CC 5.23	PC 5.84
Combined Dogmatism	CP -14.71	PP -10.47	CC - 9.70	PC - 3.87
Otis-I.Q.	PC 101.85	PP 109.89	CC 113.83	CP 114.53
Wechsler M-F	CC 2.46	PC 2.75	CP 4.36	PP 6.41
MMPI M-F	PP 23.08	CP 24.66	PC 24.72	CC 27.22

Note: Means not underlined contiguously differ at the $p < .05$ level or better. PP = Plain
Police; PC = Plain Civilians; CP = College Police; CC = College Civilians.

(least masculine), with college police and plain civilians being intermediate and
not different from each other.

The results of the dogmatism measures are less salient, the Rokeach, Piven,
and Combined scales each having five significant discriminations. The Rokeach
and the Combined scores give rise to identical situations. Plain civilians are in
both cases higher in dogmatism than are the other three groups. On the Piven
scale by itself, the important distinction is between police and civilians, with
police lower in dogmatism, college being irrelevant.

The Eysenck measures seem to be less affected but they do yield some signi-

TABLE III

EDWARDS SCALES

Summary of Differences Between Police and Civilians, Plain and College, on the 16 Scales of the Edwards Personal Preference Schedule

	Achievement	Deference	Order	Exhibitionism	Autonomy	Affiliation	Intraception	Succorance	Dominance	Abasement	Nurturance	Change	Endurance	Heterosexuality	Aggression	Consistency	Number of Variables Where Significant
Police vs. Civilians	(c)	(a)	(b)														3
College vs. Plain																	0
Plain Police vs. College Police	(c)	(a)	(b)			(a)	(a)				(a)			(b)			7
Plain Police vs. college Civilians	(a)					(c)	(a)	(b)	(a)		(a)			(a)			7
Plain Police vs. Plain Civilians				(a)				(a)		(a)	(c)			(c)			5
College Police vs. College Civilians	(a)	(c)	(c)		(b)	(c)	(a)	(a)	(a)	(c)			(a)				10
College Police vs. Plain Civilians	(c)								(a)	(c)	(a)		(a)	(b)			6
College Civilians vs. Plain Civilians		(a)	(b)			(c)				(b)			(a)	(b)			6
Degree of association (η^2)	.074	.031	.038	.018	.028	.072	.016	.028	.024	.050	.043	.003	.031	.072	.014	.013	
Number of significant comparisons	5	4	4	1	1	4	3	3	3	4	4	0	3	5	0	0	

(a) Significant at p < .05 level.
(b) Significant at p < .01 level.
(c) Significant at p < .001 level.

ficant distinctions. On the lie scale ("faking good,") plain civilians distinguish themselves from all others as the highest, while plain police are slightly but significantly higher than their collegiate counterparts. In terms of extroversion, the extreme groups are college civilians (lowest) and plain police (highest). The neuroticism scale, perhaps the most important, shows a pattern similar to that for the lie scale, but here it is plain civilians who are the highest and different from the other groups; plain police and college civilians are slightly but significantly different.

On the Edwards Personal Preference Schedule, three of the scales—aggression, consistency, and change—can be dealt with summarily since they show no meaningful difference. Exhibitionism and autonomy show only one significant difference each; plain police surpass plain civilians in exhibitionism, while college civilians surpass college police in autonomy. At the other end, achievement and heterosexuality seem to be the most prepotent variables. In achievement, college police excel all others, while college civilians excel plain police. In heterosexuality, plain police are clearly the highest, with plain civilians being clearly the lowest; in between and not different from each other are the college students, both police and civilian.

The remaining variables show intermediate strength. Deference and order are identical: college civilians are the lowest and different from the other three groups, who are indistinguishable. In abasement, plain civilians are distinguishably the highest, and in nurturance college police are the lowest by themselves. In affiliation, college civilians are higher than the other groups. In interaception, college police are uniquely high, as they are in dominance. In endurance, the important distinction seems to be between college civilians (lowest) and plain civilians (highest). In succorance, it is plain police who are lowest, with college civilians being the highest.

DISCUSSION

Intelligence

Clearly, the Otis-I.Q. was the most puissant and should be considered first. The results of this study clearly indicate that the stereotype of the "dumb cop" is completely out of keeping with the intelligence of the average New York City patrolman. While the average I.Q. of a member of the general population was 102 (55th percentile) in our study, the mean I.Q. was 110 (75th percentile) for the non-college-educated policeman and 115 (82nd percentile) for the college-educated policeman.

As has already been noted, this study used policemen with varying amounts of experience, as opposed to limiting itself to newly appointed recruits. Evidence presented by McManus et al. (1969) makes it abundantly clear that dif-

TABLE IV

Means of Four Groups on the 16 Scales of the Edwards Personal Preference Scale

Achievement	PP	PC	CC	CP
	14.40	14.72	15.77	17.14
Deference	CC	PP	PC	CP
	9.91	11.06	11.25	11.78
Order	CC	PC	PP	CP
	9.49	11.72	11.74	11.98
Exhibitionism	PC	CP	CC	PP
	13.64	14.43	14.91	15.08
Autonomy	CP	PP	PC	CC
	13.79	14.66	14.86	15.19
Affiliation	CP	PC	PP	CC
	11.34	12.17	12.46	14.36
Intraception	PC	CC	PP	CP
	15.64	15.73	15.83	16.99
Succorance	PP	CP	PC	CC
	9.57	10.05	11.33	11.55
Dominance	CC	PP	PC	CP
	14.82	15.12	15.22	16.59
Abasement	CP	CC	PP	PC
	10.70	11.39	12.10	13.77
Nurturance	CP	PP	PC	CC
	12.29	13.61	13.81	15.09
Change	PC	CP	PP	CC
	15.17	15.38	15.61	15.97
Endurance	CC	PP	CP	PC
	12.28	13.20	14.29	15.00
Heterosexuality	PC	CP	CC	PP
	16.80	19.06	19.22	20.81
Aggression	CC	CP	PP	PC
	13.47	14.01	14.77	14.94
Consistency	PC	CC	PP	CP
	11.12	11.28	11.65	11.66

Note: Means not underlined contiguously are significant at the $p < .05$ level or better.
PP = Plain Police; PC = Plain Civilians; CP = College Police; CC = College Civilians.

ferent graduating classes in the police academy have differed markedly in I.Q. Testing policemen who vary widely in experience minimizes fluctuations in the quality of new policemen due to cyclical variations in crime, as well as political, economic, and other social conditions. Thus it can safely be said that the intelligence of the average policeman in New York City is significantly higher than that of the general population.

Another important finding of the present study is that the intelligence quotient of the average college-educated policeman (I.Q. = 115) is significantly higher than that of the non-college-educated policeman (I.Q. = 110). This would indicate either that the more intelligent policeman goes on to college or that college education improves one's I.Q. score. However that may be, it is important to realize that, while statistically significant, the difference in I.Q. scores between college and plain police is relatively small (i.e., only 5 points) This is in sharp contrast to the difference in I.Q. scores shown by college (I.Q. = 116) and plain civilians (I.Q. = 102), where a 14-poin difference exists. Thus, while it is probably true that intellectual ability is a key factor in determining whether or not a civilian goes to college, motivational and other personality factors probably play an even more crucial role in determining whether or not a policeman decides to go to college. Also, whereas Leonard (1964) showed that patrolmen who are college graduates are three or four times more likely to attain promotion, it is quite likely, here too, that motivational personality factors play a greater role than native intellectual ability (since the I.Q. difference between college and plain police is only 5 points). Perhaps the same motivational and personality differences which propel policemen on to college are also at work, causing the patrolman to achieve greater professional success (i.e., promotion). Further research is clearly needed, however, as these conjectures may well be premature. In fact, many policemen question the suitability of college graduates as patrolmen (Niederhoffer, 1967). Also, Levy (1966) and Thurstone (1922) claim that the more highly educated policemen experience greater difficulty, and are more often unsuccessful, in adjusting to police department life. More recently, Wilson stated that routine police work provides "far too little challenge for an imaginative college-trained man" and that less-educated officers are often better-suited for the position (Washington *Post,* Dec. 17, 1970, p. D-1).

It should be noted that this study is consistent with other research in that it shows college-educated civilians to possess I.Q.'s clearly superior to the mean I.Q. (102) of the general population (see Noll, 1965; Thorndike & Hagen, 1961), which is insignificantly different from the norm of 100 (t = 1.30). Some insubstantial increase in I.Q. scores would be expected in this sample, since it is exclusively urban and since educational opportunities have increased significantly since the Otis Mental Abilities Test was first standardized.

Another interesting finding in this study is the fact that many (both college and plain) policemen have I.Q.'s which clearly give them the potential to perform well in college. Nonetheless, many of these very bright individuals choose police work instead of careers requiring more education. The authors of this study feel that as-yet-unknown personality factors play a role in this occupational choice and have consequently carried out further research in the area of police personality.

Masculinity

This was the second most powerful dimension in the study, and the two different measures of masculinity yielded only somewhat different results.

The results of this study clearly indicate that problems of sexual identification are not characteristic of the average New York City policeman. It is felt that in light of the methodological improvements in this paper (*e.g.,* the use of 722 *S*s instead of 22) the results of the Terman & Miles study appear highly questionable. The hypothesis that policemen as a group suffer from a deficit of masculinity has not been substantiated.

In fact, if anything, the reverse is true. The Wechsler M-F scale is one of the few measures on which police align together vis-à-vis civilians. On the MMPI M-F scale, college police and plain civilians were intermediate and similar, while plain police were highest and college civilians lowest. The plain police are far and away the most masculine on both measures, which could give rise to speculation on the part of police detractors or the psychoanalytically oriented. The speculation would be that plain police have an overcompensated masculine self-image in reaction to feelings of inadequacy as a male; however, this level of inference would have to be supported by more clinical research.

Dogmatism

In a previous study (Smith et al., 1967) it was demonstrated that college-oriented police are significantly less authoritarian than non-college-oriented police. Later (Smith et al., 1968), it was established that police in college were considerably lower on the authoritarian scale than were their non-police fellow students. The present study shows that on the whole police are lower in dogmatism than are civilians, and college police are less authoritarian than their civilian classmates. In fact, it is plain civilians who, on all measures, are the most authoritarian and dogmatic. Studies purporting to show the contrary should perhaps be reevaluated in the light of these findings.

Neuroticism

The results of this study clearly indicate that neuroticism is *not* a major characteristic of the average New York City policeman. When compared with civilians, police, on the whole, scored lower on the neuroticism scale of the Eysenck Personality Inventory.

In fact, plain civilians obtained neuroticism scores ($\overline{X}$ = 10.47) which were significantly higher than those of any of the other three groups tested: college civilians ($\overline{X}$ = 8.98; p < .05), college police ($\overline{X}$ = 7.95; p < .001), and non-college police ($\overline{X}$ = 7.49; p < .001).

When college police scores ($\overline{X}$ = 7.95) are compared with those of college civilians ($\overline{X}$ = 8.98), results fall just short of significance (p < .10). This situation is complicated by the fact that college civilians have a significantly higher lie score than do college police. Dahlstrom & Welsh (1960) indicate that a high lie score tends to artificially lower an individual's neuroticism score because "faking good" involves answering questions in a socially desirable—and generally less neurotic—direction. Since college police scored *almost significantly* (p < .10) less neurotic than did college civilians *without* lie score differences taken into account, it is likely that any formula incorporating these differences would show college police to be significantly less neurotic than college, as well as plain, civilians.

Both plain civilians ($\overline{X}$ = 10.47; p < .001) and college civilians ($\overline{X}$ = 8.98; p < .05) scored significantly higher in neuroticism than did plain police ($\overline{X}$ = 7.49). A possible, and perhaps surprising, implication of this finding is that when two of the groups (college students and non-college-educated police) met at the barricades of Columbia University in 1968 (see Fact Finding Commission on Columbia Disturbances, 1968), the students probably constituted the more neurotic group. On the other hand, when hardhats beat students in the lower Manhattan area (New York *Times,* May 9, 1970, p. 1), the results of this study would indicate that the hardhats (non-college-educated civilians) were more neurotic than the students—or than the police, who were alleged to have passively tolerated this abuse.

In reference to the recent report (Berman, 1971) indicating that neurotics often apply for positions in the field of criminal justice, the present study (which finds less neuroticism among police groups than is found in the general population) indicates that the intensive screening of police applicants probably (advertantly or inadvertantly) eliminates many neurotics. At least until 1967 (Niederhoffer, 1967) police screening procedures were so strict that only about 15% of those applying for New York City police positions were appointed. The results of this study would indicate that such strict screening is probably beneficial.

The Edwards Personal Preference Schedule Scales

In general, the Edwards scales seemed somewhat less sensitive to the group differences included in this study than were the measures of neuroticism, dogmatism, intelligence, and masculinity. One way to examine the findings is to look at those measures where a group or groups stood alone, away from the other groups.

(1) College civilians were uniquely low in deference and order, and uniquely high in affiliation. Though these students were older than the typical student, they seemed almost to fit the stereotype of the disorganized, rebellious, gregarious student of the sixties.

(2) College police were singularly high in achievement, dominance, and intraception, and singularly low in nurturance. This picture is very healthy indeed, suggesting a person who is motivated, assertive, and psychologically minded. The only blemish is a lack of interpersonal giving. (The authors, who teach police students, can attest to the achievement motivation needed for those employed full-time in police work to complete college work.)

(3) Plain civilians were the highest in abasement and the lowest in heterosexuality. This suggests that, compared with police and college civilians, plain civilians have a retiring though somewhat guilt-ridden approach to life.

(4) Plain police are distinctive as the highest scorers on heterosexuality. Combined with their being the highest on both measures of masculinity, this suggests a mild kind of "macho trip." It also fits the popular conception of policemen as "womanizers," "tail chasers," or "Don Juans," an image more common in smaller towns than in New York City. This trait cluster suggests no particular pathology; those engaging in full-time police work and not attending college merely perceive and present themselves as "real men."

CONCLUSION

It may fairly be said that differences appearing in the data presented tend to redound to the credit of police and to suggest that they may represent a *superior* subsample of the general population (a) self-selected by the demands of the job role, and (b) socially selected by the increasing prestige, desirability, and selectivity of police employment. This appears to be even more emphatically true in the case of policemen who are attending college.

Nevertheless, the study is limited by three factors. First, the applicability of the results of this study were necessarily limited by the experimental design employed. Underwood (1957) has pointed out that whenever subject variables are being compared, randomization of all possible relevant variables is impossible. Only subsequent research with different population samples and confirmatory results can make the original findings more tenable. Second, the ages of the different subject groups were not identical. College-educated civilians were significantly younger than each of the other three groups. This particular deviation from the age norm is not regarded as crucial because the major findings of this study mainly concern differences among the other three groups, whose ages were not significantly different. It is possible, however, that other relevant variables, such as prior mental health problems, may contribute to the differences that were found. Finally, while this study found many highly significant differences, the measures of association tended to run low (only the Otis-I.Q. was in double figures). Nonetheless, one can be confident that in the population the group means are truly different.

FOOTNOTES

[1] Detailed tables of the results of the analyses of variance and means are available by writing to the first author: Department of Psychology, John Jay College of Criminal Justice, 445 West 59th Street, New York, New York, 10019.

REFERENCES

Adorno, T.W., Frenkel-Brunswick, E., Levenson, D.J., and Sanford, R.N. *The Authoritarian Personality*. New York: Harper & Row, 1950.

Anastasi, A. *Psychological Testing* (3rd ed.). New York: Macmillan, 1968.

Astor, G. The New York cops. New York *Post*, June 19, 1971.

Baehr, M.E., Saunders, D.R., Froemel, E.C., & Furcon, J.E. The prediction of performance for black and for white patrolmen. *Professional Psychology*, 1971, *2*, 46-57.

Bain, R. The policeman on the beat. *The Scientific Monthly*. 1939, *48*, 452.

Balch, R.W. The police personality: Fact or fiction? *Journal of Criminal Law, Criminology, and Police Science*, 1972, *63*, 106-119.

Banton, M. *The Policeman in the Community*. New York: Basic Books, 1964.

Bayley, D.H. & Mendelsohn, H. *Minorities and the Police: Confrontation in America*. New York: The Free Press, 1969.

Berman, A. MMPI characteristics of correctional officers. Paper presented at Eastern Psychological Association. New York City, April 16, 1971.

Black, D.J. & Reiss, A.J., Jr. Patterns of behavior in police and citizen transactions. In *Studies of Crime and Law Enforcement in Major Metropolitan Areas* (Vol. 2). Washington, D.C.: U.S. Government Printing Office, 1967.

Bohardt, P.H. Tucson uses new police personnel selection methods. *FBI Law Enforcement Bulletin*, 1959, *28*, 8-12.

Brown, W.P. A police administration approach to the corruption problem. New York: State University of New York, 1971 (NTIS No. PB-218 936).

Buckley, F.R. *Eye of the Hurricane*. Garden City, N.Y.: Doubleday, 1967.

Calame, B.E. Man in the middle. In W.H. Hewitt & C.L. Newman (eds.), *Police-Community Relations: An Anthology and Bibliography*. Mineola, N.Y.: Foundation Press, 1970.

Carlson, H., Thayer, R.E. & Germann, A.C. Social attitudes and personality differences among members of two kinds of police departments (innovative vs. traditional) and students. *Journal of Criminal Law, Criminology and Police Science*, 1971, *62*, 564-567.

Clark, J.P. Isolation of the police: a comparison of the British and American situations. *Journal of Criminal Law, Criminology, and Police Science*, 1965, *56*, 307-319.

Cory, D.W. & LeRoy, J.P. *The homosexual and his society*. New York: The Citadel Press, 1963.

Dahlstrom, W.G. & Welsh, G.S. *An MMPI Handbook*. Minneapolis: University of Minnesota

Press, 1960, 47-49.

Dodd, D.J. Police mentality and behavior. *Issues in Criminology,* 1967, *3,* 47-67.

Edwards, A.L. *Experimental Design in Psychological Research.* New York: Holt, 1960, 136-140.

Ellbert, L., McNamara, J., & Hanson, V. *Research on Selection and Training for Police Recruits: First Annual Report.* New York: American Institute for Research, 1961, 6.

Eysenck, H.J. *Crime and Personality.* Boston: Houghton Mifflin, 1964.

Eysenck, H.J. & Eysenck, S.B.G. *Manual for the Eysenck Personality Inventory.* San Diego: Educational and Industrial Testing Service, 1968.

Fact Finding Commission on Columbia Disturbances, *Crisis at Columbia.* New York: Vintage Books, 1968.

Fenster, C.A. & Locke, B. The "dumb cop": myth or reality? An examination of police intelligence. *Journal of Personality Assessment,* 1973, *37,* 276-281.

Ferdinand, T.N. & Luchterhard, E.G. Inner-city youth, the police, the juvenile court, and justice. *Social Problems,* 1970, *17,* 510-527.

Feuer, L.S. *The Conflict of Generations.* New York: Basic Books, 1969.

Genet, J. *The Thief's Journal.* New York: Grove Press, 1964.

Glaser, D. The sociological approach to crime and correction. *Law and Contemporary Problems,* 1958, *23,* 683-702.

Gray, H. Freud and Jung: their contrasting psychological types. *Psychoanalytic Review,* 1949, *20,* 22-44.

Guller, I.B. Higher education and policemen: attitudinal differences between freshmen and senior police college students. *Journal of Criminal Law, Criminology and Police Science* 1972, *63,* 396-401.

Heussenstamm, F.K. Bumper stickers and the cops. *Trans-action,* 1971, *February,* 32-33.

Horwitz, J. *The W.A.S.P.* New York: Atheneum, 1967.

Johnson, D. & Gregory, R.J. Police-community relations in the United States: a review of recent literature and projects. *Journal of Criminal Law, Criminology and Police Science* 1971, *62,* 94-103.

Jung, C.G. *Psychological types.* New York: Harcourt, Brace & World, 1933.

Kaplan, M.F. & Singer, E. Dogmatism and sensory alienation: an empirical investigation. *Journal of Consulting Psychology,* 1963, *27,* 486-491.

Kates, S.L. Rorschach responses, Strong blank scales and job satisfaction among policemen. *Journal of Applied Psychology,* 1950, *34,* 252.

Kelly, R.M. & West, G. The racial transition of a police force: a profile of white and black policemen in Washington, D.C. In J.R. Snibbe & H.M. Snibbe (eds.), *The Urban Policeman in Transition.* Springfield, Ill.: Charles C. Thomas, 1973.

Kramer, C.Y. Extension of multiple range tests to group means with unequal numbers of replications. *Biometrics,* 1956, *12,* 307-310.

Lefkowitz, J. *Job Attitudes of Police.* National Institute of Law enforcement and Criminal Justice, U.S. Department of Justice, 1971.

Lefkowitz, J. Psychological attributes of policemen: a review of research and opinion. *Journal of Social Issues,* 1975, *31,* 3-26.

Leiren, B.D. Validating the selection of deputy marshals. In J.R. Snibbe & H.M. Snibbe (eds.), *The Urban Policeman in Transition.* Springfield, Ill.: Charles C. Thomas, 1973.

Leonard, G.M. The undergraduate police science program and its relationship with the New York City Police Department. Unpublished master's thesis, Bernard M. Baruch School of Business and Public Administration, The City College of The City University of New York, 57-61, (1964).

Levy, R. Retrospective study of peace officer personnel files. San Jose City Health Department, n.d.

Marshall, J. & Mansson. H. Punitiveness, recall, and the police. *Journal of Research in Crime and Delinquency,* 1966, *3,* 129-139.

Matarazzo, J.D., Allen, B.V., Saslow, G., & Wiens, A.N. Characteristics of successful policemen and firemen applicants. *Journal of Applied Psychology,* 1964, *48,* 123-133.

McGaghy, C.H. Cops talk back. *Urban Affairs Quarterly,* 1968, *4,* 245-256.

McManus, G.P., Griffin, J.I., Wetteroth, W.J., Boland, M. & Hines P.T. *Police Training and Performance Study.* Washington, D.C.: U.S. Government Printing Office, PR-70-4, Grant No. 339, 75-80 (1970).

Mills, R.B. Use of diagnostic small groups in police recruit selection and training. *Journal of Criminal Law, Criminology, and Police Science,* 1969, *60,* 238-241.

Murphy, J.J. Improving the law enforcement image. *Journal of Criminal Law, Criminology and Police Science,* 1965, *56,* 107.

Myrdal, G. *An American Dilemma.* New York: Harper & Row, 1944.

New York *Times,* 19 (September 3, 1964).

New York *Times,* 1 (May 9, 1970).

New York *Times,* 16 (July 23, 1970).

Niederhoffer, A. *Behind the Shield: The Police in Urban Society.* New York: Doubleday, 1967.

Noll, V.H. *Introduction to Educational Measurement.* Boston: Houghton-Mifflin, 1965, 83-84.

Otis, A.S. *Manual of Directions for Gamma Test of Otis Quick-Scoring Mental Ability Test* (Forms C and D). New York: Harcourt, 1939.

Pilliavin, J. *Police-Community Alienation: Its Structural Roots and a Proposed Remedy.* Andover, Mass.: Warner Modular Publications, 1973.

Piven, H. Professionalism and Organizational Structure. Unpublished D.S.W. dissertation, Columbia University School of Social Work, 1961.

Preiss, J.J. & Ehrlich, H.J. *An Examination of Role Theory: The Case of the State Police.* Lincoln, Neb.: University of Nebraska Press, 1966.

Radano, G. *Walking the Beat.* New York: World, 1968.

Rankin, J.H. Psychiatric screening of police recruits. *Public Personnel Review,* 1959, 20, 191-196.

Rapaport, D. *Diagnostic Psychological Testing.* Chicago: The Yearbook Publishers. 1949, Vol. I.

Rechy, J. *City of Night.* New York: Grove Press, 1963.

Rhead, C., Abrams, A., Trasman, H. & Margolies, P. The psychological assessment of police candidates. *American Journal of Psychiatry,* 1968, *124,* 1575-1580.

Roberts, E.F. Paradoxes in law enforcement. *Journal of Criminal Law, Criminology and Police Science,* 1961, *52,* 224-228.

Roe, A. *Psychology of Occupations.* New York: Wiley, 1956.

Rokeach, M. *The Open and Closed Mind: Investigations into the Nature of Belief Systems and Personality Systems.* New York: Basic Books, 1960.

Rotter, J.B. & Stein, D.K. Public attitudes toward the trustworthiness, competence and altruism of twenty selected occupations. *Journal of Applied Social Psychology,* 1971, *1,* 334-343.

Sayre, W.S. & Kaufman, H. *Governing New York City.* New York: Russell Sage Foundation, 1960.

Schleifer, C.B., Derbyshire, R.L. & Martin, J. Clinical change in jail-referred mental patients. *Archives of General Psychiatry,* 1968, *18,* 42-46.

Shaffer, L.F. & Shoben, E.J. *The Psychology of Adjustment.* Boston: Houghton-Mifflin, 1956.

Sikes, M.P. Police-community relations laboratory: the Houston model. *Professional*

Psychology, 1971, *2,* 39-45.

Skolnick, J.H. *Justice without Trial: Law Enforcement in Democratic Society.* New York: Wiley, 1966.

Smith, A.B., Locke, B. & Walker, W.F. Authoritarianism in college and non-college graduates and non-college police. *Journal of Criminal Law, Criminology and Police Science,* 1970, *61,* 313-315.

Smith, A.B., Locke, B.M. & Walker, W.F. Authoritarianism in college and non-college oriented police. *Journal of Criminal Law, Criminology and Police Science,* 1967, *58,* 128-132.

Smith, A.B., Locke, B., & Walker, W.F. Authoritarianism in police college students and non-police college students. *Journal of Criminal Law, criminology and Police Science,* 1968, *59,* 440-443.

Smith, R.L. *The Tarnished Badge.* New York: Thomas Y. Crowell Co., 1965.

Steffens, L. *The Autobiography of Lincoln Steffens.* New York: Harcourt, Brace & Co., 1931.

Stern, M. What makes a policeman go wrong? *Journal of Criminal Law, Criminology and Police Science,* 1962, *53,* 98-99.

Stoddard, E.R. The informal "code" of police deviance: a group approach to "blue-coat" crime. *Journal of Criminal Law, Criminology and Police Science,* 1968, *59,* 210-213.

Super, D. *The Psychology of Careers.* New York: Harper, 1957.

Symonds, M. Emotional hazards of police work. *American Journal of Psychoanalysis,* 1970, *30,* 155-160.

Terman, L.M. & Miles, C.C. *Sex and Personality: Studies in Masculinity and Femininity.* New York: McGraw-Hill, 1936.

Terman, L.M., Otis, A.S., Dickson, V., Hubbard, O.S., Norton, J.K., Howard, L., Flanders, J.K., & Cunningham, C.C. A trial of mental and pedogogical tests in a civil service examination for policemen and firemen. *Journal of Applied Psychology,* 1917, *1,* 17-29.

Thorndike, E.L. & Hagen, E. *Measurement and Evaluation in Psychology and Education.* New York: Wiley, 1961.

Thurstone, L.L. The intelligence of policemen. *Journal of Personnel Research,* 1922, *1,* 64-74.

Trojanowicz, R.C. The policeman's occupational personality. *Journal of Criminal Law, Criminology and Police Science,* 1971, *62,* 551-559.

Turner, W.W. Crime is too big for the F.B.I. *The Nation,* 1965, 201-325.

Underwood, B.J. *Psychological Research.* New York: Appleton-century-Crofts, 1957.

U.S. Riot Commission. *Report of the National Advisory Commission on Civil Disorders* (Kerner Commission). New York: Bantam Books, 1968.

Verini, J.S. & Walker, V. Policemen and the recall of criminal details. *Journal of Social Psychology,* 1970, *81,* 217-221.

Wallach, I.A. *The police function in a Negro community* (2 vols.). McLean, Va.: Research Analysis Corporation, 1970, 81, 217-221.

Walther, R.H., McCune, S.D. & Trojanowicz, R.C. The constrasting occupational cultures of policemen and social workers. In J.R. Snibbe & H.M. Snibbe (eds.), *The Urban Policeman in Transition.* Springfield, Ill.: Charles C. Thomas, 1973.

Washington Post, Dec. 17, 1970, D-1.

Westley, W.A. *The Police: A Sociological Study of Law, Custom and Morality.* Unpublished doctoral dissertation, University of Chicago, 1951.

Westley, W.A. Violence and the police. *American Journal of Sociology,* 1953, *59,* 34-41.

Westley, W.A. Secrecy and the police. *Social Forces,* 1956, *34,* 354-357.

Westley, W.A. *Violence and the Police: A Sociological Study of Law, Custom and Morality.* Cambridge, Mass.: MIT Press, 1970.

Whelton, C. Cooling the rage of the cop in the street. *The Village Voice,* June 24, 1971.

Wilson, D. Psychiatric evaluation in the selection process. In R.H. Blum (ed.), *Police Selection.* Springfield, Ill.: Charles C. Thomas, 1964, 152.

Yalom, I.D. *The Theory and Practice of Group Psychotherapy.* New York: Basic Books, 1970.

Zion, S. The police play a crime numbers game. New York *Times,* June 12, 1966, Section IV, 6.

7

Aspects of the Parole
Experience[1]

JOHN J. BERMAN

Although social scientists have been studying people convicted of crimes for many years, most of the research has been done on juvenile delinquents (*e.g.*, Matza, 1964; Korn, 1968; Van Dyke, 1970) or on prisons and prisoners (*e.g.*, Clemmer, 1940; Cressey, 1961; Sykes, 1958), while relatively little has been done on parole and parolees. The work by Glaser (1964), who reported the results of a survey of parolees from federal prisons, and Irwin (1970), who studied parolees in the San Francisco area, represent major theoretical research done specifically on parolees. Most other studies of this population have been limited to the prediction of whether or not an ex-offender will recidivate (*e.g.*, Glueck, & Glueck, 1930; Gottfredson et al., 1965). The purpose of this paper is to report certain aspects of the results of a study of parolees. The paper focuses on parolees' experiences with stigma, their unrealistic job expectancies, the extent to which they feel controlled by fate, the frequency with which they seek assistance from agencies, and the relationship between race and employment. These particular facets of parolees' experiences were chosen to be included in this report either because there is speculation but no data on the topic or because some data do exist but are scarce and in need of replication.

METHOD

The present study was conducted as part of a larger research project, the purpose of which was to evaluate the effects of a new parolee program in Illinois. The data reported in this paper are the results of a pre-test conducted before the program began. Ninety men who had been paroled from Illinois state prisons and who had been nominated by their parole agents for a parolee program were interviewed, and further data were collected on the group from parole office files. Eighteen agents had been instructed to nominate from their case load five parolees who the agents felt "could benefit most from the program." From conversations with each agent it appeared that some nominated their best people, some nominated their worst, and some nominated people more or less randomly. It was felt, therefore, that this group was reasonably representative of all Illinois parolees. In fact, the background characteristics of this group were representative when compared to those of the entire Illinois parolee population on those dimensions for which state averages were available. More specifically, this sample and the entire Illinois population were identical in racial composition, in the distribution of types of crimes for which they had been convicted, and in the proportion who were recidivists.

Fifty-seven respondents were interviewed by a white psychology graduate student; 30 were interviewed by a black male who had worked previously as an interviewer for a nationally known research group. Fifty-three percent of the respondents were black; 43%, white; 3%, chicanos. The median time out of prison was six months. Thirty-two percent had been convicted of assault crimes; 59%, of property crimes, including robbery; 9%, of narcotics offenses. Twenty-seven percent had been to prison before. Ten percent were married.

Most of the interviews were conducted in the parolee's place of residence, although a few took place in restaurants or bars. Each respondent was told that any information given would be held in the strictest confidence by the researchers and that no names would be used in any reports. Three types of questions were asked: those requiring the respondent to answer in his own words; those requiring a response on a 6-point scale ranging from "completely agree" to "completely disagree"; those requiring a probability or percentage response on an 11-point scale ranging from 0% to 100%. Respondents were taught to use the 6-point scales in the following way: They were given a card containing the appropriate response categories. After each item was read to them, they first stated which half of the scale best reflected their attitudes; then they indicated which of the small categories within that half of the scale best fit them. Thus, rather than making one decision from among six categories, they made two decisions from among two and three categories, respectively.

One problem faced by anyone trying to interview parolees is that they may not give accurate information about themselves. Several steps were taken to alleviate this validity problem. One was to construct the questionnaire so that sensitive questions were avoided. For example, respondents were not asked about their salary, their criminal experience, or their sex life. Questions such as "Do you like yourself?" or "Do you usually talk to strangers on a bus?" were avoided lest the respondent get the idea he was being psychoanalyzed. For the same reason the interviewers introduced themselves and the research project as being sponsored by a social scientist rather than a psychologist. Also, at the beginning of the interview several questions were asked to which the author did not particularly want responses but which would be reasonable questions for an interviewer to ask and would be easy for the respondent to answer. The purpose of this was to set a tone of straightforwardness, to relax the respondent, and to establish the roles each would play in the interview.

Another aspect of the research relevant to the validity of the data is that, before the interviewing began, the author spent two months doing participant observation at a halfway house for parolees. This experience provided an education in the mannerisms, language, and attitudes of ex-offenders. It also provided an excellent group of acquaintances with whom pilot tests of the interview schedule could be conducted. Four different drafts of the interview questions were piloted on the parolees at the halfway house, and the final schedule was very much a product of those parolees.

RESULTS AND DISCUSSION

Stigma

The stigma associated with being an ex-offender can be problematic for a parolee both in attempting to secure employment and in his social life. Both of these areas were studied in this research. In the area of employment, one difficulty produced by the stigma of being an ex-offender is that the parolee is in a double bind when it comes to admitting to a prospective employer that he is on parole. If he says he is, he runs the risk of not getting the job; if he hides the facts, he runs the risk of his record being discovered and of being fired because of it or because he lied on the application. During the participant observation phase of this research, it became apparent that two approaches were in use by the parolees studied. One was to be perfectly truthful on the job application. The reasoning used here was that if an employer wants to hire a particular person, he will—record or no record. A common variation of this approach was to leave blank any application questions concerning a criminal record or past working experience, but to tell the employer personally about the situation when handing in the application. The second approach was to avoid telling the employer anything about the past; then, if and when it came out, a good work record would have been established and one would not be fired. Apparently the two approaches are used about equally often: in response to the question "When you apply for a job, do you usually tell the employer you are on parole?" 51% of those surveyed said yes, and 49% said no.

Another way in which stigma can pose employment problems for a parolee is that the parolee's record might inhibit him from even trying to get certain jobs. In order to determine the extent of such inhibition, respondents were asked if they had ever not applied for a job they wanted because they were afraid their police record would keep them from getting it. Forty percent answered affirmatively. Those who said yes were then asked what kinds of jobs they had avoided. Most of them responded that they were city or state jobs or jobs requiring the worker to be bonded. The fact is that at the time of the survey city and state jobs had been opened to people with felony convictions, and Illinois had an agency which provided bonding for ex-offenders if they could not secure it through regular channels. A reason for a discrepancy of this type may lie in the distinction between subjectively experienced job discrimination and actual discrimination. Irwin (1970) felt that in many instances, because of the past history of extreme discrimination, the ex-offender feels that many doors are still closed which are actually open or at least partially open. The parolee sees the situation as one in which there is no opportunity and, therefore, does not try to obtain many kinds of jobs.

Another survey question relevant to the distinction between real and anticipated discrimination asked whether a respondent felt that any employer had actually discriminated against him because of his record. Since it is commonly thought that parolees are discriminated against, it seemed worthwhile to obtain an estimate of the proportion of ex-offenders who felt that they had in fact experienced such discrimination. Of the 68 men for whom the question was applicable, 55% said yes. The interesting aspect of this result is that 45% said they had not experienced any job discrimination. Such a finding supports a conclusion by Glaser (1964) that for a very large number of parolees the stigma of a criminal record is not as much a barrier to employment as is his lack of extensive or skilled work experience. The seriousness of this latter problem is reflected in Glaser's finding that regular work in prison even for as short a time as one year provides the longest and most continuous employment most prisoners have ever had. Irwin (1970) agreed that inexperience rather than stigma is the biggest obstacle to parolees' employability, but he suggested another less obvious way in which a parolee's lack of work experience hinders him. He felt that the routine of seeking and applying for work is one at which the parolee is particularly inexperienced and inept. In other words, in order to obtain a good job one must fill out forms, be interviewed, and take tests, and most parolees find such activities very difficult if not actually painful.

The stigma of being an ex-offender is a potential liability not only when looking for a job but also when meeting people in a social setting. Most parolees can get by in almost all social situations without their past being known. However, problems still remain because, as Goffman (1963) noted, when a person's stigma is not immediately obvious, the issue becomes one of managing information. There are constant decisions about whether to tell or not to tell, to lie or not to lie, to let on or not to let on, and, in every case, when, how, and to whom.

To get an indication of the extent to which social stigma created a problem for parolees, respondents were asked to agree or disagree with the following two questions: "When people find out you've been to prison, they do not give you the respect they give to other men" and "When people find out you've been to prison, they do not act any differently towards you because of it." They were also asked to estimate the percentage of people they meet who shy away when they find out they are talking to an ex-offender. The results showed that only 39% of the respondents agreed that people gave them less respect, while 59% agreed that people do not act any differently toward them. These results are similar to those of Irwin (1970), who found that two-thirds of the parolees he interviewed in San Francisco never felt awkward in a social setting because of their ex-convict status. The responses to the question about what percentage of people they meet shy away from them indicated that the percentage of people who give ex-offenders any trouble is relatively small, the median for that question being approximately 5%.

If it is assumed that there is in fact a social stigma associated with being an ex-offender, then an explanation of why relatively few ex-offenders reported experiencing such a stigma is required. There seem to be several plausible explanations, and these can be divided into two types. The first type posits that parolees do not encounter embarrassing situations. One way this could be true is if, both before and after imprisonment, parolees are part of a segment of society in which having a police record is unimportant or even prestigious. Another way is if ex-offenders employ an information management strategy of letting their parolee status be known only when they feel fairly sure that they will not be discredited. That is, they simply avoid the types of people, places and situations where the probability is high that their record will be discovered and/or make a significant difference in how they are treated. In such a case the label "ex-con" is indeed a problem in that it restricts activities; however, the use of this strategy ensures that actual discrimination need never be faced. It is important to note that the avoidance of people and places where ex-offender status is taboo might very well do more than reduce embarrassment. It might keep an ex-offender in a criminal subculture and thus contribute to recidivism. Reasoning along these lines, Irwin (1970, p. 138) writes:

> An effect of the stigmatization experienced by those ex-deviants who desire to move out from under the protective umbrella of a deviant perspective is to encourage the brethern to remain under its protection. Consequently, stigma is perhaps an important force in maintaining commitment to deviant social worlds.

The second type of explanation for ex-offenders' not experiencing stigma posits that the parolee encounters potentially embarrassing situations but is in fact not embarrassed by them. In discussing strategies for coping with stigma of any type, Goffman (1963) suggests that it is possible for an individual to become insulated by his alienation and/or protected by identity beliefs of his own. Such a person feels he is a normal human being and that it is the rest of society which is not quite human. This person may bear a stigma but does not seem to be impressed or repentant about it. The insulating alienation which Goffman discusses is similar to Matza's (1964) idea of a state of drift which is brought about by a neutralization of the moral bind of the law and which is a necessary condition for committing a crime. This suggests that the majority of parolees do not feel much stigma for the same reasons they committed a crime in the first place; *i.e.,* they are operating under a value system different from that of the rest of society. It is also possible, however, that the mechanisms for dealing with the stigma of being an ex-offender are developed not before prison but during and as a result of it. Sykes (1958), among others, has argued that the threat to one's self-concept, that is, the constant reminders that one has been rejected and condemned, is the most painful aspect of prison, and that somehow a prisoner must cope with this constant threat to his self-esteem. It could be, then, that the parolee's experiences in prison equip him to interact with the rest of society without embarrassment, and that, therefore, he does not experience stigma in situations where one might expect him to.

Unrealistic Expectancies

Past research on parolees (*e.g.,* Erickson et al., 1973) suggests that men come out of prison with very high—in fact, unrealistic—expectancies about what kind of job they can get, how much money they can make, and how much money they need in order to live comfortably. One reason for the formulation of these unrealistic expectancies might be that while in prison a person is free to fantasize about the outside world without the usual check on such fantasies that is provided by reality. Such high expectations are viewed as harmful to ex-offenders because they make it highly probable that the parolee will experience the disillusionment and despair of having one's expectancies about the future cruelly disconfirmed. Indeed, several studies in social psychology have documented the negative effects of having expectancies of even minor importance disconfirmed (Carlsmith & Aronson, 1961; Aronson & Carlsmith, 1962).

In an attempt to measure unrealistic thinking, each parolee in this study was asked, "How much money would you need to be making a week in order to be living comfortably?", "How much money do you think you'll be making a week in five years if things go the way you've planned?" and "What are the chances that you will eventually be an executive or vice-president of some company?" Respondents were also asked to indicate the extent of their agreement with two statements: "It's possible for you to stay within the law and make 15 to 20 thousand dollars a year" and "No matter how hard you tried you could *not* work your way up to be an executive of some company."

The mean response to how much money a parolee would need to be living comfortably was $139 a week; responses ranged from $50 to $350 with a standard deviation of $50. The interesting aspect of the average is that it does not reflect an extravagant aspiration. Much more extravagant is the average estimate of how much money the respondents would be making five years from now. Three hundred thirty-three dollars a week was the mean, with a minimum of $90, a maximum of $1,000 and a standard deviation of $242. Responses to the question about being able to make $15,000 to $20,000 a year showed that 79% of those interviewed felt they could. Also, answers to the question about not being able to become an executive of a company showed that 71% disagreed. Finally, in response to the question about the chances of actually becoming an executive of some company, 42% of those interviewed felt that their chances were 50-50 or better.

The extravagant estimates of salary in five years, the high percentage of respondents who felt they could make $15,000 to $20,000 a year, and the relatively high proportion of respondents who felt their chances of being an executive were quite high were produced largely by those who felt they would own their own business in five yeras and, therefore, would be the president of a company which would be producing large profits. An inspection of these answers showed that owning a cocktail lounge and being a free-lance artist or photographer were the most frequently expected ways of being in business for oneself. Considering the life situation of most ex-offenders, it is clear that these expectations about making money, becoming an executive, and owning one's own business are highly unrealistic.

The pattern of results found here replicate those of Erickson et al. (1973). These authors administered Cantril's (1965) Self Anchoring Scale—a measure of aspirations and expectations in life—to 60 parolees, asking them to indicate their aspirations for the present and for five years hence. The authors then com- pared these results with those Cantril obtained by asking the same questions of a national sample of Americans. The data indicated that the mean aspiration level for the present was significantly lower among parolees than among the general public; however, the mean expectations for five years hence were signifi- cantly higher among parolees than among the general public.

Several personality theorists have felt that unrealistically high expectations are a major source of maladaptive behavior. Rogers (1969), for example, placed a great deal of emphasis on the congruity, or lack of it, between what a person felt he should be and what he felt he actually was. Rotter & Hochreich (1975) theorized that a person's expectancies are one of three major determinants of behavior. Furthermore, Rotter (1966) felt that unrealistically high expectations lead to a lack of action or to inappropriate action. He felt that the lowering of a person's expectancies should often be a prime focus of attention in psycho-

therapy because it would allow the individual to obtain greater personal satisfaction and increased self-confidence. Thus the fact that many parolees have
such high expectations might well be cause for concern among people in corrections, and the lowering of ex-offender's expectancies about what they can
accomplish in the future would seem to be a worthwhile goal of any parolee
program.

Fate Control vs. Self-Determination

Rotter & Hochreich's (1975) ideas about the effects of expectancies on behavior are only one part of their theory of behavior. Their theorizing also includes a discussion of the concept of locus of control of reinforcements, which
they define as the degree to which an individual sees himself in control of his
life and the events that influence it. Rotter (1966) and his colleagues have
presented considerable evidence that people behave differently in situations
where rewards depend on chance or luck than they do in situations where they
perceive that skill or their own attributes determine whether reinforcements will
occur. Those people who see themselves as exerting significant influence over
their own lives are called "internals," and those who believe that events are
caused by forces outside of themselves are called "externals."

One aspect of the theory that has not been extensively tested is the question
of how the tendency to be internal or external is acquired and/or changed.
Rotter & Hochreich (1975) hypothesize that a person becomes an external by
being subjected to a series of specific situations in which he has little control.
They feel that a person then develops a generalized expectancy that he has
little control over his environment. One of the few studies relevant to this issue
was done by McArthur (1970), who found that college students who had their
draft status changed by the first draft lottery (a random event) exhibited a
stronger external orientation then did students whose draft status remained the
same after the lottery.

If people do indeed develop an external orientation after a series of experiences in which their lives are externally controlled, one would expect that ex-
prisoners would exhibit a strong external orientation since prison consists of
one long series of externally controlled events. Besides the external experiences
of prison, another reason for the likelihood of becoming externals is that it provides a rationalization for having been to prison. More specifically, if a parolee
develops the attitude that what happens to people is not under his control but
is caused by the forces of fate, he can then tell himself and others that it was not
his fault that he had been to prison; it was simply bad luck.

In order to get an indication of whether ex-offenders were indeed externals,
they were asked to agree or disagree on 6-point scales with these statements:
"Becoming a success in life is mainly a matter of luck; hard work has little to do
with it" and "Your staying out of trouble depends entirely on your own atti-

tudes and efforts; the breaks you get will have nothing to do with it." The distributions of answers to these questions showed that 89% of respondents disagreed that becoming a success in life was mainly a matter of luck, and 88% agreed that their staying out ot trouble depended entirely on their own attitudes and efforts.

These data obviously suggest that parolees do not attempt to rationalize their situation by saying that success and failure in life is caused by fate. On the contrary, they seem very extreme in their view that these outcomes are determined by one's own efforts. It would be a worthwhile project to study how parolees learn to feel so strongly about this, and why they do not use this rationalization. These results also suggest that prison does not make a person externally oriented, at least not when it comes to expectations about future success. These data, then, do not support the idea that a series of externally controlled situations produces an external person.

Clearly, one can not conclude on the basis of this study that Rotter's ideas about the development of locus of control are wrong. It is possible, for example, that externally controlled experiences which take place in an isolated environment like prison do produce generalized external expectations for that environment but not for a totally different one like the outside world. Another possibility is that the extreme internal orientation exhibited by these parolees is part of the unrealistic expectancies they have about what the outside world is like and what it takes to get ahead in it.

Assistance-Seeking

Most parolees are in the type of financial situation where they qualify for public aid of some kind. Also, since many of them are unemployed, the state unemployment service and day-labor agencies are logical places for them to go. Consequently, respondents were asked whether or not they had been to a welfare or public-aid office, the state employment service and/or a day-labor agency. If they answered affirmatively to either of the first two places, they were then asked whether or not they were satisfied with what the agency had done for them. The results are presented in Table I.

One interesting feature of Table I is the relatively low percentage of parolees who used welfare or public aid. Less than a third had done so, even though almost two-thirds did not have a job set up for them when they came out and, therefore, at least that many qualified for public assistance at some time since they had been out. This result would be a comfort to those worried that the release of prisoners swells the welfare lines. On the other hand, those concerned about recidivism might, on the basis of this result, propose that parolees be encouraged to make better use of the legal avenues which are available when they get into financial difficulty, thus reducing the need to resort to illegal channels. Parolees themselves should take note that out of the 27 who went to

TABLE I

Parolees' Assistance-Seeking Behavior

	Yes	No
Been to welfare or public aid	30%	89
Were you satisfied with what welfare did for you?	68%	27
Been to state employment service	42%	88
Were you satisfied with what the employment service did?	50%	38

welfare or public aid, over two-thirds were satisfied with the results.

Another noteworthy feature of Table I is that only 10% of the sample had engaged in day labor even though at least two-thirds were out of work at one time or another. This could be taken as evidence for one of Irwin's (1970) observations that in many cases merely "making it," that is, staying out of prison, is not enough for the parolee. He must "do all right" as defined by a group of very harsh judges—the prison yard. Evidently, the low-paying, low-status day labor does not fit the yard's definition of "doing all right."

Racial Differences in Employment

The pervasiveness of black/white differences in employment in the general population is well-documented. There are, however, no studies known to the author which have investigated black/white employment differences among men on parole. On the one hand, it makes sense that the differences found in studies of the general population would be reflected in the parolee population; after all, men on parole compete in the same job market as everyone else, and thus the same racial discrimination ought to be found. On the other hand, because blacks and whites who are ex-offenders have more in common than blacks and whites in the general population, it could be that there are no racial differences in employment among men on parole.

Actually, there are several ways in which black and white parolees are more similar than their non-parolee counterparts. First, they share whatever background characteristics are common to men who have been convicted of a felony and sent to prison. According to Glaser (1964), these generally include a low socioeconomic status, a relatively low level of education, a lack of job skills and work habits, a life style which includes unsuccessful deviance from the law, and so on. Secondly, because black and white parolees have had the common experience of a prison subculture, they share a certain vocabulary, certain mannerisms, and certain self-presentations (Sykes, 1958). Furthermore, it seems safe to assume that vocabulary, mannerisms, and self-presentations determine to a rather large extent what type of job a person gets, or whether he gets one at all. Thus the common experience of prison may produce fewer differences in employment opportunities between blacks and whites on parole than is the case in the general population. Third, black and white parolees may be similar because they share the stigma of being an ex-convict, a stigma which is obviously associated with unemployment (Schwartz & Skolnick, 1962) and which may well be a stronger influence on employment than is race.

In order to test these ideas, only data from black and white respondents were used. This meant that the three chicanos in the sample were dropped from this analysis, and the results were based on 87 ex-offenders. The data were collected in several ways. Whether or not a man was working and, if so, how much money he made in January, 1972, were determined from the records kept by the parole office. Also, during the individual interviews each respondent was asked to agree or disagree on a 6-point scale with the following two statements: "It's almost impossible for a parolee to get a job" and "It's not any harder for a parolee to get a job than for anyone else." Also, each parolee was asked these two open-ended questions: "What advice would you give a young man just coming out of prison and starting on parole?" and "How could the parole system be improved?" On both questions the interviewer probed for as many suggestions as he could get from the respondent. To code these items, dummy variables were created for each of the dimensions most frequently mentioned (employment was the most frequently mentioned category in response to both questions), and 1 was coded if the respondent made that suggestion, while 0 was coded if he did not. Two raters coded the responses to each of these questions, and the interrater reliabilities on the employment dimension were .95 for the question concerning advice to a new parolee and .89 for the question concerning ways the parole system could improve.

Respondents who were working were also asked three questions about their present job. "How do you feel about your present job?" and "How do you feel about your salary?" required responses on a 6-point scale ranging from completely dissatisfied to completely satisfied. The third was an open-ended item which again asked how they liked their job, and the responses were coded as either positive, negative, or neutral. The interrater reliability between two raters on this last item was .85. The intercorrelations among these three questions ranged from .50 to .67, which was higher than their correlations with any of the other items in the interview schedule; consequently, the responses were standardized and summed to form an index of job satisfaction

Table II shows the separate responses to these seven indices for black and

TABLE II

Responses to Questions Concerning the Employment
of Black and White Parolees

	Black	White	χ^2
1. Percentage working	46% (48)	69% (39)	3.88[a]

	Black	White	t
2. Average salary for January, 1972	$381. (21)	$379. (25)	.60

	Black	White	t
3. Average agreement with: "It's almost impossible for a parolee to get a job"	3.06 (47)	2.45 (38)	1.69[b]

	Black	White	t
4. Average agreement with: "It's not any harder for a parolee to get a job than for anyone else"	2.51 (47)	3.21 (39)	2.04[a]

	Black	White	χ^2
5. Percent suggesting that the parole system could improve by providing more jobs	58% (48)	38% (39)	2.65[b]

	Black	White	χ^2
6. Percent whose advice to new parolees concerned employment	73% (48)	49% (39)	4.37[a]

	Black	White	t
7. Average score on index of job satisfaction	-.41 (22)	.27 (26)	.95

Note: The number of respondents on which each data point is based is indicated in parentheses.

[a] $p < .05$.
[b] $p < .1$.

white parolees. A significantly larger proportion of whites were employed; on both agree-disagree questions, whites were not as negative as blacks in their opinions of how hard it is for a parolee to get a job; significantly fewer whites mentioned job procurement as a way the parole system could improve; and significantly fewer whites mentioned employment in their advice to a new parolee. However, no racial differences were found among those working either in the amount of money they made or in their job satisfaction.

Because race of interviewer was correlated both with race of respondent (*i.e.,* the black interviewer interviewed more blacks than whites and vice versa for the white interviewer) and with many of the employment indices, further analyses were required in order to check on the possibility that the pattern of differences among those questions asked during the interview was due not to race of respondent but to interviewer differences. Thus the above analyses were performed separately among those parolees contacted by the white interviewer and those contacted by the black interviewer. These results showed means and proportions almost identical to those in Table II, which ruled out the possibility of interviewer differences having produced the above outcomes. It should be noted that the other background variables used in the study, namely, marital status, age, time in prison, time out of prison, type of crime, education, and first-timers vs. recidivists, were found not to be significantly related to both race and these employment indices, and thus are not plausible causes of the findings.

The fact that more blacks were unemployed, that blacks had more negative attitudes toward how hard it is to get a job, and that blacks more frequently mentioned employment problems in response to open-ended questions suggests that among parolees blacks have a harder time in obtaining and/or keeping a job than do whites. Apparently, then, sharing the background characteristics of men who have been convicted of a felony and sent to prison, having in common the vocabulary, the mannerisms, and the self-presentations learned in prison, and sharing the stigma of being an ex-convict do not equate black and white parolees on their chances of getting a job. This conclusion is more significant than it might at first seem when one considers that most researchers feel employment is the number one problem faced by men returning from prison (*e.g.,* Irwin, 1970) and that employment is highly correlated with recidivism. Glaser (1964), for example, found that rates of unemployment were over twice as high for parolees who were considered recidivists as for those considered successful. Thus it appears that the black parolee does indeed have two strikes against him. Schwartz & Skolnick (1962) have shown that being an ex-convict significantly reduces one's chances of getting a job, and the present study has shown that being a black ex-convict reduces one's chances even more.

It is of interest that although there were these racial differences in employment rates, there were no racial differences among those who had a job in the amount of money made or in job satisfaction. An explanation of the lack of relationship between race and both money made and job satisfaction is that there is a limitation on the kinds of jobs available to ex-offenders regardless of race. That is, it seems reasonable that in the types of jobs parolees can get (*e.g.,* dishwasher, mover, gas station attendant) there is little room for promotion or raises in salary, which are conditions that allow racial prejudice or differences to operate. In this way the stigma of being an ex-offender, the common experiences in prison, and the shared background characteristics of felons could indeed be reducing the racial differences in income and job satisfaction among parolees from what those differences are in the general population.

Thus the overall pattern of these data could be interpreted as showing that race does affect which ex-offenders get jobs and which do not; however, once a parolee has a job, race does not influence his pay or job satisfaction because the causes and effects of being an ex-convict have channeled him into a very narrow range of low-level employment. It seems, then, that race is a significant determinant in obtaining a job; with regard to what type of job is obtained, however, the causes and effects of being an ex-offender may be more significant than race.

FOOTNOTE

[1] The present report represents part of the author's Ph.D. dissertation. This research was financed by a Woodrow Wilson Dissertation Year Fellowship, a Russell Sage Foundation Grant to Northwestern University, and National Science Foundation Grant GS 302734 (D.T. Campbell, principal investigator).

REFERENCES

Aronson, E. & Carlsmith, J. Performance expectancy as a determinant of actual performance. *Journal of Abnormal and Social Psychology,* 1962, *65,* 178-182.

Cantril, H. *The pattern of human concerns.* New Brunswick, N.J.: Rutgers University Press, 1965.

Carlsmith, J. & Aronson, E. Affectual consequences of the disconfirmation of expectancies. *American Psychologist,* 1961, *16,* 437.

Clemmer, D. *The prison community.* Boston: The Christopher Publishing House, 1940.

Cressey, D. *The Prison.* New York: Holt, Rinehart & Winston, 1961.

Erickson, R., Crow, W., Zurcher, L. & Connett, A. *Paroled but not free.* New York: Behavioral Publications, 1973.

Glaser, D. *The effectiveness of a prison and parole system.* Indianapolis: Bobbs-Merrill, 1964.

Glueck, S. & Glueck, E. Predictability in the administration of criminal justice. *Harvard Law Review,* 1929, *42,* 297-329.

Goffman, I. *Stigma.* Englewood Cliffs, N.J.: Prentice-Hall, 1963.

Gottredson, D., Ballard, K., Mannering, J. & Babst, D. *Wisconsin base expectancies for reformatories and prisons.* Vacaville, Calif.: Institute for the Study of Crime and Delinquency, 1965.

Irwin, J. *The felon.* Englewood Cliffs, N.J.: Prentice-Hall, 1970.

Korn, R. *Juvenile delinquency.* New York: Crowell, 1968.

Matza, D. *Delinquency and drift.* New York: Wiley, 1964.

McArthur, L. Luck is alive and well in New Haven: A serendipitous finding on perceived control of reinforcement after the draft lottery. *Journal of Personality and Social Psychology,* 1970, *16,* 316-318.

Rotter, J. Generalized expectancies for internal versus external control of reinforcement. *Psychological Monographs General and Applied, 80* (1, Whole No. 609), 1-28.

Rotter, J. & Hochreich, D. *Personality.* Glenview, Ill.: Scott, Foresman, 1975.

Schwartz, R. & Skolnick, J. A study of legal stigma. *Social Problems,* 1962, *10,* 133-138.

Sykes, G. *The Society of captives.* New York: Random House, 1958.

Van Dyke, H. *Juvenile delinquency.* Boston: Ginn, 1970.

8

Children's Conception of Intentionality and the Criminal Law

CHARLES BLAKE KEASEY
BRUCE DENNIS SALES*

THE LEGAL ISSUE

In almost all criminal laws, the intent of the alleged criminal to perpetrate the act, or at least foresee the reasonable and probable consequences of his actions, is a necessary ingredient in proving that individual guilty of the crime. As the famous English legal commentator Blackstone noted, "An unwarrantable act without a vicious will is no crime at all" (as cited in Kadish & Paulsen, 1969, p. 214). It is this element of intent that the law refers to as the mens rea.

The Problems in Finding Mens Rea

The problem of determining mens rea is manifold. First, many observers argue that judges do not initially try to seek a clear demonstration of the mens rea, but rather seek to make their findings conform to their desire to reach a particular result. Second, mens rea itself has received a multiplicity of definitions, including the use of such similar but differing words and phrases as "intentionality," "purposefulness," "knowingly," "with awareness," and "of choice." Third, determining if in fact the mens rea existed is particularly difficult because the mens rea that pertains to the law is that which occurred at the time of the crime and not presently.[1] Fourth, and finally for this discussion, valid and reliable techniques for making that assessment do not exist.

In a typical criminal case, the jury is allowed to find the mens rea from the totality of the evidence without the aid of psychological testimony. When this happens, the first problem noted above, namely, making the findings fit the desired result, may occur very easily. Where a psychologist or psychiatrist is called upon to testify, the evidence that is usually presented is based upon direct observation of the defendant and/or an interview with him and/or a summary of the results of projective tests. The use of this type of information suffers from the third problem listed above. Furthermore, most of this testimony lacks credible empirical verification as to its reliability or validity,[2] the fourth criterion above. Therefore, the probability greatly increases that the judge or jury will be deciding not upon a factual determination but an unsubstantiated belief.

Mens Rea as Applied to Juveniles

Whatever the problems in assessing mens rea for the adult, they are often compounded when applied to the juvenile. Since juveniles are most often not equal to adults in their capacity to rigorously pursue their defense, the law should be extra careful in ensuring that the child is afforded the greatest protection from capricious state action, or, as we define it in this case, state action based upon invalid methods of determining mens rea or methods which have never been subjected to validity checks. Although lawyers are usually not well-acquainted with validity tests, these procedures of empirical assessment are not new to psychologists and are indeed available for use in the legal process.

Instead of attacking this problem directly by developing procedures to assess mens rea, legislatures via statutory law and judges via case, or common law, have attempted to create certain legal protections for juveniles. For example, the prevailing rule is that children under the age of seven are incapable of committing a crime due to a conclusive presumption that such persons are unable to formulate the appropriate mens rea. For persons between the ages of seven and fourteen, the presumption of no mens rea is rebuttable. Finally, persons fourteen years old and over are treated as adults.

Although the purpose of the above rule is to protect those children who had no intent from being found guilty of a crime, its approach to the problem is inadequate. First, to presume that children below a certain age can have no intent, without that age being based upon scientific fact, arbitrarily exculpates some, possibly many, when in fact they may have possessed the requisite mens rea. Second, even if one eliminates all those under seven and creates a rebuttable presumption for those between seven and fourteen, there remains the problem of no procedure to adequately assess mens rea and thereby rebut or maintain the presumption in the middle age grouping. Clearly, the fourteen-and-over rule suffers from the same problems that are attendant to the other two classifications.

The History of the Rule

A look at the history of this rule and the varieties of its manifestation in this country amply demonstrates that the seven- and fourteen-year-old classifications were based not upon careful scientific investigation but rather upon arbitrary pronouncements by judges and legal commentators going back to antiquity. For a more detailed discussion of the history of this rule see Kean (1937) and Woodbridge (1939). Briefly, conceptions of the best way to deal with children varied. However, around A.D. 407 the age of infancy in Roman law was fixed at seven years because until that age children did not speak.[3] Similarly, the age of adult responsibility began at fourteen, which appears to be based on the age of puberty. It is ironic that the rule which now persists according to which children are or are not liable for their acts supposedly because of the presence or lack of mens rea was based on a lack of speech or puberty. Arguably, a lack of speech makes assessment difficult, but that difficulty in measuring mens rea should not be equated with its absence. Most likely, puberty was chosen because of its (historical) relation to manhood, and this in turn may have been assumed to be related to mens rea. It appears that pragmatics and myth, not science, dictated the creation of the age classifications.

In later English law (1400's) the seven-year age was believed to relate to lack of knowledge between good and evil and not to one's speech capacity, but how that relationship was determined is not stated. Similarly, at fourteen years of age or older the child was assumed to have "discretion," but no proof is apparent. The lack of clear and objective proof in these instances is matched by a lack of precision in exactly what it was that excused a child from liability. For example, is a lack of mens rea equivalent to a lack of speech, a lack of intellect, a lack of discretion, or a lack of knowledge of the difference between good and evil or right and wrong? All of these phrases appear in the records. Unfortunately, as noted above, a similar lack of precision persists today.

As mentioned earlier, the creation of a method to assess mens rea is particularly difficult given the multitude of words and phrases that are used to define it, including: (1) knowledge of the nature and illegality of the offense; (2) consciousness of the wrongfulness of the act; (3) capability of entertaining a criminal intent; (4) comprehension of the act's consequences; (5) powers to discriminate right from wrong; (6) demonstration of intelligent design and malice in execution of the act; (7) a mischievous inclination or disposition. With this multitude of definitions, courts have further compounded the problem both by not stating what evidence demonstrates mens rea and by admitting into evidence on this point a plethora of circumstantial evidence (*e.g.*, education, habits, general character, moral and religious instruction, circumstances surrounding the act) while never directly assessing the mens rea.

The absence of a standard criterion subjected to measurement easily accounts for the fact that various countries at various times throughout history modified the age classifications. However, legal comentators felt the need to draw fixed boundaries and not leave the issue to be resolved locally; hence the predominant seven- and fourteen-year-old rule. Since courts varied in their initial beliefs as to proper age limits, however, this same variation took place in the development of American law. Some states have adopted the seven- and fourteen-year-old rule in total, while others have adopted certain modifications.

The Current Status of the Law

A review of the law in each of the fifty states shows that twenty-six states have statutes which speak to this issue,[4] sixteen states and the District of Columbia have case law on point,[5] while eight states have never had an official ruling.[6] The stated law in the forty-two states and the District of Columbia can be broken down into six categories. States in the first category have enacted no provision regarding age limits of capability; instead, they have uniformly elected to follow the common-law age classifications (under seven, seven to fourteen, over fourteen). States in the second category differ from the common law in two ways. First, they raise the age of the conclusive presumption from seven to eight, ten, twelve, thirteen, fourteen, fifteen, or sixteen. Second, they eliminate the intermediate age group, where the presumption against giving the requisite mens rea is rebuttable. In the third category, the states have eliminated the conclusive presumption. Instead, persons under a given age, usually fourteen, are presumed incapable of committing a crime in the absence of clear proof that they knew the wrongfulness of the act. The presumption of incapacity is thus rebuttable. States in the fourth category follow the common-law pattern establishing an age of conclusive presumption and an intermediate age of rebuttable presumption against capacity. They differ in that the age limits are different from the original common-law rule.

States in the last two categories speak to the relationship of juvenile to adult courts. In the fifth category, the states provide for an age of conclusive presumption against capability and then provide that no person in the intermediate age group shall be prosecuted in criminal court unless jurisdiction is waived by juvenile courts. In the sixth and last category are those states that choose to deal with the question of capacity exclusively through the juvenile courts. In these jurisdictions various procedures are followed. Usually, exceptions to jurisdiction of juvenile court are enumerated for certain heinous crimes, and in the discretion of the court a youthful offender can be turned over to the adult authorities.

The procedures followed in juvenile courts are particularly vexing. The statutorily prescribed jurisdiction of juvenile courts differs from state to state and from county to county within each state. In addition, all states with the exception of New York and Vermont have established statutory provisions for discretionary transfer of jurisdiction from the juvenile court to the adult criminal court. If the case is tried in criminal (adult) court, the mens rea and the actus reus (the overt act) must both be proved. The basic tenet of the juvenile courts is that the state in a delinquency proceeding acts as parens patriae and not as an adversary. The United States Supreme Court in *In re Gault* (1967) and in *In re Winship* (1970) clearly stated that the actus reus element of a crime must always be proven beyond a reasonable doubt in juvenile court; however, no clear-cut dictate has emerged regarding whether the mens rea element must also be proven.

Two views prevail on mens rea in juvenile courts. The first view is that the best interests of the child are of paramount consideration. Although, following *Gault* and *Winship,* full due process procedural safeguards must be granted in all juvenile court proceedings, the proceedings take on a peculiarly civil nature. The juvenile is not prosecuted for a crime even though a crime is the basis on which the delinquency petition is formulated. The important element, rather, is that the juvenile committed the antisocial act (actus reus), and if that is found the court will turn its attention to a determination of what rehabilitative process should follow. Intent in fact, the mens rea, is irrelevant. (See, *e.g., In re L.B.,* 1968; *In re Steenback,* 1961; Frey, 1973; Westbrook, 1965). The second view is that intent in fact is relevant in the determination of delinquency—an ajudication of juvenile delinquency should be based on a stronger foundation than that of the juvenile's "accidental deed." (*In re Glassberg,* 1956; *People in the Interest of J.S.C.,* 1972; *United States v. Costanzo,* 1968).

A similar splitting of judicial opinion has emerged concerning whether the defense of insanity is permissible in juvenile court proceedings, and thus, in a roundabout fashion, whether intent (or lack of intent) is a relevant consideration for the court. One juvenile court has dismissed a delinquency petition subsequent to proof of insanity. In *In re Winburn* (1966) the Wisconsin Supreme Court held that the juvenile judge had the duty to dismiss the delinquency petition on its merits when the fact of insanity was proved. Another juvenile court, however, was forced to ignore insanity as a defense (*In re H.C.,* 1969), since the statute which authorizes commitment of an adult who is acquitted by reason of insanity applied only to indictable offenses, and was not applicable in juvenile courts (see, generally, Frey, 1973; Popkin & Lippert, 1971).

Although the juvenile courts split over whether or not to search for the mens rea in juvenile proceedings arising out of a criminal act, three facts continue to make mens rea a critical element in proceedings against juveniles. First, many juveniles accused of criminal conduct are still tried in adult court. Second, even if the juvenile is sent to juvenile court, many of these forums still search for the mens rea. Third, the juvenile court judge has the power to send the juvenile back to adult court and may do so when particularly serious crimes are in contention. The need for an empirical procedure to assess the mens rea in juveniles, as in adults, is thus present.

The Central Concerns of This Chapter

Considering all the above information, we can focus on two interesting and important scientific questions. First, does the development of the ability to have the requisite mens rea conform to the common-law rules or their modifications? For example, are children under seven always incapable of having the requisite mens rea? Second, can a valid and reliable scientific test be created that would directly assess the mens rea? Obviously, any scientific analysis must begin with a clear definition of what one is assessing. As amply demonstrated above, that is no easy task in this case. However, after a careful reading of the statutes, cases, and historical commentary in this area, we concluded that the key element underlying a court's inquiry into the mens rea is the search for the child's *intent* to commit the act. The study of intentionality and its development in children is not new to psychology.

PSYCHOLOGICAL LITERATURE

Piaget's Early Observations on Intentionality

Almost all psychological research dealing with children's developing conceptions of intentionality derives from the pioneering efforts of Piaget (1932). For him, intentionality represents only one of at least eleven different aspects of moral reasoning that differentiate two general stages of moral thinking evidenced by children. An excellent review of Piaget's theory and observations is presented by Hoffman (1970).

Piaget distinguished children's active or practical moral thinking from their theoretical moral thought. The former is evidenced in real-life situations in which the child is directly involved, whereas the latter is required when children are presented with hypothetical situations about other children and are asked to make judgments. Piaget believes that the development of theoretical moral thinking lags behind that of active moral thought.

Piaget's own intensive day-to-day observations of his three children's active moral thinking led him to conclude that children succeed "fairly soon (at three-four, when the first 'whys' and the interest in motivation begin) in differentiating intentional faults from involuntary breaches of the moral code" (p. 180). His observations on the usage of intentionality in children's theoretical moral thinking are based on interviews with about one hundred children between six and ten years of age. Procedurally, Piaget presented children with pairs of stories which always constrasted good intentions resulting in high amounts of damage with bad intentions resulting in low amounts of damage. He used story pairs that involved lying, clumsiness, and stealing. The following story pair is an example of clumsiness (p. 118):

> A little boy who is called John is in his room. He is called to dinner. He goes into the dining room. But behind the door there was a chair, and on the chair there was a tray with fifteen cups on it. John couldn't have known that there was all this behind the door. He goes in, the door knocks against the tray, bang go the fifteen cups and they all get broken!

> Once there was a little boy whose name was Henry. One day when his mother was out he tried to get some jam out of the cupboard. He climbed up on to a chair and stretched out his arm. But the jam was too high up and he couldn't reach it and have any. But while he was trying to get it he knocked over a cup. The cup fell down and broke.

At the end of each pair of stories, Piaget assessed the child's comprehension of the stories and repeated them if necessary. He then asked the child if one of the main story characters was naughtier than the other and why. On the basis of children's responses to various story pairs, Piaget concluded that with increasing age children shift from objective to subjective responsibility. The objective responsibility evidenced by six- and seven-year-olds is characterized by judgments based on damage even though many of the children are well aware of the intentional or accidental nature of the behaviors producing the varying amounts of damage. In contrast, by age nine, a majority of children were basing their judgments on the issue of intentionality rather than damage. These children were fully aware of the differing amounts of damage produced by the main characters, but considered it less important than the issue of intentionality.

Summarizing Piaget's early observations, we find that between three and four years of age children's active moral thinking distinguishes between accidental and intentional acts of their own. Soon after this, they evidence use of this distinction by excusing their own accidents. However, most children under the age of nine, although aware of intentionality and using it at least in reference to their own behavior, fail to consider it more important than consequences when presented hypothetical situations about the behavior of others. Thus it is not until the age of about nine that intentionality is considered to be more important than consequences in the theoretical moral thinking of most children.

Replication Studies of the 1950's and 1960's

Initially, Piaget's theory of moral development met with the same degree of skepticism that his more encompassing theory of cognitive development received. As a result, numerous replication studies were undertaken to check on the existence of the multitude of phenomenon observed and reported by Piaget.

All six of the replication studies (Boehm, 1962; Boehm & Nass, 1962; Grinder, 1964; Johnson, 1962; MacRae, 1954; Whiteman & Kosier, 1964) conducted in the 1950's and 1960's found empirical evidence of an increasing preference for intentionality in children from six through seventeen years of age. Significant positive correlations between age and preference for intentionality were reported by Johnson (1962) and MacRae (1954): .35 and .53, respectively. Of all the other possible correlates, only I.Q. has been consistently found to be positively related to preference for intentionality (Boehm, 1962; Boehm & Nass, 1962; Johnson, 1962; Whiteman & Kosier, 1964).

Only one study (Johnson, 1962) has looked at important measurement issues such as reliability and construct validity. Johnson obtained respectable test-retest reliabilities on a short scale of only four intentionality stories ($\overline{X}$ = .44. range = .30-.58). The intercorrelation of performance across the four stories was also respectable ($\overline{X}$ = .36; range = .30-.42). These correlations were higher than those obtained between intentionality and five of the other aspects of morality within Piaget's system ($\overline{X}$ = .22; range = .09-.29). Thus Johnson has obtained evidence of moderate reliability for intentionality stories and evidence for both convergent and discriminate construct validity.

In some of the replication studies, data are presented in sufficient detail so as to provide useful norms (Boehm, 1962; Boehm & Nass, 1962; Whiteman & Kosier, 1964). Since the two studies by Boehm administered the same two intentionality stories to comparable samples of children (N's = 237 and 160), the findings have been combined. The following percentages represent the proportion of all responses given at each age that explicitly included intentionality: six (35%), seven (49%), eight (54%), nine (84%), ten (77%), and eleven (71%). Whiteman & Kosier (1964) administered three intentionality stories to 126 children and obtained the following percentages of responses reflecting intentionality: seven (45%), nine (60%), and eleven (89%).

Some reasonable generalizations can be drawn from the response patterns of this rather large combined sample of children (N = 523). Clearly, the usage of intentionality seems to increase systematically with age. It is not until age eight, however, that the majority of responses focus explicitly on intentionality. At the age of seven, slightly less than half of the responses incorporated intentionality. Finally, it should be noted that even as late as age eleven a sizable minority of responses are still being based on consequences rather than intentions.

In concluding this section, it should be noted that the norms found in the replication studies are only slightly more advanced than those reported by Piaget some twenty-five to thirty-five years earlier. Even these slight differences might reflect nothing more than cultural changes occurring over a quarter of a century. Indeed, this is suggested in a personal communication from B. Inhelder to Boehm (1962) stating that Piaget's staff now finds Swiss children developing more rapidly in moral reasoning.

Methodological Innovations of the 1970's

Although the basic assessment procedure that Piaget introduced over forty years ago was appropriate for assessing a child's relative preference for consequence or intentions, it was not sensitive to detecting the child's usage of intentionality. A number of investigators (Armsby, 1971; Buchanan & Thompson, 1973; Chandler et al., 1973; Costanzo et al., 1973; Gutkin, 1972; Hebble, 1971; King, 1971) have attempted to overcome this problem by means of various modifications in Piaget's basic procedure.

Perhaps the most serious problem with it is that intentionality and consequences are confounded (Costanzo et al., 1973). This occurs because Piaget's story pairs always contrast a high-damage/good-intent story with a low-damage/bad-intent story. Consequently, such story pairs provided the preference data Piaget sought but failed to indicate if a child was using both parameters simultaneously (Buchanan & Thompson, 1973). Two somewhat different procedures have been devised for avoiding this confounding. Children are asked either to rate each of the four story types (good-intent/high-damage, good-intent/low-damage, bad-intent/high-damage, bad-intent/low-damage) separately (Costanzo et al., 1973; Hebble, 1971; Buchanan & Thompson, 1973) or to identify the naughtier central character in each of the six possible pairings of these four basic story types (Gutkin, 1972; Keasey, 1977; Keasey & Sales, 1975, 1976). Berg-Cross (1975) used both procedures with first-graders and obtained more intentionality responses with the single-story procedure.

Using these improved procedures, Hebble (1971) found that intent and consequence were considered equally important by first-graders. In higher grades (two through six), intent was judged more important than consequence. Similarly, Gutkin (1972) found that a majority of first-graders (25/45) attended to both components, with more than half judging intent to be more important (seventeen vs. eight). Gutkin concluded that his findings suggested a four-stage developmental sequence: (1) intent irrelevant, (2) intent relevant but consequences more important, (3) both relevant but intent more important, (4) only intent relevant.

Related to the above problem of confounding has been the failure of many of Piaget's original story pairs to clearly contrast a purposive act with an accidental one (Armsby, 1971; Berg-Cross, 1975). For example, in the cup-breaking stories presented earlier, the breakage in both cases is accidental; however, one boy was being disobedient. Armsby found that revised story pairs elicited significantly more intentionality among six-, eight-, and ten-year-olds than Piaget's did original stories. Similar findings were obtained by Berg-Cross with six-year-olds. Armsby found that intentionality judgments were made by 75% of the six-year-olds, and by 85% of the eight- and ten-year-olds.

Another possible drawback with Piaget's original story pairs was that the consequences were always negative and varied little in magnitude. Costanzo et al. (1973) and Imamoglu (1975) both employed stories involving positive as well as negative consequences. Costanzo et al. found that although kindergarten children failed to focus on intentionality when the consequences were negative they clearly did so when they were positive. Imamoglu also found that positive consequences elicited more intentionality responses, but not among children as young as kindergarten age. The issue of magnitude was investigated by Armsby (1971), who employed four levels of damage. He found that the usage of intentionality by six-year-olds decreased significantly as the amount of damage increased. The trend among eight-year-olds was not as strong and the findings were very mixed among ten-year-olds.

An additional modification in Piaget's original technique has focused upon the mode of presentation (Berndt & Berndt, 1975; Chandler et al., 1973; Farnill, 1974; King, 1971). Through the employment of videotapes, Farnill found that boys as young as kindergarten age could differentiate their moral judgments on the basis of intent in situations of negative outcome. By using both verbal stories and videotapes of these same stories, Chandler et al. were able to demonstrate greater usage of intent in first graders when the videotape medium was used. Berndt & Berndt, however, failed to find any difference between films and stories among either preschoolers, second-graders, or fifth-graders.

Taken as a whole, the above studies have important implications for the issues of assessment and age norms. Clearly, an assessment procedure that would be maximally sensitive to intentionality should be one in which consequences and intentionality are not confounded. Stories should clearly contrast purposeful acts with accidental ones, and positive as well as negative consequences need to be included. The magnitude of the negative consequences should not be so great as to override the influence of intentionality. No firm recommendations can be made concerning modes of presentation (stories vs. videotapes) until the conflicting findings can be resolved.

The employment of these different methodological innovations has clearly raised the age norms over those originally obtained by Piaget and the subsequent replication studies. Whereas the replication studies found that slightly less than half of the responses of seven-year-olds focused on intentionality, this newer set of studies found that between 50% and 75% of the responses of six-year-olds evidenced intentionality. Keasey (1977) obtained 49% intentionality-oriented responses from kindergarteners (mean age = 6-0) exposed to the traditional other-oriented stories. Thus it seems that assessment procedures using various innovations have lowered the age at which intentionality responses are given at least half of the time by about two years (from seven to five).

Extensions of the Paradigm

The importance of a third variable, provocation, has emerged from three studies (Hewitt, 1974, 1975; Rule & Duker, 1973) that have examined moral evaluations of aggressive acts. Consistent with earlier research, both good intentions and less serious injury received more positive evaluations than bad intentions and more serious injury. Furthermore, younger children (eight-year-olds) were more influenced by consequences than older children (twelve-year-olds), and differentiation due to intentionality was less when consequences were serious (Rule & Duker, 1973).

Hewitt (1975) found that the provoked harm-doer was rated less naughty than one who was not provoked. However, the impact of provocation seems to vary with age. This is seen by the finding that the evaluations of twelve-year-olds clearly differentiated intentionality under both high and low provocation, but eight-year-olds failed to differentiate intentionality when provocation was high. In other words, high provocation overrides consideration of the harm-doer's intentions in eight-year-olds but not in twelve-year-olds. Using a somewhat different procedure, Shantz & Voydanoff (1973) found that older children (nine- and twelve-year-olds) reported that they would rataliate more against intentional as opposed to accidental aggression from another child. In contrast, seven-year-olds failed to make such a distinction. The findings of this set of four studies of aggression suggest that the addition of provocation lowers the saliency of intentionality. This effect seems most pronounced for children eight years and under.

The final extension has been in terms of age rather than methodology. Twelve stories representing three levels of intentionality and four levels of consequences were administered to over 1,000 children between the ages of eleven and seventeen (Breznitz & Kugelmass, 1967; Kugelmass & Breznitz, 1968). The researchers found evidence that some aspects of the concept of intentionality and their usage continue to develop systematically through adolescence. Their findings suggest that children's understanding of intentionality moves from a preverbalized usage of the principle to a stage of verbalization, then to the capacity to spontaneously recall the principle of intentionality, and finally to a very refined usage of the principle. Only about 10% of the 69 seventeen-year-olds in their sample evidenced usage of the highest level, and about 28% achieved the next highest level.

INTEGRATING THE LEGAL AND PSYCHOLOGICAL KNOWLEDGE

The legal analysis presented in the first section of this chapter posed two questions that psychologists should attempt to answer. First, does the common-law rule (that children under seven years are irrebuttably presumed to lack the necessary mens rea to commit a crime, that children between the ages of seven and fourteen are rebuttably presumed to lack the mens rea, and that children fourteen and over are treated as adults), or its variants, conform to our scientific knowledge of the cognitive development of intentional behavior in children *and* their awareness of it? Second, whatever the answer to the first question, can a reliable and valid scientific procedure be developed that will provide an objective technique for assessing a child's capacity to entertain the requisite mens rea *and* did that mens rea exist at the commission of the criminal act?

In this final section, we will try to answer both questions. Before we do, however, it is important to consider the possibility that the common-law rule was created with some purpose in mind not heretofore considered.

Alternative Justifications for the Common-Law Rule

It is clear from legal history that the choice of the common-law ages was not based upon science or a clear knowledge of the age at which mens rea developed. The fact that knowledge of cognitive development was not the yardstick for the creation of the rule is no justification, however, for leaving the rule unchallenged and appears to us to be ample reason to question its desirability. Rules should have a rational relation to that which they are supposed to achieve. If the goal of the common-law rule is to protect those who have no mens rea (under seven) or who may have no mens rea (between seven and fourteen), then the rule should accurately reflect the reality of the age at which mens rea develops in most children and the variance among the remaining part of the population. For example, if many children at the age of five years have the ability to entertain the requisite mental state to commit the crime, what purpose is served by legally presuming a lack of that capacity?

One could argue that is is better if the court cannot determine if the child had the requisite mens rea since that prohibits the court from labeling the child a "criminal." If there is no proof of the existence of mens rea, then a crime cannot be proved. Since the literature is replete with arguments that labeling results in stigma, this argument would hold that it is better never to be able to label the child in court. Rather, the child should be released without conditions or released and sent for psychological assessment. Both of these solutions are troubling.

It is conceivable that a child who committed a criminal act could be set free without conditions if the mens rea of the individual was not determined. Thus the court may assume that the act was done innocently (without evil intent) or accidentally. In that case, unconditional release may be appropriate. But what if the judge was wrong and the child did possess the intent to commit the act? Release without rehabilitation allows the individual's "problem" to continue and possibly grow while increasing the probability that society will be harmed again.

What if the court decides to grant release on condition that the child undergo some form of education? This could happen hypothetically if the judge believed that the child committed the act innocently but not accidentally. Remedial education could help ensure that the child would not commit the act again. But this training may all be for naught. How can the court, the educator, or society rely on a decision to train an individual that was based upon incomplete evidence? If evidence of mens rea was admitted, the court may have found out that the child intended the act and realized that the court-ordered training was inappropriate. Thus, once again, not searching for mens rea could be costly to society both financially (providing irrelevant training) and socially (the child may commit the same act again). Similarly, if part of the focus of the decision was to provide therapy to help the child accept the act that he committed without suffering self-recriminations, that therapy would be ill-planned if the therapist was assuming that no evil intent existed if in fact it did.

It could also be argued that society should excuse children under seven from their acts as a matter of policy. This position might be justified on the grounds that prosecuting everybody is not feasible economically and would overburden our court system. Such an argument is inadequate on several grounds. There has never been a showing that the number of alleged crimes for children under seven is so high that eliminatiing this group would either substantially decrease the case load burdens on the courts or substantially decrease the costs of our court system. Even if it could be shown, is society benefiting in excess of these costs by ignoring the very young offender who has both a high probability of repeating the crime or engaging in new ones over his entire life? It makes more sense for society to attempt to rehabilitate the very young first offender since that individual does not have a long history of maladaptive behavior that needs to be changed and therapy may have a higher probability of success. Additionally, if therapy is successful, then society is protected against years of crime by this individual during his lifetime. Although there are no data on this point, we would estimate that the cost savings to the court system of ignoring very young offenders cannot nearly match the cost that society will bear if the young individual spends the rest of his life as a criminal.

Excusing the young offender as a matter of policy may also be based on the belief that, no matter what the nature of the crime or the intentions of the criminal, a child under seven should not be punished because his tender years make punishment morally wrong. This position is similar to the age-old assumption that lack of age goes hand in hand with lack of mental capacity and society should not punish the incapacitated. This position is clearly inadequate. The mental capacity necessary to form the requisite mens rea may exist in children as young as three years of age (Piaget, 1932). If that is the case, what benefit does society derive from excusing these children? Surely, excusing these children to help them avoid labeling and stigma would only prolong their and society's problems. Excusing them because they are of tender years makes about as much sense as denying women the vote because they are of the gentle sex.

Moreover, if the child did commit a criminal act with the requisite mens rea, then society should provide the appropriate psychological intervention and rehabilitation. The disturbed child should have a right to treatment. If so, how can a judge accurately dispense justice and act in the child's best interests if he does not know whether or not the child had the "evil" intent or committed the act innocently or accidentally? Intent would have to be assessed either in the judicial proceeding or afterward so that the child's need for therapy and the particular type can be accurately determined. Alternative explanations and justifications for the common-law rule are inadequate.[7] It can only be related logically to protecting the child who lacks the mental capacity to hold the mens rea, or the child who had that capacity but did not have the mens rea when he committed the particular act that is in contention.

Do the Psychological Data Support the Common-Law Age Divisions?

Although the literature reviewed in the last section involved studies on children's intent in general, and not intent to commit crimes in particular, it seems logical and appropriate to generalize their findings to the current problem. As Piaget observed in 1932, the active moral thinking of young children succeeds "fairly soon (between three and four) in differentiating intentional faults from involuntary breaches of the moral code" (p. 180). Subsequent studies have found widespread usage of intentionality in children as young as five and six years old (Chandler et al., 1973; Costanzo et al., 1973; Gutkin, 1972; Hebble, 1971). Keasey (1977) has recently suggested that investigators may be able to empirically confirm Piaget's observation of intentionality in three- and four-year-old children if they employ more naturalistic methods of assessment. It appears that one part of the common law rule, the irrebuttable presumption against a finding that the child who is under seven years of age could have the requisite mens rea, is completely without scientific justification. Furthermore, without repeating the arguments noted above, it seems irrational to automatically exclude children in this age group from a finding of guilt.

Two additional issues should be kept in mind at this point. First, a finding of guilt may be desirable so that the aggrieved party may exact his restitution or retribution. It may also be desirable for the defendant. If guilty, a clear determination of that fact could help force the individual into an appropriate rehabilitation program. Second, if the court could or would order rehabilitation without the guilty determination, this might also be a desirable result. The offender could be rehabilitated without the necessity of creating a criminal record for him. This approach is not alway feasible, however. Criminal (adult) courts must make the determination of mens rea and make a finding of guilt in order to impose a sentence or other dispositional alternative. Similarly, the same process must take place in many juvenile courts. In the remaining ones, the juvenile judge could impose a rehabilitation program on the child where only a showing of the child's commission of the actus reus is made. However, the mens rea would still have to be found by the therapist in order to accurately formulate the therapeutic plan.

The scientific evidence relating to the rebuttable presumption of no mens rea in children seven to fourteen is much more favorable. Several of the studies reported demonstrated that awareness and usage of intentionality increases with age (*e.g.*, Piaget, 1932; Boehm, 1962); seven-year-olds showed 45% of their responses reflecting intentionality, with the percentage increasing to 89% among eleven-year-olds (Whiteman & Kosier, 1964). Although it is highly probable that most thirteen-year-olds have the capacity to entertain the requisite mens rea, the use of the upper limit for the middle grouping is not inconsistent with the data. Additionally, this allows the defendent some measure of protection, expecially in those few cases where the individual had not developed intentionality, since the state has the burden of proving its existence.

Similarly, the fourteen-and-over rule seems reasonable in light of the scientific evidence since almost all adolescents show an understanding of their own intentional behavior by this age. This conclusion is also consistent with the findings of Breznitz & Kugelmass (1967) and Kugelmass & Breznitz (1968). Although these authors suggest that the principle of intentionality in moral judgment continues to develop during adolescence (children eleven to seventeen in their studies), the development was one of refinement of its usage and not in its existence vs. nonexistence.

In summary, then, the scientific evidence demonstrates that there is no rational basis to support the irrebuttable presumption of no mens rea in children under seven years of age, but that the two other age divisions of the rule conform to the results of moral development studies in children.

These conclusions strongly reinforce the need for the development of a valid and reliable test to assess mens rea in children. If mens rea must be proved, then an objective technique for conducting that assessment is needed. In the common-law rule, the rebuttable presumption for children between seven and fourteen necessitates this test if the state is to rebut the presumption. If our above conclusions are correct, states should abolish the lower classification or lower it to children under four years of age. This result would increase the need for such an assessment device. Finally, even if states persist in maintaining the lower age division in spite of the scientific evidence, the assessment device is still needed for therapists working with those children as well as children who are processed in those juvenile courts where a showing of mens rea is not necessary.

Can a Valid and Reliable Procedure Be Developed to Assess Mens Rea?

As suggested above, Piaget's story pairs could be used as the basis for the development of a valid and reliable procedure to assess mens rea. This technique involves short stories in which the character acted either intentionally or accidentally. By asking the child which character is naughtier, we have a direct means of assessing that child's understanding of intentionality.

Refining, modifying, and then testing this procedure to establish reliability and validity coefficients seems particularly promising for a number of reasons.

First, the procedure is simple to administer and would be easy to score. Second, the response required of the child could involve nothing more than his simply pointing. This would correct for deficiencies in speech. Third, the stories can be created to conform very closely with real-life situations or even the act the child is alleged to have committed. Fourth, the stories or the language could be modified and standardized for minority cultures and subcultures. Finally, the creation and standardization of such an assessment device does not have to begin from scratch but rather has a substantial history of research upon which to begin its development.

This research shows that such tests can be used to assess intentionality and its development in children (*e.g.,* Piaget, 1932; Boehm, 1962; Boehm and Nass, 1962), but that several methodological issues will have to be studied and resolved in the development of procedures. Costanzo et al. (1973) have demonstrated that Piaget's original stories confounded intentionality with damage. Thus the effect of these two variables must be assessed independently and in their interaction. Furthermore, studies should isolate the levels of these two factors. For example, does the child really distinguish between evil intent (the intent to commit the bad act), innocent intent (the intent to commit the act, not realizing that it was wrong), lack of caution (not intending to commit the act but, understanding that if it was committed it would be wrong, doing so because of lack of caution), accident 1 (taking reasonable precautions but the act still occurs by accident), accident 2 (same as accident 1 except that even if the child intended the act his intent would have been innocent), and insanity? Similarly, does the child really differentiate the seriousness of the consequences of different criminal acts (death, serious injury, minor injury, destruction of valuable property, etc.)? Lastly, does the magnitude of the damage interact with the "cause" variables?

The "magnitude of the damage" variable is akin to and suggests the need for also assessing the "objective of the act." Was the actus reus hurting another person or damaging property? It may be that the development of intentionality is specific to particular classes of objectives. For example, parents may attempt to train a respect for life before they emphasize property. This may be reflected in the child's cognitive development. Similarly, does the child understand evil intent when by accident it gets tied to a positive or good consequence? What if the evil intent was tied to a good consequence not by accident but because the child did not realize that his method of carrying out his intent was inappropriate?

Another methodological innovation that will be necessary to incorporate is having the central character of the stories be the person being questioned. Keasey (in press) demonstrated that children are aware of their own intentionality much before they distinguish between the intentional and accidental nature of the behavior of others. If the assessment device to to test whether the child had the requisite mens rea, and not some other person, then the use of the child as the central character in the story seems mandatory. Parenthetical to this discussion, it might be desirable to create a variant of this procedure using characters who are not the child being questioned, for testing the child's capacity to act as a witness against others on this issue.[8]

The content of these stories should also be modified to contain legal vignettes as opposed to other moral dilemmas. This would increase the test's external validity by having it more closely approximate that which it is testing—mens rea for criminal acts as defined by the law. The type of crime committed in these stories should also be modified. This reflects the concern stated above that intent may develop differentially to specific objectives (hurting people vs. hurting property).

Methodological concern should also be focused upon the presentation procedures and response modes. For example, should pairs of stories vs. individual stories be presented for a response? Should children be asked to say who's naughtier of the pair or rate the degree of naughtiness on a 5-7 point scale? Should the reason for their responses be required? Keasey & Sales (1976) present some data to indicate that these purely procedural methodological variations can affect results. If the concern is with developing a valid and reliable assessment technique than these issues like the more substantive methodological concerns must be clarified and standardized.

Choice of presentation and response modes may also be important for the various age groups that need to be tested. For example, assessing a four-year-old accurately may require a simplier form of the technique than that which might be chosen if only children were involved. Additionally, the effect of written or oral stories, as compared to more naturalistic methods of presentation such as videotape or film should be evaluated, keeping in mind cost effectiveness for developing and using each procedure.

When studies such as these are carried out, followed by the testing of large samples of children at all ages, normative data should be available for future test users to rely on, and a valid and reliable procedure for assessing mens rea should result. This test should allow for an accurate assment of the child's capacity to entertain the requisite mens rea and, if administered soon after the criminal act took place, using stories that are similar to the actual crime, could present strong circumstantial evidence of whether or not the child had the mens rea at the time of the crime.[9]

Some Final Considerations of the Law of Mens Rea

If the law of mens rea is to maintain its authority, it must be rational and admit to valid and reliable evidence. At this point in history, neither of these goals is being completely met. Although it appears that mens rea is best defined as evil intent or intent to commit the bad act with knowledge that it is wrong, other definitions have been used by courts. It is possible that courts felt the need to couch their opinion in language approximating that presented by the witnesses, and since no standard test is available the explanatory language used by witnesses may have varied. But such variance in analysis can only foster confusion and suspicion as to what the law requires or what the court is really searching for.

Similar problems exist in   proving mens rea existed. Since no tests are currently available, courts rely primarily on circumstantial evidence as opposed to a direct assessment. If experts are called on to testify on this issue, which appears to be infrequent if not rare, their methods are equally suspect since no test currently exists to measure mens rea, especially no test that has been standardized with a demonstration of high reliability and validity. Surely, a search for a mental state that relies on nonpsychological evidence that is of dubious reliability or validity should be carefully scrutinized—if not in the past, at least in the future. This holds true whether the defendant is a child or an adult.

FOOTNOTES

*We thank Robinsue Frohboese whose work as a research assistant aided us immensely in this project.

[1] Present intent may be used in determining sentence or other dispositional alternatives after a determination of guilt has been made.

[2] For an excellent discussion of how to cross-examine this type of testimony, see Zisken (1975).

[3] It is unclear whether the rule was laid down because children could not speak or because they were not sufficiently fluent until seven years of age. Obviously, the latter is more reasonable to assume.

[4] Arizona, Arkansas, California, Colorado, Connecticut, Florida, Georgia, Hawaii, Idaho, Illinois, Louisiana, Massachusetts, Minnesota, Missouri, Montana, Nevada, New Hampshire, New Jersey, New York, North Dakota, Oklahoma, Oregon, South Dakota, Texas, Utah, Washington.

[5] Alabama, Delaware, District of Columbia, Indiana, Iowa, Kentucky, Maine, Maryland, Michigan, Mississippi, North Carolina, Ohio, Pennsylvania, Tennessee, Vermont, Virginia, West Virginia.

[6] Alaska, Kansas, Nebraska, New Mexico, Rhode Island, South Carolina, Wisconsin, Wyoming.

[7] Each of the hypothetical arguments could only be partially accurate, at best, since they only explain the under seven group and do not account for the rebuttable presumption that is attached to children between seven and fourteen.

[8] Although this evidence would probably be inadmissible since it is unsubstantiated opinion testimony by a non-expert, it could often be sought and relied upon in other situations, such as pre-trial investigations by law enforcement officials.

[9] Lying or deception checks will have to be built in, as is done on other inventories such as the Minnesota Multiphasic Personality Inventory.

REFERENCES

Armsby, R.E. A reexamination of the development of moral judgments in children. *Child Development*, 1971, *42*, 1241-1248.

Berg-Cross, L.G. Intentionality, degree of damage, and moral judgments. *Child Development*, 1975, *46*, 970-974.

Berndt, T.J. & Berndt, E.G. Children's use of motives and intentionality in person perception and moral judgment. *Child Development*, 1975, *46*, 904-912.

Boehm, L. The development of conscience: A comparison of American children of different mental and socioeconomic levels, *Child Development*, 1962, *33*, 575-590.

Boehm, L. & Nass, M.L. Social class differences in conscience development. *Child Development*, 1962, *33*, 565-574.

Breznitz, S. & Kugelmass, S. Intentionality in moral judgment: Developmental stages. *Child Development*, 1967, *38*, 469-479.

Buchanan, J.P. & Thompson, S.K. A quantitative methodology to examine the development of moral judgment. *Child Development*, 1973, *44*, 186-189.

Chandler, M.J., Greenspan, M. & Barenboim, C. Judgments of intentionality in response to videotaped and verbally presented moral dilemmas: The medium is the message. *Child Development*, 1973, *44*, 315-320.

Costanzo, P.R., Coie, J.D., Grumet, J.F. & Farnill, D. A reexamination of the effects of intent and consequence on children's moral judgments. *Child Development*, 1973, *44*, 154-161.

Farnill, D. The effects of social-judgment set on children's use of intent information. *Journal of Personality*, 1974, *42*, 276-289.

Frey, M.A. Intent in fact, insanity and infancy: Elusory concepts in the exercise of juvenile court jurisdiction. *California Western Law Review*, 1973, *9*, 273-289.

Grinder, R.E. Relations between behavioral and cognitive dimensions of conscience in middle childhood. *Child Development*, 1964, *35*, 881-891.

Gutkin, D.C. The effect of systematic story changes on intentionality in children's moral judgments. *Child Development*, 1972, *43*, 187-195.

Hebble, P.W. The development of elementary school children's judgment of intent. *Child Development*, 1971, *42*, 1203-1215.

Hewitt, L.S. Children's evaluations of harmdoers as a function of intentions and consequences. *Psychological Reports*, 1974, *35*, 755-762.

Hewitt, L.S. The effects of provocation, intentions, and consequences on children's moral judgments. *Child Development*, 1975, *46*, 540-544.

Hoffman, M.L. Moral development. In P.H. Mussen (ed.), *Carmichael's manual of child psychology*, Vol. 2. New York: Wiley, 1970.

Imamoglu, E.O. Children's awareness and usage of intention cues. *Child Development*, 1975, *46, 39-45.*

46, 39-45.

In re Gault, 387 U.S. 1 (1967).

In re Glassberg, 230 La. 396, 88 S.2d 707 (1956).

In re L.B., 99 N.J. Super. 589, 240 A.2d 709, 713 (Juv. & Dom. Rel. Ct. 1968).

In re Steenback, 34 N.J. 89, 102, 167 A.2d 397, 403 (1961).

In re Winship, 397 U.S. 358 (1970).

Johnson, R.C. A study of children's moral judgments. *Child Development*, 1962, *33*, 327-354.

Kadish, S.H. & Paulsen, M.G. *Criminal Law and its Processes.* Boston: Little, Brown, 1969.

Kean, A.W.G. The history of the criminal liability of children. *Law Quarterly Review*, 1937, *LIII*, 364-370.

Keasey, C.B. Young children's attribution of intentionality to themselves and others. *Child Development*, 1977, *48*, 261-264.

Keasey, C.B. & Sales, B.D. *A minor's intentionality as imputed in civil and criminal law: Some current research findings.* Paper presented at American Psychology-Law Society meeting, Chicago, 1975.

Keasey, C.B. & Sales, B.D. An empirical investigation of young children's awareness and usage of intentionality in criminal situations. *Law and Human Behavior,* 1977, *1,* 45-61.

King, M. The development of some intention concepts in young children. *Child Development,* 1971, *42,* 1145-1152.

Kugelmass, S. & Breznitz, S. Intentionality in moral judgment: Adolescent development. *Child Development,* 1968, *39,* 249-256.

MacRae, D. A test of Piaget's theories of moral development. *Journal of Abnormal and Social Psychology,* 1954, *49,* 14-18.

People in the Interest of J.S.C. 493 P.2d 671 (Colo. App. 1972).

Piaget, J. *The moral judgment of the child.* New York: Harcourt, Brace, 1932.

Popkin, A. & Lippert, F. Is there a constitutional right to the insanity defense in juvenile court? *Journal of Family Law,* 1971, *10,* 421-442.

Rule, B.G. & Duker, P. Effects of intentions and consequences on children's evaluations of aggressors. *Journal of Personality and Social Psychology* 1973, *27,* 184-189.

Shantz, D.W. & Voydanoff, D.A. Situational effects of retaliatory aggression at three age levels. *Child Development,* 1973, *44,* 149-153.

United States v. Costanzo, 395 F.2d 441 (4th Cir. 1968).

Westbrook, J. Mens rea in the juvenile court. *Journal of Family Law,* 1965, *5,* 121-138.

Whiteman, P.H. & Kosier, K.P. Development of children's moralistic judgments: Age, sex, IQ, and certain personal-experimental variables. *Child Development,* 1964, *35,* 843-850.

Woodbridge, F. Physical and mental infancy in the criminal law. *University of Pennsylvania Law Review,* 1939, *87,* 426-454.

Zisken, J. *Coping with psychiatric and psychological testimony* (2nd ed.). Beverly Hills, Calif.: Law and Psychology Press, 1975.

9

The Concept of
Dangerousness: Criticism
and Compromise[1]

DAVID LEVINE

"... laws were never meant to be understood, and it is foolish to make the attempt."

The Tin Woodman in *The Land of Oz*

Despite this Ozmian admonition, many lawyers and psychologists are engaged in an attempt to understand the use of the word "dangerousness" in Anglo-American law. The endeavor is frequently a frustrating one—and perhaps the Tin Woodman is right. Nevertheless, the attempt needs to be made: despite recent extensive criticism, the idea of "dangerousness"—or something very much like it—has been important in most legal systems and is central to many of the decisions made in our own system.

Whether or not an offender is considered dangerous is a factor in his disposition at almost every stage of the criminal justice and mental health process: it is a factor in laws governing arrest, bail, preventive detention, sentencing, release, and involuntary civil commitment. It is likely to become an even more critical factor in mental health statutes as litigation concerning the rights of mental patients leads state legislatures to correct the ambiguity and lack of due process features of current statutes.

The idea of dangerousness has been a factor in civil procedures as well (*e.g., Underwood v. United States,* 356 F. 2d 92 (1966); *Fair v. United States,* 234 F. 2d 288 (1956); *Greenberg v. Barbour,* 322 F. Supp. 745 (1971)). Most recently, in *Tarasoff v. The Regents of the University of California* (520 P. 2d 553 (1976)), the court found that

> a patient with severe mental illness and dangerous proclivities may, in a given case, present a danger as serious and as foreseeable as does the carrier of a contagious disease. . . . We conclude that a doctor or a psychotherapist treating a mentally ill patient, just as a doctor treating physical illness, bears a duty to use reasonable care to give threatened persons such warnings as are essential to avert foreseeable danger arising from his patient's condition or treatment. (599)

As a final example of the legal significance of the term "dangerous," we note that in the area of civil liberties the Supreme Court has not improved upon the "clear and present danger" test as the one to be considered when balancing individual liberties with the needs of national security. Elsewhere (Levine, in press), I have developed at some length the manner in which the concept of dangerousness is involved in the area of civil liberties, in the working of the democratic political process, and even in the subtleties of family law and interpersonal processes.

Since the concept appears so often in our own legal system, it is not surprising to find that Classical, Oriental, and Moslem law have also relied heavily on the idea (Ancel, 1965, p. 28ff). The goal of "protecting the public from danger" is at the heart of the Positivist and the Social Defense schools of Criminology (Garofalo, 1914; Ancel, 1965) and is included in almost all Model Criminal Codes (Morris, 1974, p. 62ff). Katz (1969, 1972) goes so far as to set the concept of dangerousness as the essential cornerstone of a just and rational legal structure.

CRITICISMS OF THE CONCEPT

Although the term is widely used, it has not been free from criticism. Thirty-five years ago Michael & Wechsler (1940) wrote that

> the concept . . . of the criminal law as an instrument for social protection against dangerous persons . . . is neither as alien to our present law nor as helpful in solving its problems as many believe it to be. (p. 3)

However, it is only within the past fifteen years that the concept has been attacked vigorously (Goldstein & Katz, 1960)—and the tempo of the attacks seems to be accelerating (Dershowitz, 1970; Ennis & Litwack, 1974; Morris, 1974; Monahan, 1973, 1975; among others). Criticism has taken three forms: (1) The commonsense meaning of the term is too vague and ambiguous to permit the promulgation of a specific legal definition. (2) Legal definitions of the term have been rare, circular, misguided, or irrelevant. (3) Attempts to predict dangerousness have failed—and must fail for various methodological and theoretical reasons.

Commonsense Use of The Word is Ambiguous

Several writers (*e.g.*, Morris, 1968; Walker, 1969) have pointed out that when, in everyday speech, we refer to an offender as being dangerous we mean there is a high probability that in the future he will harm himself or another. This usage, they say, has two built-in ambiguities: What is meant by "harm"? And how probable is probable? Neither of these questions can be answered in a satisfactory manner.

While some people will want to restrict the use of the word to physical harm, others will include psychological harm. Still others will want to consider as dangerous those people with a predilection toward crimes involving theft of large sums of money or extensive property damage. A subsidiary ambiguity—but an important one—involves the question of how much harm needs to be done before the word "dangerous" is applicable. A black eye? A broken jaw? Disfigurement? How much psychological strain is dangerous?

Walker (1968) has suggested that one way to answer these questions is to determine the extent to which the harm is remediable. Although this removes some ambiguity, Walker recognizes that it does not completely resolve all the problems: How does one estimate the remediability of psychological harm? And, more basically, how does one compare a minor irremediable harm (a slight scar) with major remediable harm (severely painful injury which puts a person's life at risk, but does not leave a physical scar)? A particularly thorny difficulty is the fact that what causes one person irreparable harm may not bother another person at all, *e.g.*, the effect of indecent exposure on two different women, one an adolescent of rather strict upbringing and the other a more mature woman with a rather wider range of experience. This is not a problem, however, if one restrict dangerousness to physical harm (as, we shall see later, is done by the Scottish Council on Crime).

Willis (personal communication) has suggested that the word "dangerous" performs a function in everyday speech which is based on the very kind of ambiguity I have been describing. Once we know precisely the risk involved and the nature of the harm effected, we do not use the word "dangerous" but select a more specific word—perhaps "violent" or "habitual" or "homicidal," and so on.

Willis concludes that there is no sense trying to define dangerousness specifically because any definition will not accord with the use of the word in everyday speech and it is this use of the word that the public wants in the laws. Presumably, there are times when the law needs to be somewhat general.

Continuing this line of linguistic analysis, Messinger (personal communication) suggests that when we say a person is dangerous we are emphasizing the heinousness of the act (Znaniecki, 1936, pp. 356-357) rather than the likelihood of its occurrence. Thus, even when the likelihood is very small that a person will commit a particularly evil or harmful act, we speak of that person as being very dangerous, while if we are reasonably certain that a person will be a nuisance, but not seriously injure anyone, we do not usually call him dangerous.

Sarbin (1967) and Steadman (1973) refer to the etymology of the word in an attempt to clarify its meaning. Their writings are of interest in terms of an attributional analysis of the word, *i.e.,* under what circumstances the attribute "dangerous" is likely to be applied. Further research on this question is likely to be particularly fruitful (*e.g.,* Monahan & Cummings, 1974). The results thus far support the criticism that the everyday use of the word is too vague to be useful in a legal context.

But the word is used in the law.

Legal Definitions of Dangerousness

Judge David L. Bazelon has recently supplied us with a summary of the situation:

> Even more problematic [than diagnosing mental illness] is proof of dangerousness to self and others. Remaining largely undefined, application of these concepts [mental illness and dangerousness] by judge and jury may unduly reflect clinical definitions and conclusions rather than the appropriate judicial exegetics and community values. (*In re Bailey,* 482 F 2d 648, 665, 1973).

Although Bazelon is correct about the terms being largely undefined, there have been some attempts at legal definition both in England and in the United States. Unfortunately, these definitions have been circular, misguided, or irrelevant.

A typical example of a *circular* definition is that written into the U.S. Organized Crime Control Act of 1970 (18 U.S.C.A. 3575), which reads in part:

> ... (f) A defendant is dangerous for purposes of this section if a period of confinement longer than that provided for such felony is required for the protection of the public from further criminal conduct by the defendant.

Or consider the New York State Criminal Procedure Law as revised effective September 1, 1971. Section 730.10 defines a "dangerous incapacitated (incompetent) person" as an incapacitated person who is so mentally ill or mentally defective that his presence in an institution run by the Department of Mental Hygiene is dangerous to the safety of other patients therein, the staff of the institution or the community.

Both statutes—like many others—do not furnish *independent* procedures for determining if an offender is dangerous and must therefore be considered circular definitions.

Irrelevant legal definitions are those which have defined the dangerous offender in terms of a record of repeated offenses not necessarily related to the ones in question (*e.g.,* American Law Institute, 1962; Council of Judges, NCCD, 1972; Criminal Justice Act, 1967). It has become clear that these statutes—and ones modeled on them—are identifying the inadequate habitual offender rather than the person with a high potential for causing a particular serious harm (Hammond & Chayen, 1963; Home Office *Criminal Statistics*). The idea of using past behavior to predict future behavior makes much sense and deserves careful consideration. If one wants to predict serious assaultive behavior, however, one should probably not be concerned with a past history of burglary—or vice versa.

Judicial interpretation of the law has not helped matters—quite the contrary, on occasion. In *Overholzer v. Russell* the defendant had been found not guilty by reason of insanity on a charge of writing bad checks. He appealed the continuing medical decision that he needed to remain in the mental hospital. In denying his appeal, the court held:

The danger to the public need not be possible physical violence or a crime of violence. It is enough if there is competent evidence that he may commit *any* criminal act, for any such act will injure others and will expose the person to arrest, trial, and conviction. There is always the additional possible danger—not to be discounted even if remote—that a nonviolent criminal act may expose the perpetrator to violent retaliatory acts by the victim of the crime. (238 F. 2d 195, 1960)

The potential injustice of such a ruling seems clear.

The English Criminal Court of Appeals has also grappled with the problem of defining under what conditions

it is thought the protection of the public is required. . . . . for example the case of crimes of violence, and of the more serious sexual offenses, particularly if the prisoner has a record of such offenses, or if there is a history of mental disorder involving violent behavior. (Practice Note, Gardiner's Case, 1967 Crim. L. R. 231)

Critics will note that the examples cited leave untouched the crucial definitional problems: What is a crime of violence? Does any use of physical force define behavior as violent? How serious is a "more serious sexual offense"? And finally the Practice Note reintroduces the highly controversial notion that mental disorder and dangerousness are somehow related. (See Ennis & Litwack, 1974, for a recent summary of this controversy.)

The most recent attempt by the court of Appeals, Criminal Division, to clarify the matter (*Regina v. Turner and Others*) occurs during the justices' consideration of lengthy prison sentences:

> Criminals have tended to become more and more sophisticated. They had become a bigger danger to the public.... serious crimes fall into [two] categories. [The first category is serious crimes] which are quite abnormal, their circumstances [are] horrifying and they [may] lead to danger to the state. [Into] this category fell the Great Train Robbery, bad cases of espionage, and cases of very great or horrid violence such as were instanced in the Richardson "torture trial" in the 1960's ... [as well as] bomb outrages, acts of political terrorism and, possibly in the future, political kidnapping.

> [The second category is crimes which] could not be regarded as wholly abnormal ... such as bank robberies ... such as the present one ... where in general violence was not inflicted although it was threatened.... a girl cashier who attempted to ring the alarm bell was kicked in the head ... a man was injured when a firearm was discharged. (Law Report, *The Times*, March 12, 1975)

Although the judges use the term "bigger danger," which suggests they have a continuum of danger in mind, they so emphasize the dichotomous classification that one is uncertain as to their meaning. Their attempt to give concrete illustrations of the two categories can be considered a positive step in the direction of "pouring substantive content" (Goldstein & Katz, 1960) into a conception of dangerousness. However, their reliance on the notion of "normality" will probably lead to further confusion and their selection of examples does highlight the continuing importance of subjective value judgments in determining what behavior will be labelled "dangerous."

This very brief review suggests that little progress has been made since Goldstein & Katz (1960) claim that dangerous behavior [has been] construed to include:

(1) only the crime for which [an] insanity defense was successfully raised;
(2) all crimes;
(3) only felonious crimes (as opposed to misdemeanors);
(4) only crimes for which a given maximum sentence or more is authorized;
(5) only crimes categorized as violent;
(6) only crimes categorized as harmful, physically or psychologically, reparable or irreparable, to the victim;
(7) any conduct, even if not labelled criminal, categorized as violent, harmful, or threatening;
(8) any conduct which may provoke retaliatory acts [probably *Overholzer v. Russell*];
(9) any physical violence toward oneself;
(10) any combination of these.

Predicting Dangerousness

Despite all this ambiguity, much of the criticism would be silenced could an empirical demonstration be made of the possibility of identifying in advance those people who are prone to commit seriously violent criminal acts. Therefore, when Kozol et al. (1972) claimed to have demonstrated that "dangerousness in criminal offenders can be reliably diagnosed and effectively treated with a recidivism rate of 6.1%," critics analyzed their research carefully. Morris (1974) and Monahan (1973), among others, have decided that Kozol's conclusions are unwarranted. Some critics have gone further and, citing the series of Baxstrom studies (*e.g.,* Steadman & Keveles, 1972) and the Wenk et al. study (1972), have stressed the futility of continuing the attempt to identify dangerous offenders.

Although the critics' case is a strong one, there are complexities in the methodology which deserve further consideration before this line of research can be abandoned. In support of their arguments, Kozol's claims obviously capitalize on the *base rate* phenomenon (Meehl & Rosen, 1955) which will always plague this kind of prediction research: only about 10% of his released patients became recidivists.

Although the concept of *base rate* is a relatively simple one, surprisingly few people are alert to the situations in which it may lead to inflated claims of predictive or therapeutic efficiency. The Kozol et al. claim that "treatment [of dangerousness] was successful in modifying the dangerous potential of 94% of the patients we recommended for discharge after treatment for an average of 43 months" is a perfect illustration of *base rate* error. It is a result of the fact that of the 82 patients for whom they recommended release, 77 did not commit a further serious crime of violence during the follow-up period (Table I). 77/82 x 100 = 94%. However, 72% (13 divided by 18) of the inmates whom they considered still dangerous but whom the courts released against the psychiatric advice also did not commit further crimes of violence.

A much more parsimonious interpretation of the findings is that 90% of the inmates kept in the institution for four years (on the average) will not commit further crimes of violence—and that "treatment" or "psychiatric recommendations" are of only minor importance. This 90% figure is the *base rate* for further crimes of violence and is the most reasonable figure against which to make any claims of predictive efficiency. Elsewhere in this chapter, I point out the importance of assigning social values and costs to the correct and incorrect predictions in this kind of situation. Kozol et al. may perhaps claim that their diagnostic opinion was better than the court's, *i.e.,* 94% compared to 72%—but that is the very most they can claim.

Thus the critics correctly attack these and similar claims of very high predictive accuracy because these claims capitalize on the very high percentage of "hits" when one predicts that a person will *not* act in a violent manner, but this high percentage of "hits" conceals the relative inaccuracy of positive predictions,

TABLE I[a]

**Inmates of Bridgewater Center for Dangerous Persons
Incarcerated for an Average Period of
Four Years and Then Released**

	No Recidivism During Follow-up	Recidivism During Follow-up	Total
Recommended for release by psychiatric staff	77	5	82
Released by court against psychiatric recommendation	13	5	18
Total	90	10	100

[a]Data from Kozol et al. (1972).

i.e., predicting that a person *will* act in a violent manner. However, some critics lead their readers to infer that because the claims based on "hit rate" are misleading, the predictions are no better than chance. This is going too far: although clinical methods are not successful at a level of 94% efficiency, the predictions made by Kozol's team are more accurate in terms of simple hit rate than those which the court made against the staff's recommendations—and the difference is statistically significant (Kozol et al., 1972).

Second, the Kozol data—like the Baxstrom results—are based on the hard-to-predict cases; where the courts and the psychiatrists agree that an offender is dangerous, he remains incarcerated and there is no way to evaluate the accuracy of these predictions. Approximately 25% of Kozol's group remain in Bridgewater Center for Diagnosis and Treatment of Dangerous Offenders and almost 50% of the Baxstrom patients remain in civil mental hospitals. There is most likely a great deal of overprediction of dangerousness involved, but releasing these people would probably lead to higher recidivism rates.

Third, although there is this overprediction, the rate of assaultive behavior among these patients does seem higher than one would expect from a random sample of citizens: 26% of the Baxstrom women and 20% of the men were assaultive after their transfer to a civil mental hospital (Halfon et al., 1972, p. 2). This rate might have been even higher had the patients been transferred or released years ago, when they were younger, since Steadman & Keveles (1972) have substantiated, in the Baxstrom sample, the expected relationship between age and recidivism. (Also see Cocozza & Steadman, 1974).

Furthermore, the criterion of reconviction leads to an overestimation of the number of false positives. Steadman & Keveles (1972) note:

> When an individual is known at the time of his apprehension or becomes known after the arrest as an ex-mental patient, he is often rehospitalized rather than booked. . . . we found a number of instances documented in clinical notes where the police apprehended an individual for assault and property damage but rehospitalized him rather than charged him.

Thus there is the lingering possibility—which will die hard—that the claims of clinical psychiatrists and psychologists have some validity, that there are some few—perhaps very few—people about whom a valid prediction can be made (see Panel Report, 1973, for a relatively convincing case). I have recently come across some substantiation of this notion (Steer, personal communication). Walker et al. (1970) showed that—although there were the usual false positives—the probability of further convictions for crimes of violence increased directly with the number of previous convictions for crimes of violence, e.g., from 12% after one conviction to 67% after four convictions. What is relevant here is that after five convictions the rate goes to 100%—but on the basis on only 2 cases. In other words, from the original sample of 4,301 men, 264 committed one or more crimes of violence. Of these 264, 2 men committed five crimes of violence; both of them went on and committed a sixth and a seventh crime of violence. If one would have predicted that five convictions leads to further convictions, there would have been no false positives and no false negatives. I cite this only to emphasize the complexity of this kind of research; I have critized it in other ways (Levine, in press).

THE DILEMMA RESTATED

The scaffolding for the dilemma has now been erected. On the one hand, society through its laws, policies, and regulations has been developing procedures for its self-protection which rely heavily on the use of predictions of dangerous behavior. On the other hand, it has been shown that these predictions are bound to be in error some—if not most—of the time. Under the Fifth and Fourteenth amendments every *individual* is guaranteed a right of due process such that he may not be deprived of his liberty if the decision process involved is arbitrary, capricious, or discriminatory. In those countries without these written protections, principles of justice and fairness raise the same barrier. If our predictions are accurate only in extreme cases (Morris, 1968; Walker, 1969), any use of predictions of dangerousness as a criterion for incarceration runs afoul of these constitutional safeguards or principles of justice.

COMPROMISE

We have seen, then, that the word "dangerousness" defies simple definition and prediction; leading critics recommend a moratorium on its use. Some scholars have suggested that since trying to predict dangerousness is bound to fail because of the overwhelming importance of situational and contextual variables, research with this as its aim should be discontinued (Sarbin, 1967; Tedeschi, 1974). Nevertheless, the public still wants to be protected, Model Penal Codes continue to use the concept, and clinicians and researchers still believe they can make a contribution for dealing with a serious social problem. Compromise between these opposing camps seems desirable from the perspective of research planning and from the perspective of legislative reform.

Research Planning

A compromise position recognizes that research can be useful if it supplies new information but that it can be harmful if its results are misinterpreted because of improper methodology. I will outline briefly some requirements of sound design in prediction research:

(1) *The Criterion*
   (a) The criterion to be predicted needs to be specified clearly and operationally, *e.g.*, number of convictions for crimes involving physical assault. Dangerousness, as such, is too general a criterion to be predicted.
   (b) The possibility of a complex criterion must be taken into account. Predictor variables related to one aspect or definition of the criterion might be unrelated to another, *e.g.*, the person who will commit planned acts of violence is probably different from the person who will commit impulsive violence (*e.g.*, Megargee, 1966).
   (c) The criterion should be quantified on a scale which includes more than 2 points so that nonlinear relationships might be uncovered.
   (d) The question of *criterion validity* should not be taken for granted. (See above note concerning diversion of Baxstrom patients from the criminal justice system.)

(2) *Predictors*
   (a) Besides being operationally clear, the predictors in any study should probably include both clinical and statistical measures (Sawyer, 1966).
   (b) One should consider the possibility that moderator variables would be effective in improving prediction (*e.g.*, Bem & Allen, 1974).
   (c) Some consideration needs to be given to the difficult problem of

utilizing ecological variables, in interaction or covariation with personality variables, as predictors. One can, for example, easily imagine some people who are provoked by authority when it is present and others who are cowed by it. Those cowed by authority, however, may be particularly dangerous when they are in control while those who are provoked by authority may not be dangerous at all when they are in power (*e.g.,* Toch, 1969; Tedeschi, 1974).

(3) *Statistical Analysis*
   (a) Care should be taken with sample selection so that one ends up using a sample with a sizable base rate, and does not exclude a subsample about whom predictions have a greater chance of success.
   (b) Cross-validation, if original relationships were not specified in advance, need to be undertaken.
   (c) Possibility of nonlinear relationships should be explored.
   (d) The problem of assigning value and cost estimates to correct and incorrect predictions will need to be faced (*e.g.,* Bishir & Drewes, 1970, pp. 576-578). Simple hit rates are pragmatically useless (Buchwald, 1965).

What this outline implies is that thorough research on this subject has not been done and may not be feasible. Thus any conclusions should be studied carefully and social planning based on these conclusions undertaken with extreme caution. Because the fact that no research has been particularly successful in eliminating false positives does not mean that dangerousness is completely unpredictable. It means that some of the variance—perhaps a substantial amount—remains unexplained.

Legislative Reform

This leaves us, as a society, in the uncomfortable position of wanting protection from danger but being advised that it is unfair to imprison those we feel might harm us. Morris' (1974) recommendation that

> as a matter of justice we should never take power over the convicted criminal on the basis of unreliable predictions of his dangerousness

is unpersuasive—despite its appeal on a moral plane and from a constitutional perspective—because: (1) the research which he cites to support his recommendation is, as I have discussed, open to alternative interpretations; (2) even if the research demonstrated that dangerousness is unpredictable, such a finding goes against people's intuitive beliefs that they can predict dangerousness (Bem & Allen, 1974); and (3) in any event, the need for a feeling of safety is very powerful (Levine, in press; Sarbin, 1967).

What is likely to happen is a series of compromises: legislation will be passed which does allow for a special category of "dangerous offender" but which also has built-in safeguards against the abuse of civil liberties in the name of public protection or national security (Ginsberg & Klockhars, 1974). The most carefully developed example of such legislation with which I am familiar is the Scottish Council on Crime's recent recommendation for the establishment of a "public protection order" (1975).

Like most attempts at legislative compromise, it will satisfy neither extreme position. Its aim, however, is stated clearly enough:

> to secure the continued detention of a violence-prone offender until it is safe for him to be released, to protect the country from such offender. (39)

(1) *Selection of offenders:* The order can only be obtained "where the accused is convicted of an offense involving physical harm." This definition of dangerousness will not satisfy those who want to be protected from all dangers, but the Scottish Council apparently decided that, as a first step toward legislative reform, it might be well to concentrate on physical violence, leaving to some future date the difficulties of psychological harm, property damage, and sexual offenses.

In addition, it must be

> established, by evidence... that there is substantial likelihood that the offender is the sort of person who... will, if set at large, commit acts causing or threatening physical harm to others and there is no other adequate means of protecting the public. (66)

This evidence must include written opinions by a psychiatrist and a clinical psychologist, plus a social inquiry report. It is, of course, this feature of the proposal which is anathema to critics like Morris and Monahan; they will say that no one—not even, perhaps especially not, the experts—can make this kind of prediction. But unless one goes to determinate sentences and no parole, courts and parole boards cannot be prevented from taking this variable into account, and there is probably some advantage in having an independent person (why not then a trained one?) review the complete file of the offender and advise the judge or the prison administrator.

Furthermore, in this regard, the proposal is no different from a hospital order (Mental Health Act, 1959) or civil commitment proceedings in the United States, except that under a "public protection order" there is no need to find the defendant "mentally ill." In fact, the public protection order cannot be used with mentally ill offenders. Given the increasing controversy surrounding that label, perhaps the substitution of "dangerousness" for "mental illness" is neither progress nor regress. Proponents of the new recommendation will argue that judgments of dangerousness are no *less* reliable or valid than diagnoses of mental illness; critics will reply that they are no *more* reliable either.

(2) *Safeguards:* Although the proposal recommends that detention may be indefinite, there are three kinds of safeguards:

(a) The order *must* be reviewed every two years by a body such as the parole board.

(b) A positive case must be established for continued detention.

(c) A right of appeal against the making of the order, as well as a right of appeal at the stage of every two-yearly review, is granted to the offender.

For those who object to any legislation of this kind, these safeguards will not be sufficient. The proposal will be more palatable, however, than most "habitual offender," "dangerous sexual offender," or civil commitment legislation.

One final note: the extent to which the concept "dangerousness" and the concept "mental illness" are in fact related or in social and legal policy should be related to one another is a continuing controversy. Most attempts at improving mental health laws so that they do not violate due process considerations are placing increasing emphasis on the concept of "dangerousness."

A more reasonable solution, it seems to me, is to change our sentencing and commitment regulations, procedures, and laws so that they are tied strictly to past acts of serious physical violence. What little research is available justifies such a step (*e.g.,* Walker et al., 1970) and it is a recommendation which does not present any constitutional hinderances. Concretely, while a first offense involving serious physical violence might be punishable by a sentence of one to two years, the second offense of this kind would lead to a term of two to five years, a third to four to seven, etc.

No social or legal policy will guarantee the public safety against all dangers since it is well established that some acts of very serious physical violence are unplanned, explosive outbursts by people who have spent many years overcontrolling their emotions (Megargee, 1966; Blackburn, 1968). Furthermore, a conflict theory of social and human behavior suggests that danger is inherent in human life. Nevertheless, it is clear the substantial legislative and judicial activity is under way and that a reasonable balance between public safety and individual rights is a not-unrealistic goal.

FOOTNOTE

[1] This chapter is based on a paper presented at the National Criminology Conference, Institute of Criminology, Cambridge University, July 9-11, 1975. Much of the work on the chapter was completed during the academic year 1974-75 while the author was Visiting Fellow, Institute of Criminology, Cambridge University. Appreciation is expressed to Nigel Walker, D.J. West, David Thomas, and David Farrington for their help and support. I am also indebted to Bruce Sales for his assistance, especially with regard to constitutional issues, but then my indebtedness to Bruce far transcends his assistance on this chapter. Of course, the responsibility for any errors is the author's.

REFERENCES

American Law Institute. *Modern penal code: Proposed official draft.* Philadelphia: ALI, 1962.

Ancel, M. *Social defense.* London: Routledge, 1965.

Bem, D. & Allen, A. On predicting some of the people some of the time. *Psychological Review,* 1974, *81,* 506-520.

Bishir, J.W. & Drewes, D.W. *Mathematics in the behavioral and social sciences.* New York: Harcourt, Brace & World, 1970.

Blackburn, R. Personality in relation to extreme aggression in psychiatric offend rs. *The British Journal of Psychiatry,* 1968, *114,* 821-828.

Buchwald, A.M. Values and the use of tests. *Journal of Consulting Psychology,* 1965, *29,* 49-54.

Cocozza, J.J. & Steadman, H.J. Some refinements in the measurement and prediction of dangerous behavior. *American Journal of Psychiatry,* 1974, *131,* 1012-1015.

Council of Judges, National Council on Crime and Delinquency. *Model Sentencing Act,* 2d ed. Washington, D.C.: NCCD, 1972.

Dershowitz, A.M. The law of dangerousness: Some fictions about predictions. *Journal of Legal Education,* 1970, *23,* 24-47.

Doremus et al. v. Farrell et al., U.S. District Court, Nebraska Civil No. 75-0-168.

Ennis, B.J. & Litwack, T.R. Psychiatry and the presumption of expertise: Flipping coins in the courtroom. *California Law Review,* 1974, *62,* 693-752.

Garofalo, R. *Criminology.* Boston: Little, Brown, 1914.

Ginsberg, P.H. & Klockars, M. "Dangerous offenders" and legislative reform. *Willamette Law Journal,* 1974, *10,* 167-184.

Goldstein, J. & Katz, J. Dangerousness and mental illness: Some observations on the decision to release persons acquitted by reason of insanity. *Yale Law Journal,* 1960, *70,* 225-239.

Halfon, A., David, M. & Steadman, H.J. The Baxstrom women: A four-year follow-up of behavior patterns. *Psychiatric Quarterly,* 1972, *45,* 1-10.

Hammond, W.H. & Chayen, E. *Persistent criminals.* London: HMSO, 1963.

Katz, A. Dangerousness: A theoretical reconstruction of the criminal law. *Buffalo Law Review,* 1969, *19,* 1-33.

Kozol, H.L., Boucher, R.J. & Garofalo, R.F. The diagnosis and treatment of dangerousness. *Crime and Delinquency,* 1972, *18,* 371-392.

Kozol, H.J., Boucher, R.J. & Garofalo, R.F. Dangerousness: Letter to the editor. *Crime and Delinquency,* 1973, *19,* 554-555.

Levine, D. Crime, mental illness, and political dissent. In J. Tapp & F. Levine (eds.), *Legal socialization: Issues for psychology and law,* 1976a, in press.

Levine, D. Careers of violence: Further comments. *British Journal of Criminology,* 1976b, in press.

Meehl, P.E. & Rosen, A. Antecedent probability and the efficiency of psychometric signs, patterns, or cutting scores. *Psychological Bulletin,* 1955, *52,* 194-216.

Megargee, E.I. Undercontrolled and overcontrolled personality types in extreme antisocial aggression. *Psychological Monographs,* 1966, *80* (3).

Michael, J. & Wechsler, H. *Criminal law and its administration.* Chicago: University of Chicago Press, 1940.

Monahan, J. Dangerous offenders: A critique of Kozol et al. *Crime & Delinquency,* 1973, *19,* 418-420.

Monahan, J. The prevention of violence. In J. Monahan (ed.), *Community mental health and the criminal justice system.* New York: Pergamon Press, 1975.

Monahan, J. & Cummings, L. Prediction of dangerousness as a function of its perceived consequences. *Journal of Criminal Justice*, 1974, *2*, 239-242.

Morris, N. Psychiatry and the dangerous criminal. *Southern California Law Review*, 1968, *41*, 514-547.

Nebraska State Bar Association. Committee on Mental Health. *A Proposed Nebraska Mental Health Commitment Act*. October 4, 1975.

Panel Report: When is dangerous, dangerous? *Journal of Psychiatry and Law*, 1973, *1*, 427-461.

Report of the Committee on Mentally Abnormal Offenders. Cmnd. 6244. London: HMSO, 1975.

Sarbin, T.R. The dangerous individual: an outcome of social identity transformation. *British Journal of Criminology*, 1967, *7*, 285-295.

Sawyer, J. Measurement and prediction, clinical and statistical. *Psychological Bulletin*, 1966, *66*, 178-200.

Scottish Council on Crime. *Crime and the prevention of crime*. London: HMSO, 1975.

Steadman, H.J. Some evidence on the inadequacy of the concept and determination of dangerousness in law and psychiatry. *The Journal of Psychiatry and Law*, 1973, *1*, 409-426.

Steadman, H.J. & Keveles, G. The community adjustment and criminal activity of the Baxstrom patients: 1966-1970. *American Journal of Psychiatry*, 1972, *129*, 302-310.

Tarasoff v. Regents, 529 P. 2d 553.

Tedeschi, J.T. et al. A reinterpretation of research on aggression. *Psychological Bulletin*, 1974, *81*, 540-563.

Toch, H. *Violent men*. Chicago: University of Chicago Press, 1969.

Walker, N. *Sentencing in a rational society*. London, 1969.

Walker, N., Hammond, W. & Steer, D. Careers of violence. In *The violent offender: Reality or illusion*. Occasional paper No. 1. Oxford: Oxford Penal Research Unit, 1970.

Wenk, E.A. et al. Can violence be predicted? *Crime and Delinquency*, 1972, *18*, 393-402.

Znaniecki, F. *Social actions*. New York: Russell & Russell, 1936.

10

Sentencing: Discretion and Justice in Judicial Decision-Making[1]

WILLIAM AUSTIN
MARY KRISTINE UTNE

A SOCIAL PSYCHOLOGICAL VIEW OF THE LEGAL PROCESS

In recent years, observers of the American legal system have begun to focus less on its structural aspects and more on the social psychological processes which operate within the legal system. Rather than studying the static components endemic to the study of legal codes, jurisdictions, or legal roles, legal scholars are now pointing to the dynamic, fluid nature of relationships among legal actors. For example, researchers have: (1) isolated factors which predispose police officers to exercise their discretion to warn instead of arrest offenders; (2) studied the effect of personal characteristics of arrested individuals on the likelihood of being granted bail, the amount of bail stipulated, and the length of sentence they receive if they are found guilty; (3) studied the impact of judges' background on the kinds of sentences they impose; and (4) studied the effect of defendants' personal qualities and case histories on jurors' decisions.

Recent studies on what can be called the social ecology of the courtroom demonstrate the value of juxtaposing and integrating interpersonal and structural dimensions of the court. This research (cf. Blumberg, 1967; Suffet, 1967; Sudnow, 1965; Newman, 1966) provides an accurate view of the metropolitan court. It indicates that the quality of those social relationships among legal actors, which operate amidst the court's formal structure (*i.e.,* reccurrent roles, laws, norms), often function as the most important variable in the final disposition of a court case. In this regard, the descriptive work of Blumberg (1967) and others thoroughly documents the mutual influences processes in the court and reveals how the social interaction patterns affect judicial decisions. This research describes how law enforcers (police and prosecution) and members of the court (judges, clerks, public defenders, defense attorneys) regularly interact with one another under a common set of experiences and expectations. While many new individuals appear and old ones disappear as new arrests are made, the judicial process retains a large measure of interpersonal continuity. The main actors usually remain, and their behavior is constantly influenced by their shared past and future. Police, prosecutors, judges, and defense attorneys alike must conform to and cope with the recurring demands of their system in and around the courtroom. For example, since nine out of ten cases are resolved via plea bargaining the prosecutor must be sensitive to his/her future dealings with a particular defense attorney; the defense attorney must learn to coexist with the prosecutor and his/her staff, and each in turn must learn to coexist with various courtroom personnel.

One salient aspect of the courtroom and the judicial system is the judicial decision, particularly the judicial sanction. In the remainder of this chapter we will concentrate on it exclusively. We will consider judicial decisions as system outcomes, the result of personal and interpersonal influences, and structural restraints (or lack thereof) of the court and the larger judicial system. The interpersonal dynamics of judicial decision-making are complex, largely because of the amount of *discretion* at the disposal of judges. Discretion can be loosely defined as the ability to make decisions and perform acts which are not subject to review by outside authorities (see Reiss, 1974). This discretionary power means that a plethora of variables—legal and extralegal—often affect judges and jurors' appraisal of a case and their ultimate decision. Thus we will look at judicial discretion and review research on extralegal factors which seem to influence judicial decisions. We will then assess the implications of legal goals of judicial punishment for the exercise of that judicial judgment.

OVERVIEW OF JUDICIAL DECISION-MAKING: SOURCES OF TENSION

The General Law vs. the Specific Case

As with the general operation of the court as a social system, the trial proceeding and its culmination in the judicial decision can be properly viewed as a social psychological process. The judicial decision is the product of an interaction among the judge, jury, defendant, defense attorney, and prosecutor—with the shadow of the nature and severity of the alleged offense tempering the quality of the relationships. Modern criminologists seem to agree that exposing the interpersonal dynamics surrounding the judicial decision places it in a "realistic" perspective. For example, Richard Quinney (1970), a noted criminologist, states:

> The criminal trial may be most profitably analyzed as a system of human actions that entails perceptions and behaviors the like of which are found in any social situation. The persons involved in the trial are acting according to their own pasts, their present perspectives, and their future expectations; and their actions are oriented to the behavior of others. (158)

While the judicial decision is influenced by inputs from all of the main courtroom actors, the judge is the central influential character. Even in jury trials the judge's presence predominates. The pervasiveness of this influence is manifested by the way the judge exerts centralized *control over the flow of information:* he/she rules on admissibility of evidence, oversees courtroom procedure, instructs the jury on matters of law, and finally may impose a "gag rule" preventing participants and/or media people from discussing the case outside the court. An even more vivid demonstration of the judge's power lies in his/her sentencing capacity. In the vast majority of cases, it is judges who set the sentences for convicted offenders.

Although the judge's power contributes continuity to the court, each judicial decision evolves from an unpredictable social process. This assertion may confuse the naïve observer whose impression is that a judicial decision is arrived at in a relatively straightforward manner: facts are presented, the defendant is judged guilty or not, and a "reasonable" sentence is imposed. However, there are a number of factors which add considerable complexity and variability to judicial decision, making them not so "straightforward" at all. First, the very general nature of most laws often results in vagueness, forcing the judge to impose his/her own interpretation on these laws. Second, the fact of the "uniqueness" of each legal case—perhaps conforming to Leibnitz's "principle of indiscernables" that no two cases are alike—means that jurors and judges consider each case and its remedy in the context of its own peculiar circumstances. Third, the amount of judicial discretion (*i.e.,* judges' control over information, jurors' *absolute* discretion to convict or acquit, and judges' sentencing powers) is the structural variable through which all sources of unpredictability are funneled.

These three sources of legal uncertainty act together to produce the major challenge facing judges and jurors: to fairly apply the law in light of the specific "facts of the case." This stands as the main point of tension in the decision-maker's mind. He/she must be sensitive to the principles reflected in the mottos "Treat similar cases similarly" and "Make the punishment fit the crime," both of which call for *strict application* of the "letter of the law." On the other hand, decision-makers must be mindful of the legal dicta, "Treat each case on its own merits" and "Fit the punishment to the criminal," which call for *flexible interpretations* of the law.

This tension between the simultaneous generality of the *law* (*i.e.,* structural consideration) and the specificity of the *legal case* (*i.e.,* personal and interpersonal factors) has been discussed by legal philosophers and theorists for centuries. Since this is one of the central issues in judicial decision-making, it may be useful for us to pause here and examine the views of two legal philosophers, Aristotle and Kant, on the dialectic between application and interpretation of the law. For both philosophers, this dialectic, or tension, was embodied in the concept of "equity," meaning in this instance "the consideration of special mitigating circumstances before rendering a legal decision." Aristotle (1912) emphasized the importance of equity in his defense of judicial flexibility.

> Equity, though just, is not legal justice, but a rectification of legal justice. The reason for this is that law is always a general statement, yet there are cases which it is not possible to cover in a general statement. In matters, therefore, while it is necessary to speak in general terms, it is not possible to do so correctly, the law takes into consideration the majority of cases, although it is not unaware of the error this involves. And this does not make it a wrong law; for the error is not in the law or the lawgiver, but in the nature of the case: the material of conduct is essentially irregular. When therefore the law lays down a general rule, and thereafter an exception arises which is an exception to the rule, it is then right, where the lawgiver's pronouncement, because of its absoluteness, is defective and erroneous, to rectify the defect by deciding as the lawgiver would himself decide if he were present on the occasion, and would have enacted, if he had been cognizant of the case in question. (1137b)

Thus Aristotle's criterion in the evaluation of a judicial decision was its "justness," and only when a judge considered all the facts—legal and extralegal—could a just decision be reached. Kant, on the other hand, was less "permissive;" he emphasized "strict justice." Kant believed that laws were formed by "reasonable men" and that in the vast majority of cases justice and the "good of the state" were served by strict adherence to laws. In this regard, Kant's (1965) logical analysis led him to the following extreme position:

> It is the people's duty to endure even the most intolerable abuse of supreme authority. The reason for this is that resistance to the supreme legislation can itself only be unlawful. (86)

However, Kant maintained that individuals also had a *right* to appeal to equity in individual cases—with the implication that judges had an obligation to consider mitigating circumstances. In fact, he referred to equity as "a silent goddess who cannot be heard" (p. 40) and took the strong position that "The strictest justice is the greatest injustice" (p. 40). Thus Kant seemed to strongly favor both strict application of the law and judicial flexibility—at first glance a strange position for one who courted logic in the way Kant did. This contradiciton is more apparent than real. Kant was merely advocating a strong position which we can call "structured equity"—a compromise between dialectical opposites of strict application and flexibility. Kant simply believed judges should exercise their discretion frugally; he implied that judges should consider only certain selected mitigating factors.

It is reassuring that the case for judicial flexibility rests on the writings of distinguished philosophers because this seems to be the norm among contemporary judges. Numerous legal scholers have described the "activist" positions of judges in interpreting the law (Jacob, 1965) and the movement toward a "realist" decision-making style (Chambliss & Seidman, 1971) which emphasizes making punishment consistent with the needs and circumstances of the individual offender. Moreover, while we acknowledge that the *degree* of latitude in judicial decision-making is a politically sensitive issue, there is growing evidence in psychology that consideration of contextual factors prior to decision-making is indicative of "advanced" stages of cognitive and moral development (cf. Kohlberg, 1969). Surely, we want our legal decisions to reflect the best qualities of human judgment. Judicial discretion allows for this potential. However, discretionary power can just as well result in arbitrariness as justice in prejudice as well as sympathy. Discretion thus makes the decision a *human* process. Quinney (1970) aptly summarized this fact:

> The decisions during the trial, including the decision that ultimately defines the defendant as a convicted criminal, are made by men as social beings. That is to say, though the criminal trial is not an exercise in fact finding and logical deduction, it is a product of human action. Could something else be expected? (159)

We will examine judicial discretion in more detail below. But first we will review some other sources of tension in the decision-making process.

Reconciliation of Expectations

In the previous section we focused on tension stemming from the decision-maker's attempt to apply the general law in light of information specific to the case at hand. The decision-maker, principally the judge, faces pressures from still other sources, also calling upon him/her to render discretionary judgments. For one, the judge must satisfy legal stipulations and expectations regarding "procedural safeguards." The judge must determine if the rights of the accused have been violated prior to trial and ensure that they be protected during the trial. Evidence obtained by illegal means must be excluded *(Weeks v. United States);* confessions obtained prior to arraignment before a magistrate cannot be admitted *(Mallory v. United States);* information obtained from illegal searches and seizures must be invalidated *(Mapp v. Ohio);* defendants must be granted a right to legal counsel *(Gideon v. Wainwright; Escobedo v. Illinois);* and the accused must be informed of his rights at the time of arrest *(Miranda v. Arizona).*

At the same time, the judge (as well as jurors, to a lesser extent) confronts often contradictory expectations regarding the proper function of punishing convicted criminal offenders. The decision-maker has his/her own views, and senses, or is made explicitly aware of, the expectations of the prosecutor, the defense, and the community. The task of the judge is to reconcile these divergent views: Should the offender be punished to deter crime in general? To deter the specific offense for which he/she was convicted? To establish equity? To gain retribution for society and the victim? To rehabilitate the offender? Should pragmatic considerations of efficient functioning of the court system be a relevant consideration? These pressures force the decision-maker, and especially the judge in his/her sentencing capacity, to develop a personal "Theory of Punishment," an articulation of the goals of punishment against which to evaluate competing demands for action. It is not an easy task and apparently not often achieved. In fact, the court system is in a state of confusion today. New procedural safeguards such as dictated by the Miranda case ruling and recently enacted "gag rules" compete with public demands to "get tough" with criminals, all in an arena where the goals of punishment are uncertain. These pressures are still further compounded by judicial discretion.

THE ROLE OF DISCRETION IN JUDICIAL DECISION-MAKING

Models of Judicial Decision-Making

The amount of discretion at the disposal of judges makes the task of rendering a decision a complex one. Not only must the judge render a verdict and impose sentence, but he/she is required to make a multitude of decisions in pre-trial hearings and during the conduct of the trial, each of which has varying degrees of impact on the final decisions. The judge's task is thus made difficult by the number of decisions and their summary effect. Still more important in creating the complexity is the sheer amount of information and different types of pressures impinging upon the judge. There are three types of forces bearing on the judges: *structural* factors stemming from the judge's role (judicial canons, law, the judge's status), *personal* variables regarding the judge's background (his attitudes, experiences, personality), and *information* coming from associated legal actors regarding the specific case.

The variability of these forces makes judicial decisions unpredictable as well as complex. Structural or role factors are fairly stationary, but personal factors vary among judges, and the judge is often at the mercy of others for the quantity and quality of information. For example, a judge's case load prohibits his/her direct involvement in preparation of a pre-sentence report—often the basis for sentencing. Therefore, a judge's sentence is often heavily influenced by the investigation and report of a single probation officer.

The judge's task, then, is to integrate personal qualities with structural guidelines and to forge case-relevant information into a fair and efficacious decision. The judge in his/her role as a third party must synthesize assorted inputs into a finished product. The noted jurist Jerome Frank iterates this point: "The judge, at his best, is an arbitrator, a 'sound man' who strives to do justice to the parties by exercising a wise discretion with reference to the peculiar circumstances of the case."[2]

Legal theorists have proposed various decision-making models of judicial behavior with the goal of eventually *predicting* the outcomes from legal proceedings. These theorists have presented frameworks for identifying types of *input* factors *(i.e., judges' attitudes, pre-sentence report, severity of offense)* and their importance for the judicial decision *(i.e., the outcome)*. These theoretical models vary in sophistication and level of analysis. Chambliss & Seidman (1971) present a sociological picture of the legal system. They identify the effect of *structural inputs,* such as the court structure in appellate courts, and their impact on the *court system (i.e., structural outcomes)* as well as on the individual case. Hood & Sparks (1970) present a more social psychological view by focusing on the courtroom instead of the court system, identifying what they call the "flow of information" in the courtroom (see Fig. 1). The final decision is presented as the joint product of structural inputs of the court and personal and case-relevant informational inputs of the actors. Finally, Kaplan & Kemmerick (1974) offer a psychological representation of the judicial decision. They attempt to apply Anderson's "information integration theory" (see Anderson, 1974) to judicial judgment. This technique may help researchers uncover how judges and jurors code and weight relevant information into one total judgment. Extrapolating from Kaplan & Kemmerick, the general formula for integrating evidential and nonevidential information on a guilt dimension with a previous impression stands as

$$J = \frac{W_o S_o + K W_e S_e + K W_{ne} S_{ne}}{W_o + K W_e + K W_{ne}}$$

where J = judicial judgment; S_o = the preexisting impression; W_o = weight assigned to preexisting impression of K stimuli; S_e = guilt value for evidential factors; S_{ne} = guilt value for nonevidential factors; W_e and W_{ne} = the respective weights. This model assumes that decision-makers can scale and weight all of the relevant information on the same dimension and combine it in a linear fashion. Kaplan & Kemmerick (1974) are thus attempting to capture the essence of judicial decision-making utilizing a conception of the judge or juror as a rational processor of measurable information. While this formal model certainly possesses heuristic utility, we should anticipate an imperfect fit to many individual cases. The "myth" of a rational decision-making model has been discussed by Quinney (1970), Levi (1949), and Hart (1961). Hood & Sparks (1970) maintain there are *limits to judicial rationality:*

> ... the judge must decide whether or not the rule applies to the particular facts before him, and this is not simply a "mechanical" process of deduction. But it is not necessarily arbitrary like tossing a coin either. ...judicial decisions on questions of law *can* (logically) be both rational and consistent, even though certain judges' decisions may in fact occasionally be neither. (155)

Taken together, these models provide a valuable schematic with which to view the *general* process of judicial decision-making. Use of this multidimensional input-outcome framework should allow observers to get a coherent picture of the offender processing system and the courtroom in particular; it should enable researchers to gather more intensive data on idiosyncrasies of each phase of the judicial process.

Extralegal Factors and Sentencing Disparity

A basic theme of this chapter is that judicial discretion ensures that a great many factors—legal and extralegal—may influence a decision. An extralegal factor can be defined as information not directly bearing on an individual's guilt or innocence, nor on the nature of a convicted offender's crime or the situational context within which the offense was committed (*i.e.,* precipitating causes, etc.). They are factors not directly entered into evidence during a trial. Extralegal factors can be either positive or negative, mitigating or incriminating, consequently, they can either help or hurt a defendant. Some nonevidentiary factors are clearly either uniformly positive or negative in their effect. Positive factors include no prior criminal record, genuine remorsefulness, personal suffering due to conviction, and making restitution to the victim. The following are examples of the positive effects of two different extralegal inputs (cooperation with prosecution and restitution to the victim);

> Former Nixon re-election campaign aid Frederick LaRue was sentenced to six months in prison (a comparatively light sentence) yesterday for his role in the Watergate coverup. LaRue pleaded guilty to one count of conspiracy to obstruct justice ... to delivering more than $200,000 in hush money to the lawyers of the Watergate burgulars .... He was one of the first ... aides to cooperate in the investigation .... He had been free on personal bond since his guilty plea and was a leading witness in last year's coverup trial of former

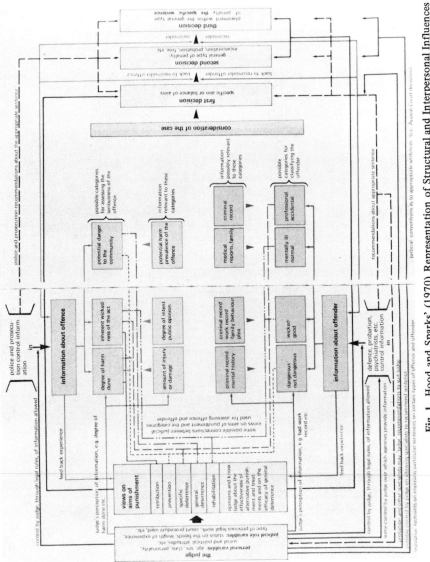

Fig. 1. Hood and Sparks' (1970) Representation of Structural and Interpersonal Influences on the Judicial Decision.

Attorney General John Mitchell and other Nixon associates. (Boston *Globe,* March 15, 1975)

LOUISA—A group of gypsies charged with stealing the $11,000 life savings of an elderly Louisa couple are free. ... the charges were dropped after [the gypsies] agreed to make restitution and pay other costs which totalled more than $700. The group gathered in front of the sheriff's office. ... along with ten young children who had been taken into custody at the time of their arrest, [they] departed for Chicago, from where they said they came. (*Daily Progress,* May 7, 1975)

Negative factors include a criminal record, indignant attitude, and personal aggrandizement from the crime (*i.e.,* an "instrumental" crime). A judge's background and attitudes will determine the impact of such other extralegal factors as a defendant's race, sex, education, income, and church attendance, community pressures, status of judge, and whether the judge is elected or appointed.

Procedural safeguards (admissibility of evidence, right to jury trial, etc.) are built into the judicial system to diminish the influence of extralegal factors on the decision to convict or acquit a defendant. But latitude in sentencing (and therefore the *potential* influence of extralegal information) is deliberately written into the legal system. Thus discretion and the subsequent influence of nonevidentiary factors are most conspicuous in *sentencing disparity.*

The widespread disparity in sentences for similar crimes among countries, between federal and state court systems, among states, and within each of these systems is an accepted fact (President's Commission on Crime and the Administration of Justice, 1967). The Prison Reform Committee of the Florida Bar Association provides one example of disparity.[3]

Case 1 (Harsh)	*Case 2* (Lenient)
Age: 20 County: Escambia	Age: 18 County: Dade
Offense: Robbery	Offense: Robbery
Circumstances: Robbed male individual of $18.52	Circumstances: Robbed male individual of $12
Weapon Used: Knife	Weapon Used: .38 caliber revolver
Sentence: Life	Sentence: Five years. Credit for 50 days jail time.
Prior Felony Convictions: None	Prior Felony Convictions: None

Research on sentencing disparity has a long and arduous history with the net result that researchers are not quite certain about the relative impact of a plethora of legal and extralegal variables. This uncertainty stands as one of the strangest paradoxes in legal research. Since the sentence is obviously of paramount importance to the offender, the inability of researchers to predict judicial outcomes is surprising. For years this "knowledge gap" was simply due to a lack of research on sentencing. Researchers seemed to forget about the offender once a guilty verdict was reached (see McQuire & Holtzoff, 1940). However, in recent years researchers have addressed the issue of sentencing disparity and the reasons behind it. The current challenge is to interpret often conflicting results and to isolate the relative importance of the relevant social psychological and structural variables which affect sentencing.

Research in this area has focused on the effect of defendant characteristics. Numerous studies have found a relationship between sentencing and educational level, property ownership, race, sex, marital status, and residence (Bullock, 1961; Green, 1961; Rubin, 1966; Carter & Wilkins, 1967). However, an ample number of studies suggest that many of these variables are not major factors in sentencing. Green (1961) found this to be the case with age, sex, and education; Carter and Wilkins (1967) argue that race and religion are minor influences. Conclusions from the most recent reviews of the research on race, social class, age, and sex (Hagan, 1974; Chiricos & Waldo, 1975) indicate that race is not a factor in sentencing for noncapital offenses when prior criminal record is held constant. However, race does produce sentencing disparity in capital offenses in some Southern states. Social class, similarly, is important only in capital cases when prior record is controlled. Age and sex seem to be minor variables in all types of cases. Thus it seems safe to conclude that demographic variables *in themselves* are unimportant for noncapital cases. They may exert an impact *in combination with* other variables, however. Much more research needs to be done. Moreover, demographic variables compose only a portion of all extralegal variables acting on legal decision-makers.

Another difficulty in reconciling conflicting data on sentencing disparity arises from the divergent research methods employed. Hood & Sparks (1970, pp. 143-151) survey three such methods: "crude comparisons between courts" (Grunhut, 1956; Patchett & McClean, 1965), "random sample studies" (Gaudet, 1949) in which samples of cases are drawn from representative courts, and "matching studies" (Green, 1961) in which offenders are matched according to a similar "risk category" (*e.g.,* race, sex). Each of these approaches represents a different strategy for isolating the relevancy and strength of factors which influence sentences in order to *equate* offenses and offenders. Variety on both dimensions renders data-gathering and interpretation problematic.

Austin & Williams (1977) employed yet another approach to the study of judicial sentencing which solves the problem of equalizing cases but at the expense of "realism." In this study, Virginia district court judges attending an educational workshop responded to the *same* hypothetical cases by recommending a verdict and sentence.[4] For example, in one case, the judges read:

Debbie Jones, 18 years of age, appears in court. She was apprehended with her boy friend, in the apartment of an acquaintance of theirs. There were seven boys and girls present. Seven roaches or butts were found, none in Debbie's hands, and ten unused cigarettes of marijuana were found in a paper bag on the coffee table.

Debbie is charged with "Possession of Marijuana"
Guilty or Not Guilty?
As charged or what?

Debbie has no previous record. She attends high school regularly as a senior. She does not appear particularly apologetic for her use of marijuana, but neither does she appear rebellious against "the establishment." Her father, in court with her, is branch manager of national manufacturer of duplicating equipment.

Punishment?

The variability of judges' responses to this case is quite dramatic: twenty-nine judges noted "Not Guilty" while eighteen "Guilty" recommendations were recorded; of the eighteen guilty verdicts, eight judges recommended probation, four would impose a fine, three would issue probation *and* a fine, and three were in favor of a jail term. The lack of consensus on both the verdict and the sentence is readily apparent. It is perhaps "appropriate" that data for this rather striking illustration of sentencing disparity was gathered at a "judicial work-shop," designed, among other things, as a forum for judges and "experts" to discuss the complexities of sentencing because a number of observers have called for such workshops as one way to reduce sentencing disparity (cf. Remington & Newman, 1962).

In attempting to explain sentencing disparity researchers have concentrated on individual differences among judges (cf. Hogarth, 1971) often referred to as the "personal equation" (Gaudet, 1949). This focus on personal attributes of judges often leaves the impression that "the sentencing process is unjust, inefficacious or both" (Hood & Sparks, 1970, p. 154). For example, Jerome Frank (1950) maintains:

When it comes to "finding" the "facts" in lawsuits where the oral testimony is in conflict, these obscure indiosyncrasies in the trial judge are bafflingly at work. The judge's *sympathies* and *antipathies* are likely to be active with respect to the witnesses. His own past may have created plus or minus reactions to women, or blond women, or men with beards, or Southerners, or Italians, or Englishmen, or plumbers, or ministers, or college-graduates or Democrats. A certain facial twitch or cough or gesture may start up memories, painful or pleasant. Those memories of the trial judge, while he is listening to a witness with such a facial twitch or cough or gesture, may affect the judge's initial hearing, or subsequent recollection, of what the witness said, or the weight of credibility which the judge will attach to the witness' testimony. (151)

Judicial values and prejudices undoubtedly do play a major role in decisions. However, Hood & Sparks (1970) assert that if we are to gain a workable insight into sentencing, researchers need to study other components of the "personal equation." Specifically, they point to three other differences among judges: (1) Judges have different sentencing policies, including priorities and weighting of different goals and theories of punishment. (2) Judges may receive different types of information about offenders. Carter & Wilkins (1967) document how pre-sentence reports vary in quality. (3) Judges may classify offenders and offenses differently in terms of type of crime and its severity. Thus researchers should probe these types of differences in their efforts to explain sentencing disparity. Once descriptive data are gathered on judicial practices of *classification* and the *bases for punishment* (*e.g.,* deterrence, rehabilitation), the possibility for predicting and structuring judicial decisions can be entertained.

Less personal factors also add to sentencing disparity. For example, sentences reflect jurisdictional differences in laws, penalties (absolute and minimum-maximum), community values, political pressures, public scrutiny,[5] and probability of appeal. A vivid demonstration of this last variable is the course of most divorce proceedings. Although divorce is a civil law proceeding, it shows that when the probability of appeal is low, lower court judges hold near-absolute discretionary power. Divorce law generally allows for flexible interpretations with several different "types of divorce" open to the litigants. The net result of vagueness in law and near impossibility of an appeal being granted is that divorce decrees are more discrepant than most types of decisions; lawyers jockey for the "right judge" in light of a client's case. Traffic courts represent another dramatic illustration of the impact of structural factors on sentencing disparity. In this case, the *type of court* facilitates disparate sentences. The case load on traffic judges demands quick judgments, a situation which can only enhance the effect of personal factors. This is compounded by the unlikelihood of an appeal being filed or granted.

Discretion in Appellate Courts

Discretionary power among appellate judges is perhaps even more striking than that exercised by trial judges. But since appeal decisions are not embellished with the "drama" of a trial and since appellate action occurs a considerable time after the initial trial, it has received less scrutiny from researchers and public alike.

Three aspects of state and federal appellate courts facilitate and compound their judicial discretion. First, the *authority* of appeal judges *is not diffused* among other interested parties as it is in lower courts. Prosecutors and probation officials, for example, are not around to share in the decision-making. Second, *judges can deny appeals without any accompanying opinion.* However, this is mainly an option available only to supreme courts. Lower appeal courts cannot deny an appeal because of its "lack of significance." Third, the tremendous case loads that burden virtually every appeal court docket encourage *quick judgments,* a fact that can only increase the discretionary aspect of judicial decision-making. This is particularly true of the United States Supreme Court, where justices usually can spend only a few minutes reviewing each prospective appeal. A reasonable hypothesis is that the less time spent on a case, the more likely the judgment is to reflect the personal qualities of the judge instead of the "facts of the case" or interpretation of the law.

These three facets of appeals act together to imbue lower court decisions with a greater *finality* than is generally recognized. Consequently, the de facto operation of the appellate court may actually solidify instead of act as a check upon the discretion of lower court judges. It is impossible to determine exactly how much the low probability of a successful appeal affects the actions of lower court judges. But it creates a paradoxical situation in the judicial system: the illusion that most appeals receive careful consideration, which further enhances the perceived legitimacy and fairness of the judicial system.

This pardox is perhaps most apparent in the Supreme Court, which is shrouded in the image of "blindfold justice" and "the court of last resort"—the ultimate guarantee of fairness of law and decision. This image is entrenched by "landmark decisions" and media exposure. However, there exist no guidelines, outside of the history of the Supreme Court, to help justices decide when to grant an appeal. The result is that appeals are often granted because of their implications for public policy, not because an unjust decision may have befallen a litigant.

Restraints on Judicial Discretion

Judicial discretion does not go unchecked. Jacob (1965) classifies factors which restrain judges into two types. He refers to the first type as "internalized" pressures. These factors include the influence of local norms, judicial canons and ethical guidelines, the norm of respect for legal precedent *(stare decisis),* and the norm to avoid political questions. The second group of restraints are "external." These refer to the structure of separation of powers *(i.e.,* dependence of judiciary on the executive branch to carry out its decrees), limitations on the jurisdiction of courts, recall of appointed judges and political defeat of elected judges, and the nullification of court decisions by constitutional amendment.

Despite these built-in safeguards, enormous latitude exists for judges in many of their decisions. For example, many of the external restraints are applicable only in response to the most blatant abuses of discretion *(e.g.,* recall). Consequently, many observers have advocated changes in the legal system in an effort to curb judicial discretion. Critics have focused principally on the areas of sentencing disparity and judicial activism or policy-making by judges. Regarding sentencing, U.S. Attorney General Edward Levi has recently proposed a restructuring of federal sentencing practices and the abolition of the parole system. Levi claims that inconsistencies in sentencing and the uncertainty of length of sentence due to parole undermines the deterrent effect of the law. Levi thus proposed the establishment of a permanent federal sentencing commission that would set up sentencing guidelines. A judge would have to specify his/her reasons if a sentence did not conform to the guidelines and the sentencing decision could be appealed under such circumstances. The abolition of parole would mean that *the judge,* not a parole board, would set the real prison term after a statutory minimum sentence was met (UPI, *The Flint Journal,* February 4, 1976). A proposal similar to Levi's is contained in a bill currently pending before the U.S. Senate Judiciary Committee (S.1) which recommends appellate review of sentences. Thus changes in judicial sentencing may become a reality.

A strong argument can be made that it is only fair that offenders should be able to challenge the magnitude of their punishment (or at least the reason behind it) as well as the verdict (*i.e.,* the "right to punish" at all). After all, proposals which would instruct judges and juries to justify their sentences are merely extensions of the judicial opinion regarding verdicts and they may produce a number of benefits to the judicial process. Specifically, guidelines and "sentencing opinions" could greatly reduce the influence of unwarranted extra-legal factors on sentencing—such as judge and defendant characteristics. In addition, the publication of sentencing opinions would comprise almost an ideal survey of judges' rationales for punishment—a key factor in sentencing disparity.

Judges, principally appellate judges, have also be criticized on the grounds that they too often attempt to "make policy" instead of merely applying existing law to a particular case (see Jacob, 1965, for a review). Few observers would not agree that judges shoulder a difficult burden as they attempt to interpret the vagaries of modern laws. However, some people see judges as going too far in this task.[6] It is a question of the proper *degree* of judicial activism and disagreements about the proper role of judges in modern society. The recent controversy over mandatory busing of school children to achieve racial balance exemplifies this controversy. In this case, the controversy involves judges *interpreting a previous interpretation* of the Fourteenth Amendment (*Brown v. Board of Education,* 1954). In another clear example of judicial initiative it was reported that U.S. District Judge Frank M. Johnson "put Alabama on notice that he would close every prison in the state if it did not correct conditions that have caused 'the rampant violence and jungle atmosphere.' Johnson . . . established a set of minimum constitutional standards: every prisoner should have 60 square feet of living space, a change of bed linen every week, three nutritious meals a day, the opportunity to perform a meaningful job, at least 30 minutes of outdoor exercise daily, and medical treatment. He also demanded that the state nearly double the number of guards at its prisons" (*Newsweek,* January 26, 1976, p. 43).

It is difficult to deny that Judge Johnson is establishing "policy" here. However, many legal theorists would support his action. For example, Chambliss & Seidman (1971) would classify this case as a "trouble case"—one where the law is undeveloped and there exist only a limited number of precedents for the judge to use as guidelines. Because appellate judges are constitutionally *charged with* interpreting law and lower court decisions, the controversy surrounding the question of "how active" judges should be is probably a permanent issue. Unless the *structure* of the American judicial system is altered, which is doubtful, policy-making by judges is likely to continue. In fact, this legislative function of judges may be the inevitable and desirable result of the inability of legislatures to anticipate social change in modern society.

JUSTICE AND OTHER MOTIVES IN JUDICIAL DECISION-MAKING: THE JUDICIAL THEORY FOR PUNISHMENT

Public disagreements concerning the use or misuse of judicial discretion largely arise from divergent views on the proper goals of judicial sanction. It is not surprising that judges, legal observers, and scholars disagree about the length of prison sentence when they don't see "eye to eye" on the basic objectives of legal punishment itself. Identifying these objectives and agreeing on their relative importance are necessary steps before an evaluation of judicial decision-making can be completed and proposed changes in the judicial process can be seriously considered.

Criticisms of judicial discretionary judgments follow two themes: justice and efficacy. An argument based on justice points to questions of either procedure, distribution, or retribution. Statements on efficacy usually refer to the evaluative criteria of deterrence, rehabilitation, or the efficient functioning of the legal system.

Justice

Dimensions of Justice

The concept of justice, whether we define it as a value, a right, or a norm, has probably always served as the central standard with which to evaluate judicial acts. Rawls (1971) in his recent classic book makes this point:

> Justice is the first virtue of social institutions, as truth is of systems of thought. A theory however elegant and economical must be rejected if untrue; likewise laws and institutions no matter how efficient and well-arranged must be abolished if they are unjust. Each person possesses an inviolability founded on justice that even the welfare of society as a whole cannot override. (3-4)

Justice is a global concept which is put to many different uses and enshrined in a plethora of meanings. Despite this complexity there appears to be a growing consensus among both philosophers and social scientists that a common thread runs through the many faces of justice. The key to operationalizing justice—to making it a concrete, useful concept—is *fairness*. "Justice as fairness" thus permeates both philosophy (Rawls, 1971) and social psychology (cf. Thibaut et al., 1974; Leventhal, 1976a).

Austin (1974) tested this conception of justice via a simple descriptive study. Subjects were asked merely to define the term "fairness" and to supply examples. In scoring the protocols, Austin consistently found that subjects conceived of fairness along five overlapping dimensions: (a) "playing by the rules," (b) "meeting one's expectations," (c) "equity" (*i.e.,* rewards and punishment apportioned according to individual differences), (d) "equality," and (e) "deserving." A close inspection of these dimensions reveals two general "factors": procedural justice and distributive justice.

Procedural justice covers perceptions of fairness specifically concerning *rules* which regulate the *operation* of groups and organizations. In Austin's study this element of fairness covers all of dimension (a) and parts of (b) and (e).

An evaluative judgment that procedures are fair or unfair requires both that the rules themselves are seen as just and that the rules are being implemented in the prescribed manner. In legal terms, procedural justice confronts questions regarding the substance and implementation of laws. For observers of individual court cases, this orientation means, first, that perceptions of fairness are governed by the "justness" of the law allegedly violated. As observers make judgments of laws according to personal and community values, some laws inevitably enjoy more social support than others. For example, laws regulating marijuana possession enjoy relatively little public endorsement partly because people disagree with the *concept* of the law (regulating victimless crimes where the degree of personal and social harm is low). Observers also may feel that a law is unjust even when they agree with the concept behind the law. For example, until recently many marijuana laws were criticized because the penalties were too severe. Second, the remaining elements of procedural justice in legal settings concern protection of the accused such as right to a jury trial, a lawyer, an adversarial proceeding, and so on. These considerations of procedural justice thus guide observers and participants' perceptions up to the point where a verdict is reached.

Distributive justice concerns the fairness of the verdict, viz., an offender's punishment, or lack of it. Does it match the harm done? Is it appropriate to this particular offender? Does it approximate decisions in similar cases? It focuses on the final outcome of a case, or all of dimensions (c), (d) and parts of (b) and (e) in Austin's (1974) study above.

The concept of distributive justice was originated by Aristotle, who implicitly identified two main subsets or "rules" of distributive justice. The first such rule is equity. As we discussed at the beginning of the chapter, "equity justice" refers essentially to individual differences. In a legal case, this means two things: offenders should be punished according to the gravity of their crime and factors specific to the circumstances of the case. Regarding the second aspect, Aristotle stated: "The same thing, then, is just and equitable, and while both are good, the equitable is superior. What creates the problem is that the equitable is just, but not legally just but a correction of legal justice" (1966, p. 1137a). Making an equitable decision, however, is a difficult matter—whether it is an employer deciding on a rate of pay or a judge imposing a sentence. The most obvious problem is to decide what inputs, or factors in the situation, should be counted. Aristotle tells us: " . . . all men agree that what is just in distribution must be according to merit in some sense, though they do not all specify the same sort of merit, but democrats identify it with the status of freemen, supporters of oligarchy with wealth and supporters of aristocracy with excellence" (1966, 1131a). Thus the exercise of judicial discretion in deciding what inputs to consider relevant and at what weight (often determined by probation officer reports) rests on a series of value judgments and is bound to produce disparate sentences. In a specific case, the two facets of equity probably do not combine additively. That is, when the crime is of high severity (*e.g.,* murder) a judge probably accentuates negative factors and when the crime is less serious (*e.g.,* petty larceny) favorable factors should be enhanced. A related problem concerns the evaluation of the equitableness of a given decision because it depends on which frame of reference—which social comparison—is used to make the judgment. Aristotle conveyed to us that "The just, then, must be both intermediate and equal (according to merit) and relative. . . . The just involves at least four terms; for the persons for whom it is in fact just are two, and the things in which it is manifested, the objects distributed, are two" (1966, p. 1131a). This problem thus concerns the issue of equalizing similar cases discussed above. Should a case be judged relative to all other cases involving the same crime, or be restricted to the same crime by the same type of person? It is a difficult matter, for the answer as to how fair the outcome is depends on how we ask the question. In summary, Aristotle defined equity justice as rewards and punishments distributed according to differences in *merit* and *relative* to other similar persons. It is an "equality of proportions" in this sense.[7]

The second rule of distributive justice is *equality*. In legal terms, this means that "similar cases should be treated similarly." It means that cases regarding violations of the same law are subject to the same potential punishment. However, when an individual judicial decision is rendered, the equality rule is often inconsistent with and subservient to an "equitable" decision. This leads us to ask the obvious question "How much equity?" In response, a recent report[8] on discretion in the legal system states:

> . . . the use of discretion, even when humanity, justice, equity, or expediency is served by doing so, has a negative side. That is, it increases the punishment of those for whom no exception is made.

Consequently, we face another paradox in judicial decision-making: the frequent incompatability of equity and equality as decision rules. They are two faces of distributive justice, and each carries its own problems. Thus a judge who consistently acts in terms of the equity rule will treat differently defendants accused of the same legal violation, in accordance with the different favorable or unfavorable mitigating factors each presents. Legally this is unfair, in a relative sense. Another judge may favor strict equality, choosing not to exercise his discretion. He/she may thus create injustice by failing to intervene and rectify the inflexibility of universal rules.

While procedural and distributive justice involve distinctly separate processes, they are interrelated. The separate evaluations must be joined together to form an overall impression of a judicial case. And violations of procedural expectations imply that distributive justice will be affected because when procedural safeguards are broken outcomes may be altered. For example, if an accused is denied the right to counsel, he/she is probably more likely to be found guilty. The significance of procedures is mostly indirect because they are colored by the judicial outcome. Fair procedures are small consolation in the face of an unjust verdict or sentence. However, procedures are directly important through their *symbolic value*. They represent the role of the state in preserving the ideal of a lawful society; just procedures legitimate and evoke confidence in the judicial process.

Retribution is a concept closely related to distributive justice. Acts of retribution play a central role in judicial sanctions and are often shrouded in the term "retributive justice" (see Golding, 1975, for a review of traditional treatments of retribution in the law). However, we have not included it in our definition of justice because it is not easily captured by a conception of "justice as fairness."

Scholars have traditionally conceived of retribution in two ways. First, it has been equated simply with retaliation for harm done: giving an offender "what he deserves," making him "pay for his crime," and expiating his guilt (Rose & Prell, 1953; Fry, 1956). When retribution is used in this sense of proportional retaliation, then it is totally redundant with the notion of distributive justice which dictates that balance must be restored in the relationship between offender and society. This usage refers to Austin's (1974) dimension (e) of deserving. In this sense, distributive justice is the more general and parsimonious concept, encompassing the distribution of rewards as well as punishments. However, laws spelling out punishment for certain crimes usually do not merely specify an equal amount of punishment. They often insist on a punishment greater, in an absolute sense, than the harm caused by the crime. For example, the sentence for theft may be a fine *and* a prison sentence. It is in this sense that retribution gains its originality. It implies something more than distributive justice. Thus retribution is defined here as the "extra" amount of punishment administered to a harm-doer. This distinction has been made by other theorists (Tillich, 1954; Piaget, 1965).

It is logically possible to treat retribution as a simple act of retaliation in which qualitative assessment of an act (*i.e.,* heinousness of the crime) serves as a *negative input* demanding proportionately more punishment. In this sense, it would be an application of the equity principle. For example, stealing $100 from a poor elderly lady cannot be adequately rectified by simple restitution of the money. However, the concept of retribution is steeped in rich scholarly tradition so that it cannot be discarded so easily even in the name of parsimony. For instance, Kant (1965), the best-known "retributionist," proclaimed that criminals needed to be punished "in proportion to their inner viciousness' (p. 103). In less vivid terms, many still agree.

The second usage of retribution defines it in terms of the motive of vengeance. It is *the reason* for retaliation. In contrast to a motive of a simple equity restoration, retribution refers to the value of expiation, vindication, and the satisfaction of seeing one's enemy suffer. In distributive justice, the concern was with implementing a clear rule with the emphasis on *material* balance. Retribution points to the *psychological* satisfaction of retaliation. The distinction is important. For small crimes, material balance suffices, but this is not the case for more serious offenses. The reaction to a recent case involving the kidnap-murder of an eight-year-old boy in France illustrates this point:

> PARIS—The atmosphere of lynch law was so thick in Troyes that the arrested man was moved to greater safety. ... Not a single lawyer in Troyes came forward to conduct the defense. ... Hundreds of people signed a petition demanding a death sentence. "Let him be guillotined" Henry's [the accused] mother told a journalist. "And the day they cut off his head, let him expect nothing from me. At the foot of the scaffold, I renounce my son." ... Letters ... insisted the guillotine was too merciful ... demanding the cross. (*Washington Post,* March 10, 1976)

While the distributive and retributive goals of punishment are distinct, they combine to exemplify the "moral indignation" inherent in judicial sanction (see Golding, 1975). When they guide judicial decisions, they restore balance between offender and society and they gain a measure of vengeance for the victim. While theorists criticize retribution as "backward-looking" and unrepresentative of modern penal theory (see Golding, 1975), it remains a basic motive behind human behavior. We should not expect judges and jurors to escape its influence.

Research on Interpersonal Justice

Procedural justice. Researchers have documented the impact of procedural factors on observers, and participants' perception of the judicial process. Thibaut & Walker (1975) have identified several dimensions of procedural justice. First, they have shown that perceptions of fairness are affected by implicit or explicit rules on the *collection* of information (Friedland et al., 1973), on the *utilization* of information (Thibaut et al., 1972; Lind et al., 1973), and on *control* over information exchange (Thibaut et al., 1974). Through the use of experimental simulations this research indicates that fairness and bias are affected by illegitimate procurement of evidence, presence of an attorney, and an adversarial as opposed to an inquisitorial mode of adjudication. Similar findings have been reported on the illegitimacy of rule-breaking in nonlegal encounters (cf. Horowitz, 1958; Leventhal et al., 1964).

Distributive justice. Social psychologists have extensively documented the fundamental role which equity and equality rules play in all types of interpersonal encounters. They regulate the distribution of outcomes in business relationships (Leventhal, 1976b), less formal social situations (Walster et al., 1973), judicial decisions (Austin et al., 1976; Macaulay & Walster, 1971) and even in intimate relations (Walster et al., in press).

This research has been guided by an elaboration of Aristotle's conception into what is generally called "equity theory" (Adams, 1965; Walster et al., 1973). The basic thesis of the theory is that the perception of an unfair distribution causes distress in participants and observers of a relationship inducing them to rectify the situation or to justify it somehow. This statement pertains to both instances of underreward (*e.g.,* being the victim of a crime) or overreward (*e.g.,* the criminal receiving an inadequate sentence). According to one equity theorist (Adams, 1965) a relationship is fair when

$$\frac{\text{Outcomes Person A}}{\text{Inputs Person A}} = \frac{\text{Outcomes Person B}}{\text{Inputs Person B}}$$

where outcomes = rewards - costs and inputs are anything which entitle a person to a fair outcome. Thus merit and social comparison comprise the central process of reward evaluation.

In a legal case, the most salient comparison is between the offender and society (as embodied by the victim). The victim's outcomes are established by the magnitude of the crime, with inputs presumably constant. As we have seen, the inputs of the offender are many and diversified, including magnitude of offense, heinousness of act, personal characteristics, and prior record. Other salient comparisons can be made as well. For example, DeJong et al. (1976) found that simulated jurors assign less punishment when a guilty accomplice of an offender had already escaped punishment.

Assuming that relevant inputs and outcomes can be roughly measured and scaled quantitatively, the "equity formula" provides a valuable heuristic with which to describe the judicial decision vis-à-vis a criterion of justice. Austin et al. (1976) suggested that researchers should use this framework for gathering descriptive data on those input factors that affect judicial outcomes. Important steps in this direction have been taken. Survey data, such as Kalven & Zeisel's (1966) analysis of the specific factors affecting jurors' decisions, provide a prototype. To test the utility of the equity theory conception we conducted four experimental simulations. The first three studies (Austin & Utne, 1975) tested the hypothesis that jurors would be less likely to consider the extralegal input of offender-suffering as the severity of the crime increased in magnitude. In each study, the salient comparison was between how much the offender suffered during commission of the crime and how much the victim suffered. Each study used a different crime: simple robbery, robbery and felonious assault, or robbery and rape. The offender was depicted as suffering excessively relative to his crime, about the same amount, or not at all. The hypothesis was confirmed. For robbery, jurors assigned significantly less punishment for each successive level of offender-suffering. However, for crimes of assault and rape only excessive suffering was effective in lowering sentences. In a fourth experiment (Austin & Utne, 1976), the effect of the "relevance" of the offender's extralegal suffering was explored. The offender was convicted of robbery and assault and suffered excessively or moderately either as a direct result of the crime (relevant) or while he was released on bail (irrelevant). The results were identical to the first three studies. Offender-suffering mitigated sentences only in the presence of excessive suffering. In addition, irrelevant suffering was equally effective. These data warrant three concludions. First, they experimentally substantiate Kalven & Zeisel's extensive descriptive data on the impact of offender-suffering. Second, although any act of judicial punishment will be affected by several motives simultaneously, these results *suggest* that as crimes increase in severity the motive for retribution takes precedence over a motive for simple distributive justice. Third, the utility of conceiving of judicial decisions as the dividend of differentially valued inputs is demonstrated. For a petty crime, offender-suffering always acts as a positive input, but for serious acts this input factor is ignored. This framework does not imply an overly rational view of judicial decision-making. It simply provides a descriptive tool for calibrating how any number of input factors should be integrated to predict a "just" decision.

Procedural justice vs. distributive justice. A recent study by Austin and his colleagues (1976) demonstrates the uneasy truce between these two components of justice. In an experimental simulation, we examined observers' perceptions of different modes of adjudication in the presence of either a favorable or unfavorable verdict. Subjects viewed a viedotaped enactment of an actual traffic case (leaving the scene of an accident). The courtroom procedure was either adversarial or inquisitorial, with a defense lawyer present or not present. The judge ruled the violation either a misdemeanor (low penalty) or a felony (high penalty). The results confirmed our suspeicions that the standard preference for adversal proceedings (cf. Walker et al., 1974) was qualified by the judicial outcome. Subjects apparently approached the proceeding with a negative view, uniformly expressing that the general nature of the trial was unfair (see Fig. 2). But this attitude was qualified by a procedure X outcome interaction. Subjects consistently rated adversarial-lawyer-misdemeanor most positively, with adversarial-no lawyer-misdemeanor closely behind. The most unfair was inquisitorial-felony, but, perhaps surprisingly, inquisitorial-misdemeanor was rated higher than ad-

Observers' Reactions to Adversarial and Inquisitorial Modes of Adjudication Under Conditions of Felony and Misdemeanor Offenses[a]

	Overall Outcome		How fair facts presented?	Given facts, how good verdict?	Defense	
	Fair	Biased			Bias	Useful
Adversarial-lawyer-misdemeanor	2.65	1.60	4.10	3.75	3.45	4.20
Adversarial-lawyer-felony	2.60	1.50	2.20	1.95	3.45	4.20
Adversarial-w/o lawyer-misdemeanor	2.50	1.50	3.55	3.32	3.30	4.13
Adversarial-w/o lawyer-felony	2.50	1.50	2.18	2.09	2.50	3.09
Inquisitorial-misdemeanor	2.55	1.50	3.05	3.96	2.55	3.70
Inquisitorial-felony	2.48	1.48	2.72	2.60	2.83	2.83

[a] All scales were 7-point bipolar, with low scores representing less fair, biased, etc.

Fig. 2.

versarial-lawyer-felony. Thus the fairer procedure of adversary with lawyer was less important than the outcome.

Other Goals

While Rawls's (1971) claim that "justice is the first virtue of social institutions" may be true, other objectives of judicial sanction often displace or act in combination with justice as determinants of legal punishments. We have already discussed retribution as one such motive. Four additional considerations are discussed below.

Value Affirmation

As mentioned previously, trials which satisfy the public's expectations of procedural, distributive, and retributive justice serve as rituals where numerous specific values are reaffirmed. This function of labeling and censoring offenders has been noted by other theorists (Golding, 1975). In this respect, Roche (1958)[9] remarks:

> The criminal trial is an operation having religious meaning essential as a public exercise in which the prevailing moral ideals are dramatized and reaffirmed. The religious meaning is the adjusting of tensional moral conflict within the law abiding. The conflict is materialized in the actions of the criminal, and dissipated in the ritual of guilt fastening, condemnation, and punishment. ... The criminal trial has the function of public edification rather than the welfare of individual wrong-doers who pass over its stage in an endless procession. (245-246)

We conducted a final laboratory simulation on offender-suffering to determine the strength of the urge to censor an offender. Subjects read highly incriminating evidence about a defendant in a robbery-assault case. However, in this study the subjects' task was not to assign a sentence but to recommend a verdict of conviction or acquittal. Perhaps unexpectedly, not a single subject voted for acquittal. Even in the excessive suffering condition, all subjects were in favor of conviction. In the previous experiments. more than half of the subjects recommended a suspended sentence in the excessive condition. But apparently jurors are willing to indicate a sympathetic response in a serious offense only after public condemnation (*i.e.,* a guilty verdict) has been reached.

Deterrence

When the goal of punishment is the deterrence of future offenses, we again are asking the question *How much* punishment is appropriate? In the case of justice, the answer involved trying to reconcile an individual case with traditional normative rules of fairness. However, when deterrence is the goal, the answer is more difficult to ascertain because it must be directed at many unknown faces instead of one specific case. The result is that deterring crime through laws and individual judicial decisions is a vocal social issue.

Deterrence as a basis for punishment arises from the utilitarian tradition of Jeremy Bentham and rests on an image of man as a profit-maximizer who deploys a hedonistic calculus prior to important personal decisions. According to Bentham, the key to determining an appropriate level of punishment for each offense is to find that amount which is *just necessary* to eliminate the temptation of crime for other citizens. The simple utilitarian-deterrence rule dictates that punishment is justified by what is good for society, not for the individual.

Utilitarian doctrines have been subject to ardent criticisms by legal philosophers for centuries (Kant, 1965; Rawls, 1971), mainly on the grounds that deterrence is incompatible with justice as a basis for judicial sanction. The three central criticisms are that (1) deterrence logically allows us to punish the innocent to deter crime (Kant, 1965), (2) the amount necessary to deter crimes of a certain type may be grossly unjust to an individual case (Rawls, 1971), and (3) it is impossible to calculate how much punishment is adequate to deter crime due to variation in values (Golding, 1975). Critics have also pointed to the high rate of recidivism as an indicator of the inability of sentences to deter (Chambliss & Seidman, 1971); they have maintained that crime is deterred mainly through values (American Friends Service Committee, 1971) and may result in legal actors refusing to impose sanctions (Vidmar, 1972).

As with most controversial issues, the critics of deterrence as a legitimate goal and its effectiveness have stated the "strong case." Some of the criticisms assume deterrence will be the *major* goal of sanction and many of the issues are exacerbated by the inadequacy of research on deterrence. The question should be not whether we should try to deter crime but how we should integrate deterrence with other objectives. We believe that deterrence is so thoroughly ingrained in the modern legal system that this is the only realistic approach. The proposal by Attorney General Levi (cited above) indicates that policy-makers are willing to propose radical judicial reforms to bolster the deterrent effect of the law. Moreover, it was recently reported by the U.S. Bureau of Prisons that there has been an upsurge in the number of offenders sent to prison and the magnitude of sentences given to them, suggesting that deterrence may be emerging as more salient to judges. This trend appears to be fairly uniform across the country (UPI, *The Flint Journal,* February 1, 1976).

It appears that judges and jurors are likely to continue to attempt to deter crime by their decisions. The burden, then, seems to be on researchers to convey which penalties and practices act as most effective deterrents and for which types of crimes. Researchers have begun to accumulate some evidence (see Gibbs, 1975) and theorists are beginning to formalize hypotheses on certainty, severity, and timing of punishment (see Geerken & Gove, 1975). In addition, legislators need to provide guidelines as to the purpose of deterrence (to deter the particular offender, to deter violations of a particular law, or to deter crime in general) and guidelines on the relative importance of justice and deterrence for various types of offenses.

Rehabilitation

The trend in modern penal theory, and policy, has been toward an individualized approach—making the punishment fit the criminal rather than the crime and attempting to rehabilitate offenders. This philosophy was benignly motivated as a reaction to abhorrent treatment of criminals in correctional facilities. The result has been a "treatment approach" emphasizing judicial discretion, commonly labeled a "realist" judicial decision-making style (Chambliss & Seidman, 1971).

This policy is most clear in juvenile courts, where until recently the treatment orientation has resulted in almost absolute judicial discretion. Such a system has led one observer (Matza, 1964) to equate juvenile courts with a Kadi system of justice. Kadi refers to ancient Moslem courts where local magistrates would decide each law violation truly "on its own merits" and without regard to precedents or guidelines. Criticisms of the real and potential abuses of such a well-meaning system have led to supreme Court decisions guaranteeing juveniles the right to an attorney. In *Gault v. Arizona,* 1967, the Supreme Court stated: "Juvenile court history has again demonstrated that unbridled discretion, however benevolently motivated, is frequently a poor substitute for principle and procedure."[10] In this case, a 15-year-old boy was charged with making an obscene phone call. His juvenile court proceeding resulted in his imprisonment for four years in a state facility. If he had been 18 years old, the maximum sentence would have been a fine of $5 to $50 and not more than two months in jail.

In adult courts, the individualized orientation has operated in a more de facto sense rather than as an explicit ideology, as in juvenile courts. This is illustrated best by the indeterminant sentence, which affords judges great latitude to fit the prison sentence to the specific case (*i.e.,* the "needs" of the individual). The extreme form of this position is found in proposals that sentencing should be handled exclusively by panels of "experts" (Wooton, 1963). The State of California currently delegates much sentencing responsibility to "sentencing boards" (see Glaser, 1973).

A number of specific criticisms have been directed at the inefficacy of treatment approaches. First, overcrowding and generally brutal prison conditions make genuine psychological rehabilitation impossible and vocational rehabilitation infeasible. Second, a treatment approach emphasizes individual pathology rather than environmental causes of crime. Critics claim it makes little sense to try to "cure" an offender only to send him back to the same crime-generating social millieu. Third, treatment of individuals assumes that practitioners can reliably classify criminals and that they understand the etiology, or causes, of crime. Criminologists readily acknowledge researchers' weakness on both accounts. Fourth, the treatment produces a "sick" label which can become a self-fulfilling prophecy if offenders come to view themselves in such terms. Critics view this strategy as working against the goals of building confidence and self-renewal. Fifth, high recidivism rates suggest that the number of offenders who are genuinely rehabilitated is a small minority. Sixth, critics stress that calling incarceration "treatment" does not make it less punishing. Finally, the treatment ideology allows for "too much" discretion across the spectrum of the offender processing system. The uncertainty produced by indeterminant sentences impresses most prisoners as cruel; they feel the rationale of release contingent upon a cure is a disguise for arbitrary reasons for denial of parole. It is seen as ex post facto law enforcement. Critics maintain that these seven factors combine to undermine the trust and legitimacy which are absolutely essential to any helping relationship and which are the bases of the treatment approach (see Quinney, 1970; Wilkins, 1969; Ward, 1973; American Friends Service Committee, 1971; Hood & Sparks, 1970; Clinard, 1968). Perhaps the most convincing testimony on public and professional disenchantment with rehabilitation as a goal of judicial sanction is the data from the U.S. Bureau of Prisons discussed above on the increasing number of prisoners and the average length of prison terms.

Efficiency

This consideration in judicial sanctions is rarely explicit, but it is just as real as other motives. Law enforcement officials and judges must be sensitive to the goal of smoothly processing the accused and the convicted. The reaction of court officials to their burdensome case loads has led some observers to characterize judicial decisions as focusing on efficiency to the exclusion of other goals (see Downie, 1971). The clearest example of the influence of efficiency considerations is plea bargaining, a case resolution process which is more the rule than the exception in criminal cases. The bureaucratic machinery of the court would become overwhelmed without such negotiation and compromise in the processing system.

Efficiency considerations often have implications for other goals of judicial sanction. For example, plea bargaining may undermine the potential deterrent effect of the law by producing a lower probability of a prison term and shorter sentences. Plea bargaining may also cause inconsistent outcomes such as in the highly publicized case of former Vice-President Spiro Agnew and his fellow conspirators. Agnew plea-bargained for a suspended prison sentence and a fine for tax evasion. His co-conspirators, on the other hand, whose testimony was instrumental in building the case against Agnew, were given both a fine *and* a prison sentence. The judges, in their ruling, stressed the the Agnew plea bargain was not relevant, although former Attorney General Elliot Richardson, who supervised the case, protested the relative unfairness of the punishment for Agnew's co-conspirators. Thus efficiency-based decisions may be difficult to reconcile with justice. Macaulay & Walster (1971) describe how "equity considerations" (*i.e.,* the wrongdoer compensating for his offense in exact proportion) may be compromised by more pragmatic considerations. In civil cases, damage awards often are settled out of court, with the amount representing a compromise between what is owed and what is feasible.

Summary

We have described six general goals of legal sanction: justice, retribution, value affirmation, deterrence, rehabilitation, and efficiency. We have discussed some of their interrelationships. Any one of several objectives may be salient in any given decision. For example, a particularly heinous crime may accentuate retribution, deterrence, and value affirmation. Evidential factors may encourage plea bargaining and efficiency. Researchers need to accumulate descriptive evidence on the relative weights assigned to these different motives for different types of offenses and offenders. This will allow theorists to begin to decipher the nature of judges' "theories of punishment."

FUTURE PROSPECTS

In this chapter, we have described the structural, personal, and interpersonal factors which influence the judicial decision-maker. The judge's discretion is most obvious in his/her sentencing capacity where he/she generally operates under a loose statutory mandate of, say, sentencing from 2 to 20 years. In reaching a decision, the judge may focus on the offender, the circumstances surrounding the offense, or the offense itself, and the decision may be grounded in considerations of justice, retribution, deterrence, rehabilitation, efficiency or any differential combination of these factors.

We have noted that this kind of judicial flexibility, which is the norm, has been extensively criticized. In the last few years, the number of books and advisory reports on the judicial process has multiplied, with sentencing practices receiving most of the critical attention. Substantial changes of some kind thus may be imminent. All contemporary proposals for changing the character of judicial decision-making involve curtailing the judge's discretion. However, before we can reasonably expect judges, scholars, policy-makers, and the public to reach some degree of consensus on what changes are necessary and how they might be implemented, interested parties must confront some basic questions.

We perceive at least four such questions. *First,* the logical starting point is the philosophical and motivational basis of judicial sanction. We must closely inspect why we punish offenders. As we suggested above, descriptive research on practicing judges' theories of punishment will prove instrumental in this regard. Observers need to make hard decisions as to which objectives are most important. *Second,* we need to ask what is the best way to integrate philosophy and policy. Perhaps legislators need to provide judges with guidelines on the relative weight to give various objectives in different types of cases. This is a burdensome task due to the difficulty of constructing a typology of similar cases. *Third,* the general issue of the degree of structure must be resolved. Will the goal be to completely curb judicial discretion in sentencing? If we eliminate judicial capacity to intervene positively in behalf of defendants, then we might witness judges and jurors freeing guilty offenders if they feel the only available punishment is too harsh. Researchers have experimentally verified this possibility (Vidmar, 1972). Thus the goal would best be to put some checks on judicial discretion *and* to make the system subservient to a criterion of justice. Davis (1971) elucidates the principles behind such a policy. He makes the perhaps obvious observation that reforms should concentrate on removing *unnecessary* discretion, not discretion per se. *Fourth,* we need to ask what positive and negative factors should legitimately influence sentences. Is it realistic to attempt to define the relevancy of extralegal factors? Answers to these questions should yield a rational basis for regulating judicial discretion in sentencing.

FOOTNOTES

[1] Work on this chapter was supported in part by National Institute of Mental Health Grant No. MH27203-01.

[2] J. Frank, *Law and the Modern Mind.* New York: Tudor Publishing Co., 1936, P. 121.

[3] These examples are cited in American Friends Service Committee, *Struggle for Justice.* New York: Hill & Wang, 1971, p. 127.

[4] We would like to thank the American Academy of Judicial Education and the organizers of the Judicial conference of Virginia District Court Judges for making accessible the data for this study.

[5] The structure of juvenile courts exemplifies the impact of lack of public scrutiny on sentencing disparity. Until recently the closed-door hearings, lack of record keeping, and lack of defense counsel magnified judicial discretion in juvenile courts.

[6] See for example, A.S. Miller, Supreme Court: Time for Reforms, Washington *Post,* January 11, 1976.

[7] Some theorists have pointed to need as a separate distribution rule (Lerner et al., 1976; Leventhal, 1976a), but we feel that need is merely a case of equity being properly considered. A person's obvious need constitutes a positive input which identifies a special mitigating set of circumstances.

[8] American Friends Service Committee, *op. cit.,* p. 134.

[9] *Ibid.,* p. 60.

[10] Cited in L.T. Empey, Juvenile justice reform: Diversion, due process, and deinstitutionalization. In L.E. Ohlin (ed.), *Prisoners in America.* Englewood Cliffs, N.J.: Prentice-Hall, 1973, p. 21.

REFERENCES

Adams, J.S. Inequity in social exchange. In L. Berkowitz (ed.), *Advances in experimental social psychology,* Vol. 2. New York: Academic Press, 1965, pp. 267-299.

American Friends Service Committee. *Struggle for justice.* New York: Hill & Wang, 1971.

Anderson, N.H. Cognitive algebra: Integration theory applied to social attribution. In L. Berkowitz (ed.), *Advances in experimental social psychology,* Vol. 7. New York: Academic Press, 1974, pp. 1-101.

Aristotle. *Nicomachean ethics.* H. Rackham, Translator. Cambridge: Harvard University Press, 1912.

Austin, W. Studies on "equity with the world": A new application of equity theory. Unpublished Ph.D. dissertation, University of Wisconsin-Madison, 1974.

Austin, W. & Utne, M.K. Simulated Jurors' responses to a defendant's suffering: How much is enough? Paper presented at the American Psychology-Law Society meetings, Chicago, Illinois, 1975.

Austin, W. & Utne, M.K. The differential impact of an offender's suffering on simulated jurors' conviction and sentencing behavior. Unpublished manuscript, University of Virginia, 1976.

Austin, W. & Williams, T. A survey of judges' responses to simulated legal cases: A research note on sentencing disparity. *Journal of Criminal Law and Criminology,* in press, 1977.

Austin, W. Walster, E., & Utne, M.K. Equity and the law: The effect of a harmdoer's "suffering in the act" on liking and assigned punishment. In L. Berkowitz & E. Walster (eds.), *Advances in experimental social psychology,* Vol. 9. New York: Academic Press, 1976a, pp. 163-190.

Austin, W., Williams, T., Adler, A., Warshel, S. & Siegel, D. Effect of mode of adjudication and favorability of verdict on observers' evaluation of a trial proceeding. Unpublished manuscript, University of Virginia, Department of Psychology, 1976b (mimeo available from author).

Blumberg, A. *Criminal justice.* New York: Quadrangle Books, 1967.

Bullock, H.A. Significance of the racial factor in the length of prison sentences. *Journal of Criminal Law,* 1961 (November-December), 411-417.

Carter, R.M. & Wilkins, L.T. Some factors in sentencing policy. *Journal of Criminal Law, Criminology, and Police Science,* 1967, *584,* 503-514.

Chambliss, W.J. The deterrent influence of punishment. *Crime and Delinquency,* 1966, *12,* 70-75.

Chambliss, W.J. & Seidman, R.B. *Law, order and power.* Reading, Mass.: Addison-Wesley, 1971.

Clinard, M.B. *Sociology of deviant behavior,* 3rd ed. New York: Holt, Rinehart & Winston, 1968.

Clinard, M.B. & Quinney, R. *Criminal behavior systems: A typology.* New York: Holt, Rinehart & Winston, 1967.

Chiricos, T.G. & Waldo, G.P. Socioeconomic status and criminal sentencing: An empirical assessment of a conflict proposition. *American Sociological Review,* 1975, *40,* 753-772.

Davis, K.C. *Discretionary justice: A preliminary inquiry.* Baton Rouge, La.: Louisiana State University Press, 1969.

DeJong, W., Morris, W.N. & Hastorf, A.H. Effect of an escaped accomplice on the punishment assigned to a criminal defendant. *Journal of Personality and Social Psychology,* 1976, *33,* 192-198.

Downie, L. *Justice denied: The case for reform of the courts.* New York: Praeger, 1971.

Empey, L.T. Juvenile justice reform: Diversion, due process, and deinstitutionalization. In L.E. Ohlin (ed.), *Prisoners in America.* Englewood Cliffs, N.J.: Prentice-Hall, 1973, pp. 13-48.

Frank, J. *Courts on trial.* Princeton, N.J.: Princeton University Press, 1950.

Friedland, N., Thibaut, J. & Walker, L. Some determinants of the violation of rules. *Journal of Applied Social Psychology,* 1973, *3,* 103-118.

Fry, M. Justice for victims. In M.H. Rubin (ed.), 1956 Compensation for victims of criminal violence: A round table. *Journal of Public Law, 8,* 155-253.

Gaudet, F.J. The sentencing behavior of the judge. In V.C. Burnham & S.B. Kutash (eds.), *Encyclopedia of criminology.* New York: Philosophical Library, 1949, pp. 449-461.

Geerken, M.R. & Gove, W.R. Deterrence: Some theoretical considerations. *Law and Society Review,* 1975, *9,* 497-514.

Gibbs, J.P. Crime, punishment and deterrence. *Southwest Social Science Quarterly,* 1968, *46,* 515-530.

Gibbs, J.P. *Crime, punishment and deterrence.* New York: Elsevier, 1975.

Glaser, D. Correction of adult offenders in the community. In L.E. Ohlin (ed.), *Prisoners in America.* Englewood Cliffs, N.J.: Prentice-Hall, 1973, pp. 89-116.

Golding, M.P. *Philsoophy of law.* Englewood Cliffs, N.J.: Prentice-Hall, 1975.

Green, E. *Judicial attitudes in sentencing.* London: Macmillan, 1961.

Grunhut, M. *Juvenile offenders before the courts.* Oxford: Clarendon Press, 1956.

Hagan, J. Extra-legal attributes and criminal sentencing: An assessment of a sociological viewpoint. *Law and Society Review,* 1974, *8,* 357-383.

Hart, H.L.A. *The concept of law.* Oxford: The Clarendon Press, 1961.

Hogarth, J. *Sentencing as a human process.* Toronto: University of Toronto Press, 1971.

Hood, R. & Sparks, R. *Key issues in criminology.* New York: McGraw-Hill, 1970.

Horowitz, M. The veridicality of liking and disliking. In R. Taguiri & L. Petrullo (eds.), *Person perception and interpersonal behavior.* Stanford: Stanford University Press, 1950, pp. 191-209.

Jacob, H. *Justice in America.* Boston: Little, Brown, 1965.

Kant, E. *The metaphysical elements of justice.* New York: Bobbs-Merrill, 1965 (originally published in 1797).

Kalven, H. & Zeisel, H. *The American Jury.* Boston: Little, Brown, 1966.

Kaplan, M.F. & Kemmerick, G.D. juror judgment as information integration: Combining evidential and nonevidential information. *Journal of Personality and Social Psychology,* 1974, *30,* 493-499.

Kohlberg, L. Stage and sequence: The cognitive developmental approach to socialization. In D. Goslin (ed.), *Handbook of socialization theory and research.* New York: Rand McNally, 1969.

Leventhal, G.S. Fairness in social relationships. In J. Thibaut, J.T. Spence & R. Carson (eds.), *Contemporary topics in social psychology.* Morristown, N.J.: General Learning Press, 1976a.

Leventhal, G.S. The distribution of rewards and resources in groups and organizations. In L. Berkowtiz & E. Walster (eds.), *Advances in experimental social psychology,* Vol. 9. New York: Academic Press, 1976b, pp. 92-131.

Leventhal, G.S., Reilly, E. & Lhrer, P. Change in reward as a determinant of satisfaction and reward expectancy. Paper presented at Western Psychological Association Meetings, Portland, Oregon, 1964.

Levi, E.N. *An introduction to legal reasoning.* Chicago: University of Chicago Press, 1949.

Lind, E.A., Thibaut, J. & Walker, L. Discovery and presentation of evidence in adversary and nonadversary proceedings. *Michigan Law Review,* 1973, *71,* 1129-1144.

Macaulay, S. & Walster, E. Legal structures and restoring equity. *Journal of Social Issues,* 1971, *27,* 173-188.

McIntyre, J. Public attitudes toward crime and law enforcement. *Annals of the American Academy of Political and Social Science,* 1967, *374,* 34-46.

McQuire, M.F. & Holtzoff, A. The problem of sentence in criminal law. *Boston University Law Review,* 1940, *20,* 423-434.

Matza, D. *Delinquency and drift.* New York: Wiley, 1964.

Newman, D. *Conviction: Determination of guilt or innocence without trial.* Boston: Little, Brown, 1966.

Patchett, K.W. & McClean, J.D. Decision making in juvenile courts. *Criminal Law Review,* 1965, 699-710.

Piaget, J. *The moral judgement of the child.* New York: The Free Press, 1965.

President's Commission on Law Enforcement and Administration of Justice: Public Attitudes toward crime and law enforcement. *Task force report: Crime and its impact—an assessment.* Washington, D.C.: U.S. Government Printing Office, 1967.

Quinney, R. *The social reality of crime.* Boston: Little, Brown, 1970.

Rawls, J. *A theory of justice.* Cambridge: Harvard University Press, 1971.

Reiss, A.J., Jr. Discretionary justice in the United States. *International Journal of Criminology and Penology,* 1974, *2,* 181-205.

Remington, F.J. & Newman, D.J. The Highland Park Institute on sentence disparity. *Federal Probation,* 1962, *26,* 4-9.

Roche, P.Q. *The criminal mind.* New York: Wiley, 1958.

Rose, A.M. & Prell, A.F. Does the punishment fit the crime? *American Journal of Sociology.* 1955, *61,* 247-259.

Rubin, S. Disparity and equality of sentencing—a constitutional challenge. *Federal Rules Decisions,* 1966, *55,* 65-67.

Sudnow, D.D. Moral crimes: Sociological features of the penal code in a public defenders' office. *Social Problems,* 1965, *12,* 255-276.

Suffet, F. Bail setting: A study of courtroom interaction. *Crime and Delinquency,* October, 1966, 318-331.

Thibaut, J. & Walker, L. *Procedural justice.* Hillsdale, N.J.: Erlbaum, 1975.

Thibaut, J., Walker, L., LaTour, S. & Houlden, P. Procedural justice as fairness. *Stanford Law Review,* 1974, *26,* 1271-1289.

Thibaut, J., Walker, L. & Lind, E.A. Adversary presentation and bias in decision making. *Harvard Law Review,* 1972, *86,* 386-401.

Tillich, P. *Love, power, and justice.* New York: Oxford University Press, 1954.

Vidmar, N. Effects of decision alternatives on the verdicts and social perceptions of simulated jurors. *Journal of Personality and Social Psychology,* 1972, *22,* 211-218.

Walker, L., LaTour, S., Lind, E.A. & Thibaut, J. Reactions of participants and observers to modes of adjudication. *Journal of Applied Social Psychology,* 1974, *4,* 295-310.

Walster, E., Bersheid, E. & Walster, G.W. New directions in equity research. *Journal of Personality and Social Psychology,* 1973, *25,* 151-176.

Walster, E., Utne, M.K. & Trapumann, J. Equity theory and intimate relationships. In W. Stroege (ed.), *Friendship and love: Psychological approaches to the development of inter-relationships,* in press.

Ward, D.A. Evaluative research for corrections. In L.E. Ohlin (ed.), *Prisoners in America.* Englewood Cliffs, N.J.: Prentice-Hall, 1973, pp. 184-206.

Wasserstrom, R.A. *The judicial decision.* Stanford: Stanford University Press, 1961.

Wilkins, L. *Evaluation of penal measures.* New York: Random House, 1969.

Wooton, B. *Crime and the criminal law.* London: Stevens and Sons, 1963.

IV

Policy and Professional Issues

11

Community Psychology and Public Policy: The Promise and the Pitfalls

JOHN MONAHAN

Of all the groupings of individuals who call themselves psychologists, none is in a greater state of conceptual flux or a more frantic search for professional roles than those who preface their activities with the term "community." The tenth anniversary of the birth of community psychology has just been celebrated by a National Training Conference in Austin, Texas (Iscoe, 1975). Of the many admonitions offered at that exceedingly fruitful meeting, the one which recurred most frequently was the necessity for meaningful involvement in social change. Community psychology, many argued, is not the provision of old clinical services in new "community" settings; psychoanalysis in Spanish is still psychoanalysis and street-corner token economies are token economies nonetheless. What characterizes a genuine community psychology, it was held, is its unrelenting emphasis on ameliorating those situational and social forces which give rise to problem behavior, and enhancing those community factors conducive to psychosocial strength and competence.

The purpose of this paper is to propose that a valuable and often overlooked role for this kind of activist community psychology can be found in the realm of public policy. Charges of *Walden Twoism* and social engineering are sure to follow any such suggestions, and merely by raising the possibility that community psychologists may contribute to the formation of public policy I risk unfavorable mention in the writings of Thomas Szasz. Nonetheless, the attempt will be made to articulate the rationale and justification for policy involvement, and to answer its critics straightforwardly. As well, three public policy roles that the community psychologist legitimately may assume shall be proposed, and a model for the assumption of one of them shall be offered.

POLICY INVOLVEMENT: THE PROMISE AND THE PITFALLS

The number of definitions of community psychology currently in use approaches the number of its definers. Zax & Specter's (1974) delineation of the field, however, appears to be gaining some consensual validation. They regard community psychology as "an approach to human behavior problems that emphasizes contributions made to their development by environmental forces as well as the potential contributions to be made toward their alleviation by the use of these forces" (p. 3). While it is the task of etiological research to ferret out the contribution of environmental forces to the development of behavior problems, there would seem to be no more efficient large-scale method of alleviating undesirable environmental influences on behavior than through public policy intervention.

Public policy is "whatever governments choose to do or not to do" (Dye, 1975, p. 1). It is the official means by which an organized society prioritizes and responds to the issues confronting it (Kahn, 1969a,b). Many policy decisions, such as the creation of Head Start, and the Community Mental Health Centers Act, are of obvious importance to the concerns of community psychology. For the ecologically minded community psychologist (Kelly, 1966; Catalano & Monahan, 1975), however, it is not difficult to see that a vast number of federal, state, and local policy actions also have significant psychological implications. Policy concerning schools, housing, police, and welfare, for example, will have an immense impact—for better or worse—upon the nature of community problems and the provision of direct and indirect services to meet community needs. Sarason (1974) uses the example of public transportation to make a similar point:

> For most people, perhaps the demise of this service, or a drastic reduction in service, would be akin to losing a convenience. For many others it is to lose a necessity. Young people would be most adversely affected. What the near- and long-term consequences would be for these groups is no trivial question either for them or for the larger community. [But] I have never met a psychologist or psy-

chiatrist with a "community" orientation who was even interested in the problem of public transportation or who understood its differential relationship to various groups in the community. As long as one has a purely psychological orientation, as long as one focuses primarily on the individual, as long as one conceives of the environment narrowly or in interpersonal terms, one can never comprehend how much of an individual's "psychology" reflects nonpsychological factors and processes. (p. 147)

Policy decisions play a pivotal role in community functioning and community problem-solving. To the extent that the community psychologist wishes to affect the total community, public policy offers him or her a unique and powerful opportunity to do so (cf. Reiff, 1970).

The arguments against community psychologists becoming active in the formation of public policy are no more difficult to come by. The objections to policy involvement by community psychologists fall into two broad categories. One asserts the lack of a knowledge base from which to launch policy intervention, and the other claims that such interventions are of a dubious ethical and moral nature. Stated as bald accusations, the charges are that community psychologists have little knowledge to contribute to policy decisions (*e.g.,* Halleck, 1969) and that policy intervention by community psychologists is elitist and undemocratic (*e.g.,* Keniston, 1973).

Since it is unfortunately the case that these charges are sometimes true, it would be futile to offer a blanket denial. Community psychologists and community psychiatrists have taken stands on issues concerning which they knew precious little, and they have sometimes acted in what to my mind is an elitist and undemocratic way. (See, *e.g.,* Bellack's [1971] plan for "legislated psychotherapy" or Hutchnecker's [1972] proposal for a mental health overseer for the president.) The issue, however, is not whether community psychologists and their psychiatric colleagues are capable of abusing the public policy arena. Obviously, they are. Rather, the question is whether such acknowledged abuses are *intrinsic* to policy involvement by community psychologists or whether they can be excised from the endeavor, leaving intact a viable, if cautious, role for the community psycholoigist.

It is painfully evident to anyone reading the research literature in community psychology that nontrivial empirical findings are in short supply and "established facts" are nonexistent (Cowen, 1973; Kessler & Albee, 1975). How different this is from other applied areas of psychology (*e.g.,* psychotherapy, behavior change), or even from traditional areas of psychological theorizing (*e.g.,* attribution theory, the "risky shift"), is an arguable albeit ad hominem point. Clearly, the community psychologist or other behavioral scientist cannot offer to the policy-maker knowledge of the same degree of precision as can his or her colleague in the physical or biological services (*e.g.,* in setting public standards for bridge construction or public health measures). The community psychologist who holds his or her breath until all facets of a complex policy issue have been empirically researched will unfortunately but inevitably die a dark shade of blue.

Again, the question needs reframing. The issue is not whether the community psychologist has all the empirical knowledge necessary to formulate rational public policy. He or she doesn't, and neither does anyone else. *The issue is whether public policy will be more intelligently formed if the decision-makers have input from community psychologists.* Here the answer depends on the policy area under consideration, and on the particular expertise of the individual community psychologist.

While humility concerning the current level of psychological knowledge is certainly called for, it would be a false humility to claim that psychologists know nothing of behavior or its development. Research abounds in the policy-relevant areas of socialization, education, aggression and behavior change, among many others. Disagreements as to the interpretations of these findings, to be sure, are rife. *But would it not be better if conflicting psychological positions were presented to policy-makers along with the evidence upon which these positions were based, so that the policy-makers could reach their own conclusions, rather than leaving policy decisions to be made in total ignorance of psychological research and theory?* The decision-makers are always free to reject the views of the community psychologist—and frequently do—but they also may be presented with information of which they were unaware, and that information may prove to be very useful in forming the policy under consideration (Horowitz & Katz, 1975).

Assuming that at least on occasion he or she may have something relevant to say, the issue remains as to whether the community psychologist *should* have an input into the public policy decision-making process. should policy involvement be viewed as an avocation, a hobby indulged in "off duty," or should it be viewed as legitimate and even central to the role of community psychology? Since no one questions the right of the community psychologist as a citizen to become involved in public policy, the question concerns the appropriateness of his or her participation as a community psychologist.

There are some who would take the position that legitimizing a policy role for the community psychologist would result in an undemocratic and elitist form of government of "experts." The well-known views of Thomas Szasz on community psychiatry and community mental health are pertinent here. Szasz sees community intervention as part of a medical model whose values are "collectivism and social tranquility" and whose goals are to make people "uncomplainingly submissive to the will of the elites in charge of Human Engineering" (1970, p. 224).

Several points need to be made in response to this criticism of policy involvement by mental health professionals. The most obvious one is that the medical model is a straw man in this context. I have yet to meet a community psychologist of any ability who conceptualized community problems in medical terms. The more germane issue of the unintended consequences of "psychologizing" social problems must indeed be considered. Competent analyses of this problem already exist (Caplan & Nelson, 1973). Suffice it to say that it is possible for a psychologist to address a social problem without necessarily implying that its remedy must be found at the level of the individual. While they often do it, there is no necessity for psychologists always to "blame the victim" for his or her own plight (Ryan, 1971).

In arguing for a role for community psychologists in the formation of public policy, I am not advocating that they should ever be given *control* over policy decisions, but rather that they should aggressively seek out for themselves opportunities for creative *input* into the democratic decision-making process. It would, for example, be elitist for the state to choose a community psychologist simply because he or she was a community psychologist, and give that person complete discretion on the allocation of day-dare monies in a state. What I would argue is that it is as much within the role definition of a community psychologist to advocate a certain state program for day care before a legislative committee—with the elected representatives making the policy decision—as it is to consult to an individual day-care center.

The danger that psychologists or other social scientists will be placed in positions of excessive control over social policy is a real one, and we are better for having watchdogs such as Szasz keep the mental health professions on their democratic toes. But social control by psychologists is an outcome to be avoided in policy involvement; it is not the inevitable result of such involvement. Horowitz & Katz (1975) have put the issue well:

> The best arguement for the widest possible implementation of social scientists in legislative, executive, and judicial branches of government at national and subnational levels is the brake they provide on idiosyncratic decision making that results from too narrow a consideration of evidence and contexts. The worst reason for more widely using social science talent is to avoid or bypass the democratic process—a situation in which the role of expertise comes to displace the will of the people on major issues. Between these two polls the tightrope must be walked. (p. 168)

THREE PUBLIC POLICY ROLES

It is possible to identify three generic public policy roles for the community psychologist. The roles focus on the *administration* of policy programs, the *evaluation* of policy choices, and the *formation* of policy decisions themselves.

The first two are relatively straightforward activities, and their parameters can be quickly sketched. The last will require a more detailed elaboration.

Policy Administration

One powerful but underutilized policy role open to the community psychologist lies in the actual administration of an ongoing public program. In this role, the community psychologist is not a consultant "with the luxury of giving advice without responsibility for implementation" (Sarason, 1974, p. 248). He or she is accountable for day-to-day program performance and for long-term program impact.

While the administration of a community mental health center may be the most obvious exemplar of this policy role, programs in many other areas, such as social service, education, urban planning, and criminal justice, are equally open to being administered by community psychologists who have educated themselves in the subject matter (Monahan, 1976).

Administrative responsibility for an important public attempt at community problem resolution can be an exceedingly creative and scholarly enterprise. Often the decision to implement a policy program is hastily arrived at. In the surge of political pressures surrounding the policy decision, it is frequently the case that the substance of the program is only vaguely delineated. It is left to the administrator to fashion meaningful policies within the broad mandate which has been provided. However good a policy decision may be, it is rarely better than the person implementing it.

Precautions must be taken in order to maintain one's identity as a community psychologist rather than degenerate into becoming merely another faceless government bureaucrat. Chief among these precautions may be the adaptation of what Sarason (1974) terms "time-limited administration." According to this procedure, the community psychologist would commit himself or herself full-time to the administration of a public program, but with an explicit end-point in sight. After this time had been reached, the community psychologist would conceptualize and disseminate his or her experience so as to contribute to a body of policy knowledge from which others might draw.

Policy Evaluation

Program evaluation is a field of endeavor that has recently come into its own. The methodological literature on evaluating social programs has been steadily increasing since the appearance of Campbell & Stanley's classic monograph in 1963. The pace of publication has increased drastically in the past few years, until now there is little but lethargy or expedience to keep almost any policy program from being empirically evaluated (Heller & Monahan, 1977).

The rationale for promoting an evaluative role in public policy for the community psychologist needs little elaboration. "The social change process," Fair-weather et al. (1974) note, "must involve continuous feedback to decision-makers based on scientific inquiry. Thus, the scientist himself must help society improve its decision-making processes so that needed problem-solving change can occur in an orderly and systematic manner" (p. 203). In the "experimenting society," the empirical evaluation of public programs is essential "as an aid in helping society decide whether or not its innovations have achieved desired goals without damaging side effects" (Campbell, 1973, p. 72).

While the issues involved in the evaluation of policy programs are numerous (see, *e.g.,* Rossi & Williams, 1972), one bears mention in the current context. Daniel Moynihan (1969), in his otherwise excellent description of the involve-ment of social scientists in the Kennedy and Johnson administrations' "war on poverty" programs, arrives at the conclusion that the *only* role for the social scientist vis-à-vis public policy is that of evaluation: "What institutional role may the social sciences expect to play in public affairs? The answer seems clear enough. The role of social science lies not in the formation of social policy, but in the measurement of its results" (p. 193).

It is difficult to overestimate the importance of program evaluation in the public policy process. It is, in addition, the policy role for which psychologists are best trained, given the empirical traditions of our field. But Moynihan's attempt to restrict psychologists and other social scientists to evaluative roles is unjustified. That social scientists failed in developing one set of social programs does not mean they must fail in all others (Zúniga, 1975). That social scientists in the past, when they have tried to develop policy rather than simply evaluate its, have frequently been co-opted and manipulated by political forces (Sarason, 1975b) does not mean that such patterns must persist into the future. At the very least, based on their knowledge of the negative evaluations of many of the social programs of the 1960's, community psychologists and other social scien-tists are in a position to suggest to policy-makers what probably will *not* work, because similar programs have been tried and have failed. As one of the nation's leading program evaluators has put it, "given the record of largely ineffective social programming, I think the time has come to put more of our research talents into even earlier phases of the policy process, into work that contributes to the development of ideas and prototypes" (Weiss, 1973, p. 45). This contri-bution to the development of ideas and prototypes, to the *formation* of public policies, is the final role to be examined.

Policy Formation

The most ambitious policy role to which a community psychologist can aspire lies in contributing not to the administration or evaluation of a policy program, but to the formation of policy decisions themselves. Involvement in the social planning process can be viewed as community psychology at its most distinctive and powerful level, for here, if anywhere, one can influence the shape and direction of large-scale social change.

With the wisdom of hindsight, I will propose a six-stage process for formative policy input by the community psychologist. The process is offered both as a heuristic vehicle for explicating the issues involved in policy formation and as a working guide for those who wish to fashion their own policy role. The stages are (1) problem choice and definition, (2) articulation of values, (3) investigation of attempted solutions, (4) selection of the best feasible policy alternative, (5) design of empirical policy evaluation, and (6) adopting a strategy for action.

Problem Choice and Definition

The initial step in becoming involved in the formation of public policy is deciding upon precisely which area of public policy one wishes to address. There are, of course, existing policy positions on almost every issue, and it is impera- tive to narrow one's focus at the outset to a problem of manageable proportions, lest one succumb to the politician's occupational disease of being a jack-of-all- trades and master of none. The target of policy intervention need not be a "problem" in the pathological sense. Strengthening existing community re- sources is a tack long overlooked by community psychologists (Rappaport et al., 1975). The target issue must have an "empiric component" (Reiff, 1970, p. 9), since without some relevant data or theory base, there is no rationale for pro- fessional psychological input. "We need to develop generic criteria suggesting the kinds of social problems that can be approached intelligently from the stand- point of psychology. Psychology is not relevant to everything" (Rappoport & Kren, 1975, p. 840). But psychology, as has already been argued, is relevant to some things, and from among the universe of issues which can be approached intelligently from the standpoint of psychology, two factors may assist the com- munity psychologist in choosing one for policy intervention. The factors are community priorities and ecological importance.

It would appear essential that a community psychologist allow the com- munity itself substantial leeway in setting the priorities and directions for policy action, rather than responding to one's own pet issues (Rappaport & O'Conner, 1972). Only be respecting the autonomy of a community and acting as a facilita- tor of community sentiment and a resource for community action can the com- munity psychologist escape the accusation of elitism discussed earlier. Com- munity control, to be sure, is not an unqualified good. In many communities, there are issues (*e.g.,* racial equality) on which one could not in good conscience facilitate the prevailing community sentiment or serve as a resource for the kinds of action the majority of the community would wish to pursue. At such times, the policy-oriented community psychologist must either switch target issues or switch communities of allegiance. But while such ethical impasses do sometimes arise, the more usual case is that the priorities of the community fall within the psychologist's range of moral acceptance, and should take precedence in planning policy interventions.

The notion of community priorities can be illustrated by the recent moves by myself and others in several states to abolish the indeterminate prison sentence. The indeterminate sentence involves sentencing convicted offenders for vaguely specified periods of time (*e.g.*, 1 to 20 years), with the actual release date determined by a parole board on the basis of psychological or psychiatric reports. As a psychologist, I was aware of the data on the failure of involuntary treatment (Geis & Monahan, 1976) and the inability of mental health professionals to predict with any accuracy when an offender was violence-prone (Monahan, 1975b; Monahan & Cummings, 1975a). But persuasive as these data were, they did not tell me how highly the community in question—prisoners, in this case— prioritized *this* policy issue as compared with others. It was only through reading the literature of prisoner advocates (American Friends Service Committee, 1972; Mitford. 1974). talking with officials of the Prisoners' Union, and seeing the thousands of letters written to legislators by prisoners themselves urging abolition of the indeterminate sentence that I became aware that this was not just one among many issues of community concern, but an extremely high-priority issue as well. Convinced that my choice of a target problem was consistent with the priorities of the community, and marshaling all the available empirical evidence, I advocated both in the popular media and before legislative committees (Monahan, 1975a) that the indeterminate sentence should be abolished. While the effect of any one person's testimony was doubtlessly marginal, the legislature did take the evidence into account when it voted to abolish the indeterminate sentence effective July 1, 1977.

When a reliable sense of community priorities has been obtained, it remains to place the designated target of policy intervention into its ecological context. The relevance of ecological constructs to community psychology has been suggested for some time (Kelly, 1966), and they appear especially pertinent at the level of public policy. Questions raised by an ecological perspective include: What other problem areas are interdependent with this problem? Will change in this problem area affect change in others, and, if so, in what direction? From among a group of problems which the community prioritizes as urgent, an ecological perspective would suggest that one select for intervention that problem which plays the most central role in maintaining other problems. Regardless of which problem is selected, an ecological perspective alerts the community psychologist to investigate the "unintended consequences" of the policy intervention upon other phenomena in the community.

The value of an ecological perspective in problem choice and definition can be seen in the policy changes in the area of civil commitment that are currently being carried out in many states. What one finds is that commitment in a mental hospital is interdependent with incarceration in jail in a number of ways. When commitment statutes are narrowed so that it becomes more difficult to hospitalize (and thereby isolate) those of whom the community is intolerant, community pressure is brought to bear on the police to enforce unwritten social norms by effecting a criminal arrest in cases where previously they would have taken the individual to a mental hospital (Abramson, 1974; Monahan, 1974a; Monahan & Geis, 1976).

If incarceration in jail is hydraulically interdependent with commitment in a mental hospital, an ecological perspective would suggest that change in public policy regarding mental hospitalization could not be made without simultaneously affecting change in the criminal justice system. Using such an ecological perspective, I have argued before legislative committees in California and Washington that while policy *should*, for civil libertarian reasons, be changed in the direction of narrowing eligibility for involuntary commitment, such policy change will have little beneficial effect on those it was meant to help unless one simultaneously upgrades psychological services in jails for those disordered persons who have actually committed a crime, and in addition creates on the community level new and voluntary alternatives to both mental hospitals and jails for those who have committed no offense other than being "different" (Monahan, 1974b; Monahan & Cummings, 1975b).

Articulation of Values

That any form of psychology can be value-free is a pernicious myth that many have helped put to rest (Smith, 1969; Halleck, 1971; Stier, 1975). In community psychology, values are not merely "relevant," they are pervasive (Vallance, 1972). If the community psychologist is to escape the charge of disguising personal values as scientific conclusions and then foisting them upon an unsuspecting public, he or she must be explicit about the values to be maximized in any given policy intervention. This means being explicit both on what one's values are and on the fact that they *are* values and not scientific truths. It is not enough, however, to list a long catalog of the virtues to be optimized, or to offer Barnum statements about improving "the quality of life." The *relative ordering* of values is what is called for here. One cannot maximize everything at the same time. Precisely *which* values will be weighed most heavily—*which* qualities of life will be maximized more than others—must be articulated at the outset (Cowen, 1973). Each intervention may have a different set of guiding values, or the same values may be weighted differently in different projects. It is honesty, not consistency, which is most demanded.

As an illustration of the principle of value articulation, I have recently begun a policy consultation program with the local (Irvine, California) police department. After numerous meetings and in the context of a growing and friendly professional relationship with the police chief, but before any formal agreements were reached as to the nature of my role as a community psychologist, I sent him a memo which read in part:

> I would like to be explicit about the values that will guide our future interaction. I see them as three:
>
> (a) *Autonomy*. A primary function of the Irvine Police Force shall be to guarantee every citizen the right to live a life free of unnecessary state interference in their decision-making.
> (b) *Safety*. A primary function of the Irvine Police Force shall be to guarantee every citizen the right to lead a life free of fear for his or her physical safety.
> (c) *Justice*. The value by which competing claims for individual autonomy and community safety shall be mediated is that of justice. In its most basic sense, justice can be defined as "fairness" to all citizens in the application of the law.

To be sure that the implications of these values were clear, I specified six operational principles which would guide my involvement in the formation of police policy:

> (1) *Community input*. The citizens of Irvine should have maximum input at every stage of the policing process.
> (2) *Openness*. Police policies and procedures should be open to public review. Secretiveness is to be avoided whereever possible.
> (3) *Least forceful alternative*. When several courses of police action are available, the least forceful alternative consistent with community safety shall be chosen.
> (4) *Legal rights*. Whatever action is taken, the maximum protection of the individual's legal and psychological rights shall be afforded.
> (5) *Diversity*. The Irvine Police Force shall show a high degree of respect to cultural and sub-cultural diversity within the community.
> (6) *Experimental social innovation*. The explicit philosophy of the department shall be one of responsible experimentation with ways to maximize the values of autonomy, safety, and justice. Policies are made to be changed by empirical data on their effectiveness.

Investigation of Attempted Solutions

An important policy issue will quickly generate a range of proposed solutions, each generally predictable from a knowledge of the self-interest of those generating the proposals. More importantly, since community problems rarely arise de novo, each is associated with a history of attempts at policy remediation (Sarason, 1975a). "A careful exploration of these attempted solutions not only shows what kind of change must *not* be attempted, but also reveals what maintains the situation that is to be changed and where, therefore, chaange has to be applied" (Watzlawick et al., 1974, p. 111). Indeed, it is often the case that the attempted solution has itself become more problematic than the original difficulty which prompted it, the prohibition of alcohol in the 1930's and of marijuana today being cases in point. At such times, "radical non-intervention" (Shure, 1973) may be the best strategy. "Those who are ignorant of history," Santana wrote, "are condemned to repeat it." Detailed answers to the questions "Why has this problem resisted previous attempts at resolution?" and "What will I do *differently* so that I will succeed where others have failed?" may help to isolate the overlooked variables that have caused past attempts to flounder. In the ecological literature, this concept is referred to as "succession" (Trickett et al., 1972), but the moral is the same: the wise community psychologist learns from the mistakes of others.

In designing a program to voluntarily divert early-offending juveniles from the justice system to a family problem-solving project (Binder et al., 1976), for example, my colleagues and I surveyed the literature on previous attempts to change police policy in regard to juvenile incarceration and found that they had failed for two reasons: they lost the cooperation of the police, who saw such activities as usurping police authority, or they lost the faith of the community, which saw diversion from juvenile hall as being "soft" on delinquency (Lemert, 1971). Knowing the history of attempts at resolving our target problem, we were able to design a project from the start with these two pitfalls in mind. We established procedures for close relationships with feedback to the police (within the limits of confidentiality), to discourage the perception that we were working behind their backs, and we secured a strong community board of directors, as well as launched a public relations campaign, to assure the community that we were not condoning delinquency. The success of the project to date in voluntarily diverting more than a thousand juveniles from further police processing has much to do with these initial historically based moves.

Selection of the Best Feasible Policy Alternative

When the reasons for past policy failure have been ascertained, the community psychologist is in a position to choose which of the proposed policy options should be promoted, or what new option must be created, consistent with the priorities of the community and the values that have been espoused. It is at this point that the community psychologist can be at his or her most scientific. Rallying the most solid data and theory available, he or she must arrive at a scientifically sound and politically feasible proposal for action.

Given the uniqueness of each policy problem, it is not possible to present an accounting of all the variables which must go into the selection of the optimum policy alternative. That the chosen alternative must be a "feasible" one should be emphasized, however. I would agree with Fairweather and his colleagues (1974, p. 210) when they state that it is "exceedingly important that decision makers understand the weakness of decisions arrived at through political compromise when the future of man is at stake." But I would also concur with Ardrey that "the pursuit of the unobtainable makes impossible the realizable." One must strive for the best policy alternative capable of being implemented at the given moment in history. Utopian fantasies can be extremely counterproductive when rigidly pursued (Monahan, 1973).

Design of Empirical Policy Evaluation

In proposing or supporting a course of policy action, the allegiance of the community psychologist must always be to "experimental social innovation" (Fairweather, 1969). Solutions to community problems should be promoted not because they will work—a fact of which no one can be sure—but because based on the best available evidence, they appear to have the highest probability of success. Campbell (1973) cogently advises that psychologists "avoid cloaking their recommendations in a specious pseudo-scientific certainty, and instead acknowledge their advice as consisting of but wise conjectures that need to be tested in implementation" (p. 73). He justly berates those "scholar-advisors" who fall into the "overadvocacy trap" and "fail to be interested in finding out what happens when their advice is followed" (p. 72).

In the ideal case, a course of proposed policy action would be chosen, and a prospective experimental or quasi-experimental evaluation design would be constructed and included in the cost of the program being promoted. The results of this evaluation would later be disseminated back to the policy-makers, who would then be in a position to make a genuinely informed decision as to the program's continuation, demise, or modification.

Adopting a Strategy for Action

After all is said, something must be done. Following the choice of a policy alternative and the inclusion of an evaluation design, steps must be taken to heighten the probability of the policy's being actually implemented.

While the choice of strategy, like the choice of the policy alternative itself, is highly specific to the given issue and the particular group of decision-makers, it is generally advisable to begin strategy planning by first analyzing the potential sources of support and of resistance in the decision-making body. Who is likely to support a given course of action on the face of it, because it dovetails with their expressed positions or interests, and who can be counted among the opposition? Most importantly, how can those without a clear or vested interest in the given issue be moved in support of it? This latter question is often the crucial one. There are few issues which engage the interest of the majority of people. Most issues evoke a serious response from a self-interested minority and apathy from the rest of us. In planning strategy, the community psychologist must consider what ethical and open tactics of persuasion can be employed to move fence-sitters into his or her own yard.

The planning of strategy and the earlier choice of the best feasible policy alternative are highly interdependent: if the strategy fails, then one must move back a step and reassess whether the chosen tack was indeed a "feasible" one, or whether one must move down a peg on the hierarchy of preferred policy alternatives.

One difficulty at this final stage of policy formation which often dissuades community psychologists from ever becoming involved in the policy process is the problem of entry or access to decision-makers. Even if a policy issue can be chosen, underlying values made explicit, previous solutions researched, a feasible position taken, and an empirical evaluation designed, how is the politically inexperienced community psychologist to gain access to the ears and minds of those in a position to take action on his or her recommendations?

While not wishing to demean what can at times be a serious problem, especially if it is national policy one desires to affect, it has been my experience that access to state and local decision-makers is more generally available than is commonly believed. Most policy-makers of my acquaintance are perpetually badgered by "input" from those special interests who have a financial stake in policy decisions. They have welcomed the contribution of someone with academic credentials who could summarize and evaluate the available data on a policy issue, and who could offer recommendations that did not involve personal financial gain. As I have become more involved in policy issues and better known in decision-making circles, the issue of access has ceased to be a problem, and, in fact, the opposite difficulty has arisen: more requests to have input into policy decisions than I can accommodate with integrity (*i.e.,* taking the time to do the necessary background research and documentation). It should be noted that before most important policy decisions are made, open public hearings are held where any citizen can testify. These hearings may be a good entry point for the community psychologist who wishes seriously to adopt a role in policy formation.

CONCLUSIONS

Public policy is surely not the only vehicle for affecting social change. Strategies which take place at the individual or group level undoubtedly have much to offer and should be pursued vigorously by community psychologists. But to the extent that public policy decisions have a large-scale and enduring impact on the community, work at the policy level provides an unparalleled opportunity for bringing about the kinds of environmental change that are the very core of community psychology.

Policy intervention is a highly collaborative task. It involves working closely with community groups, lawyers, agency administrators, other social scientists, and politicians, and so necessitates an attitude of interdisciplinary and jargonless ecumenism. It is also a prolonged task and requires a deep commitment to social change. Often years elapse between the genesis of a policy recommendation, its enactment, and its final implementation. Those in need of weekend publications had best look elsewhere, as should those with a low tolerance for failure.

But although frustration, disappointment, and, at times, despair, are the companions of the community psychologist who forays into the politicized world of public policy, the partial reinforcement effects are no less real. To appear before a legislative committee and later watch the roll call vote support the position which you have advocated produces a surge of adrenalin the likes of which are not often found in the laboratory or the consultation room.

A final observation: There are many who will read and agree with the sentiments expressed in this chapter, and yet will protest, "All well and good, *but this is not psychology!*" Surely public policy intervention is not what I or most community psychologists have been trained to do or have been led to believe is within the purview of our professional role. Yet I would argue now that it is the nature of training and the prescription of roles which must change, not involvement in the public decision-making process. In the spirit of the Bicentennial, I would answer the Tories of the psychological establishment by paraphrasing Patrick Henry: If this is not psychology, then let us make the most of it.

FOOTNOTES

Parts of this chapter were originally presented to the annual convention of the American Psychology-Law Society, Chicago, Illinois, 1975. I am fortunate to have had the benefit of insightful comments on this manuscript by my colleagues Linda Monahan, Raymond Novaco, Joseph DiMento, David Dooley, Kenneth Heller, and Eileen Raffaniello.

[1] People v. Burdick, Sup., 121 *Cal. Rptr.* 488 (1975).

REFERENCES

Abramson, M. The criminalization of mentally disordered behavior. In A. Brooks (ed.), *Law, psychiatry, and the mental health system.* Boston: Little, Brown, 1974, pp. 491-496.

American Friends Service Committee. *Struggle for justice.* New York: Hill & Wang, 1971.

Bellak, L. The need for public health law for psychiatric illness. *American Journal of Public Health,* 1971, *61,* 119-121.

Binder, A., Monahan, J. & Newkirk, M. Diversion from the juvenile justice system and the prevention of delinquency. In J. Monahan (ed.), *Community mental health and the criminal justice system.* New York: Pergamon Press, 1976, pp. 131-140.

Campbell, D. The social scientist as methodological servant of the experimenting society. *Policy Studies Journal,* 1973, *2,* 72-75.

Caplan, N. & Nelson, S. On being useful: The nature and consequence of psychological research on social problems. *American Psychologist,* 1973, *28,* 199-211.

Catalano, R. & Monahan, J. The community psychologist as social planner: Designing optimal environments. *American Journal of Community Psychology,* 1975, *3,* 327-334.

Cowen, E. Social and community interventions. *Annual Review of Psychology,* 1973, *24,* 423-472.

Dye, T. *Understanding public policy* (2nd ed.). Englewood Cliffs: Prentice-Hall, 1975.

Fairweather, G. *Methods for experimental social innovation.* New York: Wiley, 1967.

Fairweather, G., Sanders, D. & Tornatzky, L. *Creating change in mental health organizations.* New York: Pergamon Press, 1974.

Geis, G. & Monahan, J. The social ecology of violence. In T. Lickona (ed.), *Moral development and behavior: Theory, research, and social issues.* New York: Holt, Rinehart & Winston, 1976.

Halleck, S. Community psychiatry: Some troubling questions. In L. Roberts, S. Halleck & M. Loeb (eds.), *Community psychiatry.* New York: Anchor Books, 1969.

Halleck, S. *The politics of therapy.* New York: Science House, 1971.

Heller, K. & Monahan, J. *Psychology and community change.* Homewood, Ill.: Dorsey Press, 1977.

Horowitz, J. & Katz, J. *Social science and public policy in the United States.* New York: Praeger, 1975.

Hutchnecker, A. The stigma of seeing a psychiatrist. *New York Times,* July 4, 1973, p. E-15.

Iscoe, I. *Report on the Austin conference: The future of community psychology.* Symposium presented at the meeting of the American Psychological Association, Chicago, September, 1975.

Kahn, A. *Studies in social policy and planning.* New York: Russell Sage, 1969a.

Kahn, A. *Theory and practice of social planning.* New York: Russell Sage, 1969b.

Kelly, J. Ecological constraints on mental health services. *American Psychologist,* 1966, *21,* 535-539.

Keniston, K. How community mental health stamped out the riots (1968-78). In B. Denner & R. Price (eds.), *Community mental health: Social action and reaction.* New York: Holt, Rinehart & Winston, 1973, pp. 341-351.

Kessler, M. & Albee, G. Primary prevention. *Annual Review of Psychology,* 1975, *26,* 557-591.

Lemert, E. *Instead of court: Diversion in juvenile justice.* Washington, D.C.: Government Printing Office, 1971.

Mitford, J. *Kind and usual punishment: The prison business.* New York: Vintage, 1974.

Monahan, J. Abolish the insanity defense? Not yet. *Rutgers Law Review,* 1973, *26,* 719-740.

Monahan, J. The psychiatrization of criminal behavior. In A. Brooks (ed.). *Law, psychiatry, and the mental health system.* Boston: Little, Brown, 1974a, pp. 696-699.

Monahan, J. Dangerousness and civil commitment. In Committee on the Judiciary, United States Senate. *Reform of the Federal Criminal Laws.* Washington, D.C.: Government Printing Office, 1974b, pp. 7083-7093.

Monahan, J. *Abolishing the indeterminate sentence.* Testimony before the California Senate Select Committee on Penal Institutions, Sacramento, April, 1975a.

Monahan, J. (ed.). *Community mental health and the criminal justice system.* New York: Pergamon Press, 1976.

Monahan, J. The prediction of violence. In D. Chappell & J. Monahan (eds.), *Violence & criminal justice.* Lexington, Mass.: Lexington Books, 1975b, pp. 15-31.

Monahan, J. & Cummings, L. The prediction of dangerousness as a function of its perceived consequences. *Journal of Criminal Justice,* 1975a, *2,* 239-242.

Monahan, J. & Cummings, L. Social policy implications of the inability to predict violence. *Journal of Social Issues,* 1975b, *31,* 153-164.

Monahan, J. & Geis, G. Controlling "dangerous" people. *Annals of the American Academy of Political and Social Science,* 1976, *423,* 142-151.

Moynihan, D. *Maximum feasible misunderstanding.* New York: Free Press, 1969.

Rappaport, J. & O'Conner, R. Advocacy and accountability in consultation to the poor. *Mental Hygiene,* 1972, *56,* 39-47.

Rappaport, J., Davidson, W., Wilson, M. & Mitchell, A. Alternatives to blaming the victim or the environment: Our places to stand have not moved the earth. *American Psychologist,* 1975, *30,* 525-528.

Rappoport, L. & Kren, G. What is a social issue? *American Psychologist,* 1975, *30,* 838-841.

Reiff, R. Psychology and public policy. *Professional psychology,* 1970, *1,* 1-10.

Rossi, P. & Williams, W. (eds.). *Evaluating social programs.* New York: Seminar Press, 1972.

Ryan, W. *Blaming the victim.* New York: Pantheon, 1971.

Sarason, S. *The psychological sense of community: Prospects for a community psychology.* San Francisco: Jossey-Bass, 1974.

Sarason, S. *Community psychology, networks, and "Mr. Everyman."* Address presented to the National Training Conference in Community Psychology, Austin, April, 1975a.

Sarason, S. *Community psychology and the anarchist principle.* Address presented to the meeting of the American Psychological Association, Chicago, September, 1975b.

Shure, E. *Radical non-intervention: Rethinking the delinquency problem.* Englewood Cliffs, N.J.: Prentice-Hall, 1973.

Smith, M.B. *Social psychology and human values.* Chicago: Aldine, 1969.

Stier, S. Psychology and public policy. In S. Nagel (ed.), *Policy studies and the social sciences.* Lexington, Mass.: Lexington Books, 1975, pp. 107-123.

Szasz, T. *The manufacture of madness.* New York: Harper & Row, 1970.

Trickett, E., Kelly, J. & Todd, D. The social environment of the high school. In S. Golann & C. Eisdorfer (eds.), *Handbook of community mental health.* New York: Appleton-Century-Crofts, 1972, pp. 331-406.

Vallance, T. social science and social policy: A moral methodology in a matrix of values. *American Psychologist,* 1972, *27,* 107-113.

Watzlawick, P., Weakland, J. & Fisch, R. *Change: Principles of problem formation and problem resolution.* New York: Norton, 1974.

Weiss, C. Where politics and evaluation research meet. *Evaluation,* 1973, *1,* 37-45.

Zax, M. & Specter, G. *An introduction to community psychology.* New York: Wiley, 1974.

Zúniga, R. The experimenting society and radical social reform: The role of the social scientist in Chile's Unidad Popular Experience. *American Psychologist,* 1975, *30,* 99-115.

12

Federal Regulation of Psychological Devices: An Example of Medical-Political Drift

R.K. SCHWITZGEBEL

The use of devices to observe, measure, and change behavior has a long history in psychology. For example, Sir Francis Galton, who is well-known for his early work in assessing intelligence, was also interested in measuring aspects of character which often involved the use of various devices. In the *Fortnightly Review,* Galton described an apparatus for determining when two persons have an inclination toward one another.[1] He suggested that at a dinner table they visibly incline or slope toward each other while sitting side by side. He placed pressure gauges on the legs of their chairs to measure this inclination.

Devices have also been important in the work of B. F. Skinner. Even as a child, he was a skilled gadgeteer. He developed a flotation device to sort green elderberries from ripe ones. His attempt to develop a perpetual motion machine was less successful—or perhaps awaits some further development. His design for the cumulative recorder as a graduate student was central in the development of his theory of operant conditioning.

Psychologists have continued and considerably increased their use of instruments to measure behavior, thought, and emotion. Now, however, devices are also being developed by psychologists to change these processes. It is the use of devices for the purposes of treatment which has most concerned the public and the federal government. The federal regulation of the sale and use of these psychological devices could have an extremely great impact upon psychological research and practice.

POTENTIAL REGULATION BY THE FDA

The most immediate, likely source of federal regulation is the Food and Drug Administration (FDA). Legislation has been passed and is now being implemented which would greatly clarify and expand the authority of the FDA in regulating "medical devices." This legislation would pose no great difficulty for psychology except that it includes an extremely broad definition of a medical device. In H.R. 5545, known as the Rogers bill, the definition of a medical device includes the words "intended to affect the structure or any function of the body of man or other animals."[2] This definition of a medical device as one which affects "any function" of the body is certainly overly broad. A handgun clearly affects the functioning of the body, but it is not a medical device even when it is used by a physician. A teaching machine might improve the reading ability or mental functioning of a student, but that is not sufficient to make it a medical device. A baseball pitching machine might improve eye-hand coordination, clearly a function of the body, but it cannot reasonably be considered a medical device. Nor can alarm clocks or traffic lights be considered medical devices, although they also affect the functioning of the body. These are psychological or behavioral devices.

A medical device must be a device which is (or claims to be) of substantial importance in supporting, sustaining, or preventing impairment of human life or health. This definition could encompass some devices developed and currently used by psychologists. The Mowrer pad, for example, which sounds an alarm immediately upon a child's wetting the bed, is commonly used to treat enuresis. This device was developed expressly with learning principles in mind. The child was to learn to contract his urethral sphincter muscles while experiencing relevant bladder pressure cues.[3] One could characterize this device in current terminology as a primitive type of biofeedback device. Modern biofeedback devices used to treat medical disorders such as migraine headaches or hypertension could appropriately by considered medical devices when so used. Their use or misuse could substantially affect human health.

When a device has multiple uses, some of which are nonmedical, its classification should take into account this fact. The primary intended use of the device by the ultimate user may determine its classification in a particular situation. A thermometer used to measure a patient's temperature is a medical device, but if it is used to measure atmospheric temperature it is a meteorological device. A biofeedback unit used only for purposes of meditation is not a medical device, but if it is used to treat migraine headaches it is a medical device.

As with drugs, the FDA is concerned primarily about two characteristics of medical devices: their safety and their effectiveness (or efficacy). In current practice and under present regulations, the FDA may place a medical device into one of three major categories. Class I devices are those regulated by general controls. These controls may include, for example, the registration of the manufacturer with the FDA, factory inspection, record and report keeping by the manufacturer, good manufacturing practices, notification to certain purchasers of defects found in the device, and repair or replacement of defective devices. A typical medical device in Class I is a tongue depressor.

A Class II device would be one regulated by performance standards because in the opinion of the FDA general controls are not sufficient to assure the safety and effectiveness of the device. In cooperation with outside groups and experts, the FDA is to establish and enforce standards regarding matters such as indicated uses, proper labeling, instructions for use, and warnings to users. There should be periodic reviews of the standards to see that they are appropriate. Devices not meeting the established standards are not permitted in interstate commerce. These standards usually apply to general classes of medical devices such as hypodermic needles of a particular type.

A Class III device is one which requires premarket approval by the FDA because in the opinion of the FDA standards could not be developed which would assure the safety and effectiveness of the device. A device in this category would be subject to scientific review before being permitted in interstate commerce. A medical device in this class would be a new cardiac pacemaker.

If a device is classified as Class II (standards) or III (premarket approval), the Secretary of the FDA may establish special requirements concerning the sale and use of the device. In the case of a device which has potentially harmful effects, the FDA may limit its sale and distribution so that it is available "(A) only upon the written or oral authorization of a practitioner licensed by law to administer or use such device, or (B) upon such other conditions as the Secretary may prescribe in such regulation."[4] This gives the FDA very broad discretionary and undefined authority. A device subject to this regulation would be considered a "prescription device."

FDA DRIFT TOWARD PSYCHOLOGY

It has often been said that nature abhors a vacuum. Apparently, the federal government abhors administrative vacuums. The fields of medical and psychological devices have not been extensively regulated and most observers would agree that some additional professional and federal intervention is probably needed to protect consumers. Overall, the present medical device law and the classification of medical devices into three classes as just described seems reasonable. One of the most frequent difficulties with this type of legislation, however, is its interpretation and implementation by the administrative group.

The FDA has already established panels to begin screening and classifying medical devices. Among these panels are those considering cardiovascular, orthopedic, and neurological devices. Over 3,000 devices have been classified by these panels into the three major classes just described. These panels are composed primarily of physicians and the outlook is primarily medical. This results in a "medical-political drift" in which risks to consumers, psychological problems, and even behavior are viewed primarily in medical terms. This medical view tends to be accepted, not because of any malice or clear logic, but merely because it is familiar to the FDA. Alternative conceptualizations and procedures for regulation are missing from consideration. One effect of this medical-political drift is the overly broad classification of psychological or behavioral devices as medical devices.

One example of this drift begins with the testimony of Dr. Charles C. Edwards. As Assistant Secretary for Health of DHEW, he testified on behalf of medical device legislation and in that testimony listed several FDA classification panels. Among these panels he mentioned one on "neurological disease"[5] which is called the Panel on Review of Neurological Devices. The term "disease" has now disappeared—or Congress was not correctly informed and that panel recently held a meeting on biofeedback and behavioral devices. One could ask whether any FDA panel is properly authorized to examine "behavioral" devices.

The effects of medical-political drift are found not only in the classification of devices but also in the regulation of the sale and use of devices following their classification. The FDA is not authorized to regulate the practice of medicine or psychology. That is regulated by state law and professional organizations. The decisions made by the FDA regarding the sale and use of devices can, however, have indirect and substantial effects upon professional practice. As previously noted, the Secretary of the FDA may restrict the sale or distribution of a device to "a practitioner licensed by law to administer or use such device." The FDA is very likely to consider such a practitioner to be a physician. But physicians are not the only persons who treat diseases. They are surely not the only persons who treat "mental diseases"—to the extent that such a concept has any logical meaning and includes emotional and behavioral problems.

The Panel on Review of Neurological Devices has classified both biofeedback and aversive conditioning (electrical stimulus) devices as medical devices subject to standards to be established subsequently by the FDA.[6] The Panel has recommended that the following warning be affixed to or accompany an aversive conditioning device: "If this device is used in the treatment of a disease, it shall be used only in consultation with a physician."[7] Missing from this recommended label is the possibility of consultation with "a person licensed by law to administer or use such device" who is not a physician. Only the term "physician" is used. If the disease is a physiological disorder, limiting the use of a device to consultation with a physician may be appropriate. If disease is broadly interpreted, then limiting the use of aversive conditioning equipment to consultation with a physician may be clearly contrary to present psychological practice and may also be an illegal infringement by a federal agency upon the right to professional practice. Does the aversive conditioning of homosexual impulses or impulses to shoplift involve the treatment of a disease? Is homosexuality or shoplifting a disease? Because neither the term "medical device" nor the term "disease" is clearly defined, the FDA drifts toward the regulation of psychological practice in a sea of conceptual ambiguities.

ALTERNATIVE REGULATORY APPROACHES

Development of Standards by Psychological Organizations: Self-Regulation

Psychology as a profession has not been well organized with regard to the use of psychological devices. Standards or guidelines for assuring the safety and effectiveness of psychological devices have not been formally developed and accepted. In the absence of such standards, psychological entrepreneurs may have a field day. It is not that entrepreneurs are bad; they are in fact needed in order to bring to the public the benefits of technological innovation. They should not, however, be permitted to benefit from the sale of devices which are unsafe or ineffective. We are indeed fortunate that more serious accidents have not occurred in the use of psychological devices. Standards of safety, particularly regarding shock hazards, urgently need to be developed. Some preliminary test procedures and safety specifications for devices used for aversive shock therapy have been developed by Butterfield.[8]

Standards related to the effectiveness of devices in achieving their claimed purposes also need to be developed. Some so-called psychological devices come close to being "quack" or fraudulent devices. For example, an organization is currently marketing a "mood" ring which allegedly indicates mood. The ring is claimed to be "your liaison between real life and nature's mystical contingencies."[9] Variations in skin temperature apparently change the color of the ring. Different colors are to give the wearer different "mood warnings." A yellow color is to indicate that the wearer is "easily bothered; mind is difficult to focus and control; time for concern and extra caution." No evidence is presented in the small paper accompanying the ring that it in fact "Helps you control your emotions and plot your destiny" as claimed. This ring is not a medical device nor noes it seem to be a psychological device. It is probably best characterized as a toy and should be so labeled.

Cooperation with Consumer Organizations

Issues regarding the safety and effectiveness of consumer products are not exclusively in the jurisdiction of the FDA. Physical injury, even death, from a product does not necessarily make that product one suitable for regulation by the FDA. Some people will be electrocuted by flying kites into high-power lines. Many people will be injured by power lawn mowers, and many will be killed by automobiles. Kites, lawn mowers, and automobiles are not medical devices. Psychology as a discipline is uniquely capable of collecting data and running controlled experiments to determine the extent to which people are deceived by misleading claims or advertising, how well consumers understand and follow instructions, and how accidents occur. The interests of consumers are not incompatible with psychology. In fact, a major trend in psychology has focused upon measuring the effectiveness of psychotherapeutic interventions and has raised serious doubt about the effectiveness of psychoanalysis as generally applied by psychiatrists. Empirical findings by psychologists about treatment effectiveness have frequently been used in policy formation and judicial decisions.[10] Ironically, it has been psychologists rather than physicians or psychiatrists who have most emphasized accountability and effectiveness in treatment and thus protected the interest of mental health consumers.

More generally, the Consumer Product Safety Commission can remove from interstate commerce those products presenting unreasonable risk to consumers. The Federal Trade Commission has authority to stop excessive and fraudulent claims in advertising. These agencies could use standards and information developed by recognized psychological organizations in their enforcement activities. This in turn could reduce the need to classify devices as medical devices to obtain adequate public protection.

Development of Interdisciplinary Evaluation and Treatment Programs

Under present law, the effectiveness of medical devices is to be determined "on the basis of well-controlled investigations, including clinical investigations where appropriate, by experts qualified by training and experience to evaluate the effectiveness of the device."[11] Psychologists could contribute much to the evaluation of devices. The usual training of a physician does not qualify him to conduct valid evaluation studies.

As medical and psychological devices become increasingly complex, it becomes increasingly inappropriate to expect that any one practitioner, whether physician or psychologist, will have sufficient skill and knowledge to use a device in an optimal manner. In the case of devices which are primarily psychological, but which may involve some medical risks, it would seem inappropriate to have the treatment conducted "under the supervision" of a physician who was not specially trained or skilled in the psychological treatment procedure. But a labeling requirement, as previously discussed, which stated that the device should be used "only in consultation with a physician" (or other properly licensed practitioner) would seem appropriate.[12] The goal should be the development of an interdisciplinary treatment situation which, as a whole, maximally utilizes the unique skills of the various practitioners in order to safeguard or promote the health of the patient.

It should be remembered that not all serious problems or risks in this world are medical in nature. Driving a car may result in serious injury or even death, but cars may be purchased and used without medical prescriptions. Some devices are medical devices; some are not. In the area of product safety and effectiveness, no one discipline can rightfully claim a monopoly on skill, virtue, or moral authority. Psychology should assume its responsibility and psychologists should be permitted to practice freely and collaboratively within the domain of their special expertise.

NOTES

[1] Galton, *Measurement of Character*, 42 Fortnightly Review 179 (1884).

[2] H.R. 5545, 94th Cong., 1st Sess. § 520 (e) (1) (1975); Federal Food, Drug, and Cosmetic Act, § 201 (h) (3) (1976).

[3] Mowrer & Mowrer, *Enuresis: A Method for Its Study and Treatment*, 8 Am. J. Orthopsychiatry 436 (1938).

[4] H.R. 5545, 94th Cong., 1st Sess. § 520 (e) (1) (1975).

[5] Hearings on H.R. 6073, H.R. 9984, H.R. 539, H.R. 10061. Before the Subcomm. on Public Health and Environment of the House Comm. on Interstate and Foreign Commerce, 93rd Congress, 1st Sess. 156 (1974).

[6] See Summary Minutes, 7th meeting, Panel on Review of Neurological Devices, FDA, December 12-13, 1975.

[7] *Id.* at 4.

[8] Butterfield, *Electric Shock—Hazards in Aversive Shock Conditioning of Humans,* 3 Behavioral Engineering 1 (1975).

[9] McGrath Hamin Inc., *New Spectra • Stone,* Providence RI 02901 (1975).

[10] See O'Connor v. Donaldson, No. 74-8, U.S. (June 26, 1975), Chief Justice Burger concurring, at 7 (Slip Opinion).

[11] H.R. 5545, 94th Cong., 1st Sess. §513 (a) (3) (1975).

[12] *Supra* note 6 at 4.

13

The Fallibility of the Eyewitness: Psychological Evidence

ALVIN G. GOLDSTEIN

Despite improvements in and discoveries of sophisticated new scientific methods of criminal investigations, it is still true that in certain kinds of crimes simple eyewitness identification retains its traditional importance among law enforcement workers. A recent article in the New York *Times* emphasizes both the extent to which law enforcement agencies depend on eyewitness identification and the risks which are still inherent in the use of eyewitness identification procedures. In this case, a 19-year-old high school youth was arrested and charged with robbing a woman. The only evidence was the victim's identification. While out on bail, the youth read in a newspaper story of a man, accused of rape by an eyewitness's (mis)identification, who was subsequently freed because the real rapist confessed to the attack. From photographs which accompanied the news article, it was evident to the youth that *both* men resembled him. As a result of further investigation by the youth's lawyer, the rapist also confessed to the robbery, and the charges against the youth were dropped (New York *Times,* 1974).

These comments emphasize the dilemma faced by law enforcement agencies, lawyers, and the courts whenever eyewitness testimony is the sole and decisive evidence in a criminal trial. On the one hand, nearly all criminal investigators would argue against abolition of eyewitness identification testimony in criminal trials because eyewitnesses are often valuable sources of evidence, more often than not they correctly identify the culprit, and finally, under special circumstances, the testimony of an eyewitness may be the *only* evidence apparently linking the criminal suspect to the scene of the crime. On the other hand, as the *Times* story dramatizes, and as anyone familiar with court proceedings or the history of criminal justice must know, eyewitnesses have recurrently identified the wrong individuals, and the consequences of these errors often have been appalling (Wall, 1965).[1] In trials where both disconfirming and corroborating evidence were totally absent, the defendant sometimes has been wrongfully convicted solely on the basis of the eyewitness testimony. Moreover, the existence of these known and documented errors of identification implies the inescapable conclusion that misidentifications and subsequent convictions have occurred in other criminal trials but remain undiscovered. This can only mean that innocent people have served (and are serving) prison sentences, and some unknown number have been executed.

The dilemma is clear: eyewitness identification is a powerful but extremely dangerous tool and its use is always a mixed blessing. Continued acceptance of uncorroborated eyewitness identification testimony in the long run will inevitably lead to two opposing consequences: criminals who would otherwise remain free because all other kinds of evidence were lacking will be apprehended and convicted on eyewitness testimony; and innocent people will be convicted of crimes they did not commit. The question facing all branches of law enforcement is also clear: how to maximize the possibility of apprehending and convicting the guilty, but minimize both the possibility of convicting the innocent and the possibility of *accusing* the innocent. It is important to recognize that accusation, although not equal to conviction, is still an appalling error quite capable of causing enormous losses to the individual in both money and prestige.

In this chapter, a radical but effective solution to the dilemma will be suggested. I will propose that no official action against a suspect be permitted unless the eyewitness testimony connecting him to the crime is corroborated by another type of evidence. In other words, I propose that with *direct* evidence *alone* no charges can be brought against a suspect.[2] I will offer an extended argument to defend this proposal, but the defense will not be based on legal or procedural grounds: instead it will be supported by logical considerations and psychological research data. Although the chapter is organized around this solution, it is necessary, in order to lay the groundwork and develop the relevant arguments, to explore several related aspects of the psychological problems surrounding recognition memory. These explorations will be presented in subsequent sections, in the following sequence. First, I will begin with an analysis of the reasons the criminal justice system depends so heavily upon eyewitness testimony. Second, examples of laboratory evidence documenting the invalidity of face recognition performance will be presented. This will be followed by a statement and clarification of the central proposal of this paper. A discussion of the futility of "improving" personal identification procedures to make them "foolproof" will come next. Finally, the use of expert witnesses in eyewitness cases will be analyzed, and its employment discouraged. A concluding statement completes the chapter.

FAITH IN EYEWITNESS TESTIMONY

As an outsider looking in, as it were, at the working of the criminal justice system, I am astonished to discover that testimony concerned with personal identification by eyewitnesses is accorded at least equal status with several other kinds of evidence. It is obvious that the courts assume humans are capable, in their day-to-day activities, of almost errorless registration and subsequent reporting of events. This faith in human perceptual and memory performance is all the more surprising since, from my vantage point as a perceptual psychologist, most of the information at my disposal forces me to conclude that almost any human performance involving perceptual registration and memory processes must be riddled with error. Moreover, the probability of error would be greatest among people who lacked training in observation, that is, the vast majority of people. There is almost no disagreement among present-day experimental psychologists: the perceptual and memory systems do not produce high-fidelity output (*e.g.,* Berkowitz, 1975, Ch. 5; Erdelyi, 1974, p. 12; Trankell, 1972).

Why, then, do the courts seem not to share the psychologists' mistrust of the abilities of the human observer? My analysis of this question has led me to the following series of hypotheses. Criminal law, from its beginnings in antiquity, was totally dependent upon what people saw and what people said they saw. There was little else available to those whose job it was to gather evidence to convict the wrongdoers. The analysis of physical evidence for use in the prosecution of criminals is a modern innovation. Strong evidence demonstrating the unreliability of eyewitness testimony has been readily available for at least 50 years, most probably much longer, but this evidence has been largely ignored because the legal system, similar to other complex institutions, accrued static inertia over its long history of development. Too much past history weighed heavily in favor of continuing to do things in the way they had always been done. In a sense, no one even noticed that there were other, more reliable ways to get evidence or that direct evidence need no longer be a keystone in the structure of facts making up a case against a suspect.

It is reasonable also to wonder whether the legal profession really did have an appreciation for the inexact nature of human testimony—whether the evidence implicating eyewitness testimony as unreliable was available to the workers in the legal profession. It is quite clear from innumerable reviews, briefs, articles, a few books, and judicial opinions that the legal profession *was* and *is* aware of the error-ridden nature of human testimony about events, things, and people, but this awareness if necessarily distorted by at least two important unstated considerations. The fundamental workings of the entire judicial system is squarely based on the transfer of information obtained through perceptual processing (observing, remembering, reporting, thinking, etc.). Were these processes known to be highly unreliable, or unpredictably biased, or riddled by random error, this knowledge should have over the years caused considerable pressure to make extensive modifications in the way certain kinds of evidence are obtained and used. Little change within the criminal justice system was accomplished because of the enormity of the problems which would be generated by overt acceptance of the principle of perceptual error. Thus there would be subtle but nevertheless powerful reasons to keep the status quo. Remember, our knowledge of perceptual distortion and error is relatively recent when compared to the length of time juries have listened to eyewitness testimony. Again, tradition would be more influential than newly discovered information generated in an unrelated discipline.

Furthermore, the legal professions' awareness of this kind of human error has not focused on the *degree* of error; it could be said that the awareness has been vague, not specific. This situation arose as a natural consequence of the fact that there is no simple way to obtain valid data pertinent to the overall efficiency of the methods involved in eyewitness testimony. Readily available facts about the ratio of identification error to total number of identifications is completely lacking. Without firm, easily available statistical information there would be little motivation to scrutinize carefully a police procedure which appeared to be working adequately in the vast majority of cases. This complacency is understandable; it is, moreover, fed by the fact that there is every year an enormous number of criminal cases which are conducted to successful conclusion through the courts without notoriety, and the reasonable presumption here would be that justice was served, witnesses did not misidentify innocent people, recognition was accurate. This knowledge—faulty logic and all—would serve to balance the score against those few cases that get national attention in the newspapers because misidentification by a witness has caused an innocent person to be convicted of a crime. However, the general impression created by this kind of reasoning supports the belief that errors of identification are rare, that personal identification procedures are accurate in almost every case where they are used.

Further support for the apparent reliability of eyewitness testimony comes from our collective personal experience. Face recognition is a highly practiced natural skill which we all share. It is, however, a skill which is not under conscious control, and thus we have almost no insight into the limits of our capability or the conditions under which our capability is measurably affected. It is for these reasons that judges, juries, and lawyers have not seriously questioned either the general assumption, implicit in all trials where eyewitness testimony is the key issue, that eyewitnesses *can* recognize faces, or the specific assumption that *face recognition following a single exposure is equal to face recognition following multiple exposures.* In other words, everyone involved in the legal process seems to believe, without question, that recognition memory for a face seen only once is equal to recognition memory for a face seen many times. The importance of this assertion can not be overemphasized. Because we as individuals are not aware of the exact limits of our recognition memory capacity, we have developed an overall impression that "once seen, never forgotten," but even if this impression were true, it would be based on experiences where we had many exposures, not just one exposure, to a face (see Bahrick et al., 1975, for evidence pertaining to the extraordinary lengths of time familiar faces are remembered). In other words, if we, collectively, think we can almost always recognize faces correctly, this belief is based on those experiences where we *have* accurately recognized faces, but in these instances the faces were highly familiar. I am suggesting two propositions: first, we do not have adequate experiential data to make accurate estimates of our performance with faces seen only once; second, we are totally unaware that we extrapolate inappropriately from multiple-exposure to single-exposure situations.

Finally, motivation to exhaustively examine the accuracy of personal identification testimony would be weak because criminal justice workers may believe, rightly or wrongly, that *truly innocent* people are rarely, if ever, wrongfully convicted of a crime. The argument behind this belief is quite logical. Suspects almost always have criminal records. *This* suspect may not have committed this *crime* for which he is accused, but he surely has committed other crimes for which he was not apprehended; therefore, he "deserves" to go to prison anway.

Up to this point, covert and self-serving motives have been offered as reasons for the continued acceptance of eyewitness identification testimony. But pressure to maintain the status quo also comes from less hidden sources of motivation. As I will show in a later section of this paper, face recognition following a single exposure, although far from perfect, *is* more often accurate than not. Thus there are data—albeit unconscious data—available to each of us suggesting that even with single exposures we often make correct recognitions. Undoubtedly, much of this apparent accuracy is not in response to physiognomic features alone. Recognition would be immensely helped if the person were seen twice in the same location, or seen on both occasions talking to the same friends, or even if on both occasions some article of clothing were identical. Nevertheless, this past history of recognitions would tend to support our belief in the reliability of eyewitness testimony. But the crucial point at issue here is that we fail to distinguish between the almost perfect, extremely long-term recognition memory for faces which have been seen on innumerable occasions, and the relatively poorer recognition accuracy for faces seen only once or twice and for brief periods of time. This blurring of two different situations and our responses to them are responsible for our mistaken belief in, or our almost unquestioned faith in, the ability of an eyewitness to correctly recognize a once-seen face.

In summary, in today's trial court eyewitness testimony falls erroneously within the realm of judicial notice. "Everyone" knows that after looking at a man, he can recognize him at a later date. He may not know his name, but he knows he saw him earlier. It is this collective belief in our ability to recognize faces seen before which is the reason for admitting eyewitness identification into evidence without challenging the general accuracy of recognition memory, nor demanding proof of its reliability equal to the proof demanded from, say, firearms analysis or voice print analysis. Undoubtedly, we humans must know we are not infallible, but our collective experience gives us the impression that people rarely mistake one person for another, that we more often than not recognize a person we met for the first time and see again a day or so later. For these reasons, and others presented later in this chapter, we have developed the folklore that eyewitness identification is acceptably reliable as a "method" of criminal identification. Because the procedures used to obtain eyewitness identification do not closely resemble a "method" or a scientific technology, judges may never have felt the need to demand rigorous, experimental proof of its reliability, or to impose standards for its admissibility. Needless to say, the record of the misidentifications which have caused people to be convicted of crimes they did not commit stands in mute testimony to the need for at least some systematic understanding of face recognition performance (Wall, 1965).

EXPERIMENTAL EVIDENCE FOR FACE RECOGNITION

The variety and scope of the evidence implicating the *general* unreliability of eyewitness testimony is so well documented that it would be almost impossible to find a psychologist (or, for that matter, a sociologist or psychiatrist) who did not believe that most eyewitnesses are untrustworthy reporters of what happened, how it happened, and to whom it happened. But are eyewitnesses untrustworthy reporters only when memory reconstruction of scenes or events are required, or is the fallibility of their memory a more general phenomenon, encompassing recognition memory also?[3] More specifically, how unreliable is the testimony of an eyewitness when identifying a suspect in a line-up or a mug book?

How often in laboratory studies will an observer commit errors in face reconnition for a face seen only once for a short period of time? The evidence available to answer that question is clear and remarkably consistent: an average error of about 30% can be expected to occur, and only rarely will the average error in a single experiment fall below 15%. This conclusion is based on data from many experiments, using a variety of faces and a broad sample of observers. In the following section, I will summarize the results of a small sample of the literature on face recognition memory (for a more comprehensive review, see Ellis, 1975). Before beginning that task, it is necessary to describe briefly the typical experiment from which these findings have been derived.

Nearly all recognition memory experiments are composed of two parts, a study session followed by a recognition (or test) session. During the study trials, subjects (most often college students) are shown face portraits (slides or photographs), usually called "target stimuli." Both the number of targets and the length of time each portrait is exposed may vary from experiment to experiment. In these studies, from one to more than 40 targets have been employed, and the exposure duration has varied from less than a second to 10 seconds per face. Although the instructions given subjects at the beginning of the study session typically inform them of the purpose of the experiment, some investigators have been interested in measuring recognition performance without alerting their subjects to the subsequent recognition test. The instructions usually describe the purpose of the study, and also ask the subject to pay attention to the faces so that they will be able to pick out the targets from among other faces to be shown to them during the recognition test. It is not unusual also to inform the subjects of the exact length of time between the study and test sessions. During the recognition phase of the experiment, which follows the study phase by several minutes or by much longer periods of time (days or weeks), either the target faces and distractor faces are presented one at a time in a randomly arranged sequence, or target and distractor faces are presented simultaneously in pairs or in larger sets composed of one target with several distractors. Whichever method is used, the subject is required to designate which of the faces are targets ("old," or seen before) and which are the distractors ("new," or not seen before).

Accuracy of recognition is not a simple concept nor is it a simple matter to measure since its level depends on many factors, some acting within the observer and some acting on the observer but coming from the environment. In addition, as a moment of thought will prove, accuracy as an index of performance must be measured by more than the raw number of correct recognition responses: accuracy must be evaluated also as a function of the number of false recognition responses. More about this problem later; now, to present the findings of a representative sample of face recognition experiments.

What level of accuracy can be expected if white faces are briefly viewed on only one occasion and recognition memory is measured immediately following the study trials? Shepherd & Ellis (1973) report 89% correct recognition; Scapinello & Yarmey's (1970) subjects on the average recognized 75% of their targets; Cross et al. (1971) found average performance levels to be approximately 54% correct; Goldstein & Chance report 71% correct in one study and 68% correct in another investigation (Chance et al., 1975; Goldstein & Chance, 1971); Elliott et al. (1973) obtained accuracy levels of 75% from each of two groups of subjects; white subjects in an investigation by Malpass & Kravitz (1969) never exceeded 79% of correct recognition of white faces.

What happens to accuracy when the delay interval between the study trials and recognition test is increased beyond a few minutes? Accuracy of performance deteriorated after 6 and 35 days in the Shepherd & Ellis study to 80% and 71% recognition, respectively, from 87%, the level obtained when the test followed the study trials by only a few minutes (Shepherd & Ellis, 1973; Shepherd et al. 1974) report 71% correct recognition following 24 hours delay; Goldstein & Chance (1971) found accuracy to be unaffected by increasing delay from zero to 48 hours, with mean accuracy in both cases 71% correct. Parenthetically, it is important to note that subjects in experiments investigating the effects of increasing the study-test delay interval are tested only once. For example, one group of subjects is tested immediately after the study trials, and a second group is tested, say, 24 hours after the study trials.

Is recognition accuracy for all kinds of faces equal? Several investigators have reported finding reliable decrements in white subjects' performance when black or Oriental faces are used as stimuli. For example, Malpass & Kravitz (1969) found that both white and black subjects performed best with own-race faces, Chance et al. (1975) have shown that white subjects' recognition memory was best for white faces (68%), next-best for black faces (55%), and least accurate for Oriental faces (45%). In contrast, black subjects recognized more black faces (60%) than either white faces (49%) or Oriental faces (43%). Elliott et al. (1973) also report reduced recognition accuracy by white subjects for Oriental faces compared to white faces.

Are children less accurate than adults in face recognition? Only one investigation seems to have relevant information here. Recognition accuracy increases with chronological age; kindergarten children averaged 36% correct; third-graders, 60% correct; and eighth-graders, about 73% correct (Goldstein & Chance, 1964).

In all experiments just reviewed, subjects were presented with multiple targets, and these targets were always pictures (slides or photographs) of faces. Is it reasonable to generalize from the results of laboratory studies to real-life situations? Isn't it much more likely that a single live "target" or, at most, two or three "targets" would be encountered by an eyewitness? Unfortunately, there is little experimental evidence which bears directly on this question, but the facts which are reported suggest that the level of recognition memory performance with live targets is similar to the level of performance found in the multiple picture-target research. Laughery (1972, Ch. 5) reports 84% correct recognition of a single, live target exposed for 30 seconds. Recognition was tested immediately by using 2 portraits of the target distributed among 148 distractors. Laughery (1972) reports the results of a second experiment in which a black man and a white man served as targets. As the data reported earlier would lead one to expect, recognition memory for the black target (by white subjects) was inferior (52% correct) to the level of performance on the white target (96% correct), with the overall performance approximately 75% correct. In a related experiment, Alexander (1972, Ch. 3) investigated recognition memory for one target person, but during the study session subjects were shown 4 candid color photographs depicting various poses of the target face for a total of 30 seconds. Performance was measured with one target and 149 distractor slides; overall accuracy of recognition was 55%. Several demonstrations of eyewitness fallibility conducted by Buckhout are also relevant to this discussion, primarily because he employed techniques designed to resemble real-life crime situations. Once again, recognition memory performance was no better—in fact, much worse—than the levels described in this review (Buckhout, 1974).

In a recently completed (but as yet unpublished) experiment, several undergraduate students under my supervision explored the effect of using either photographs (analogous to the mug book procedure) or the targets themselves (analogous to the line-up procedure) in the recognition trials (Adkins et al., 1974). All subjects looked at 3 live targets for either 5 or 30 seconds during the study trial. In the recognition session, half the subjects were asked to select out of a 5-man line-up any individual they had seen in the earlier session. The remaining subjects tried to select the targets from among 5 pictures. The distractors in the live and picture conditions were the same individuals. Overall accuracy of recognition 2 days and 2 weeks after the study session was about 77% and 85%, respectively. This unexpected reversal in level of performance remains unexplained, but large differences in performance levels from one experiment to the next are not an uncommon finding in facial recognition studies; more about this variability will be found in a later section of this article. Subjects in this study performed as well with pictures as with live targets, but, as expected, subjects given 5 seconds to look at the targets did not perform as well as those given 30 seconds to study the targets. In fact, after 15 days, the 30-second group of subjects recognized 100% of the live targets and 92% of the pictured targets.

These average levels of performance become less impressive when the number of false recognitions is taken into consideration. For example, 44% of the subjects who correctly recognized one target erroneously selected a distractor as a second target.[4] The relatively poor overall performance of subjects in this experiment may be explained by the fact that (a) the distractors were selected in accordance with accepted police procedures to resemble the targets, and (b) only one of the three targets appeared in the line-up (or among the photos) and the subjects were informed that either none, one or as many as all three of the targets were in the line-up (or in the photo display).

Are these data relevant to eyewitness testimony in a courtroom, or are they largely irrelevant because of substantial discrepancies between real-life and laboratory conditions? In essence, do these facts warrant the conclusion that recognition memory for faces, in or outside the laboratory, is unreliable and does not measure up to the minimal standards of accuracy and dependability usually demanded by our criminal courts?

Several arguments can be raised, each questioning the wisdom of using laboratory data as samples of real-life recognition memory performance.

(1) In the majority of experiments, pictures have been used in both the study and test trials, whereas in a real-life crime the criminal's face would be the "study" stimulus. Insufficient information is available to decide whether live faces or pictured faces are better recognized, but the facts which are available suggest that even though recognition performance with real faces may be better than with pictures, it is still neither perfect nor near-perfect; nor do the facts indicate that performance to live faces is consistently high, that is, performance levels vary from one laboratory to another. More importantly, in the vast majority of experiments where pictures (photographs or slides) were used, the target and test pictures were identical, thereby simplifying the subjects' recognition task. After all, the subject now has to recognize the identical picture, instead of performing the more difficult task of recognizing a person's face independent of the original pose, lighting conditions, facial expression, etc. I am suggesting that, contrary to common expectation, the use of study pictures is likely to produce higher levels of recognition accuracy than the use of live faces, and for this reason the results of the laboratory research reviewed above should be viewed as examples of the best possible face recognition memory performance.

(2) With rare exception, subjects in laboratory experiments are fully aware of the purpose of the investigation and therefore from the beginning expect to be tested in the recognition session. In contrast, eyewitnesses are seldom prepared to witness, or be the victim of a crime, and could be said to differ from laboratory subjects in their intent to remember and in their attention to the criminal's face during the incident. Also, we know the laboratory subject pays attention to the face in the experiment, but we have to assume the witness looks at the face of the criminal. Do these differences in intent and attention cause differences in memory performance? Undoubtedly they do, but once again common sense tells us that recognition memory performance of laboratory subjects should surpass the performance of an unprepared or surprised and perhaps frightened eyewitness. Evidence bearing on this question is sparse and contradictory. Some evidence suggests that pictorial recognition memory is hardly affected by the intent of the subject, whereas other findings do not support this contention (Goldstein & Chance, 1974). Although the evidence is incomplete, *nothing* suggests that *in vivo* eyewitnesses would recognize more than laboratory subjects.

(3) Distractor faces in almost all recognition memory experiments are selected "randomly" from a larger pool of face portraits usually obtained from college or high school yearbooks or similar sources. The point here is that in the experiments reviewed the distractors were not intentionally selected to be similar to the target faces, whereas in a line-up the distractors are—or should be—similar to the suspect. Both common sense and experimental data confirm the expectation that correctly locating a target among a series of similar faces is more difficult and leads to more errors than locating a target among unselected distractors. Once again, these considerations suggest that laboratory results set the *upper limit* for recognition memory performance (Laughery et al., 1974).

(4) It has often been asserted, without benefit of evidence, that because a real-life crime produces fear, excitement, or, in more general terms, what psychologists call "arousal" in those connected with the incident, the features of the criminal's face can less easily be forgotten by the victim or other witnesses. In other words, the occurrence of a real crime emotionally affects the witness, and he is for this reason alone thought to be almost incapable of forgetting the criminal's face. Disregarding for the moment the obvious problem of determining the amount of arousal experienced by a witness in a particular interaction with a crime, it is reasonable to assume that laboratory subjects in recognition memory experiments are seldom if ever aroused to levels attained by most witnesses to a crime. The logical conclusion to this argument is that the findings in laboratory experiments cannot be used as evidence for performance levels attained in real-life situations because real-life events cause more arousal in witnesses than laboratory conditions cause in subjects. Thus the recognition accuracy levels obtained in experiments are reduced estimates of performance levels usually attained by "aroused" witnesses. The scientific evidence relating emotionality and learning-memory is inadequate and cannot offer a definitive answer to this problem. Surprisingly few studies have dealt with the effect of emotional arousal on face recognition specifically. Investigations concerned with arousal and memory for words have been reported, but it would be totally inappropriate to generalize from verbal memory findings to face recognition in real-life situations. The evidence which is available and relevant seems to point to a conclusion which is in conflict with the layman's theory that strong emotions strengthen memory. Some evidence suggests that memory is disrupted when emotional arousal is very high *or* very low, but is enhanced if arousal is at an "intermediate" or moderate level. Interestingly, problem-solving and other intellectual abilities have also been shown to be adversely affected by very strong (or very weak) emotional or motivational states. In an experiment conducted in the author's laboratory, designed to explore the possibility of using high-intensity noise (about 100 db) as a means of obtaining controllable levels of psychological arousal, face recognition memory was measured in subjects exposed to the noise and in those not exposed to the noise (Majcher, 1974). The arousal level of the experimental subjects was assumed to be affected by the noise because in pre-experimental tests noise of this intensity raised galvanic skin responses (GSR, a standard laboratory technique for measuring changes in arousal) slightly higher than levels found in subjects not exposed to the noise. Although the level of performance improved in the noise-exposed group, the amount of improvement compared to the noiseless control condition was far too small to give any real comfort to the adherents of the theory that arousal improves witnesses memory. After all, emotional factors would have to improve performance, on the average, about 20% to 30% in order to raise the level of accuracy to values close to 100% correct; it is quite unlikely that emotional arousal alone is capable of improving memory by such large amounts.

(5) The length of time subjects in experiments are permitted to view a target

face is shorter than the time witnesses typically look at a criminal during a crime. This argument asserts that subjects in experiments are poor recognizers because they are not given enough time to "memorize" the targets, whereas in real-life situations the longer exposure times would enhance recognition memory performance beyond the levels obtained in the laboratory. It is not possible at this time to decide whether the first part of this assertion is or is not accurate because the evidence needed to make this decision is not available. What is the average length of time a witness looks at the face of a criminal during the actual crime? Note carefully that the question does not ask for the average duration of a criminal act—a much easier question to answer—but instead seeks the amount of time witnesses spend looking at the criminal's face. In the absence of this information the relationship between performance in the laboratory and performance by witnesses in real-life episodes must remain unclear. However, it would be erroneous to assume that increasing exposure time from several seconds (laboratory experiment) to many seconds or even minutes (assumed real-life situation) will cause recognition memory to improve to the near-perfect levels needed to compete with other court approved methods of connecting individuals with crimes. It is also very unlikely that a simple, linear relationship will be found between exposure duration and number of errors (so that for each increase in exposure time there is a decrease in errors of recognition) because the number of factors which influence recognition memory in a real-life episode are probably enormous and all could interact with exposure time. Thus lengthening exposure time may in some situations have little or no effect on performance, while in other situations, with other factors at work, lengthening exposure time may dramatically increase accuracy.

Although these considerations rightly emphasize the importance of determining the actual length of time a criminal's face is looked at by witnesses in a real-life episode, they do not eliminate the need to discover the effect of duration of exposure upon recognition accuracy in laboratory settings. Several experiments have been described earlier in this article in which a single target face was exposed for at least 30 seconds, and in an unpublished study by the author 3 targets were viewed for 30 seconds. Recognition accuracy ranged from 100% to 55% correct, clearly emphasizing and supporting the argument outlined above, that is, there is no simple relationship between exposure duration and recognition accurarcy. This is not meant to detract from the importance of investigating the effects of exposure duration on recognition memory for faces. It should come as no surprise, however, to discover that it will be difficult to measure accurately "looking time" in real-life situations.

(6) Laboratory findings are incomplete, based as they are upon physiognomic cues alone, whereas in real-life situations witnesses would be helped in their selection of the correct individual by recognizing the suspect's walk, voice, body attitude, hand movements, etc. Although this assertion is true in principle, it is totally misleading in its implication, that is, that recognition for *non*physio-

gnomic aspects of a person are as good or better than face recognition. Another unwarranted implication is that accuracy of personal identification would be improved as the number of identifying features are increased. As far as I know, research on these two hypotheses is totally lacking. Recognition of nonphysiognomic aspects seems plausible until one wonders about the answer to the question: Are body movements, styles of walk, etc., *unique* elements, occurring in a specific identifiable manner in one individual only? Facial features are known to be rarely if ever duplicated (except for twins, of course) but what about styles of walking? Without this basic information, relevant for all nonphysiognomic attributes, it would be foolhardy to assume that recognition memory for nonfacial features of a person is any better than recognition memory for faces.

Before closing this review and discussion of face recognition studies, I will return briefly to the problem of false recognition—the misidentification of nontarget faces as targets, or its real-life equivalent, selecting a suspect in a line-up as *the* criminal in the absence of the true criminal. False recognitions were deliberately deemphasized in this discussion in order to simplify the presentation and analysis of the face recognition data. Surely, false recognition responses occur with annoying but predictable frequency in both experimental and real-life situations. But emphasizing the rate in which false recognitions occur in laboratory experiments could generate wasteful, pointless arguments over the presumed relationship between the results of an experiment and the procedures employed by the experimenter, or the subjects' attitude in a laboratory as compared to real witnesses' attitudes at a line-up, etc. Thus, by omitting repeated references to the controversial false recognition data, I had hoped to legitimately emphasize the imprecise nature of human recognition memory by referring primarily to errors of target nonrecognition. If the data described here are consistent with the accusation made earlier—that eyewitness testimony is error-ridden—then the additional information about false recognitions will only make the case against eyewitness testimony even stronger, but will add little in the way of new concepts.

Several important findings, perhaps as important to law enforcement agencies as all the data already described, have not been discussed in this review because they were not readily apparent from the reported statistical analyses. These omissions will be remedied now.

In our research, we have consistently found vast differences in recognizability among faces, so much so that we never use a single set of target faces in an experiment but, instead, use several sets, sampling from a large pool of faces. In this way, we hope to reduce the effect on average performance levels of one or two or several highly recognizable or highly unrecognizable faces. Judging from the observations of other investigators, this variability in recognizability is pervasive. Moreover, we find that certain faces in experiments (not necessarily the same faces) "attract" large numbers of erroneous "seen before" responses, yet do not seem to resemble the target faces any more than other nonselected faces.

Similarly, Cross et al. (1971) report that some individual faces were misidentified 12 times more often than the least misidentified face, and that the target face most often correctly recognized was selected 3 times more often than the target least well recognized.

Still another source of error of a different kind has been suggested by a recent investigation into the question of facial stereotypes of deviants (Shoemaker et al., 1973). In one phase of this investigation, subjects were asked to select from a set of photographs (middle-aged, white males) those faces that looked most likely and least likely to belong to people who committed each of the following deviant acts: homosexuality, murder, robbery, and treason. Their findings indicate that there is "not only a general consensual, good-bad or criminal-noncriminal stereotype, but also a stereotype for each specific type of offense under consideration" (p. 429). In short, more than 70 *potential* eyewitnesses looked at faces of noncriminals and could "see" that some of these people were or were not murderers, robbers, etc.. These findings have implications for the procedures associated with obtaining eyewitness identification evidence. Eyewitnesses could unwittingly accuse a suspect not because he looks like the culprit, but because he fits the stereotypic "picture" of what a murderer, (robber, etc.), "should" look like.[5]

These are disturbing findings. They are disturbing to psychologists because we seem—momentarily, at least—to be unable to detect and specify the reasons for the vast differences between recognizability of one face compared to that of another. These data should be disturbing to the legal profession since they suggest that, with errors of this magnitude and of this peculiar quality found in well-controlled laboratory studies, it is certain that unfortunate individuals in real-life situations will be accused by eyewitnesses of crimes they did not commit. Indeed, because certain faces seem to "attract" responses from many subjects, and, as we have just seen, certain faces may fit to a greater or lesser degree the facial stereotype of a particular criminal "type," there is good reason to expect that in a real-life situation many eyewitnesses to the same crime would select from a line-up or photographs one individual as the culprit, making it all the more difficult for this person, innocent though he may be, to deny his guilt. Further support for the contention that personal identification is at best an unpredictable criminal investigatory method comes from an analysis of the range of mean error rates reported by the various laboratories engaged in face recognition research. Mean correct recognition varied from 100% to as low as 35%. Notice that these values are average values: subjects vary in ability to recognize faces just as faces vary in recognizability. Would any court in the land accept the results of a forensic science technique with demonstrated reliability as poor as that? Would courts admit evidence derived from a technique in which technicians' ability to discriminate among possible alternatives varies by about 50%?

A SOLUTION TO REDUCE FALSE ARRESTS AND JUDICIAL ERRORS

Because of the fundamental, inherent nature of eyewitness unreliability, I propose that eyewitness identification testimony no longer be admissible to evidence when it is *the only class of evidence* available in a criminal trial.[6] I would even go further and propose that no *official* police action should be taken on the basis of eyewitness testimony alone; to be formally accused of a crime is quite serious—tantamount to guilt, according to some lawyers—and could be inordinately expensive in terms of money, time, and personal anguish even though no trial ever ensues. Furthermore, eyewitness personal identification testimony should be inadmissible unless corroborated by facts associated with another class of evidence; as implied elsewhere in this article, multiple eyewitnesses may be as unreliable as single eyewitnesses.

What are some of the arguments in support of these propositions? The laboratory-generated data discussed in the preceding section in my opinion makes a strong case against accepting uncorroborated eyewitness evidence. But the case is made more convincing by the real-life instances of mistaken identity which occur with consistent regularity. These mistakes are now understandable since they can be explained by the high error rate in recognition memory performance found in laboratory experiments. This suggests that the laboratory data cannot be ignored, nor can it be argued away by accusing the laboratory workers of generating results which are artificial and limited in generality. For if the laboratory findings are inaccurate and recognition memory for faces is really much better than the research findings seem to suggest, why do identification errors still regularly occur in courts and police line-ups?[7] One could answer the question with another question: How often have fingerprint (or firearm) identification evidence sent an innocent man to prison? The implication is clear: errors of identification will always occur with eyewitness testimony because it is less accurate, less valid, and less reliable by several orders of magnitude than any other accepted form of analyzing evidence.

But, it could be argued, eyewitness testimony and testimony derived from scientific evidence cannot be evaluated in the same manner because the rules governing one do not apply to the other; eyewitness recognition evidence is categorized as direct evidence and scientific evidence is considered to be circumstantial evidence. To a psychologist it is astonishing that eyewitness testimony is legally categorized as direct evidence, that is, evidence which proves the facts directly, without inference or presumption being drawn from any other set of facts. Doubtless, the facts of an event are direct evidence, and if the facts in dispute were recorded upon film, then surely when this material (suitably authenticated) is replayed in a courtroom it would qualify as direct evidence. But it is unreasonable—nay, irrational—to say that eyewitness testimony qualifies as direct evidence in the same way that a film record is direct evidence. Most eyewitness reports cannot be taken as "proving the facts directly" because they violate the *purpose* of the definition, viz., to *prove* the facts. The facts can be proven only if the direct evidence is impeccable, and, as emphasized earlier, there is almost total agreement in the scientific community that eyewitness reports are almost never accurate reflections of the true circumstances. As a non-lawyer, I am not at all concerned with the rules governing courtroom procedures, or the definitions of what does or does not fall into the various arbitrarily designed categories of evidence. Some of the reasons for my position on this issue have been stated in the earlier paragraphs of this article. In brief, procedural and definitive rules involved in criminal justice were devised at a time when scientific information about human behavior was unknown, and, unfortunately, there were few alternatives to eyewitness evidence. It is irrational to ignore the fact that, logically speaking, an eyewitness's testimony is *used* by the courts or police in exactly the same manner as the courts *use* a report of fingerprint analysis. Today, with the information available regarding human memory performance, it is irrational to continue to assume that eyewitness evidence is different *in kind* from other forms of evidence, and for this reason need not be measured and evaluated by essentially equal yardsticks. It is similarly irrational to continue to act as though the rules of logic do not fully apply to certain kinds of evidence. All classes of evidence are facts; all evidence can be stated in propositional terms, all is equal in logical status. Some classes of evidence, for a variety of reasons, are more secure than others, but this fact in no way changes their logical status. The point here is that, logically speaking, in its role as evidence there is no difference between a bullet with its telltale rifling markings, or a fingerprint found on a water glass in the murdered man's room, or the eyewitness's response, "Yes, that's the killer," made while viewing a line-up. The exact steps which must be traced to connect the killer with the crime may differ in detail in the above examples, but they have in common one crucial characteristic. For all three examples, additional inferences must be drawn—a deduction of fact must be made—in order to logically connect the evidence to the suspect and the crime. Contrary to current legal usage, eyewitness personal identification testimony does *not* prove the facts in dispute without further inferential reasoning. Eyewitness testimony is, therefore, logically equivalent to, say, fingerprint evidence, which requires inferential reasoning to connect the suspect to the crime. The face recognition data described earlier no longer permit easy acceptance of the myth that eyewitness evidence is *direct* evidence. To the contrary, in order to persuasively—logically—link the suspect to the criminal event, eyewitness evidence demands that, at the very least, the following logical inferences be drawn: that the witness is naturally capable of recognizing at a later time any face briefly seen on one occasion, and that a *near-perfect* level of recognition ability is manifested by ordinary individuals (or at least a level of accuracy equal to the levels permitted in other methods used to identify individuals) in situations similar to the one in which the witness observed the criminal. In other words, prior to believing the testimony of an eyewitness, the trier of facts must assume that the witness is a normal individual, that he is capable of accurately remembering the events (or "storing" the face), that he is capable of accurately recognizing a once-seen face and of *rejecting all faces* of individuals who are in fact not the real criminal. Before the results of laboratory research on face recognition were made available, the foregoing assumptions were implicit in every personal identification made by an eyewitness, and probably remained implicit because scientific evidence regarding face recognition was relatively lacking. Now, with systematic knowledge of eyewitness unreliability, both the fiction that eyewitness testimony does not involve further deductive reasoning and the implicit assumption that recognition memory is nearly perfect are no longer tenable.

In summary, uncorroborated eyewitness evidence is a procedure designed to produce errors, and for this reason alone should be abolished as a method of criminal justice. The human observer, when he acts as an eyewitness, is being used by the courts or police in a way altogether analogous to their use of forensic techniques, to help them discriminate among a vast number of possible suspects and therefore identify a particular individual. Since the human observer in this role is logically analogous to a "technique" such as fingerprint analysis or a polygraph test, the reliability of his recognition memory performance should be evaluated by the same set of standards routinely applied by the courts to any new scientific test or as yet inadmissible method of determining the truth of the facts in dispute. If these routine evaluative procedures were employed, they would demonstrate that the human observer in his role as a face recognizer (or identifier) is far inferior in precision and reliability to all admissible police science methods, and also inferior to many inadmissible procedures and tests.

There are, of course, couterarguments which can be raised in opposition to the position expressed here. As a psychologist, I cannot foresee the legal consequences of the proposal advocated here. In a very real sense, it is not my duty to consider the legal aspects of the problem. The facts of human memory are clear. The courts' view of human memory is in total conflict with the facts. My responsibility was to attempt to reconcile the courts' view with the real facts of human memory, and the practical consequences of that reconciliation are only secondary in importance. If the proposal were adopted, it most probably would cause problems for the police, but that in itself is no reason for disqualification. For example, by forcing police to release suspects identified by eyewitness testimony alone, it would appear that many criminals will be allowed their freedom because additional corroborating evidence may not be available to connect them to the crime. This would be true as long as police are negligent in obtaining physical evidence at the scene of the crime. Various agencies have discovered that police fail to collect physical evidence in the majority of crimes they investigate. These allegations could be interpreted as evidence that police are more interested in eyewitness identification because they know it will be effective in court, and therefore they are less interested in collecting *all* available evidence at the crime scene. My proposal would, in effect, force police to increase their efficiency with regard to the collection of physical evidence. If this were done, there is no reason to suppose that the number of unconvicted felons would be increased as a consequence of the adoption of the proposal.

ALTERNATIVE SOLUTIONS

Although recognition memory for faces has been shown in the foregoing section to be in absolute terms an unreliable method of determining identification, this fact alone does not logically force one to accept the solution—abolition of uncorroborated eyewitness identification—I have suggested. One could argue that the suggested rule modification is too radical, and should not be adopted, but instead law enforcement agencies should be trying to solve the problem by (a) improving the procedures by which eyewitness evidence is collected, and (b) modifying the specific requirements governing the admissibility of expert witness testimony; *i.e.,* trial courts should permit qualified psychologists (or other perceptual or visual scientists) to evaluate and offer opinions to the jury about the reliability and accuracy of visual perception. In the following discussion, both of these alternative solutions will be shown to be inadequate.

A moment's reflection should be enough to convince the skeptics that improving the methods of collecting eyewitness identification testimony will not cure the problem. This is not to say that the line-up, mug book, and associated procedures could not be improved, but even if the improvements were carefully planned they would work to reduce *only* those errors often caused by police overzealousness, by confusions in the witness's mind caused by accidental viewing of a suspect before a line-up, etc. It is contended here that errors presumably caused by the way witnesses are treated *after* a crime has been committed are important, but even if all of these prejudicial post-crime tactics were eliminated (a very unlikely possibility) there would still remain the errors caused by the inherent faultiness of the human observer. In fact, there is some reason to believe that "improving" the personal identification procedures may have—in my view—deleterious effects on courts and juries because the "improvements" might bolster the misguided view that the possibility of error in personal identification procedures is thereby much reduced. Thus a climate of opinion would be generated in which there may be less reason for courts and juries to be cautious when convicting on the basis of eyewitness testimony. Incidentally, modifications of personal identification procedures typically have been imposed with little regard for scientific information about the causes of memory distortions, the effects of persuasive social factors on perception, etc.[8]

It is also true, as several jurists have affirmed, that one "improvement" in the line-up procedure may in itself cause increased errors of identification. In its fairest form, the line-up should include all individuals who are "look-alikes"—who resemble the suspect. If this apparently fair system were incorporated into a code to which most police would adhere to, there is the real possibility that the number of errors of identification would increase because the similarity among the faces could easily confuse a witness into misidentifying one of the members of the line-up. The reason for this is not hard to find; the recognition memory "trace" in the mind of the witness in the vast majority of instances is not a clear, unambiguous image but is—as the research reported earlier proves—a weak, poorly organized, labile structure which may well "accept" as familiar a face that only partly resembles the original face seen at the time the crime was committed.

In sum, all methods of "improving" eyewitness identification procedures may be self-defeating unless the possibility of erroneous accusation and prosecution is also reduced by making it impossible for the police to proceed against a suspect on the basis of eyewitness evidence alone. If both these actions are taken, eyewitness identification errors may be reduced—since some errors are unquestionably caused by procedural faults—and the probability of gross miscarriages of justice will be lessened appreciably since prosecution would be initiated only when two or more pieces of evidence implicate the same individual.

It cannot be overemphasized: the fundamental issue in eyewitness recognition memory is the weakness of the original memory trace laid down at the instant the witness looked at the culprit. Methods which purport to improve by large amounts the accuracy and reliability of witnesses' performance after the registration process has begun should be viewed with caution.

My proposal, to restrict the use of eyewitness identification evidence, requires a major change in the criminal justice code. Is this necessary, or is there a less controversial solution? If the legal profession is persuaded by the facts of face recognition performance to act to reduce the influence of memory distortions upon criminal justice, then isn't it reasonable to use expert witnesses (*e.g.,* experimental psychologist) to testify on the merits of each case in which eyewitness testimony is the crucial evidence? Although this solution would not require a major change in courtroom procedure, and would also have the advantage of making use of a standard method of informing the jury about controversial issues, its value for the court is overshadowed by several serious drawbacks.

First, both defense and prosecution lawyers almost certainly will use expert witnesses in *every* case involving eyewitness identification, and, as I will try to show, these experts will always disagree, one arguing that errors of human observers are too frequent to convict his client and the other that errors are too infrequent to acquit the defendant. The point of this is that, except in rare cases, neither expert will have the kind of precise information necessary to remove all reasonable doubt about the facts in dispute. Indeed, it is more than likely that neither expert will be able to evaluate scientifically the details of the case for which he was hired to offer his opinion, but instead will be forced to speak in general terms, describing the probable recognition performance of the "average" man. The jury will be given general information, when they most need specific opinion. A jury is not helped in reaching its decision by being told the theory of fingerprint identification, nor would it be helped by the theory of recognition memory, but it would be helped greatly by the expert's opinion about exactly whose fingerprints were lifted from the water glass or whether *this* eyewitness is reliably accurate in his identification of *this* defendant. The latter opinion cannot be offered by any reputable expert in visual perception. The reason for this lack of specificity is not hard to document.

Any episode involving a human observer's memory is really a series of events composed of registration, storage, and retrieval of the stored material. The outcome, or the observer's accuracy of rendition of the original events, is affected by a vast number of elements—so many, in fact, that for any single episode the pattern of elements affecting its outcome may be unique. For example, memory performance in general—and therefore recognition memory for faces as well—is known to be influenced by: the perceptual "capacity" of the observer (which varies among individuals and within the same person from time to time); the level of the observer's attention; the observer's physiological and emotional state at the time of registration, afterward, and during recognition testing; the observer's visual acuity, distance from the event, and the angle between the observer and the face of the criminal; the level of illumination at the scene; the recognizability of the face, and the familiarity of the face, *i.e.,* its ethnic membership; and so on. From these and other unlisted considerations it is clear that the task facing an expert witness is formidable. In addition to the sheer number of conditions which could affect a witness's accuracy, it must not be forgotten that all action of interest to an expert witness took place in the past, weeks or months or longer before he ever arrived on the scene. Since the evidence his expertise is best qualified to evaluate is memory, he has no *tangible* evidence to measure, weigh, analyze, or assess for accuracy and reliability because all this information resides, as it were, in the mind of the witness, but it is quite inaccessible to investigation in the usual sense of that word. He could, of course, measure the perceptual ability of the eyewitness, but this datum would tell him only the present status of the witness's ability and, for logical reasons, would only be helpful in clarifying the facts if the witness demonstrated poor perceptual performance.

These considerations strongly suggest that expert witnesses will contribute very little precise information helpful to a jury trying to decide whether *this* witness under *these* circumstances at *that* particular time could or could not identify the correct person as the criminal. This is true because there is no way for even an expert to identify and weigh scientifically the vast number of elements which could have serious effects upon a single eyewitness's identification.

The best an expert could hope to do would be to estimate the probability of error in a particular situation.

This will not be the first time that expert witnesses in matters psychological have contributed little in the way of clarification and, in fact, have caused more problems for the courts than they have solved. Psychiatric expert testimony is a notorious case in point, with its use of vague, speculative theories of behavior, unreliable testing methods, poorly articulated diagnostic categories, and faulty prognosis. If perceptual performance and memory performance are now added to the list of areas for which expert witnesses may testify, the problems spawned by expert psychiatric testimony will be doubly visited upon the courts.

Finally, expert witness will not protect the ordinary citizen from false arrest or detainment. My proposal will offer protection here as well as in the courtroom because police will be prohibited from arresting a suspect on the basis of eyewitness evidence alone.

CONCLUSIONS

Personal identification by means of recognition memory for faces is a technique similar in principle to all other forensic techniques employed by law enforcement workers in their attempt to ascertain the truth or falsity of the facts in issue. It differs in important ways from other methods: it is not a perfected skill, such as fingerprint identification; judgments by eyewitnesses are not open to either public or expert scrutiny because the witness alone "carries" the facts but in a form which makes them immune to objective measurement, whereas the hallmark of scientific methods is their public nature (all facts may be analyzed and reanalyzed by anyone concerned in the trial); the facts—the stored memory of the face—change with time, and as a function of many other imponderables, but with rare exception most facts studied by forensic scientists are permanent, or can be permanently recorded or stored so that little or no change takes place between the time they are first uncovered and when they are finally used in trial proceedings. None of these differences between recognition memory performance and other forensic techniques forces the conclusion that the logical status of one differs from the other.

As a technique, face recognition memory is untrustworthy; no trial court would admit it if it were evaluated for reliability by the standards used to evaluate forensic scientific methods. In fact, the general level of recognition memory performance is less accurate by several orders of magnitude than any accepted forensic technique, including at least one method still not admissible in all courts, voiceprint analysis. Of great importance in the administration of justice is the unreliability—the unpredictability—of the eyewitness method. It is bad enough to know that mistakes are made by eyewitnesses, but it is much worse to depend upon a technique whose results are capricious and variable, making it almost impossible to ascertain when, under what circumstances, and by whom these errors will be made.

There is almost no hope of improving the method of collecting eyewitness identification evidence so as to raise its level of accuracy and reliability, because it is not the details of the procedure itself which are the cause of the majority of errors. To the contrary, the largest proportion of error is inherent in the human observer; his memory system is simply not designed to remember small details without special practice nor is it designed to process and store enough details of a face seen only once to permit him to discriminate it from another similar face at a later time.

Assuming acceptance of the inevitable and intractable errors of personal identification, is the problem caused by eyewitness evidence serious enough to warrant modification of the rules of evidence? How often does a witness make a mistake which affects another person's life? There are two kinds of errors an eyewitness could commit: not identifying the real wrongdoer (a miss) and identifying the wrong person as the culprit (a false recognition). The frequency of occurrence of both of these errors is unknown, and a moment's thought will reveal that perhaps we will never know exactly how often misses and false recognitions take place. This is true because there just is no way to assess in all the police precincts in this country the number of times a witness fails to recognize the culprit in a line-up or from his picture; nor is it possible to count the number of false recognitions unless all the true criminals confess to the crimes they committed for which someone else was convicted. Without these facts—and we have none of them—estimates of the effects of eyewitness errors are mere guesses, but it is most likely that these facts will remain elusive. Until these data are collected, however, the documented cases of false identification are far more impressive than the abstract argument which minimizes the importance of errors of identification by denying the existence of the problem, assuming in effect that too few cases occur for any action to be taken by legal authorities.

FOOTNOTES

[1] People v. Anderson, 205 N.W. 2d 461 (1973).

[2] This solution is not unique, nor is it a new suggestion. For example, the English system of law in some cases requires corroborative evidence along with eyewitness identification. This prinicple has also been affirmed by the Court of Appeals of New York, People v. Linzy, 31 N.W. 2d 440 (1972) in rape cases. See also People v. Anderson, 205 N.W. 2d 461 (1973), footnote 14.

[3] Lest there be any misunderstanding, these terms are used here in their standard meaning. Reconstructive memory refers to an eyewitness retrospective description of events, things, etc., which were seen at an earlier period of time. In a sense, the witness tries verbally to reconstruct the event. Recognition memory, which is a far simpler, more primitive (*i.e.,* fundamental) form of memory and has been shown to exist in infants and subhuman

animals, involves only that the observer identify an object, person, thing, etc., as the one seen at an earlier time. Keep in mind that correct recognition also implies that the observer *rejects* unfamiliar objects or persons.

[4] New information obtained in a follow-up study (Egan et al., in press) suggests one of the major reasons for real-life eyewitness misidentifications. Again, 2 targets were used, and only one of the targets was present in the 5-man line-up which took place 2, 21, or 56 days after the study session (although the subject was not informed of this fact). Correct responses for 2-, 21-, and 56-day delays were, respectively, 91%, 83%, and 97%. But for these same delay intervals 48%, 63%, and *93%* of the subjects erroneously selected one of the distractors as the "second" target! These facts suggest that if the previously seen culprit *is* present in the line-up, eyewitnesses will with high probability select the correct person. But if the culprit is not present in a line-up, then after a relatively short delay (2 days) eyewitnesses will identify the wrong person about 50% of the time. After about one and a half months, eyewitnesses will almost always identify the wrong individual if the true culprit is not in the line-up.

[5] The power of the face to elicit projective responses—responding which is more a function of the observer than the observed—is truly amazing. Lombroso equated criminality and physiognomy. Szondi developed a test which was partly based on the dubious assumptions that psychopathology was reflected in a patient's portrait, and that patients diagnosed to be suffering from one kind of psychopathology could be distinguished on the basis of their portraits from patients diagnosed to have another kind of psychological disorder (cited in Anderson & Anderson, 1951, pp. 498-512). More recent psychological literature is replete with reports of a variety of investigations in which subjects have viewed portraits of unknown individuals and "judged" their honesty, intelligence, sexual habits, personality, extent and kind of psychopathology, etc. (*e.g.*, Hochberg & Galper, 1974; Morse et al., 1974; Secord et al., 1953; Toch et al., 1962). The most remarkable aspect of these investigations, in my opinion, is the subjects' docile compliance to experimenters' requests. I am not aware of any case where subjects refused to make these essentially impossible judgments about attributes which are not to be found in the human face. Furthermore, the subjects' responses in these studies routinely tend to show distinct patterns of agreement, so that, for example, a particular face is judged to be "very intelligent" by a large percentage of the subjects and almost never judged to be of "low intelligence." These considerations suggest that although face recognition memory appears to be a deceptively simple process, in fact a subject's (or a witness's) response is the result of a complex interaction of factors, of which only a minority are under the control of the original face stimulus. It is tempting to speculate that in the three factors discussed here—"attractive" distractors, facial stereotypes, and "projective" qualities of the face—may lie the explanation for the otherwise inexplicable cases where *several* eyewitnesses selected the same, totally innocent victim as the true criminal.

[6] As mentioned earlier (Footnote 2), this is not a unique solution.

[7] Justice Williams (205 N.W. 2d 461) reports that he located three recent. unreported examples of misidentification in the Michigan counties of Wayne and Macomb after only a few hours of inquiry. He believes the documented cases represent only the tip of the iceberg.

[8] Almost every word in this section is in conflict with the spirit and purpose of Sobel's recent book (1972) dealing with the body of law which has developed governing the admissibility of eyewitness identification testimony. In this volume Sobel also "thoroughly examines all aspects of eye-witness identification and *suggests identification procedures* equitable to both accuser and accused" (p. iv, emphasis added). My position is preventive; Sobel's is medicinal. Sobel is a judge; this fact makes the viewpoint he has expressed comprehensible to me. But as an experimental psychologist I perceive Sobel's position—which is

certainly representative of the vast majority of legal authorities—as totally lacking a logical or empirical base. What is being ignored is the very evidence itself—the data responsible for all the cases cited by Sobel. What is being ignored is the unreliability of the original eye-witness recognition memory performance. As I have tried to demonstrate here, *that* is the evidence which is faulty, erroneous, and unreliable, and all the post-incident procedural modifications in the world will never reduce the original error by one percentage point. There is no known way to salvage fundamentally unreliable memory evidence after the fact. The massive set of rules described by Sobel, which is being erected to "protect" the rights of the accused, will have little if any beneficial effect in alleviating the true problem, human perceptual errors caused by built-in limitations of the registration, storage, and retrieval mechanisms.

REFERENCES

Adkins, C., Egan, D., Peterson, L., Pittner, M. & Goldstein, A.G. *The effects of exposure, delay and method of presentation on eyewitness identification.* Unpublished manuscript, 1974.

Alexander, J.F. Search factors influencing personal appearance identification. In A. Zavala & J.J. Paley (eds.), *Personal appearance identification.* Springfield, Ill.: Charles C. Thomas, 1972.

Anderson, H.H. & Anderson, G.L. *An introduction to projective techniques.* New York: Prentice-Hall, 1951.

Bahrick, H.P., Bahrick, P.O. & Wittlinger, R.P. Fifty years of memory for names and faces: A cross-sectional approach. *Journal of Experimental Psychology:* General, 1975, *104,* 54-75.

Berkowitz, L. *A survey of social psychology.* Hinsdale, Ill.: Dryden, 1975.

Buckhout, R. Eyewitness testimony. *Scientific American,* 1974, *231,* 23-31.

Chance, J., Goldstein, A.G. & McBride, L. Differential experience and recognition memory for faces. *Journal of Social Psychology,* 1975, *97,* 243-253.

Cross, J.F., Cross, J. & Daly, J. Sex, race, age, and beauty as factors in recognition of faces. *Perception & Psychophysics,* 1971, *10,* 393-396.

Egan, D., Pittner, M. & Goldstein, A.G. Eyewitness identification: Photographs vs. live models. *Law and Human Behavior,* in press.

Elliott, E.S., Wills, E.J. & Goldstein, A.G. The effects of discrimination training on the recognition of white and oriental faces. *Bulletin of the Psychonomic Society,* 1973, *2,* 71-73.

Ellis, H.D. Recognizing faces. *British Journal of Psychology,* 1975, 66, 409-426.

Erdelyi, M.H. A new look at the new look: Perceptual defense and vigilance. *Psychological Review,* 1974, *81,* 1-25.

Goldstein, A.G. & Chance, J. Recognition of children's faces. *Child Development,* 1964, *35,* 129-136.

Goldstein, A.G. & Chance, J. Visual recognition memory for complex configurations. *Perception & Psychophysics,* 1971, *9,* 237-241.

Goldstein, A.G. & Chance, J. *Face recognition memory as a function of task instruction.* Paper presented at the meeting of the Psychonomic Society, Boston, November, 1974.

Hochberg, J. & Galper, R.E. Attribution of intention as a function of physiognomy. *Memory and Cognition,* 1974, *2,* 39-42.

Laughery, K.R. Photograph type and cross-racial factors in facial identification. In A.

Laughery, K.R., Fessler, P.K., Lenorovitz, D.R. & Yoblick, D.A. Time delay and similarity effects in facial recognition. *Journal of Applied Psychology*, 1974, *59*, 490-496.

Majcher, L.L. *Facial recognition as a function of arousal level, exposure and duration and delay interval.* Unpublished master's thesis, University of Missouri, 1974.

Malpass, R.S. & Kravitz, J. Recognition for faces of own and other "race." *Journal of Personality and Social Psychology*, 1969, *13*, 330-335.

Morse, S.J., Reis, H.T., Gruzen, J. & Wolff, E. The "eye of the beholder": Determinants of physical attractiveness judgments in the U.S. and South Africa. *Journal of Personality*, 1974, *42*, 528-542.

New York *Times.* Mistaken identity, sec. 4, *The week in review*, January 13, 1974, p. 18.

Scapinello, K.F. & Yarmey, A.D. The role of familiarity and orientation in immediate and delayed recognition of pictorial stimuli. *Psychonomic Science*, 1970, *21*, 329-330.

Secord, P.F., Bevan, W., Jr. & Dukes, W.F. Occupational and physiognomic sterotypes in the perception of photographs. *Journal of Social Psychology*, 1953, *37*, 261-270.

Shepherd, J.W. & Ellis, H.D. The effect of attractiveness on recognition memory for faces. *American Journal of Psychology*, 1973, *86*, 627-634.

Shepherd, J.W., Deregowski, J.B. & Ellis, H.D. A cross-cultural study of memory for faces. *International Journal of Psychology*, 1974, *9*, 205-211.

Shoemaker, D.J., South, D.R. & Lowe, J. Facial stereotypes of deviants and judgments of guilt or innocence. *Social Forces*, 1973, *51*, 427-433.

Sobel, N.R. *Eye-witness identification: Legal and practical problems.* New York: Clark Boardman, 1972.

Toch, H.H., Rabin, A.I. & Wilkins, D.M. Factors entering in ethnic identifications: An experimental study. *Sociometry*, 1962, *25*, 297-312.

Trankell, A. *Reliability of evidence.* Stockholm, Sweden: Beckmans, 1972.

Wall, P.M. *Eyewitness identification in criminal cases.* Springfield, Ill.: Charles C. Thomas, 1965.

Zavala & J.J. Paley (eds.), *Personal appearance identification.* Springield, Ill.: Charles C. Thomas, 1972.

14

Psychologists in
Child Custody

ROBERT HENLEY WOODY

Heretofore in the evolution of American society, child custody disputes between natural parents (and between other contesting adults as well) have been almost exclusively conducted within the domain of legalists. While certain statutes
and common-law decisions have pointed toward holding the welfare of the child
to be of foremost importance, the fact is that the rights and welfare of the child
have alway been viewed through the filter created by the positions of the respective parents. This is clearly exemplified in the lack of legal representation for the
child; the attorneys are hired by and for the advocacy of the parent-clients, and
the child's position receives only secondary representation.

There is, however, a major movement toward the concept of the best interests
of the child. Since about 1970, state statutes for child custody have included
definitions that emphasize that the rights and interests of the child must, in
every situation, be superior to the rights and preferences of the parents. In other
words, the child is being treated as a distinct person, and is to be accorded, by
statutory law, individual rights in the child custody proceedings.

As has been evident for years, child custody decision-making encompasses social, psychological, and legal factors. Contemporary child custody statues mandate that consideration be given to very specific factors that unquestionably derive from behavioral science. While legal professionals, such as judges and attorneys, are supposed to seek social and psychological data for the child custody proceedings, the success of this mandated search will hinge upon the effective integration of behavioral scientists into the legal context. Due to the nature of these data sources and the obvious need to maximize objectivity for the evaluation of the criteria used for child custody determinations, a special role for psychologists is inevitable.

This chapter will focus on the role of psychology and psychologists in child custody proceedings, with special emphasis on establishing an operational frame of reference (as might be needed for the provision of professional information and/or expert testimony). Consideration will be given to the legal, social, and psychological dimensions that are inherent to the child custody processes. Original data, from a rather large-scale research study on child custody criteria, will be presented. Finally, recommendations will be posited that will hopefully aid the psychologist in attaining a pragmatic, yet scientific, posture for involvement in child custody proceedings.

CHILD CUSTODY PRACTICES

That child custody is a prominent social problem is an understatement. Divorce is, of course, commonplace in contemporary society. Over the last hundred years, divorce rates have increased sharply and an increasing number of children are affected (Kadushin, 1967). It has been estimated that, nationally, one out of six first marriages ends in divorce, with about half of these involving children (Lidz, 1968; see also Ploscowe et al., 1972). An interesting fact, however, is that most divorces involving children do not result in a legal dispute over custody; for example, the Michigan Interprofessional Association on Marriage, Divorce, and the Family (1967) found that only 2% of contested divorces were over the custody of the children. To the psychologist, the latter statistic is obviously questionable. It seems highly likely that the reason the percentage is so small is that this kind of decision, *i.e.*, who will have custody, is often debated and decided upon outside of the legal confrontation. This result is supported by the fact that, historically, the mother has been viewed as always being the best guardian for children, especially if they are young.

Regardless of the number of actual legal disputes over child custody, the psychologist should be concerned with the familial conditions that can have negative effects on the child's development. More will be said about the psychological dimensions later, but at this point it should be recognized that child custody is the end-product of what is typically a long-standing turbulent familial/environmental history for the child. For example, Westman et al. (1970) point out that divorce "is a *family* rather than simply a *marital* phenomenon, because 60% of all divorces affect young children, and most separations occur five years after marriage" (p. 416). Further, less than half of marriages are deemed reasonably adequate by the couple (Lidz, 1968); thus many children are subjected to adverse factors because of the poor interparental relationship.

The psychologist looking initially at child custody proceedings may be taken aback by the high degree of subjectivity in the decision-making and the lack of advocacy for the children. Custody problems in actions for divorce and separation and problems relating to adoption "have received scant attention and analysis when compared to that given to the rights of children accused of crime" (Inker and Perretta, 1971, p. 417). This state of affairs could lead to benefits for the industrious psychologist in search of a fertile area for research, but for the practicing psychologist in the community or clinical sphere this can only be viewed as a sorry commentary on the legal system.

Definition of terms, a process typically dealt with in the first week of any undergraduate psychology course, has served to plague those attempting to analyze child custody proceedings. Sayre (1950) states that custody is a "slippery word" (p. 588) because: "The courts do not always use it to cover the same things." Sayre defines custody as a matter of varying relations, rights, and duties which can only be defined idiosyncratically, *i.e.,* according to each case.

For building a frame of reference for this chapter, a contemporary definition of child custody has been offered by Goldstein et al. (1973):

> "Child placement," for our purposes, is a term which encompasses all legislative, judicial, and executive decisions generally or specifically concerned with establishing, administering, or rearranging parent-child relationships. The term covers a wide range of variously labeled legal procedures for deciding who should be assigned or expected to seize the opportunity and the task of being "parent" to a child. These procedures include birth certification, neglect, abandonment, battered child, foster care, adoption, delinquency, youth offender, as well as custody in annulment, separation, and divorce. (5)

The focus for the rest of the chapter will be on the child custody decisions made either before or during legal divorce proceedings between the natural mother and natural father as to the placement of the child.

In terms of child custody practices, it is popularly maintained that the natural parents should be preferred over others for child placement. For example, Foster & Freed (1968) state: "It is perfectly obvious that natural parents ordinarily should be preferred over strangers and usually the mother is the best custodian for young children" (p. 41). Their opinion was derived from an extensive review of child custody, child support, adoption, rights of childen, delinquency, dependency, and neglect data sources.

Mention of preference for the mother over the father has already emerged several times, and it deserves specific discussion. A review of common or case law reveals that the mother has, in fact, been designated custodian in legal disputes more than the father (Ploscowe et al., 1972). A seemingly accurate explanation of the matter is offered by Slovenko (1973):

> The father as a rule recognizes that the mother can render better care, the children usually wish to be with the mother, and consequently he does not request child custody or possession of the family home in the divorce action. The mother is literally the housekeeper. It is observable among the human and animal species that it is generally the mother who cares for and protects the young. The father may also recognize that a custody dispute is to be a futile endeavor. Surveys of sample cases indicate that maternal custody is awarded in 85 to 95 percent of the cases. (361)

There is reason to believe that contemporary and future conditions will accommodate a more objective evaluation of the father's potential for custody. This prediction is supported by changes in societal values about sexual equality (as reflected in the women's movement and avoidance of sexist values in role definitions for both males and females) and the recent state statutes that support the rights and interests of the child.

A final area of reality and practice is the matter of what a divorce actually accomplishes, and here the psychologist finds strong evidence to link psychology with legal decision-making. Namely, it is illogical to believe that divorce terminates the psychological import of familial relationships. Ackerman (1958) states:

> It is to be remembered too that there can be no effective divorce for parents. Though permanently divided as a sexual couple, they remain permanently tied by their joined responsibility for the care of their children, and in some instances this tie becomes a source of suffering for many years. (149)

In a study of 106 divorces, Westman et al. (1970) found that 31% of those parents with children evidenced "repeated and intensive interaction . . . during the two-year period following the divorce decree" (p. 417), and they concluded that "divorce is a *process*, not an event" (p. 417). Thus divorce is not the end of a relationship; it is, more realistically, simply *"an adjustment of relationship* that does not erase the past nor create an unrelated future. . . . " (Westman & Cline, 1971, p. 1).

The theoretical significance for psychology is twofold: first, from a social standpoint, persons involved in divorce will be maintaining networks of influence that are difficult, to say the least, to handle positively; second, from a psychological standpoint, these persons will be moving through life under the continued influence of an earlier marriage. Of special concern is the fact that the children of divorce will continue to be under the powerful influence of *both* parents, whether the influence is directly or indirectly asserted. The potential for stress on the principals, both parents and children (but particularly children, since they lack sophisticated coping mechanisms), provides a practical justification for the involvement of psychologists in all stages of the divorce/custody sequence.

SOCIAL AND PSYCHOLOGICAL DIMENSIONS

Historically, the parental right to custody held sway in accord with the view that children were of monetary value; *i.e.,* custodial rights had commercial value in the feudal period and were subject to transfer and sale. Over the years, governmental power over the family has increased and changes have been made. Katz (1971) states:

> When one observes the expanding power of government into the family sphere, one must begin to readjust one's legal concept of family relationship, especially that of parent of child. It is not accurate to portray the parent-child relationship as one of the most jealously guarded in society—a frequently stated myth. Indeed, the greatest inroad the government has made in the family setting has been in the parent-child relationship. From a legal perspective, that relationship is probably the least secure in the family constellation. (5)

Katz further clarifies the nature of the state's interest in the parent-child relationship:

> For the parent-child relationship to remain free from state intervention, however, parents are expected to fulfill certain obligations. They are required to provide their children with financial security, to maintain their children's health, to ensure their children's education, and to instill in their children values of morality and respect. The statements of community expectations are abstract standards and have little concrete worth outside of individual cases. These standards are applied when some event occurs in the life of either the child or parent which prompts someone to question the parental right to custody. (140)

Relatedly, society has also demonstrated control over families when the mental health of the children is jeopardized, as reflected in Ackerman's (1958) statement:

> ... marital conflict is of significance not only of itself but also as the epitome and the very core of disintegrative trends in family life and the harbinger of distorted emotional development in the offspring. Ultimately this distortion adds to the burden of mental illness in the community. (149)

It is for these kinds of reasons that contemporary society, while accommodating divorce, is giving greater controls over the welfare of children to the professionals in the legal and health-related systems.

Divorce will have a critical shaping power for the child's social development.

Consequently, the child's intrapersonal and interpersonal conditions are signficantly dependent on the familial environment experienced. There is extensive research evidence linking the development of social beliefs and attitudes to a person's family life (Krech & Crutchfield, 1948). It should be apparent that the disruption caused by the stress of divorce and child custody could readily influence the social development of the person in the areas of beliefs, attitudes, group roles, and, more broadly, social behavior.

Turning now from social to psychological dimensions (which are obviously inextricably related), child custody proceedings seem to have special relevance for self-esteem, parental absence, and emotional and behavioral disorders.

Self-esteem or self-worth is probably one of the most global characteristics within the personality. Kleinfeld (1970a) points out that the "psychological and sociological literature on divorce seems fairly united behind the proposition that divorce tends to reduce children's self-esteem in inverse proportion to the children's ages" (p. 329). He offers a formidable psychoanalytic conceptualization: "Some of the relation between the effect on self-esteem and age of the children has been explained as meaning that a child during the Oedipal period more than at other developmental stages interprets the divorce as punishment for his hostility toward his parents or as a fulfillment of fantasy wishes which are more pronounced at that time, and so he feels guilty" (p. 329). Related to self-esteem is the need to have nurturance, and, of course, the sources for nurturance are jeopardized by divorce and child custody. It is here that the preference for the mother over the father gains some support from development theory, as exemplified by Lidz's (1968) argument that "the mother is the primary and major nurturant figure to the child, particularly the small child" (p. 56). Finally, self-esteem is linked to identification, and divorce and placement with only one parent can obviously have an impact on the developmental aspects of the identification process.

Parental absence receives considerable attention in developmental psychology. That is, divorce and child custody placements create parental absence, and research supports that parental absence has a strong impact on the child's general development (Mussen et al., 1969).

It is difficult to assess the relevance of the sex of the parent in the absence/development issue, because (as noted previously) heretofore custody decisions have overwhelmingly been for giving the mother custody and thus the father was absent; there has been too little research on maternal absence versus father absence. Mussen et al. (1969) state: "Perhaps not surprisingly—in view of the importance of the same-sex parent as an identification model—absence of the same-sex parent appears particularly important" (p. 493). Regardless of this position derived from developmental research, same-sex matchings are seldom used in child custody proceedings.

The age of the child at the time of parental absence is important. Research on parental separation during early childhood has focused on separation from the mother, primarily because of the dependency a young child typically has on direct maternal care, but in middle-childhood the greatest emphasis has been on separation from the father. The issue of age leads Mussen et al. (1969) to suggest that "boys who lose their father early, before identification can be assumed to have been clearly established, have greater difficulty in establishing a masculine sex-role identification and acquiring sex-typed traits, while absence of the father after the child reaches age five has far less effect" (p. 494). One might surmise from published research that boys are more vulnerable than girls to parental separation, but this inference may be in error because of a paucity of research on girls subjected to parental separation.

There is strong support for believing that divorce (and the resulting placement away from at least one of the parents) is a factor in the development of children's emotional and behavioral disorders. Research on parental absence reveals that there are more broken homes in the backgrounds of delinquents and children suffering from emotional disorders than in non-disturbed children, and that school performance often suffers in children subjected to divorce and/or separation of their parents (Mussen et al., 1969). Relatedly, maternal deprivation, particularly with infants, has been subjected to extensive research. Suffice it to say that Watson (1959) indicates that psychotoxic diseases are produced by the wrong kind of mother-child relationships and that emotional deficiency diseases can be traced to maternal deprivation (partial or complete absence of mother-child relations).

Regarding clinically defined psychiatric problems, Morrison (1974) believes that "divorce itself is not causative but is symptomatic of the parental illness, which operates genetically and environmentally to produce illness in the child" (p. 101). Using a psychoanalytically oriented rationale, Kleinfeld (1970a) asserts that the decreased self-esteem provoked in children by the divorce of their parents often leads to behavior problems. McDermott (1970), in a study of children from divorced families compared with children from legally intact families, states:

> The divorce, or the family stress surrounding it, seemed to serve, however, as a special stress dealt with through acting out rather than neurotic symptomatology, such as one might expect from a more typically acute traumatic event, e.g., parental death. This may indicate that a more prolonged trauma exists, one underscored by divorce and symptomatically expressed one to two years after it, a trauma that precedes and persists after as well as during the divorce experience, a trauma which soon becomes crystallized into character formation. (422-423)

Briscoe et al. (1973) found that approximately three-fourths of divorced women and approximately two-thirds of divorced men had (prior to or at the time of their investigation) a psychiatric disease (most commonly primary affective disease, antisocial personality, and hysteria). Although the research is still somewhat limited, there is certainly face validity, as well as some empirical data, for the belief that divorce has the potential of seriously disrupting the emotional and behavioral controls, patterns and development in children (as well as in their parents). It is on the basis of this rationale that recent state statutes have been prescribing criteria to be evaluated for the child custody proceedings and have set forth criteria that encompass social, psychological, educational, and health factors.

LEGAL CRITERIA

The confines of a single chapter preclude detailed review of the voluminous material that reflects criteria used in legal decisions for child custody. This section will note some of the basic legal dimensions that underlie child custody, to elaborate on the "best interests of the child" concept, and to cite the primary criteria evident in legal cases.

The concept of "parental power" is a cornerstone of child custody. Kleinfeld (1970b) provides a brief definition: "Parental power probably cannot be defined except as a residue of all power not lodged elsewhere by the law" (p. 413); he maintains that the law has still not adequately limited parental authority to protect the interests of the child, as is evident in the fact that the child usually is of little direct consequence in the divorce proceedings of the parents. Historically, parental power was reflected in the legal assignment of power and rights to the father only, with the rationale being that the children were "property" and were of commercial value, and that only males had the right to own property. Through the years, however, parental power took on a definiton of parental duty. According to Clad et al. (1964):

> Husband and wife have a fundamental duty to support, protect, and educate their children. This duty may extend beyond minority, especially when the child is indigent or handicapped. Statutes vary, but generally the father has the primary duty. (40)

Parenthetically, it should be noted that this emphasis on paternal duty appears in a reference from 1964, a time prior to the passage and initiation of contemporary sexual equality laws (pragmatically, courts still align the "primary duty" with the father, despite legal negation of this practice).

Progressively, the concept of parental power has adapted to the concept of children's rights. In other words, the contemporary view is that children have a moral right and a legal right to certain conditions; not the following proposed "Bill of Rights for Children" (Foster & Freed, 1972, p. 347): 1. To receive parental love and affection, discipline and guidance, and to grow to maturity in a home environment which enables him to develop into a mature and responsible adult; 2. To be supported, maintained, and educated to the best of parental ability, in return for which he has the moral duty to honor his father and mother; 3. To be regarded as a *person*, within the family, at school, and before the law; 4. To receive fair treatment from all in authority; 5. To be heard and listened to; 6. To earn and keep his own earnings; 7. To seek and obtain medical care and treatment and counseling; 8. To emancipation from the parent-child relationship when that relationship has broken down and the child has left home due to abuse, neglect, serious family conflict, or other sufficient cause, and his best interests would be served by the termination of parental authority; 9. To be free of legal disabilities of incapacities save where such are convincingly shown to be necessary and protective of the actual best interests of the child; and 10. To receive special care, consideration, and protection in the administration of law or justice so that his best interests always are a paramount factor. The issue of the rights of children assumes that the best interests of the child should be supreme.

This concept underlies the recent changes in child custody statutes. Significant impetus for these efforts came from the Uniform Child Custody Jurisdiction Act (Commissioners on Uniform State Laws, 1969) and the Uniform Marriage and Divorce Act (National Conference of Commissioners of Uniform State Laws, 1971). Adoption of these uniform laws is dependent upon individual state actions, and since marriage, divorce, and child custody are so controversial and dependent upon social values unique to the area it is not uncommon to find idiosyncratic statutes.

An excellent example of a state statute that encompasses the best interests of the child concept and that specifies criteria that reflect social, psychological, educational, and health criteria for custody determinations is the Michigan Child Custody Act of 1970. These include: 1. love and affection between parent and child; 2. emotional ties between parent and child; 3. capacity of parent to give child guidance; 4. capacity of parent to continue educating and raising the child in its religion or creed, if any; 5. capacity of parent to provide food; 6. capacity of parent to provide clothing; 7. capacity of parent to provide medical care; 8. capacity of parent to provide remedial care; 9. capacity of parent to provide other material needs; 10. length of time lived in an emotionally or psychologically stable, satisfactory environment and the desirability of maintaining continuity; 11. permanence of proposed custodial home (geographical stability); 12. moral fitness of parent; 13. mental health of parent; 14. physical health of parent; 15. home record of child; 16. school record of child; 17. community record of child; and 18. child's preference for parent (if court deems child sufficient in age).

Since the criteria rely heavily upon assumptions derived from the social and behavioral sciences, behavioral scientists are intended to figure prominently in the legal proceedings. Unfortunately, we must question our readiness to participate; Benedek & Benedek (1972) state:

> Since "best interests" is not a quantity ascertainable by formulas or with
> mathematical certainty, the skills and attitudes of those participating in the
> decision making process will inevitably influence their results. While it is true
> that the ultimate responsibility is that of the court, make no mistake, this
> would be equally so if the decisions were those of behavioral scientists. Al-
> though we tend to stereotype our thinking about the judicial or psychological
> outlook, in reality skills, training, and perspectives vary as widely among be-
> havioral scientists as they do among jurists. (830)

Although the Michigan law is relatively new, it is clear that the criteria have not
been adequately defined, it is not known how behavioral scientists react to the
criteria or to the law, and it appears, from yet unpublished data garnered by
Holmes (1974), that circuit judges in Michigan are not quickly incorporating behavioral science knowledge into the proceedings—despite the clear-cut direction
of the law!

The best interest of the child concept appears to be receiving greater and
greater support, to the extent that it typically is accorded "prime consideration"
in a custody decision. This may lead to the award of custody to relatives and
strangers, despite parental opposition. However, custody is often awarded to the
"successful" party in a divorce, that is, to the person who is granted the divorce.
This is particularly relied upon when the successful party is the mother. Exceptions may occur if one parent displays significantly greater willingness and ability to perform parental duties than the other parent.

One of the most obvious considerations in child custody is whether special
preference should be given to the mother or the father. One position is that the
mother has a superior role in the rearing of children, particularly those of "tender years." Conversely, another position is that the father would be best suited
to raise a son (if beyond the "tender years"). While it appears that mothers are
usually given preference, this may be a result of the father's accepting, without
question, that the mother is best prepared to care for the child. Fathers seem to
get preference when the mother has been established as being immoral, such as
committing adultery during the marriage, especially if, in the case, the father is
from an upper socioeconomic or professional eschelon.

The preference of the child is another commonly used criterion. Usually the
child has to be deemed of sufficient age to form an intelligent opinion; while
there is no set age level, it appears that greater weight is given as the child advances in age. Some state statutes specify the age that the child must achieve in
order to gain the privilege of specifying which parent is preferred for custody.

As mentioned previously, morality has proven to be an important factor in
child custody decisions. most commonly, morality seems to be defined in terms
of adultery during the previous marriage. There are, however, variations on and
alternatives to this definition; for example, if the parent with custody can be
proven to have engaged in socially unacceptable behavior, particularly of a sexual or criminal nature, the custody may be changed to the other parent. Mental

illness is sometimes integrated into this principle, such as labeling immoral behavior as a manifestation of mental illness (which would lessen that person's suitability for child custody). Similarly, the social behavior of the parent must be within acceptable limits in order to support child custody. Court decisions have specified that custody is contingent upon the parent's conforming to prescribed social behaviors, such as not having a friend of the opposite sex in the home where the child is residing.

Religion, with its powerful emotional appeal, would seem to be destined to play a significant role in child custody decisions, but very few cases reflect even secondary consideration of religion. When religion does enter into the decision, it is usually for the purpose of maintaining continuity of religious training and practices the child had experienced before the divorce. There seems to have been a clear avoidance of evaluating the mother and father on the criterion of "which is the *most* religious." Some religious denominations have church doctrines that allude to child custody, but the authority of the state has been upheld over the authority of the church. In cases that involve one religious parent and one agnostic or atheistic parent, the position is usually that religion will not be a factor.

Race, as with religion, has not directly influenced many cases. The issue would presumably be most applicable in a racially mixed marriage, with the concept being that the child with non-Caucasian features might be placed with the non-Caucasian parent. When race has been considered, it appears to have been accorded very little, if any, weight in the final custody decision.

Continuity of placement is perceived as potentially beneficial for the child, *i.e.*, affording an undisrupted existence after the divorce of the parents and after the initial custody placement. Thus consideration is given, at least in part, to the value of the child's continuing in the same geographical locale or in the same house or in the same psychological and social environment; most pronounced would be the child's continuing to be with the parent with whom he shares the best relationship. Case decisions seem to support that continuity is an important factor; this may be due, however, to the courts' attempts to avoid jurisdictional conflict.

To date, natural parents do seem to be preferred over others, such as relatives or foster families—even when the natural parents may seem less able to care for the child. Various judicial decisions have accorded natural parenthood with special rights for custody. It will be inevitable, therefore, that those who propagate the idea that "psychological" parents should be preferred over "biological" parents (Goldstein et al., 1973) will have to enter into contest with traditional legalists.

To summarize, it appears that the concept of the best interests of the child prescribes the major criteria for contemporary child custody determinations. In addition, case law also speaks to: custody being awarded to the successful party in a divorce; whether preference should be given to the mother or the father; the weighting of the preference of the child; the role of morality, social behavior, religion, and race; the value of maintaining continuity of placement; and the rights of the natural parent vs. others.

RESEARCH RESULTS

It seems prudent to assert that the law, as exemplified in the preceding section, and the published accounts (which are essentially "position statements") to date leave the behavioral scientist with little or no experimentally based guidelines for understanding and/or participating in child custody legal proceedings. As a first step, a research project was developed to investigate the attitudes and opinions of professionals (lawyers, psychiatrists, psychologists, and social workers) about the criteria used for deciding which natural parent should be awarded custody in a legal dispute. Special consideration was given to the possible relationships between the professionals' demographic variables (*e.g.,* sex, age, years of professional experience, marital status, divorce history, and parenthood) and the criteria they advocated and to the differences, if any, they aligned with evaluating the suitability of the mother vs. the father. Although this section will make reference to the comparative aspects (*i.e.,* between disciplines) of the research findings, it will concentrate on the ramifications of the findings to the discipline of psychology.

All subjects were known to have a professional background in and involvement with children, in a manner that would be compatible with participating in child custody legal proceedings.[1] A questionnaire was used to obtain responses.

Publications on child custody seem to yield four commonly held beliefs: natural parents should be preferred over foster parents; the mother should be preferred over the father; the child should be placed with the parent of the same sex; and siblings should be placed in the same home. This study found that there was strong support for placing the child with the natural parents, as opposed to foster parents (assuming an adequacy of conditions in both contexts). Of special interest, this preference was not significantly influenced by the discipline of the female professionals, but it was by the discipline of the male professionals. Psychologists gave the least support for placement with the natural parents among the four disciplinary groups of males.

Regarding placement with the mother instead of the father, 46.1% of the respondents indicated that the mother should be preferred over the father. Disciplinary identity did not significantly influence the male responses, but it did the female responses, with the psychologists again being relatively low in support of this maternal preference amongst the female groups (female social workers were somewhat lower). As a group, however (*i.e.,* both males and females), the psychologists were second only to psychiatrists in support of the notion to give preference to the mother.

The majority of the subjects indicated that it did not matter whether the child was placed with the parent of the same sex, and there did not seem to be any disciplinary relationship to the responses. Relatively few psychologists expressed clearly negative views, *i.e.*, that a child should not be placed with the parent of the same sex (more psychiatrists were negative). A large majority of the subjects, however, favored placing the siblings in the same home, and again there was no relationship between the disciplinary identity of the subjects and their preferences.

The questionnaire also incorporated the eighteen factors set forth in the Michigan Child Custody Act (1970) and asked the subjects to rate the importance of each factor for the mother and for the father separately. To summarize the findings: the disciplinary identity of the subjects was not related to their preferences; there was a strong dependence or contingency between the ratings for the mother and for the father for all eighteen factors (this would support that the subjects would not make a distinction when weighting the importance of any of the factors according to whether it was the mother or the father being evaluated); and the following factors were deemed to be of great importance for both parents by the majority of the respondents: love and affection between parent and child, emotional ties between parent and child, capacity of the parent to give child guidance, length of time child lived in an emotionally or psychologically stable and satisfactory environment and the desirability of maintaining continuity, and the mental health of the parent. These five strongly supported criteria clearly reveal the special relevance of the discipline of psychology to contemporary child custody legal proceedings. Indeed, while other professionals (such as psychiatrists and social workers) can contribute to the evaluation of these factors, it is self-evident that training in broad-based behavioral science, objective methodologies, human assessment techniques, personality theories, and clinical services prepares psychologists to contribute significantly to the evaluation of each of the factors.

The principles inherent to the Michigan Child Custody Act (1970) were also used to construct nine items regarding which parent, given certain considerations, should be given custody of the child. Overall, there were four criteria that were supported as being important in child custody determinations: mental and physical history of the parents, morality of the parents, child's preference for placement, and existing emotional ties between the parent and the child. Of special interest, only one of the nine situations (or criteria) was found to be significantly influenced by the disciplinary identity of the respondents; this was the mental and physical history of the parents. To elaborate, the item was worded as follows:

> Parent *A* has a history of "nervousness," which has resulted in mental and physical difficulties that have been treated medically; Parent *B* is in good health.

The "target"parent (*i.e.*, the one that would seemingly be best suited) was, of course, Parent *B* with a good health history. The statistical analysis revealed that the sex of the respondent was significantly related to the preference. In terms of those who favored the "healthy" parent, it was found that: for the male groups, the male lawyers gave the greatest preference, the male psychiatrists gave the least preference, and the male psychologists and social workers gave equal degrees of preference and were in the middle of the four disciplines; for the female groups, the female psychologists gave the most preference, with the female lawyers being slightly lower, followed sequentially by female social workers and female psychiatrists. Combining the sexes, the percentages favoring the healthy parent (in rank order) were: lawyers, 81.6%; psychologists, 74.7%; social workers, 62.8%; psychiatrists, 50.0%. This finding points toward how a professional's sex and/or discipline could enter into the posture assumed toward the health issue in a child custody dispute. For example, the attorney for a parent with a poor mental and physical health history might want to avoid lawyers and psychologists in favor of psychiatrists. (Of course, there are always individual differences, but the research does support that sex and discipline should be scrutinized when bringing in or cross-examining a professional in a case that involves a poor health history.)

It was revealed that there was ambivalence and ambiguity about the following criteria: geographical stability; continuity of the child's environment; fulfilling remedial education and child guidance needs. Finally, it appeared that the professionals tended to favor a stable, nonpressured life style to one that was more dynamic and achievement-oriented. This latter finding might be subject to regional and cultural influences; for example, a rural context might be more supportive of this concept than would a university-community context.

Twenty factors for evaluating parenthood suitability for child custody were derived from published accounts on child custody, the Michigan Child Custody Act, and the views expressed by mental health professionals in a pilot study for this investigation. The factors, presented in alphabetical order, were: age, aspirations, child-care history, child-rearing attitudes, criminal record, education, general life history, income, intelligence, knowledge of child development, mental health, morality, personal behavior, personality, physical health, quality of relationship with child, religion, sexual behavior, stability of residence, and vocation. The respondents were asked to designate in rank order the five factors that were most important and the five factors that were least important for assessing a mother's suitability for child custody, and to follow the same procedure (separately) for assessing a father's suitability for child custody.

The statistical analysis considered the possibility of difference according to the sex of the parent. In brief, it would appear that lawyers, psychiatrists, and psychologists do not distinguish between the mother and father for the importance of criteria, but the social workers seem to place higher expectations of the fathers. The significance between parents aligned with the rankings of psychologists revealed: male psychologists believed that knowledge of child development and the parent's sexual behavior history were more important for the father than for the mother, but that the stability of residence factor was more important for the mother than for the father; the female psychologists also believed that the parent's sexual behavior history was more important for the father than for the mother, whereas the criminal record and physical health record were more important for the mother than for the father.

Regarding the factors deemed to be most important, the combined disciplines supported the following "top five" factors for the mother: quality of relationship with child, mental health, child-rearing attitudes, child-care history, and personal behavior. The "top five" factors for the father were: quality of relationship with child, mental health, child-rearing attitudes, personal behavior and child-care history. Thus the same five factors were used (with a reversal in rank for two of them) for both the mother and the father.

DISCUSSION OF RESULTS

This research project supports that there are disciplinary distinctions regarding degree of preference given to a particular criterion-factor and that these distinctions often may be delineated further by the sex of the professionals. Although not statistically measured, there was some support for the belief that the stereotyped social philosophies attributed to particular professional disciplines could be upheld; for example, lawyers and psychiatrists seemed to be more conservative than psychologists and social workers regarding which factors were supported.

One of the most striking findings was that, overall, there was no statistically significant difference in the degree of importance attributed by professionals to various decision-making factors between the mother and the father. The traditional preference for the mother and the stereotyped social attitudes about what a mother can provide vs. what a father can provide to the development of a child seem to be changing significantly. It seems probable that this posture is a reflection of contemporary views about family structure and sexual equality.

While certain demographic variables (such as sex, age, professional discipline) were found to be significantly related to a degree of preference for a given criterion/factor, it would appear that a given demographic variable does not cut across all (or even most) criteria used in child custody determinations; thus the practical implication is that idiosyncratic consideration should be given, such as when an expert witness is being selected, to the demographic characteristics of the particular professional relevant to the specific factor that will receive emphasis in the legal proceedings.

Perhaps the most important finding was the degree of preference given to factors that have been the basis for legal decisions in the past and that are espoused by lawyers, psychiatrists, psychologists, and social workers at present. While comparative analyses between the four disciplines can assist the individual professional with getting disciplinary allegiances and biases into a reasonable perspective, the global rankings for the most valued criteria reveal the discrepancies between many legal judgments in the past (most of which were made without input from behavioral science professionals) and justify the inclusion of behavioral scientists in the child custody legal proceedings, such as in the roles of expert witness and/or provider of professional information (*e.g.,* diagnostic data).

RECOMMENDATIONS

This chapter has presented material designed to provide the psychologist a basic academic framework for child custody legal proceedings, encompassing a review of child custody practices, the social and psychological dimensions of child custody, and the legal criteria. From this, special research data revealed the possible relationship between personal/demographic factors (*e.g.,* professional discipline) and preference given to particular criteria that are maintained in evaluating the suitability of a parent for child custody determinations.

In view of the subjectivity that has characterized publications on child custody, the findings reported here only serve to underscore what should be patently clear: *Every professional involved in child custody determinations should be able to specify the criteria used, the definitions thereof, the academic rationale for selecting them, the reliability and validity of the evaluations, the safeguards against bias and unjustified subjectivity, and the best methods for interpreting and communicating the data.*

The implications of this recommendation are far-reaching for professional psychological practice. The psychologist, as a member of the profession for the *science* of human behavior, has less leeway than professionals in the disciplines that give greater prominence to the *art* of dealing with human behavior. For a psychologist to enjoy the vestiges of science, there must be fulfillment of this objectively oriented recommendation.

Can psychologists fulfill such rigorous standards? At the present point in the evolution of professional psychology training, the answer would probably be no. engaged in validated self-understanding efforts to the point that they are aware of how their own characteristics influence their judgments, that they have developed sources for checking and controlling personalized bias in judgments, and that they have acquired the formal academic knowledge that will accommodate adequate comprehension of the elements unique to child custody.

The academic knowledge of child custody and the practical familiarity of the workings of the legal system, especially as relevant to the acceptance of a non-legalist (such as a behavioral scientist), are typically not part of the professional psychology training program. Perhaps it is because the "helping activities" aligned with children's legal services are commonly considered to be within the providence of social work, or perhaps it is because there has been so little psychological research and, consequently, professional interest in child custody. Regardless, the profession of psychology is into a new era. It is therefore recommended that *the professional psychology training program should structure the curriculum to familiarize trainees with the psychological and social factors in child and family theories that would find application in child custody proceedings, the sociopolitical and organization aspects of the American legal system, and the methodologies required for effective participation in child custody legal proceedings.*

Any treatise on such a nebulous professional practice area as child custody must (if only for tradition's sake) include a recommendation that *extensive research should be conducted on child custody.* Aside from the obvious, this recommendation has special importance at this point in the evolution of the American legal system. Heretofore, there has been minimal research on judicial decision-making in general, and now child custody has been assigned a rather radically new composition, namely, the reliance on factors that behavioral scientists must evaluate and document. While perfect precision is never truly expected in "clinical services," it is both ethically and legally required that professionals participating in child custody legal proceedings must be capable of functioning according to scientific guidelines. Such guidelines have been only tenuously established—enough (in all likelihood) to rationalize continued and greater involvement in child custody practices, but definitely not enough to negate extensive and intensive research efforts. For the professional psychologist, there is no choice; there must be more research on child custody, particularly the decision-making processes involving professionals.

FOOTNOTE

[1] The sampling encompassed four professional disciplines: law, psychiatry, psychology, and social work.

The disciplinary identity of the subjects extends to an established involvement with and interest in children's services. Specifically, the lawyers were members of the Family Law Section of the American Bar Association, the psychiatrists and the psychologists designated work with children as a professional specialty, and the social workers were active members of the American Association of Marriage and Family Counselors.

All subjects were randomly selected from the most recent editions of their respective professional association directory: the lawyers were selected from the Directory of the Family Law Section of the American Bar Association; the psychiatrists were selected from the Directory of the American Psychiatric Association; the psychologists were selected from the Directory of the American Board of Professional Psychology (thus each psychologist held Diplomate status); and the social workers were selected from the Directory of the American Association of Marriage and Family Counselors. To repeat, the selection of each subject was done in a random manner (such as using a table of random numbers to select the page in the directory to be used and which name on that page to select as a subject).

Sample sizes were consistent across the professional disciplines. There were 75 males and 75 females randomly selected to receive the questionnaire from each discipline. Therefore, 150 lawyers, 150 psychiatrists, 150 psychologists, and 150 social workers, equally divided according to sex, received the questionnaire. The response rates according to professional discipline (disregarding the sex of the respondent) were: law, 25.6%; psychiatry, 22.6%; psychology, 25.2%; social work, 26.6%.

REFERENCES

Ackerman, Nathan W. *The psychodynamics of family life: Diagnosis and treatment of family relationships*. New York: Basic Books, 1958.

Benedek, Elissa P., & Benedek, Richard S. New child custody laws: Making them do what they say. *American Journal of Orthopsychiatry*, 1972, *42*, 5 (Oct.), 825-834.

Briscoe, C. William, Smith, James B., Robins, Eli, Marten, Sue & Gaskin, Fred. Divorce and psychiatric disease. *Archives of General Psychiatry*, 1973, *29*, 1 (July), 119-125.

Clad, C. Clinton, Halstead, Harry M. & Crocker, Donald W. *Family law*. Philadelphia: Joint Committee on Continuing Legal Education (American Law Institute and the American Bar Association), 1964.

Clark, Homer H., Jr. *The law of domestic relations in the United States*. Hornbook Series. St. Paul, Minn.: West, 1968.

Commissioners on Uniform State Laws. Uniform Child Custody Jurisdiction Act. *Family Law Quarterly*, 1969, *3*, 4 (Dec.), 317-330.

Foster, Henry H., Jr. & Freed, Doris Jonas. Children and the law. *Family Law Quarterly*, 1968, *2*, 1 (March), 40-62.

Foster, Henry H., Jr. & Freed, Doris Jonas. A bill of rights for children. *Family Law Quarterly*, 1972, *6*, 4 (Winter), 343-375.

Goldstein, Joseph, Freud, Anna & Solnit, Albert J. *Beyond the best interests of the child*. New York: Free Press, 1973.

Harper, Fowler V. & Skolnick, Jerome H. *Problems of the Family* (rev. ed.). Boston: Bobbs-Merrill, 1962.

Holmes, Martin M. Personal communication. March 19, 1974.

Inker, Monroe L. & Perretta, Charlotte Anne. A child's right to counsel in custody cases. *Family Law Quarterly*, 1971, *5*, 4 (Dec.), 417-423.

Jacobson, J. Myron & Mersky, Ray M. (eds.). *Ervin H. Pollock's fundamentals of legal research* (4th ed.). Mineola, N.Y.: Foundation Press, 1973.

Kadushin, Alfred. *Child welfare services*. New York: Macmillan, 1967.

Katz, Sanford N. *When parents fail: The law's response to family breakdown*. Boston: Beacon Press, 1971.

Kleinfeld, Andrew Jay. The balance of power among infants, their parents and the state. *Family Law Quarterly*, 1970a, *4*, 3 (Sept.), 320-350.

Kleinfeld, Andrew Jay. The balance of power among infants, their parents and the state, part II. *Family Law Quarterly*, 1970b, *4*, 4 (Dec.), 410-443.

Krech, David & Crutchfield, Richard S. *Theory and problems of social psychology*. New York: McGraw-Hill, 1948.

Lidz, Theodore, *The person: His development throughout the life cycle*. New York: Basic books, 1968.

McDermott, John F. Divorce and its psychiatric sequelae in children. *Archives of General Psychiatry*, 1970, *23*, 5 (Nov.), 421-427.

Michigan Interprofessional Association on Marriage, Divorce and the Family. Report of custody committee. In George G. Newman (ed.), *Children in the courts—The question of representation.* Ann Arbor: Institute of Continuing Legal Education, 1967, 49-59.

Morrison, James R. Parental divorce as a factor in childhood psychiatric illness. *Comprehensive Psychiatry,* 1974, *15,* 2 (March/April), 95-102.

Mussen, Paul Henry, Conger, John Janeway & Kagan, Jerome. *Child Development and Personality* (3rd ed.). New York: Harper & Row, 1969.

National Conference of Commissioners on Uniform State Laws. Uniform Marriage and Divorce Act. *Family Law Quarterly,* 1971, 5, 2 (June), 205-251.

Paulsen, Monrad G., Wadlington, Walter & Goebel, Julius, Jr. *Cases and other materials on domestic relations.* Mineola, N.Y.: Foundation Press, 1970.

Ploscowe, Morris, Foster, Henry H., Jr. & Freed, Doris Jonas. *Family law: Cases and materials* (2nd ed.). Boston: Little, Brown, 1972.

Ploscowe, Morris & Freed, Doris Jonas. *Family Law: Cases and Materials.* Boston: Little, Brown, 1963.

Sayre, Paul. Awarding custody of children. In the Committee of the Association of American Law Schools (eds.), *Selected essays on family law.* Brooklyn: Foundation Press, 1950, 588-607.

Slovenko, Ralph. *Psychiatry and law.* Boston: Little, Brown, 1973.

Watson, Robert I. *Psychology of the child: personal, social and disturbed child development.* New York: John Wiley, 1959.

Westman, Jack C. & Cline, David W. Divorce is a family affair. *Family Law Quarterly,* 1971, *5,* 1 (March), 1-10.

Westman, Jack C., Cline, David W. & Kramer, Douglas A. Role of child psychiatry in divorce. *Archives of General Psychiatry,* 1970, *23,* 5 (Nov.), 416-420.

15

The Mental Health Professional on the Witness Stand: A Survival Guide

STANLEY L. BRODSKY

When Wonder Woman is attacked by enemies firing bullets at her, she moves her wrists with lightning speed. Wonder Woman's bracelets deflect each of the bullets so that they zing back at the assailant or harmlessly fall to the ground. Mental health experts being cross-examined on the witness stand find themselves in a similar position under attack. The witnesses can count on receiving a number of hostile missiles; most witnesses, however, were not bred on Paradise Island or blessed by Athena, and are not able to fend off attorneys' bullets with the speed and grace of a Wonder Woman. All too many witnesses find themselves distressed by the unfamiliar field of battle, opposed by the courtroom equivalent of super-heroes and heroines (in attorneys and other witnesses alike), and sufficiently wounded that they vow to never risk such hazards again.

Hostilities with the enemy may be expected. Fierce fighting behind the lines with allies can be devastating. Fellow mental health professionals accuse expert witnesses of debasing the profession in public, inappropriately participating in ugly "battles of the experts," and attempting to appear authoritative without scientific bases. This latter criticism has especially been leveled by Ziskin (1975):

> With each additional experience of testifying, and with an increasing awareness
> of the vulnerability that existed, I become increasingly concerned with the
> deference that was accorded to me by lawyers and judges who consistently
> treated me as though *they totally believed* that *I really knew* what I was
> talking about. I knew how shaky were the grounds on which my conclusions
> rested and could not understand how lawyers could be so naive as not to be
> aware of this. (vii) ... Despite the ever increasing utilization of psychiatric
> and psychological evidence in the legal process, such evidence frequently does
> not meet reasonable criteria of admissibility and should not be admitted in a
> court of law and, if admitted, should be given little or no weight ... In the
> light of current scientific evidence, there is no reason to consider such testi-
> mony as other than highly speculative. (1)

In a thoughtful chapter on psychiatric expert testimony and the adversary
system, Slovenko (1974) notes that there are a series of common attacks that
have been made on the use of psychiatric testimony. Among these attacks are
that:

(1) Some psychiatrists and other mental health experts testify only for the
sake of publicity. Attracted to the public light and attention, they offer information far more sensationalistic than informative.

(2) Much jargon and gobbledygook appears in the testimony. So much jargon is used in presenting professional opinions that the material becomes unin-
telligible to the jury.

(3) Psychiatric diagnoses and prognoses are unreliable. They fail to be consistent over time and the definition of terms themselves are pointless and self-
defeating.

The discrediting of expert witnesses is dramatic and powerful. Dr. Carl Bingr
testified that Whittaker Chambers, major prosecution witness in the Alger Hiss
trial, had been found to be a "psychopath with a tendency toward making false
accusations." Slovenko reported that "Bingr on direct examination had pointed
out Chambers' untidiness, and on cross-examination he was made to acknowledge that the trait was found too in such persons as Albert Einstein, Heywood
Broun, Will Rogers, Owen D. Young, Bing Crosby, and Thomas A. Edison.
Bingr testified that Chambers habitually gazed at the ceiling while testifying
and seemed to have no direct relation with the psychological examiner. The
prosecutor in a turnabout told Bingr 'We have made a count of the number of times
you looked at the ceiling. During the first ten minutes you looked up at the ceiling nineteen times; in the next fifteen minutes you looked up ten times; in the
next fifteen minutes ten times; and for the last fifteen minutes ten times more.
We counted a total of fifty-nine times that you looked at the ceiling in fifty
minutes. Now I was wondering whether that was any symptom of a psychopathic
personality.' " (p. 46)

It is too late for Dr. Bingr to be rescued. It is not too late for the reader to learn the "bullets and bracelets" game. The place to begin is the pre-trial meeting with the attorney on "your" side.

MEETING WITH YOUR ATTORNEY

Why you are testifying, on what, and in what manner need to be clarified early and well. The very first task, then, is to establish a congruence of the attorney's expectations for you and your knowledge and plans to testify. Thus you should make an appointment at least a few days in advance of your testimony with the attorney who actually will be conducting the direct examination. This meeting should have been preceded by several phone calls or a prior meeting in which your role and his or her goals are clearly defined.

When you meet, ask to see a list of questions the attorney is intending to ask you during direct examination. If you do not like them, change them. Some of the guidelines this writer uses for questions include the following:

(1) They should be predominately open-ended.

(2) Avoid a "20 Questions" format (in which there is a gamelike rehearsed search for *the* answer).

(3) Avoid being put in the position of performing unnatural professional acts. That is, if something sounds sour or phony, explain firmly that you will not do it, and stick with your decision.

Some experienced witnesses come to this first meeting with a list or to draw up a list of questions that will help the attorney, if he or she is inexperienced. Keep asking what *you* wish to accomplish as you think through the purposes of the direct examination with the attorney.

SCHEDULING PROBLEMS

There is little that is more frustrating than sitting in a bare witness room for three or four hours, waiting to testify, and then being told to return the next day. Most of the time, the attorney who has called you will be cooperative in setting up a time-scheduling arrangement. Discuss your time preferences in advance, try to keep your appointments fluid that day, and finally go in with the expectation that there may be as much as an hour or two-hour discrepancy between your planned appearance and your actual testimony, even with the most careful arrangements, liaison, and notice.

THIRTEEN SUGGESTIONS FOR COPING WITH
THE CROSS-EXAMINATION

Wonder Woman and O.J. Simpson alike have an abundance of natural talents. Both, however, needed considerable training in specific techniques to utilize their talents well. Similarly every person engaged in forensic "bracelets and bullets" needs to master basic techniques for parrying the cross-examination. Thirteen suggestions are presented here:

(1) *Specific knowledge.* For each specific area of testimony involving theory, research, or practices, be knowledgeable about scientific and factual information. You should consider what you are accountable for defending, specific theories you use, and your subsequent conclusions. Both the information and the assumptions on which your conclusions are built should be defensible from research studies or major professional perspectives.

(2) *Preparation and review.* Many experts review Buros' *Mental Measurements Yearbooks* and *Psychological Bulletin* review articles prior to their testimony. You are far better prepared if you have read the most current knowledge and critiques by other experts, for reference and utilization on the stand.

(3) *Time and attention.* Your potential vulnerability means that extra time and care should be directed at the assessment process or the information-gathering process related to the court case. The extra time itself is useful when a cross-examining attorney seeks to equate time invested with your amount of knowledge and expertise. Each case should be considered special and given extra attention.

(4) *Honesty.* Always be honest! We have an ethical responsibility to be honest, and we are under oath. However, honesty is sometimes relative. There are many different ways of being honest. The courtroom situation is sometimes one in which you as the expert are seen as assuming an unequivocal advocacy role, identified with the attorney that has called you to testify. Therefore, honesty including evidence *against* the position of your side, is an impressive part of credibility.

(5) *Admit weaknesses.* When there is an area of personal or professional ignorance or weakness, you should admit it. I suggest admitting it in single words without great elaboration. The attitude with which you admit these weaknesses is even more important. If you have a long latency, are puzzled, stammer, and admit the weakness as if you have been personally defeated, this tends to discredit the whole testimony. These negative emotional messages suggest that you have many other areas related to your testimony that are of questionable value. A straightforward admission, almost with pride, and certainly with no sense of loss or deficit, impresses all observers.

(6) *Instruction.* Remember that the persons in the courtroom—the observers, the attorneys, the judge, and the jury—tend to be bored by much of what goes

on. Certainly a professional speaking in jargon or in language not meaningful to them will leave them distracted and daydreaming. It is very easy to fall into the temptation of engaging in a one-to-one relationship and conversation with either the direct-examining or cross-examining attorney. As you are on the witness stand, look around the courtroom, make eye contact with the judge, with members of the jury, with a variety of people. As you speak, speak to all of them. Consider it almost a group session in which there are many people with whom you wish to make good personal contact. There would be no greater sign of a successful witness than the jurors or attorneys speaking to their spouses or friends about things they learned in the courtroom. Your telling them about psychology and psychological principles in personally meaningful terms makes a great impact in your testimony and in the worth of the court experience for them.

(7) *The push-pull technique.* There are a great many questions that attorneys will ask in order to make you respond with a single damaging admission. The push-pull technique for dealing with such ploys consists of initially admitting and then denying the truth or the provocative question. An answer to a question about the usefulness of the Rorschach may look like this: "While there are many criticisms of the Rorschach in terms of its theoretical meaning, those of us who use it regularly have found that it is an extraordinarily meaningful and important technique." The push-pull technique is sometimes simpler. Instead of pushing against an attorney at one point, or disagreeing, one pulls in the direction he pushes, responding with great enthusiasm, "Oh, my gracious, yes!" can transform the psychological meaning of the situation to your advantage.

(8) *You as a special expert.* If the attorney actively challenges existing knowledge and research in the field, you should cite your own special areas of experience and knowledge that set you apart from the garden-variety psychologist or psychiatrist.

(9) *Anticipation.* Learn to anticipate where the attorney is headed with the cross-examination. If you know the purpose and directions of the line of questioning, you are far better equipped to help shape the outcome. Otherwise, you may find yourself having admitted a series of partial truths that cumulatively harm your testimony in major ways.

(10) *Take time to think.* The stacatto, machine-gun pace of some attorneys during cross-examination tends to lead some witnesses to give very quick, insufficiently thought-out answers. Pause, cock your head, look up into the distance for a moment, make it clear you are giving the question serious thought, and then answer.

(11) *Do not speak for other experts.* It is your testimony that is of concern. A good cross-examining attorney may raise a whole series of hypothestical questions about what other experts might say. If at all possible, stay with your own knowledge and perspectives.

(12) *Don't talk too much.* Except during direct examination or at times

TABLE I

Gambits in Expert Witness Examination and Responses that Degambitize

Title	Source	Example	Responses
1. Infallibility complex	McConnell	Do you think the new research by Smith and Jones on——might be important in this regard?	Admission of ignorance. Moving from concrete issues to abstract principles and knowledge. Responses that put the question in a broad perspective.
2. Primary source gambit	McConnell	"On this point about——, were you the first person to report this very interesting scientific finding?" "Then who did first?" "When?" "Where?" "When was the last time you read that source?" "Don't errors sometimes creep into texts?" (Theme: How do you know what you know?)	True self-preparation. Nature of cumulative scientific knowledge.
3. GOK (God Only knows)	McConnell	(Theme: Questions of how little the profession truly knows about relevant areas). "What actually causes schizophrenia?"	A state of knowledge summary. Full, detailed description of *one* key study.
4. Historic hysteric gambit (typically used only after expert's testimony has devastated the case)	McConnell	"Have you ever heard of Ignaz Semmelweiss? (Pasteur, Fleming, or other scientific geniuses who were scorned by their colleagues). (Theme: Attacks your predecessors and points out the uncertainty of professional consensus.)	Ideas *then* which are *now* considered professionally absurd. Current speed of acceptance of scientific information.

	Source	Cross-examination question	Response
5. Expert as capitalist		"How much are you being paid for your examination and testimony?" "By whom?" "How much money did you earn last year?" (Applies only to private practitioners.)	Matter-of-fact responding. May include a modest statement of integrity.
6. Subjective advocacy	Brodsky & Robey	"Isn't it true that anyone may develop subtle prejudice or biases without being aware of them?" "Is there any possibility you may have biases in this case, or any other, of which you are not aware?" "Would you personally like to see the defendant acquitted/convicted?"	Possible biases acknowledged as well as your pursuit of objectivity—and psychological techniques that help this pursuit.
7. History of advocacy		"This is not your first time in court, is it?" (Theme: Number of times expert has testified for a given side.)	Acknowledgement, noting different access by plaintiffs and defense. Answer on your terms.
8. Challenging experience	Ziskin	"Have you conducted follow-up research studies on the reliability (or validity) of your own assessment?"	Continuing contact with clients (case history research). Feedback from colleagues to enhance validity. The clinician's professional growth as result of experience and literature—a research process. Component responding: discuss *follow-ups* you do; discuss *research* (systematic accumulation of your knowledge); discuss bases of reliability or validity for you personally (not the entire profession).

when you have something of very great importance to say, keep your responses to two or three sentences. I would give a similar warning not to speak too little, but this is a rare deficit among mental health professionals on the witness stand.

(13) *Listen carefully to the questions.* There is a tendency for many attorneys to be imprecise in their use of language or their posing of questions. If you listen very carefully to the words used and the questions posed, then you will find yourself with increased options for answering the question. In addition, you can often rephrase a question an attorney asks, querying if that is what he meant. When this is done, the balance of power becomes subtly changed in the courtroom to your advantage.

CONCLUSION

Ambrose Bierce once wrote that a trial is a formal inquiry, designed to affirm the impeccable character of lawyers, judges, and juries. While Bierce was cynical about everything, his observation was astute about the attorneys' need to look good. When attacking the witness on specific content seems to be failing, then attorneys may attack on general principles and anticipated weaknesses of all mental health professionals. Table I presents eight such gambits, drawn from McConnell (1969), Brodsky & Robey (1972), and Ziskin (1975). Accompanying each gambit is a suggested response for the witness. The themes are related. The attorney sets up the witness as ignorant, irresponsible, or biased. The witness disarms the attack through demonstration of quiet competence and mastery of the situation.

REFERENCES

Brodsky, S.L. & Robey, A. On becoming an expert witness: Issues of orientation and effectiveness. *Professional Psychology,* 1973, *3,* 173-176.

McConnell, James V. A psychologist looks at the medical profession. In Albert G. Sugerman (ed.), *Examining the medical expert: Lectures and trial demonstrations.* Ann Arbor, Mich. Institute of Legal Education, 1969.

Slovenko, Ralph. *Law and psychiatry.* Boston: Little, Brown, 1974.

Sugerman, Albert G. (ed.). *Examining the medical expert: Lectures and trial demonstrations.* Ann Arbor, Mich.: Institute of Continuing Legal Education, 1969.

Ziskin, Jay. *Coping with psychiatric and psychological testimony,* 2nd ed. Beverly Hills, Calif.: Law and Psychology Press, 1975.

Index